Toward a Consensus on Military Service

Pergamon Titles of Related Interest

Daniel/Herbig STRATEGIC MILITARY DECEPTION
Etheredge CAN GOVERNMENTS LEARN?
Hunt/Shultz LESSONS FROM AN UNCONVENTIONAL WAR
Sherraden/Eberly NATIONAL SERVICE
Stiehm WOMEN AND MEN'S WARS (Special Issue of Women's
Studies International Forum)
Taylor/Olson/Schrader DEFENSE MANPOWER PLANNING

Related Journal*

BRITISH DEFENCE DIRECTORY

*Free specimen copy available upon request.

Toward a Consensus on Military Service

Report of the Atlantic Council's Working Group on Military Service

Andrew J. Goodpaster

Lloyd H. Elliott
Co-Chairmen

J. Allan Hovey, Jr.
Rapporteur

Foreword by Kenneth Rush

Pergamon Press
New York   Oxford   Toronto   Sydney   Paris   Frankfurt

Pergamon Press Offices:

U.S.A.
Pergamon Press Inc., Maxwell House, Fairview Park,
Elmsford, New York 10523, U.S.A.

U.K.
Pergamon Press Ltd., Headington Hill Hall,
Oxford OX3 0BW, England

CANADA
Pergamon Press Canada Ltd., Suite 104, 150 Consumers Road,
Willowdale, Ontario M2J 1P9, Canada

AUSTRALIA
Pergamon Press (Aust.) Pty. Ltd., P.O. Box 544,
Potts Point, NSW 2011, Australia

FRANCE
Pergamon Press SARL, 24 rue des Ecoles,
75240 Paris, Cedex 05, France

FEDERAL REPUBLIC OF GERMANY
Pergamon Press GmbH, Hammerweg 6
6242 Kronberg/Taunus, Federal Republic of Germany

Library of Congress Card Number: 82-12393

Printed in the United States of America

Table of Contents

"Among the many objects to which a wise and free people find it necessary to direct their attention, that of providing for their safety seems to be the first."

John Jay, 1788
The Federalist

"The terror of the Roman arms added weight and dignity to the moderation of the emperors. They preserved the peace by a constant preparation for war."

Edward Gibbon, 1776
The Decline and Fall of the Roman Empire

"The citizenry in general, and American youth in particular, must be given a better idea of what U.S. national interests are, of how U.S. foreign and domestic policies are designed to support those interests, and of the role that the military institution serves to protect those interests."

Martin Binkin, 1980
Military Manpower in the 1980s: Issues and Choices

List of Figures

List of Tables

Foreword

The Atlantic Council, now in its twenty-second year, is a bi-partisan educational organization which conducts programs to promote understanding of major international security, political and economic problems affecting the United States and its allies, foster informed public debate on these issues, and make policy recommendations to the Executive and Legislative branches of the U.S. Government, as well as to appropriate international organizations. On behalf of the Board of Directors of the Atlantic Council I want to congratulate General Andrew J. Goodpaster and Dr. Lloyd H. Elliott, co-chairmen of the Council's Military Service Working Group, Dr. J. Allan Hovey, Jr., rapporteur, and each of the Working Group members for the utility as well as the excellence of their assessment of U.S. military manpower problems and prospects today, and for the years ahead. The subject is critical to the security of the United States and its allies, both in terms of the credibility as well as the capability of Western defense.

The bi-partisan panel of experts recommends that President Reagan's administration prepare the American people for the probable resumption of the military draft sometime during this decade. Concluding that the requirements of security are unlikely to be met indefinitely by the present all-volunteer force, the 18-month study meanwhile proposes a generous new peacetime "GI Bill" of educational benefits to attract additional recruits. These conclusions represent a substantial consensus on the part of some fifty-five prominent Americans in education, the professions, the armed services, business, labor, high government service, and youth from both political parties, listed on pages xix–xxii.

Given the rising costs of higher education, the report states, this new "GI Bill" should attract growing numbers of college- or trade school-bound middle-class Americans who would find a temporary diversion from the world of school or work tolerable and perhaps even welcome. The cost of the program would be minimal at most and might even be zero. I personally believe that the proposed enlistment options would be good for the armed services, good for American colleges and universities, and good for the individuals choosing to take part.

The report, the latest in the Atlantic Council's series of Policy Papers on security issues, specifically emphasizes the necessity of adequate conventional forces to deter armed aggression and reduce the risks of a nuclear confrontation between the Atlantic Alliance and the Warsaw Pact. Noting that manpower is a key element in adequate conventional forces, the report welcomes the fact that in fiscal years 1981 and 1982 the All-Volunteer Force recovered from previous years and essentially achieved its recruitment goals for both quality and quantity. The report notes, however, that American military active-duty strength at the beginning of the 1980s is at its lowest ebb since 1950. Some increase in force size may become necessary (and some has been programmed) in coming years, and it will have to be obtained from a diminishing manpower pool. Economic recovery and a consequent drop in unemployment could further reduce the numbers of qualified young people who might enlist. It remains to be seen, the report warns, whether the recent improvements in recruitment can be maintained under such conditions. Moreover, higher quality of manpower becomes ever more essential with the growing sophistication of weaponry.

The purpose of adequate conventional forces, both active and reserve, in terms of their quality as much as their quantity, is to forestall the coercive threat of aggression, credibly deter such aggression, and, if necessary, combat it. The bottom line for the U.S. today is that our military manpower readiness and capability are not fully adequate to fulfill this mission. Unless we abdicate our role as leader and principal defender of the West, we cannot change that mission; we must, therefore, improve our capability and readiness. The problem is just that simple. And just that dangerous. The cure, however, as the reader will discern in the following pages, is not simple at all. The good news is that a cure is possible, indeed likely, if we follow the careful prescriptions recommended by the Atlantic Council's Working Group. Moreover, the cure is not costly, in either fiscal or political terms. It does require a significant reorientation of our manpower priorities, and a good deal of public education. This book is a fine start toward both objectives.

KENNETH RUSH
Chairman, Board of Directors
The Atlantic Council of the
United States

Preface

This book examines the experience and prospects of the nation's peacetime military volunteer force. Chapter 10 (the Policy Paper) offers a broad range of recommendations designed both to strengthen that force and to prepare the way, should circumstances require it, for a resumption of compulsory military service.

Winston Churchill is reported to have remarked that "Democracy is the worst form of government except all those other forms that have been tried from time to time." It is in one sense a weakness of democracies that important changes of policy must have the tacit consent if not the express approval of the people. One pays—willingly, gratefully—a price in delay of action, in the public airing of error, and in the organized chaos of controversy. But it is a great strength of democracy that policy thus achieved has behind it the unique power of the consensus of a free people. The United States today needs a broader and deeper consensus on the West's strategic position and on the role and needs of the military services in deterring war and protecting our vital interests. We believe the findings and recommendations in this book can help point the country in that direction.

We are fortunate to have had the benefit of an extremely well qualified Working Group to explore these issues. Their names appear following this Preface. Chapter 10 seeks to record the consensus that emerged from many hours of discussion and correspondence among a group of informed and thoughtful Americans. Not all the Working Group participants agree with everything in that chapter, of course, and a variety of comments and dissenting opinions are recorded in the notes or in Appendix I, as appropriate. We should also add that the views expressed are those of the Military Service Working Group and not necessarily those of the Atlantic Council as a whole.

Nine working papers written by 11 members of the Working Group, together with successive drafts of the Policy Paper prepared by our Rapporteur, provided the basis for our deliberations over the past 18 months. All of these working papers and the Policy Paper are published here.

The Working Group was privileged to discuss these chapters and a draft of the Policy Paper with additional participants in a Regional American Assembly held at Airlie House, Virginia, March 11 to 14, 1982. The conference was cosponsored by the American Assembly at Columbia University and the Atlantic Council with the support and encouragement of the Ford Foundation. The council is particularly grateful to Ambassador William H. Sullivan, president of the American Assembly, for his substantive participation as well as his agreement permitting the council to experiment with the assembly format and dovetail the proceedings into the evolving debate of the Working Group in a most constructive fashion. We are equally grateful to Enid Schoettle of the Ford Foundation, who originally suggested this innovative arrangement. The additional assembly participants are identified following the listing of the members of the Working Group. It should be noted that those government officials who participated in the discussions and commented on or dissented from the draft Policy Paper did so in an unofficial capacity as private citizens: neither their association with the council's policy formulation process nor their comments or dissents imply any necessary agreement of their respective departments or agencies. The reader will note in particular in chapter 10 several comments by Assistant Secretary of Defense Lawrence J. Korb. His thoughtful and detailed observations on drafts of the Policy Paper enabled us to refine and update important data and to take more adequate account of recent progress in dealing with the country's manpower problems. Dr. Korb's footnoted reservations regarding a number of the Working Group's conclusions serve usefully to point up important and timely issues and thus enhance considerably the value of the book.

The overall project has been made possible, as are all Atlantic Council projects, by the generous support of a number of U.S. corporations, foundations, labor unions, and individuals. We should like to thank, in addition to the Ford Foundation, the New York Life Foundation, Smith and Wesson, United Technologies, McDonnell-Douglas, the Charles Merrill Trust, Rockwell International, and the Prudential Foundation. Finally, special thanks go to George A. Strichman, president of Colt Industries, for his unstinting support of the council's work program on the credibility of the NATO deterrent in general, and the U.S. military manpower and readiness situation in particular.*

Our Group worked hard and well over the past 18 months to produce from diverse experience and often divergent points of view the collegial "white paper" and the related studies. Given the breadth of the issues and the range of the options, we take considerable satisfaction in having concluded the work with substantial consensus on the part of the members of the Working Group. We especially thank our Rapporteur, the authors cited above, the other members of the Working Group, and the additional partic-

---

*For the Council's most recent Policy Paper on NATO, see *The Credibility of the NATO Deterrent: Bringing the NATO Deterrent Up To Date*, a project chaired jointly by Kenneth Rush and Brent Scowcroft, with Joseph J. Wolf as Rapporteur.

ipants of the Regional American Assembly at Airlie House for their highly constructive contributions.

Only by free, honest, and informed discussion of our national security problems can we hope to find the common solutions that history now demands of us. It is in that spirit that we commend this book to the U.S. government and the Congress for action and to the interested public for study and debate.

LLOYD H. ELLIOTT   ANDREW J. GOODPASTER
Cochairmen of the Atlantic Council's
Working Group on Military Service

Members of the Working Group on Military Service

CO-CHAIRMEN:

Lloyd H. Elliott, President, George Washington University.

Andrew J. Goodpaster, former Superintendent, U.S. Military Academy, and Supreme Allied Commander, Europe.

RAPPORTEUR:

J. Allan Hovey, Jr., International Relations Specialist, U.S. General Accounting Office; former Vice–President, Radio Free Europe.

PROJECT DIRECTOR:

Joseph W. Harned, Deputy Director General, Atlantic Council.

MEMBERS:

David M. Abshire, President, Center for Strategic and International Studies, Georgetown University.

David C. Acheson, Attorney; former General Counsel, Communications Satellite Corporation.

Francis J. Aquila, Executive Director, Young Democrats of America; former Member, Democratic National Committee.

Martin Binkin, Senior Fellow, Brookings Institution.

George S. Blanchard, former Commander-in-Chief, U.S. Army Europe and Commander, NATO Central Army Group.

Kenneth Blaylock, Member, AFL-CIO Executive Council; Chairman, Adhoc Committee on Defense Manpower Needs.

Landrum R. Bolling, former President, Earlham College, and former Chairman, Council on Foundations.

William K. Brehm, Chairman, Systems Research and Applications; former Assistant Secretary of Defense for Manpower.

Lisle Carter, President, University of the District of Columbia; former Chancellor, Atlantic University Center.

Antonia Chayes, Attorney; former Under Secretary of the Air Force.

James E. Cheek, President, Howard University.

W. Graham Claytor, Jr., Attorney; former Deputy Secretary of Defense.

Richard V. L. Cooper, Director of Management Consulting Services, Coopers and Lybrand.

Mark J. Eitelberg, Senior Scientist, Human Resources Research Organization.

John H. Faris, Professor of Sociology, Towson State University.

H. Joseph Farmer, Executive Director, American Council of Young Political Leaders.*

Ellen L. Frost, former Deputy Assistant Secretary of Defense for International Economic Affairs.

Robert K. Fullinwider, Research Associate, Center for Philosophy and Public Policy, University of Maryland.

Robert G. Gard, Jr., former President, National Defense University, and Commander, U.S. Army Military Personnel Center.

Edward Hidalgo, Attorney; former Assistant Secretary of the Navy for Manpower, Reserve Affairs and Logistics; former Secretary of the Navy.

Jeanne M. Holm, retired Major General, U.S. Air Force; former Director, Air Force Personnel Council; Consultant to Defense Manpower Committee.

E. R. Jayne II, Corporate Director, General Dynamics Corporation; former OMB Associate Director for National Security and International Affairs.

Robert W. Komer, Adjunct Professor, George Washington University; former Under Secretary of Defense for Policy.

Peter F. Krogh, Dean, School of Foreign Service, Georgetown University.

James L. Lacy, Author; former Special Assistant to the Assistant Secretary of Defense for Manpower, Reserve Affairs and Logistics.

James F. Lyons, Vice–President for Strategic Planning, United Technologies Corporation.

Leonard H. Marks, Vice–Chairman, Foreign Policy Association; former Director, U.S. Information Agency.

Sanford N. McDonnell, President, McDonnell-Douglas Corporation.

David E. McGiffert, Attorney; former Assistant Secretary of Defense for International Security Affairs.

Robert S. McNamara, former President, International Bank for Reconstruction and Development, and former Secretary of Defense.

Charles C. Moskos, Professor of Sociology, Northwestern University.

Frederick E. Nolting, Jr., Professor, University of Virginia; former alternate U.S. Representative to NATO and Ambassador to Vietnam.

William C. Olson, Dean, American University School of International Service.

Bruce Palmer, Jr., former Vice–Chief of Staff, U.S. Army; Executive Director, Defense Manpower Commission.

Edmund D. Pellegrino, President, The Catholic University of America.

Paul D. Phillips, retired Army Brigadier General; former Principal Deputy Assistant Secretary of the Army; author of the Army Five-year Force Development Plan.

Robert B. Pirie, Jr., Director, Naval Strategy Group, Center for Naval Analyses; former Assistant Secretary of Defense.

Jeffrey Record, Senior Fellow, Institute for Foreign Policy Analysis.

Stanley R. Resor, Attorney; former Secretary of the Army.

Sally K. Richardson, Deputy Director, West Virginia Department of Health; former Chairperson, Defense Advisory Committee on Women in the Service.

Olin C. Robison, President, Middlebury College.

Brent Scowcroft, Consultant; former Assistant to the President of the United States for National Security Affairs.

---

*Served until his untimely death, March 10, 1982.

David S. Smith, Attorney; former Ambassador to Sweden; former Assistant Secretary of the Air Force.

Elvis J. Stahr, Jr., Educator and Attorney; former Secretary of the Army.

Curtis W. Tarr, Vice-President, John Deere & Co.; former Chairman, Defense Manpower Commission; former Assistant Secretary of the Air Force for Manpower and Reserve Affairs.

James B. Taylor, Representative of Young Republicans, Republican National Committee.

William J. Taylor, Jr., Director, Political/Military Studies, CSIS, Georgetown University; former Professor of Social Sciences and Director, National Security Studies, U.S. Military Academy.

Togo D. West, Jr., Attorney; former General Counsel to the Department of Defense.

Darnell M. Whitt II, former Executive Director, Committee of Nine, and Member, U.S. Mission to NATO.

Joseph J. Wolf, former Minister, U.S. Delegation to NATO.

R. James Woolsey, Attorney; former Under Secretary of the Navy.

EX OFFICIO MEMBERS:

Theodore C. Achilles, Vice-Chairman, Atlantic Council.
Kenneth Rush, Chairman, Atlantic Council.
Francis O. Wilcox, Director General, Atlantic Council.

SENIOR FELLOWS:

Eugenia Kemble, Atlantic Council.
Blake W. Robinson, Atlantic Council.
Richard R. Sexton, Atlantic Council.
Alfred D. Wilhelm, Jr., Atlantic Council.

PROJECT ASSISTANT:

Eliane Lomax, Atlantic Council.

Additional Participants in the Regional American Assembly

Airlie House, 11–14 March 1982

(N.B.: U.S. Government officials who participated in the discussions and commented on or dissented from the draft Policy Paper did so in an unofficial capacity as private citizens: neither their association with the Council's policy formulation process nor their comments or dissents imply any necessary agreement of their respective Departments or Agencies.)

Mark Blitz, Assistant Director and Head of the Office of Policy and Planning, ACTION.*

Julius Debro, Professor and Department Chair, Department of Criminal Justice, Atlanta University; former Staff Officer, Office of Chief, Army Reserve Mobilization.

Donald J. Eberly, Senior Program Officer, Alternative Service, Selective Service System.

Charles L. Fox, Major, U.S. Air Force; Military Assistant to the Assistant Secretary of Defense for Manpower.

William Josephson, Attorney; President, Peace Corps Institute.

Lawrence J. Korb, Assistant Secretary of Defense for Manpower, Reserve Affairs and Logistics.

P. B. Krogen, Major General, Danish Ministry of Defense; Chairman, NATO Eurogroup Adhoc Committee on Military Manpower Issues.

Carol Laise, former Director General of the Foreign Service and Ambassador to Nepal.

Bruce K. MacLaury, President, Brookings Institution.

Paul N. McCloskey, Jr., United States Representative.

Fran McKee, former Director, Human Resource Management Division, Office of the Chief of Naval Operations.

Berton R. Otto, National Security Advisor and Legislative Aide to Congressman Bill Chappell (ranking majority member, House Subcommittee on Defense Appropriations).

Bernard D. Rostker, Director, Management Processes and Implementation Program, Center for Naval Analyses.

Leonard Sullivan, Jr., Defense Policy Consultant, System Planning Corporation; former Assistant Secretary of Defense.

William H. Sullivan, President, The American Assembly, Columbia University.

Peter L. Szanton, Vice-President, Hamilton, Rabinovitz & Szanton.

Samuel F. Wells, Jr., Secretary, International Security Studies Program, Woodrow Wilson Center for Scholars, Smithsonian Institution.

Barbara Powers Wyatt, Director, Young Volunteers for Action, ACTION.*

---

*Took part only in the discussion of national service.

1

The Setting

Joseph J. Wolf

JOSEPH J. WOLF, former Minister, U.S. delegation to NATO, provides a geopolitical backdrop for the issues of U.S. military service examined in subsequent chapters. In this analysis of basic U.S. national interests, Soviet power and policy, and East-West relations, the author draws the lesson of the Second World War and its aftermath that in an anarchic system of sovereign yet interdependent states, the essential requirement for preserving peace is maintaining the balance of power. Given nuclear parity, our ability to deter aggression, avoid a nuclear confrontation, and protect vital interests depends on the existence within the Atlantic Alliance of adequate, trained, available military manpower.

- A third of a century after World War II,
- a quarter of a century after the Korean War,
- a decade after Viet Nam;

yet the United States needs over 2 million people in our armed forces in peacetime, a quarter of them overseas, as well as the ability to speedily reinforce them. All this at a time when there is no immediate fear of invasion or armed attack on any of our 50 states or dependencies.

"Why?" is certainly a reasonable question. It is all the more reasonable when it comes from the younger generation, a generation that has not personally experienced and hence can neither fully comprehend nor, more importantly, recall the fear that comes from the dangers to one's national freedom and individual liberty. Why should we have to fight overseas, rather than only if our borders are attacked? Why, to some, do we appear to be more concerned with the fate of Europe than the Europeans? These, and other similar questions, all need answers if the requisite popular support for a greater defense effort is to develop.

CHALLENGES TO UNITED STATES SECURITY INTERESTS

World War II ushered in a new era that is still with us, and that combines the evils and dangers of imperialist and repressive dictatorship with those of the threats of the horrors of modern war. The Axis powers (Germany, Japan, and Italy) were textbook examples of the way a single-ruling party political system led to the suppression of individual rights within and to the pursuit of expansionist policies through conquest abroad. Human rights under law and morality and the cause of peace itself fell victim to the readiness to employ force at home and abroad to gain the desired ends of dominion and rule, so that even genocide became excusable in the perverted view of Hitler and his gang. The Soviet Union was content to be partner to Hitler in his adventures until the latter's ill-advised sneak attack upon his erstwhile ally. Not until it was attacked at Pearl Harbor did the United States join the war as a participant, though its support for its allies-to-be had increased substantially as time went on. It was those allies, however, who had to purchase with their lives the time required to gear up America's defense industry and to dramatically increase its military manpower through the draft. From this, the costly lesson was underlined that rearming after attack is a luxury that can no longer be afforded.

An additional threat exists today in that the safety and prosperity of the United States and its allies can be dangerously impaired by a variety of measures far short of armed attack upon its territories and people, by the pressure of arms (as in Poland) and by interference with the good relations with other friendly nations on which our safety and prosperity to a great extent depend.

Respect for the freedom and dignity of individuals, the equality of citizens before the law, the independence and equality among nations—these are all fundamental to a world climate favorable to security and growth of the member nations. Reliance on processes of law, and the pursuit of peaceful means for the settlement of disputes are indispensable alternatives to the resort to force. A pluralistic family of nations, with no sanction for hegemonic domination by any one of them, is indispensable for the free and peaceful intercourse on which peace and prosperity depend.

Among the lessons of World War II were these:
- First, aggression must be deterred if possible, or, if deterrence fails, resisted at the outset. Avowedly expansive dictatorships cannot be appeased. The Munich Accords reflected but a semicolon, not a full stop, in Hitler's march toward world empire.
- Second, military power, in the last analysis, can be offset only by countervailing military power.

- Third, it is far better to undertake the trouble, cost, and sacrifice involved in maintaining forces in peacetime that can deter and foil attempts to use force for aggression than to pay the infinitely greater costs in human life of battling an aggression inspired by one's weakness.
- Fourth, a militant major power presents a threat that requires a collective response from the nations affected thereby.

These considerations were at the root of the final turning away from isolationism by this nation. This major shift in United States policy came during the Great Debate on the North Atlantic Treaty. As Senator Arthur Vandenberg put it, the job was to stop a war before it started.

The policy of turning to collective security agreements, coupled with major peacetime military forces in being, also reflected the failure of two other possible sources of security, each radically different from the other. One was the failure of the United Nations ability to cope with the recalcitrance of one of the permanent members of the Security Council, as the Soviet Union proceeded to disregard world opinion and international law. The other was the failure of the temporary nuclear monopoly of the United States to provide a deterrent to nonnuclear forms of aggression.

If deterrence and collective security are the essence of politico-military policy in the post-World War II period, the growth of the interdependence of nations at a geometric rate is the hallmark of the politico-economic scene. Raw materials from abroad are increasingly important for modern, high technology industry and for the increasing demands for supplies of energy. Manufactured products from abroad have replaced to a great extent the American domination in fields of mass production of automobiles and appliances. While service-oriented employment has increased, heavy industry and agriculture employ less of the American population than before. Agriculture and high technology products constitute a major share of our exports. International development and financial institutions still can play an essential and leading role in the fostering of international trade and the economic growth of the developing nations. Foreign trade and international finance are of greatly increased significance to the economies of virtually all nations, great and small.

This commerce among nations, this day-to-day business on which the average citizen depends for his well-being, requires open access to markets, freedom of trade, freedom of the seas, and of the air. The ancient classic phrase "freedom of commerce and navigation" has become increasingly significant as time and distance are foreshortened by modern modes of transportation and growing dependence on exports and imports. Foreign trade represented 22 percent of the gross national product of the United States in 1979, after the doubling of the price of oil. The energy crisis has underscored the lesson of interdependence for all.

To pursue fruitful worldwide economic interrelationships requires a considerable degree of world order. The flow of goods and services in commerce requires not only freedom of movement and transport, it requires a certain degree of stability in trade relations. It is for this reason, at least as much as because of the possible threat of interference with trade routes, that the mercantile nations are concerned about the danger of foreign influence, pressure, and instigation of the overthrow of friendly governments and the replacement of them with regimes less likely to continue prior friendly trade relations. For these reasons, the Soviet invasion of Afghanistan potentially endangered Western access to Persian Gulf oil.

There is also a less immediate but politically equally important spin-off of such challenges to the freedom of commerce and the independence of nations. Intervention in the affairs of other nations, no less than aggression itself, has effects which cannot be limited to the country or region targeted for such action. The relations of all nations with the transgressor nation are inevitably affected to a greater or lesser degree. Nothing brought home the lesson of the indivisibility of détente so much as the Soviet invasion of Afghanistan, arousing, for varying reasons, the peoples of the Moslem nations, the Third World, and the industrialized nations, particularly the United States.

Finally, there is an intangible but very forceful motivation that must be placed in the scale along with the more mundane interests which require our defense. The tradition, culture, and civilization of the Western nations hold that the use of force and fear, of bullying and bloodshed are repugnant to human decency. It is hence a prime tenet of United States policy that problems among peoples and nations should be solved by means short of the use of force—that the rights of individual peoples and nations can peaceably be rationalized with the needs of others. When that heritage is frontally assaulted, as in Poland, a strong reaction is inevitable.

HOW SOVIET POLICY AND POWER AFFECT US

Once again, an expansionist dictatorship—this time, the Soviet Union—has adopted a pattern of conduct that challenges the standards of human morality and international law. At one and the same time, the Soviet Union maintains the largest modern armed forces of any nation in the world, yet it certainly, so far, has not plunged into armed confrontation with the United States. If, notwithstanding this paradox, we are to understand and accept the need for greater military manpower in our armed forces, further explanation and analysis are surely indicated.

The Soviet Union derives its national policy from a blend of ideology, national interests, and the characteristics of a militant dictatorship. Its doctrine warns us that they believe that it is in the nature of things that continued struggle and, ultimately, hostilities will mark the relations between communist and capitalist nations, with ultimate communist victory. In this struggle, the "correlation of forces" will be all-important: the balance of not only military but also economic, sociological, and psychological factors between the two sides, with military power being given highest, but not sole priority. Given this doctrinal framework of continuing conflict, it follows that expansionism must be pursued, though never at the cost of security of the homeland and its regime.

At the end of World War II, although the United States and its other allies demobilized the greater share of their armed forces, the Soviet Union continued to maintain a far larger share of their considerable forces under arms. The Soviet Union continued to station massive Soviet forces outside its own borders in the Eastern European countries, particularly East Germany, far more than needed for internal security in those hostage nations and far more than needed to defend against a weakened Western Europe. The relative military weakness of the Allies had left them open to Soviet pressures, reflected in the activities of Communist parties in Western Europe, and in Soviet moves to create instability and fear in a war-ravaged Europe seeking to rebuild itself. Soviet belligerent intransigence at the United Nations and the Four Power Talks, coupled with its suppression of independence in Eastern Europe, its imposition of the Berlin Blockade, and, eventually, its support of North Korea in the invasion of the South, led the Atlantic Allies to unite for the collective defense of their homelands against the threat of a powerful and aggressive self-declared opponent. It was only as the West started to rearm in NATO that those Soviet tactics began to be less disturbing, as Western Europe attained the confidence that let it pursue the economic recovery and development needed for political stability.

Once the West attained a reasonable military posture, the Soviet Union tempered its approach toward Western Europe to the extent that it urged a relationship of "peaceful coexistence" among the industrialized nations. At the same time, it pursued two major goals: the consolidation of its Eastern European buffer zone and the extension of its influence in Western Europe.

With the passage of time, the Soviet-West German peace treaty and related international agreements, in effect recognizing Eastern Europe as a Soviet buffer area, went far to meet the overriding concern of the Soviet Union for its own security. But it should be well noted, particularly by those who wonder at the continued need to maintain United States forces abroad, that there has been no Soviet move to reduce their armed forces in Eastern Europe.

Second only to that goal of self-defense has been the Soviet objective of becoming the dominant power in Europe, to which it has recently been free to turn. Given the unity and strength of NATO, the Soviet Union does not seek a war with the NATO nations. Both Soviet doctrine and Soviet opportunistic pragmatism call, rather, for a policy of political attack. Its policy is to obtain military superiority, first of all for defense, and then in order to exploit that superiority through pressure for political purpose. Frontal armed conquest of a strong opponent could be far more costly, and inevitably involve more risks to the Soviet regime, already troubled with economic ills and the seeds of political dissent, than measures short of war. Nor is Soviet policy likely to want to see Western Europe leveled in warfare. It would undoubtedly prefer to turn it into a compliant, productive, and supportive neighbor. The most likely threat, then, is that the Soviets will try to combine fear of their military superiority with hope on the part of Western European nations for benefits from selective détente in order to support a major effort over time to split the Old World from the New.

While following a policy of aggressive political and even military intervention in the Third World, in Western Europe the Soviet policy of "selective détente" has been marked by improved economic and political relations. Communist trade with European NATO countries is now about two-thirds of the current level of trade between the United States and its European partners. The hard currency supporting the Soviet share comes largely from Western credits. With Soviet exports to Western Europe focusing on the key areas of energy and raw materials, the politically important sectors of Western European banking and industry, as well as labor, are affected more than the bare figures indicate.

Western Europe, moreover, is important to the Soviets as much as an exporter of much needed technology as of finished goods. Critically important to the deterrent are the leanings of the people of the Federal Republic of Germany. Not only economic gains, but the improvement of contacts between the hostage peoples of East Germany and those of the Federal Republic have been a natural and preeminent motive in its support of détente. Finally, the replacement of bluster and threat with more proper Soviet conduct toward Western Europe, notwithstanding its pattern of conduct elsewhere, has influenced the political climate in the capitals of Europe and has gained support from a broad spectrum of society, including both Left and Right, that not unnaturally prefers détente to a return to the cold war with its apparently greater dangers and lesser benefits.

The Soviets too have a stake in détente. It has been well said that it would be no bargain to trade the problems of the West for those of Moscow. Soviet relations with China, the still festering blunder of the Afghanistan invasion, the fundamental heresy of the unrest and change in Poland, the continuing failure to meet basic requirements for food, the increasing pressure for more consumer goods, and the rapidly growing problem of minorities that are becoming majorities — these certainly combine the characteristics of constraints with those risks always inherent in potential crises.

On balance, these factors argue against the probability of an armed attack against Western Europe. Far more likely is the use of Soviet military strength to back up pressure, whether tacit or overt, directed toward influencing and dominating Western European policies to support Moscow's ends. The recent Polish crisis speaks for itself as an example of the effective use of outside pressure.

Does it follow that it is no longer necessary to maintain a balance of military power between NATO and the Warsaw Pact?

The answer is self-evident. Both political and military measures must be available to hold in check any efforts to employ military power, whether for pressure or attack. If the balance of power were allowed to become so askew that resistance to military pressure, let alone armed attack, would be unlikely or even merely questionable, the extension of Soviet hegemony would be all too easy. The Western "values of democracy and respect for human rights and individual freedom" the alliance seeks to preserve would be, in all too short a time, seriously menaced, or indeed, snuffed out.

Moreover, some genuine risks of hostilities must be taken into account, including the following:

- The danger that the Soviets would be more likely to risk military adventures in the Middle East or elsewhere, some of which could spread to Europe, should they come to feel that the balance of power in Europe was strongly in their favor.
- The ever present possibility that, as in the past in Czechoslovakia and Hungary, or even now in Poland, the Soviets would engage their own armed forces under the Brezhnev Doctrine to preserve their hegemony in Eastern Europe with ensuing events leading to armed confrontation between NATO and the Warsaw Pact.
- The use of force or pressure in connection with Berlin could well constitute a casus belli.
- The possibility that hostilities along the Mediterranean littoral, whether instigated by Libyan militancy, Arab-Israeli confrontation, or otherwise, could subsequently lead to an East-West confrontation.
- The danger that a continually growing imbalance of military strength could, over time, and accompanied by a resulting political weakness in the West, lead the Soviets to risk a surprise attack in anticipation of early collapse and surrender by the West.

Outside the NATO area, Soviet policy has played a different tune. The Soviet doctrine that communist states have a duty to support "wars of national liberation" has provided a convenient carte blanche justification for the instigation, subornation, and military support of radical movements seeking to subvert or overthrow by force regimes currently in power. The Third World has afforded frequent examples of internal factionalism and civil war, as the newly independent peoples of these emerging nations seek to find individual, national, and regional security and well-being. Change and unrest must be expected as political institutions grow, economic development affects the structure of society, and new leadership groups emerge. In these circumstances, the Soviets have easily found targets of opportunity which permit them to work for the reduction of Western influence, and even the establishment of anti-Western and pro-Communist regimes. The story of Soviet exploitation of the situation in such places as South Yemen, Ethiopia, Somalia, Angola, and Afghanistan explains the heightened Western concern over access to Middle East and Persian Gulf oil. The potential for squeezing the Western nations by pressures on their sources of supply and trade, by intervention through proxy and not their own forces is great and still growing. Tempting targets are the politically fragile regimes, such as Saudi Arabia, Jordan, and Morocco, which remain important to the well-being of the West. The Western hemisphere, too, affords the atmosphere of political and economic ferment in Latin America and the Caribbean which is particularly susceptible to outside influence.

In Eastern Asia, too, Soviet power looms over the underarmed nation of Japan, now one of the industrial giants of the world. The USSR supports the excessively large and well-equipped armed forces of North Korea. Its growing naval presence in Pacific waters, together with Backfire Bomber bases and SS-20 intermediate range missiles, make it a power to be reckoned with in the area from Vietnam to Siberia and which, in the absence of allied strength, could dominate the vital industrial complex represented by Japan, the Republic of Korea, Taiwan, and Singapore.

In all aspects of its defense establishment, the Soviet Union presents a military posture which can and does back up its expansionist policy, particularly wherever it may be unopposed. Why manpower is so essential if that policy is to be held in check is the next step in our analysis.

THE ROLE OF MANPOWER
IN KEEPING THE PEACE
IN A NUCLEAR AGE

Trained, available military manpower is now, more clearly than ever, essential to keeping peace and stability in a troubled world, and reducing the risks of resort to nuclear weapons.

Three propositions explain the compelling need for a shift in emphasis in Western military thinking:

- Soviet attainment of superiority in battlefield and theater nuclear weapons and parity in strategic nuclear weapons should serve to reemphasize the fact that NATO's shortlived nuclear superiority is gone; that resorting

to nuclear weapons to make up for conventional deficiencies would truly
be a measure of last resort.

- Reliance on general purpose forces to deter any military threat or action
is thus increased; with increasing requirements around the globe, which
can only be met with conventional power, conventional deficiencies acceptable in a time of nuclear superiority and much lower Soviet ability to
project power abroad now offer unacceptable risks.
- The combination of weak conventional forces and lessened readiness to
resort to nuclear weapons gravely increases the chances of Soviet mis-
judgment of the risks of confrontation.

The following discussion enlarges on these points.

The Loss of Nuclear Superiority

NATO's conventional forces are supposed to be able to sustain a forward
defense sufficient to inflict serious losses on the aggressor and to convince
the aggressor of the risks of continuing his aggression. As will be seen,
NATO's forces can, in fact, sustain such an effort for all too short a period
of time. The limited extent to which, in the past, NATO relied on the use of
tactical nuclear weapons to deter and defend should its conventional capability have been proven insufficient is simply irrelevant today.

What has occurred to change the picture is the loss of that predominance
in both strategic and tactical (or theater) nuclear weapons, which in its earliest days was deemed to give the Atlantic Alliance control of the decision to
escalate to nuclear warfare. The Soviets now have superiority in theater
nuclear weapons and are threatening to surpass the West in strategic weaponry. Europe, the Middle East, most of the Indian Ocean, and the East
Asian perimeter are now within range of the Soviet SS-20 missile and the
Backfire Bomber. Clear NATO nuclear superiority is not likely to be seen
again. While the Long Range Theater Nuclear Force, when deployed,
should make Soviet planners less confident of the success of large scale conventional attack, the fact remains that, even then, a resort to nuclear weapons by the allies would be counterproductive should the Soviets respond
with their full theater nuclear power. Resort to tactical nuclear weapons by
the allies to shore up their conventional weaknesses would be likely to make
them worse off, as not only the national infrastructure and populations of
Western Europe, but also NATO's military forces themselves would be
vulnerable to Soviet nuclear counterattack.

While it is theoretically conceivable that the resort to theater nuclear
weapons even in a most limited way might not result in escalation, the
chances of the mutual exercise of restraint in such circumstances are too
questionable to constitute the basis of a responsible strategy or policy.

It must be noted that while the readiness with which the West might be prepared to initiate use of nuclear weapons is thus appreciably reduced, this by no means permits them to be eliminated from the arsenals of the allies. In the absence of effective and verifiable arms control agreements, they remain indispensable to forestall Soviet first use of nuclear weapons or resort to nuclear blackmail. They moreover leave the Soviets uncertain whether they might not be employed by the West as a last resort—terrible and mutually costly though it might be—if faced with ultimate defeat on the battlefield.

But should the West become unable to mount a serious defense with conventional weapons—whether because of increased Soviet conventional power, or declining Western capabilities, or both—the Soviets would have every reason to give less credence to the will and determination of NATO to resort to nuclear war even as a last resort. They might base their estimates of the situation on European fears that the Americans were decoupling nuclear weapons because of fear of Soviet nuclear power, as well as on American reluctance to undertake the risks of strategic nuclear war on behalf of European allies who had not undertaken a genuine conventional defense of their own lands. In the absence of NATO preparations for a more serious conventional defense level, they then might be well led to conclude that, if push came to shove, NATO would not really fight at all, with either conventional or nuclear weapons. In such an event, the temptations for a bullying or an adventurist Soviet policy would greatly increase the risks of more aggressive domination, if not confrontation.

In other words, the conventional balance has assumed far greater deterrent significance now than it did when NATO had clear escalatory control. A more genuine conventional capability is essential to make NATO's strategy of deterrence and defense responsive to today's needs.

The Need for Conventional Forces in NATO

As noted, NATO's conventional forces are supposed to be able to sustain a forward defense sufficient to inflict serious losses on the aggressor and convince him of the risks of continuing his aggression. But NATO's forces can, in fact, sustain such an effort for all too short a period of time.

The reasons are twofold: Soviet growing strength and Western growing deficiencies. The Soviet Union's program of steady quantitative as well as qualitative improvement of its military forces over the past decade has profoundly changed its conventional as well as its nuclear posture. New generations of tanks, guns, armored fighting vehicles, and aircraft, along with an impressive chemical warfare capability have transformed the Soviet military establishment into a first-class fighting force with steadily improved combat power and sustaining logistical support, increasing the need for readiness among NATO forces. Its strength and composition far exceed what might be needed either for defense of even its vast empire or to preserve internal security in the Eastern European countries. Its equipment and weaponry are, in many aspects, superior to that of the West. Unlike Western forces, Soviet ground forces are prepared to operate in a chemical warfare environment. The large, growing, and modern Soviet Navy has increased its presence along the sea lanes of the Mediterranean, the Atlantic, the Indian Ocean, and the Pacific.

It is in the European theater that the Soviets have consistently deployed their best-equipped, most ready ground and air forces with 30 combat-ready divisions and 1700 aircraft deployed in Eastern Europe. Backed up by the less-effective but numerous second echelon forces in the neighboring USSR, their presence inescapably requires a high level of countervailing forces in Western Europe.

NATO's forces, on the other hand, have simply not kept pace. A combination of economic pressures (the burden of stagflation), lack of conviction on the significance of Soviet growing military power on security in Europe and in the United States, and sheer wishful thinking have combined to keep the net NATO defense effort from balancing that of the Soviets. Escalating costs of military manpower in the West, particularly in the United States which has renounced conscription, has cut deeply into the amount of defense resources available for equipment and supplies. The Warsaw Pact states have no problem of the same nature. The decade-long decline in the United States defense effort after Vietnam more than outweighed the fact that some NATO measures have been of real significance in keeping up the NATO defenses. On balance, the trend today is toward a widening, not a narrowing, of the gap between East and West in nonnuclear capability.

It is paradoxical that the antinuclear movement in Europe and in the United States failed to sponsor the growth of conventional forces in the West as the best way to avoid ever having to resort to nuclear weapons. Yet, their focus has been narrowly antinuclear rather than on the bigger issue of how to keep peace with freedom.

The Increased Need for Manpower Elsewhere

It is where a balance of power is lacking that opportunities for the Soviet Union to extend its influence and domination at little cost exist. The areas outside of NATO are hence more vulnerable. Afghanistan not only seemed low on any list of countries in which the West had substantial interests, it was remote from any Western military stronghold. The withdrawal of Britain east of Suez left only token United States forces and a French flotilla in all the vast reaches of the Indian Ocean and the Gulf. A power vacuum existed there; hence the concern at the invitation it constituted for the application of force. The enunciation of the Carter Doctrine was a warning of intent to protect our interests in the Gulf; but a force that could afford prompt resistance if needed has not yet been developed. The Persian Gulf may be the worst place for us to wage a major war; but that is quite different from the fact that it is also the worst place to leave devoid of any ability to make the outcome of a challenge to our vital interests a serious affair.

The Persian Gulf is only one of the areas outside NATO that comes to mind. Indigenous unrest make other parts of the Middle East, the southern shore of the Mediterranean, the African continent, and, nearer to home, Central America, the Caribbean, and even South America vulnerable to external exploitation and troublemaking, particularly if no capability and purpose to respond to such activities is available.

The ability and the purpose to confront such external intervention is, then, essential to restraining Soviet intervention in areas where the power to rule may be at issue. Nuclear capability is simply not the sort of power that can be used in Third World situations (except to countervail possible Soviet nuclear threats). But not only American forces are needed to deter the employment of Soviet combat or support forces. The ability to support friendly indigenous governments is of even greater importance in a day when the use of proxy forces and the support of radical elements of the local society offer the Soviets a cheaper and more fruitful line of attack than the direct use of Soviet combat forces.

If such activities are to be checked, rather than to be allowed to progress to a critical point where regional power balances are affected, plans, programs, equipment, supply, and, above all, ready trained manpower to do the job are needed.

As these studies proceed to evaluate the best way to get adequate manpower into the United States armed forces, it may be well to consider that the most effective action in attempting to keep the peace in time of crisis and to reduce the chances of escalation to nuclear warfare could well be the ability to deploy promptly additional capable, trained, conventional reinforcements to a troubled area.

DIFFERENCES OF ATTITUDE AND POLICY AMONG THE ALLIES

There is, particularly after Afghanistan and Poland, a general awareness throughout the world of the dangers to liberty, and to all countries, great or small. But there is far greater diversity of views of what each of the allies should do about it, as might well be expected.

Indeed, it almost seems as if alliances of free states breed a sort of paradoxical diversion of attitude rather than unity of perception. For example:
• The European allies wish to be assured of nuclear protection from the United States, so long as nuclear war is not waged in Europe.

- Wishing to avoid a nuclear exchange in Europe, some Western European nations are nevertheless reluctant to increase conventional forces for fear the nuclear umbrella might be weakened, as well as because of severe political pressures to maintain social programs at present levels.
- Grateful that the United States is ready to undertake security measures to protect Middle East/Persian Gulf oil on which their economic life depends, the European allies and Japan have not yet taken concrete steps either to compensate for these calls on United States defense assets or to contribute adequately to that effort.
- Conscious of the significance of the dangers to their oil supply, the European allies are nevertheless reluctant to risk the fruits of détente in Europe by actively participating in deterrent forces outside NATO.
- Pleased that the United States has decided to devote greater effort to defense and to be clearer and more consistent in its policy, our allies nevertheless reflect concern at what they consider excessive reliance by the United States on support of military measures to resolve problems, particularly in the Third World countries.

And at the same time, our allies, looking across the Atlantic, wonder at some of our attitudes that to them do not seem easily understandable. For example:

- At the same time as the administration assumes a firmer posture on the indivisibility of détente, and urges sanctions against the USSR because of the Polish crisis, it refrains from reinstituting the embargo on the export of grain to the Soviet Union.
- While urging the allies to increase defense efforts even at some sacrifice in social benefits, the United States has itself not yet found the way to produce all the required military manpower or equipment it lacks.
- Urging its allies to accept long range theater nuclear weapons on their territory, the United States is not yet ready to accept a new generation of mobile land-based strategic nuclear weapons.

Inconsistency, then, is not a monopoly of our allies, but a trait we share ourselves. It remains to look more carefully at the implications of some of these differing points of view on the continued strength and unity of the alliances on which we all depend.

Governments of democratic nations are responsible to public opinion and must be responsive to the will of the people if they are to continue in power. The foreign policy of each nation depends, in the final analysis, on domestic politics. As the political situation varies in every case, it is impossible to speak of "allied attitudes" or "European views" without risk of overgeneralization. Even within each nation, there can be, and often is, a gap between the position of the leaders of the government and the varying views of the different elements which make up the political spectrum of the nation. But despite these disclaimers, certain trends in governmental thinking and in popular attitudes require consideration if the concerns of our allies at our course of conduct are to be taken into account, and our concerns at their approaches be recognized and understood by them.

As a first step toward becoming the dominant power in Europe, Soviet policy is directed toward splintering the NATO Alliance, and particularly splitting Western Europe from the United States. Weakening the United States' commitment to the defense of Europe is thus a fundamental Soviet goal, which it pursues through propaganda, negotiation, and threat. If different approaches within the alliance which create serious irritations are not rationalized and controlled, this could lead to major splits within the alliance. Among them are the following:

- The urgency and nature of the Soviet challenge, whether in the NATO area or outside it;
- How to interrelate arms control negotiations (a political imperative in Europe, second to security in U.S. eyes) with rearmament;
- How to balance the desirability of maintaining détente in Europe and resisting Soviet expansionism elsewhere, for example, in the Middle East/ Persian Gulf area;
- How to share the defense burden equitably, particularly if the United States now undertakes additional responsibilities outside the NATO area;
- The importance of greater Western conventional capabilities in a time when there is no longer Western nuclear superiority;
- How the United States can exercise leadership of the alliance without alienating its partners.

Periodically recurring pressures in the media and in the Congress to withdraw American troops now stationed abroad because of what is judged to be inadequate defense efforts on the part of our allies exemplify this tension. Displeasure with allied policies that do not always support American initiatives, as in the case of sanctions because of Poland, tend to have the same result. And a form of neo-isolationism, based on the desire to see the United States "go it alone," feeds on these elements of discontent. Such pressures are likely to increase as economic difficulties at home and difficulties with our allies abroad increase.

The problem is made more difficult because of the shortage of personnel to meet United States reserve requirements, so vital to the ability to speedily reinforce our forces abroad in time of crisis, as well as painful deficiencies in the active forces in the senior noncommissioned grades and technically trained personnel, which are generally viewed in Europe as bearing significantly on the combat effectiveness of the American armed forces.

Maintaining large numbers of visiting troops abroad in peacetime over an extended period of time is something new to history. It is remarkable that this concept, introduced only after World War II, has succeeded as well as it has. But it admittedly puts a strain on both the troops (and their families) away from home and the citizens who find they have foreign soldiers permanently in their midst. It seems to be a natural American feeling to wonder why the citizens of the host nation have no reaction other than gratitude that the United States is there to protect them.

We must continually remind ourselves that our troops are abroad to defend our own interests first and foremost. And that, in the last analysis, it is the 30 Soviet divisions abroad in Eastern Europe that compel our major overseas deployment. It is they, coupled with the SS-20 deployment, that have led to NATO's proposals either to limit theater nuclear weapons or to see them deployed on both sides.

Fear of nuclear warfare is generating a troublesome political movement in Western Europe, and in the United States as well. It focuses on the awesome risks of nuclear war rather than on the dedication to defending peace and freedom without recourse to force, nuclear or otherwise. It erroneously argues that there is little that smaller countries can do to affect the balance of power, overlooking the fact that "mony a mickle makes a muckle." It constitutes a neo-defeatist school of thought that recalls the "better Red than dead" slogan of some years back. While still a minority, it draws its strength from such diverse sectors as church and youth groups, and Labor and Socialist elements in a number of Western European nations. Particularly troublesome is the by-product in Europe of anti-Americanism, which seems to follow on the condemnation of nuclear weaponry without any equivalent anti-Soviet feeling. It has an all too significant constraining influence on the defense policies of every member of the alliance and will require continuing attention for the foreseeable future, both at home and abroad.

The defense policy of Japan needs some special comment. As a heritage of World War II, Japan remains loathe to undertake a significant increase in the minuscule defense effort it now sustains. While ready to support non-military security programs, the Japanese regrettably do not yet seem psychologically prepared to assume even an adequately increased role in their own self-defense, even with forces that would be purely defensive in nature.

To what extent does the manpower problem affect the allies' view of the United States defense effort? German Federal Chancellor Schmidt has said that the United States would turn to the draft, as have all the allies save the United States, the United Kingdom, and Canada, if the United States were really serious about the nature of the problem. Many consider this a facile excuse for the failure of a prosperous Federal Republic to devote more resources to defense and point to the undesirably short terms of service prevalent in the military services of the continental allies. To some extent, this may be correct. At the same time, it is also true that the average young German citizen subject to the draft cannot but feel that Germans are thereby being subjected to greater sacrifices than are their young American counterparts, particularly when American pay scales are taken into account. The European allies provide by far the greater share of the manpower for the defense of Europe.

Perhaps the paramount issue, however, is the problem of balancing defense efforts with the economic strengths and limitations of the Western nations. The manpower problem cannot be dealt with as if in a laboratory—either at home or abroad. It is only one important aspect of the whole, difficult problem of the poverty of the rich which now faces the industrialized nations, calling for a fundamental restatement of values and priorities in response to the conflicting demands of modern life if the goal of peace with freedom is to be protected and nourished.

NATIONAL SECURITY AND AMERICAN SOCIETY

It has been traditional in our society that military service be given the back of the hand in peacetime. As Kipling wrote approximately a century ago:

> I went into a theatre as sober as could be,
> They gave a drunk civilian room, but 'adn't none for me;
> They sent me to the gallery, or round the music-'alls,
> But when it comes to fightin'; Lord! they'll shove me in the stalls!

Not only the individual soldier, but the defense establishment as a whole has suffered from lack of attention in the times between wars. The Louisiana Maneuvers before American entry into World War II, with broomsticks labeled "GUNS," gave evidence of this neglect; the parsimonious Louis Johnson postwar defense budget even more recently showed that the lesson of need for peacetime preparedness is forgotten all too soon.

But from the 1950s on, circumstances have compelled a standing military establishment which is considerably different from simply being a cadre for expansion in wartime. No longer do the oceans provide the security needed for a deliberate mobilization. Instead, forces already present on the scene are needed to make a serious military engagement the price of a serious threat. And augmentation forces at home must be capable of speedy mobilization and deployment as well. In these days, training civilian soldiers only after aggression has commenced would be an extreme case of "too little and too late."

The concept of maintaining large deterrent global forces in peacetime is something new in our history and repugnant to the pattern of the past. But is this "peace"? Webster defines "peace" as "a state of tranquility or quiet." Present times certainly do not fit that bill, even though they do conform to the more limited definition that "peace is the absence of war." The distinction is no idle one. For, while short of active hostilities, the world scene today is far from what in earlier days was considered peace. Hence, it calls for greater sacrifice in order to keep the peace and provide the desired sense of security that otherwise could not be attained.

The American people tended, in the decade after Vietnam, to play down the dangers of a lessened defense posture as against the risks of another undeclared war. Nevertheless, it seemed that once they felt they were being put in a second-best position, their reaction was quick and strong, and the national emphasis on an increased defense posture was one of the elements that swept the present administration into office.

However, the total bill is not yet in, in terms of dollars, equipment, or manpower. Current defense budgets are but a prelude to increasing programs in the coming years if even the most simple plans for expansion and modernization are put through. And the shortages of material and trained men continue to be with us. How the executive and the legislature will combine to translate plans into realities as the economic and political strengths and weaknesses of the nation develop over the next several years remains to be seen. The important thing is that a beginning be made in reversing the trend toward increasing weakness.

This will depend, in the last analysis, on the pressures of public opinion — on what the American people want and how much they want it. No military establishment can be created by fiat; it must be sustained by a national commitment on the part of its citizenry. As Edmund Burke said of the British armed forces:

> It is the love of the British people; it is their attachment to their government, from the sense of the deep stakes they have in such a glorious institution, which gives you both your army and your navy, and infuses into both that liberal obedience, without which your army would be a base rabble, and your navy nothing but a rotten timber.

Is there that spirit today among the people of the United States? Is it there among those of the younger generation who would make up the bulk of the armed forces, whether volunteer or conscript? Is it there among society as a whole, reflected in our daily culture — the press, TV, the movies — in family contacts, the marketplace, the church? Is there such a feeling of participation, of responsibility, of contribution on the part of the individual? Is the idea of peace with freedom worth working for?

If those questions had been posed a decade ago, the answers would have bordered on the hopeless. The very elements that have stimulated the movement of resistance to nuclear weapons in Europe today were present even more strongly in the United States, vastly augmented by the Vietnam experience. As a result, there occurred a rebellion against the institutions which had failed to make life seem worthwhile to many of the younger generation. That list of failed institutions is distressing in its comprehensiveness and includes the family, the church, the economic and educational systems, and the government itself. With the rejection of these key institutions came the collapse of respect for authority in whatever form, fostered by the growth of that permissiveness that the younger generation inherited as part of the environment that they knew at firsthand.

There may be grounds for hope that the American youth of the ensuing decade to some extent has reversed the swing of the pendulum. While still viewing many of our institutions as they now function with the combination of optimism and cynicism that youth can and should bring to the picture, there seems to be a degree of renewed acceptance on the part of some of the need for some framework of society, for better institutions rather than no institutions, for the acceptance by the individual of his or her responsibility to the society to which we all belong.

But the conformist acceptance of authority that once prevailed should not be expected to return. It is far too early to be "Pollyannaish" about the future, particularly as it bears on the question of military manpower. It is inviting, after looking at the results of the 1980 election, to envisage a vast national consensus with full unity of approach on a conservative, defense-minded policy. It is more realistic to recognize that there is great diversity of thought as to the ways to go about the job. This study itself bears witness to that fact. It is also more realistic to remember that each individual personally affected by increased defense measures naturally has a different view of them than those who are not directly called upon for sacrifice.

When any young man is asked to devote a number of years of his life outside the mainstream of economic endeavor he wants to pursue he becomes faced with a difficult set of choices. If he comes from an underprivileged environment or believes his opportunities in life are limited, will he have the same feeling of owing a debt to society as the young man whose future is more assured? Will the young man whose prospects are better than average really be eager to risk those prospects more than he who has less to risk?

At the same time, it is important that the system adopted not violate flagrantly the American concept of fairness in sharing the burdens of society. The wartime draft of World War II provided a rough equity among the citizenry. The same cannot be said of the system that provided manpower for the Vietnam crisis. The call for an All-Volunteer Force, one supported by four presidents, can be viewed in part as an attempt to rectify that situation. In any event, it has been a politically imposed imperative, and the burden of proof will rest on the advocates of change. Whether the benefits and burdens of military service do fall reasonably and fairly throughout our society today is a question for the most careful consideration. It in turn raises the question of how closely military manpower availability should be related to the availability of jobs in the marketplace.

The issues are made more difficult because the situation lacks the compelling impetus of urgency that would accompany an unmistakable danger of immediate hostilities. The fact that trying to raise a more capable military establishment before a crisis has occurred admittedly lacks the emotional call that would speedily fill the ranks in other, more urgent, circumstances, as they were filled after Pearl Harbor.

This, then, is a political problem to be solved through the political process. It calls for that blending of leadership and reflection of popular views that issues of the public good inevitably demand. Having explained why the manpower issue needs tackling, we now turn to past experience before we analyze the pros and cons of the various possible steps.

2
Military Manpower:
The American Experience
and the Enduring Debate
James L. Lacy

JAMES L. LACY, former Special Assistant to the Assistant Secretary of Defense for Manpower, Reserve Affairs and Logistics, and currently completing a history of U.S. naval strategy at the Center for Naval Analyses, as well as finishing a book on the details of resuming a military draft, remarks toward the end of this chapter that, "The nation has rarely been as clever, duplicitous, inspired, noble, venal, passionate, or absurd as in the act of inducing its citizens to military service." The author explores from colonial times to the last draft era the "instructive antecedents" of today's force-manning issues— what the country did and said about such questions as selective service, voluntarism, the reserves, conscientious objection, universal military training, civilian "national service," and the role of women and minorities.

A page of history is worth a volume of logic, said Mr. Justice Holmes, and in terms of contemporary American force-manning, there are more than a few pages of instructive antecedents. The great military manpower issues of the 1980s may derive their urgency from Soviet foreign and military policy, and their specific formulations from contemporary American social, political, and economic science, but in several key respects they are as old as the American republic, and then some. What size armed force, drawn from which of the citizenry, how compensated and controlled, and whether drafted or entirely volunteer—have been enduring questions. To these the generation preceding World War I added two propositions—universal military training and civilian "national service"—which have spurred a host of additional, and no less durable, issues.

The pre-twentieth-century American experience with military service is fairly well traveled ground. The constant complaints of General George

Washington, the flatulent rhetoric of Daniel Webster, the great New York City draft riot of 1863 (which, in fact, seems to have had little to do with conscription) have been amply recorded in popular historical accounts and are taken up here principally by way of introduction. The fundamental debates were formed in the nineteenth century, but the wellspring of most current issues and proposals is located closer in time, in the last 90-some years. Here there are fewer accounts and less understanding, and it is here that the past is most pertinent in appreciating present choices and their complexity.

COLONIAL MILITIA TO SAN JUAN HILL

The two great military issues in eighteenth- and nineteenth-century America concerned control of military forces and the means by which their manpower was to be secured. The states vied with the national government over which would control the common defense. Conscription-versus-voluntarism was fiercely debated at several junctures.

Early colonial defense had been a local affair, reflecting a heritage of "citizen-soldier" service that reached back to King Henry II's Assize of Arms in 1181. The colonies (save for Quaker Pennsylvania) required militia service of able-bodied men, but the exceptions were extensive.[1] Moreover, routine militia duties were limited to an occasional parade or muster, and the militia's responsibilities were confined largely to matters within the boundaries of the colony: home defense, suppression of insurrections, and convening as a *posse comitatus* to pursue outlaws. While militiamen could be summoned for duty beyond the colony, this often provoked a fair amount of local commotion.[2]

A rag-tag mixture of volunteers and militia fought the Revolutionary War, and General Washington's complaints were notorious: "All the allurements of the most exorbitant bounties and every other inducement that could be thought of have had little effect other than to increase the rapacity and raise the demands of those to whom they are held out." Still, while the Constitutional Convention of 1787 empowered the Congress to raise armies, the national charter was silent concerning how this was to be done, and ambiguous in that it also provided that the states could maintain their own militia.

The national army was voluntary and small; in 1789 it had a total strength of 718 officers and enlisted men; in 1811 it barely topped 5,000.

The first great political and constitutional debate over military service did not occur until the War of 1812. President Madison had secured congressional approval of a wartime army of 166,000 men to be composed primarily of state militiamen. Three New England states opposed the war, however, and refused to provide militia forces. Regular army recruiting fared not much better. By 1814, the city of Washington, D.C. had been ransacked by an unopposed British expeditionary force, and Baltimore had been seriously threatened. Meeting in the ashes of the national capital, the Congress called on Madison for a plan to bolster the sagging fortunes of the regular army. It was James Monroe, his secretary of war, who responded.

Monroe's plan was for a national draft and contained many of the elements of twentieth-century conscription: selective service, local selections, direct conscription without regard to state militias. The free male population was to be divided into groups of 100, each to furnish 10 men for the war and to replace them in the event of casualty. For Monroe, the plan's constitutionality was obvious.

> The idea that the United States cannot raise a regular army in any mode than by accepting the voluntary service of individuals, is believed to be repugnant to the uniform construction of all grants of power, and equally so to the first principles and leading objects of the Federal compact. An unqualified grant of power gives the means necessary to carry it into effect. This is a universal maxim, which admits of no exception.

Some, notably the freshman congressman from New Hampshire, Daniel Webster, thought otherwise. With Monroe's plan, said Webster with apocalyptic foreboding, "the Constitution is libelled, foully libelled."

> The people of this country have not established for themselves such a fabric of despotism. They have not purchased at a vast expense of their own treasure and their own blood a Magna Carta to be slaves. Where is it written in the Constitution, in what article or section is it contained, that you may take children from their parents, and parents from their children, & compel them to fight the battles of any war, in which the folly or the wickedness of government may engage it?

The Senate had not acted on the Monroe plan when the war ended, and the great issue quickly lapsed from the public agenda. For the next 40 years, America maintained its national forces with volunteers, and at modest levels. The army dropped to as few as 6,000 men in the mid-1820s and was manned by not much more than 16,000 as the 1860s began.[3]

The Civil War was at first a conflict between opposing volunteer forces, but, as the casualties and manpower demands mounted, first the Confederacy, and then the Union, turned to conscription. For the South, the irony was poignant. A confederacy which seceded in order to preserve the supremacy of states' rights promptly submerged them by enacting America's first draft in the service of a central government.[4]

Editorial reaction on both sides was mixed: variously condemning the measures as unnecessary and unconstitutional, and applauding their contributions to the war effort. The Augusta *Constitutionalist*, the North Carolina *Standard*, and the *Montgomery Mail* branded the southern draft unconstitutional. (The Confederate Constitution paralleled word-for-word the Federal Constitution.) The Washington *Sunday-Times* condemned the federal draft, huffing that, "the act of Congress, ignoring the authority and control of states over their own militia, is a bag of wind let loose, and nothing more!" The *New York Herald* worried that federal conscription gave the president the "powers of the Autocrat of all the Russias, or the powers of an absolute despotism." The *New York Times*, on the other hand, praised the federal act as a "new pledge of success." Looking eastward across the Atlantic even as it peered southward, the *Times* confidently intoned:

> Now for the first time, we shall have the Power of the nation pitted fairly against the Power of the rebellion. The confederate conscriptions are nearly exhausted; ours are but just to begin. . . . It will, too, enable us to repel the armed intervention of Napoleon III, if he shall prove so infatuated as to undertake it.

On both sides there was considerable evasion, feigning of ailments, and violence. Armed bands of resisters controlled sections of western Virginia, North Carolina, Alabama, and Tennessee. Federal draft records were burned and draft enrolling officers were attacked in Ohio, Indiana, Illinois, and Vermont. For four days in July 1863, the bloodiest riot in American history erupted in New York City. How much it had to do with the draft is questionable, but the *New York Times* had no hesitancies, "its instigators and leaders are allies and agents of Jefferson Davis . . . the Left Wing of Lee's Army."

The struggle over conscription played in the courthouse as well. Several lower courts held the federal draft unconstitutional, but the matter never reached the Supreme Court.[5] Provost Marshall General Fry, summarizing difficulties in executing the federal draft, complained that it had been seriously impeded by the actions of civil courts: draft officials had been subjected to injunctions, habeas corpus writs, attachments for contempt, and other judicial processes. Indeed, a "lawyers' conspiracy" to use the judicial process to obstruct conscription law had formed around New York attorney Samuel J. Tilden, quietly encouraged by New York Governor Horatio Seymour.

Both Civil War drafts had exemptions and deferments, and both allowed a potential conscript to substitute another or pay a commutation fee in lieu of personal service.[6] The federal draft was administered by an apparatus of unbridled power. Enrollment officers sought out potential conscripts in their homes and workplaces. Each enrollment board was headed by a provost marshall who was also a captain in the army. The decision of the board concerning exemptions was final. Failure to report for service was, by law, desertion, subject to military court martial and the death penalty.

Conscription proved much more vital to the Confederacy than to the Union. Fully one-third of the South's soldiers had been draftees. The federal draft, on the other hand, produced less than 3 percent of the Union Army in conscripts, plus another 6 percent in substitutes. With the end of the war the draft was terminated.

As in 1814, conscription fell quickly from the public agenda. The regular army dropped in size again: from 1 million in 1865 to 37,240 by 1870. American forces were entirely volunteer for another 50 years. The states maintained their militias, although after the 1840s militia service was wholly voluntary.

Few Americans looked back on the draft debacle of the 1860s. Few as well looked forward with any systematic attention to future military organization or manpower needs. Two exceptions are noteworthy. An assessment of the federal Civil War draft was put together by Brevet Brigadier General James Oakes in 1866. For Oakes, the lessons were clear. Future drafts should, among other things: obligate men to come forward to register instead of using enrollment officers to track them down, bar the use of substitutes, prohibit the payment of bounties, and localize the selection determination, leaving it to local panels of neighbors and friends. In the 1870s, Emory Upton, a West Point graduate, proposed that among the "chief causes of weakness of our present system" were: reliance on voluntary enlistments, instead of voluntary enlistments coupled with conscription, and "the intrusion of the States in military affairs and the consequent waging of all our wars on the theory that we are a confederacy instead of a nation."[7]

An America seeking its "manifest destiny" waged its western campaigns against the Indians and the border skirmishes with Mexico with an army of slightly over 27,000 in the 1870s and 1880s. A private's pay was $11 a month until 1894, when it was raised to $13. Desertions were no less frequent than before the Civil War: in 1871 alone one-third of the United States Army deserted. And matters comfortably forgotten for a score and ten years returned. Unseemly, widely publicized, the confusion in the mobilization and command of U.S. forces in the Spanish-American War of 1898 was the catalyst for a period of reevaluation of old military manpower organization and methods. Upton's earlier prescriptions found a following. The first truly modern debate over voluntary versus conscripted forces, over the role of state reserve forces, and over national service began in earnest within a decade.

THE FIRST MODERN FORMULATIONS: 1900–1919

The years immediately preceding World War I set the terms of subsequent twentieth-century debate. The size, control, and manner of recruitment of the nation's armed forces became once again matters of dispute. New ideas — military training, compulsory and voluntary nonmilitary service, a military draft to influence civilian behavior as much as to man the armed forces, concerns about equity of obligation — were propounded by an extraordinarily articulate generation.

In the Franco-Prussian War of 1870–71, the Germans successfully used a mass conscript army, based on universal, compulsory military training in peacetime. By the turn of the century, most other European nations and Japan had copied the German model. Britain and the United States stood almost alone in clinging to relatively small, volunteer forces. America, as well, had its federalism to contend with. Much governmental authority, including control of the militia, reposed in the states.

Still, industrialization in the United States did produce some moves toward greater centralization of both military and civilian institutions. Defense acts of 1903 and 1916 provided for increasing federalization of the state militia. The awkward disposition of American forces in the War of 1898 added pressures on traditional military institutions.

In England, a private but prominent National Service League pressed for adoption of the European system of compulsory military training. A similar campaign began in earnest in the United States in 1912. Among its proponents were intellectuals, such as Charles Eliot and Ralph Barton Perry of Harvard, former President Theodore Roosevelt, former Secretaries of War Elihu Root and Henry Stimson, and Army Chief of Staff General Leonard Wood.

These American conscriptionists argued their case on two grounds. First, the traditional voluntary system was militarily inadequate. According to Wood:

It is uncertain in operation, prevents organized preparation, tends to destroy that individual sense of obligation for military service which should be found in every citizen, costs excessively in life and treasure, and does not permit that condition of preparedness which must exist if we are to wage war successfully with any great power prepared for war.

The second rationale was offered by Harvard's Eliot. Universal military training was not only essential "for defensive combat with any military power." According to Eliot, it also offered important social benefits.

All the able-bodied young men in the country would receive a training in the hard work of a soldier which would be of some service to them in any industry in which they might afterward engage. They would have become accustomed to a discipline under which many men cooperate strenuously in the pursuit of common objects.

Arrayed against the American conscriptionists was an unlikely coalition of progressives, liberal pacificists, anarchists, and agrarian disciples of William Jennings Bryan who argued, among other things, to make the volunteer military system stronger by increasing soldiers' pay to a point of competitiveness with civilian wages. And there was Harvard philosopher William James, with still another view.

James and National Service

To James' 1910 essay, "A Moral Equivalent of War," are commonly ascribed the beginnings of what has come to be known as "national service," an idea which has never strayed far from debates about military manpower. James wrote against a backdrop of increasing political polarization over America's foreign policy and military posture. The essay, he said, was an attempt to reconcile the two opposing philosophies: to bring together the camps of the "war party" and the "peace party." Martial virtues and pacifism need not be in opposition. The compromise, however, was not a military army, but a civilian workforce imbued with military values.

Declaring himself "squarely in the anti-militarist party," James nevertheless saw "certain deficiencies in the program of pacifism which set the militarist imagination strongly, and to a certain extent, justifiably, against it." Pacifism was soft and without direction. A peaceful economy cannot be a "simple pleasure economy." The "old elements of army discipline" were compatible with and necessary to pacifism; they needed only to be redirected to peaceful pursuits. "Martial virtues must be the inducing cement; intrepidity, contempt of softness, surrender of private interest, obedience to command; must still remain the rock upon which states are built. . . ."

In place of both the volunteer army and military conscription, James proposed a new organization of drafted youth grounded in pacifism: conscription for "a certain number of years" of all young men in an "Army enlisted against Nature." "Nature," however, was an artful term in this context.

> To coal and iron mines, to freight trains, to fishing fleets in December, to dish-washing, clothes-washing, and window-washing, to road-building and tunnel-making, to foundries and stokeholes, and to the frames of skyscrapers would our gilded youths be drafted off, according to their choice, to get the childishness knocked out of them and to come back into society with healthier sympathies and soberer ideas; they would have paid their blood tax, done their own part in the immemorial human warfare against nature; they would tread the earth more proudly, the women would value them more highly, they would be greater fathers and teachers of the following generation.

The aim was to toughen young men, to preserve "manliness of type," and to even out class distinctions by imposing similarly severe work on all.

[T]hat so many men, by mere accidents of birth and opportunity, should have a life of *nothing else* but toil and pain and hardness and inferiority imposed on them, should have *no* vacation, while others natively no more deserving never get the taste of this campaigning life at all, — *this* is capable of arousing indignation in reflective minds. It may end by seeming shameful to all of us that some of us have nothing but campaigning, and others nothing but unmanly ease.

Conscription and Universal Military Training (UMT)

While preaching much the same social values as James, Harvard's Charles Eliot was quick to dismiss James' pacifist army as naive. "A few philanthropists believe that the world would get on better if there were no armies and navies and no use of force to resist wrong-doers; but non-resistance seems to almost everybody an impracticable international policy at mankind's actual state of progress."

Eliot, too, sought hardiness and self-sacrifice in youth. With universal military training, "the whole people would soon attain a new sentiment of patriotic duty and self-sacrificing devotion to the country as the groundwork of home, kinship, and friendship, and the representative of public justice and liberty and of progress we hope for mankind."[8]

Proponents of UMT had great difficulty, however, in making a case for its military necessity before the outbreak of war in Europe. A foreign military threat seemed remote. Vast oceans, not mass conscript armies, were the first line of defense. After 1914, however, with growing fears of an invasion of the United States, or a trade war conducted by European belligerents, the UMT movement grew in numbers and influence.

The Case for Voluntarism

An ad hoc group of "antimilitarists" called the American Union Against Militarism (AUAM) preached at the same time the fundamental goodness of voluntary military service and voluntary national service. Drawing support from several labor unions, the National Grange, Quakers and other peace groups, the Women's Peace Party, some progressive Republicans, and the Socialist Party, the AUAM fiercely opposed universal military training and James' obligatory pacifist service.

A just cause and competitive pay levels were all the armed forces required, said the AUAM. The volunteer military, if it is needed at all, "can be raised by the right kind of an appeal to the American people." There was merit in James' scheme, the AUAM said, except for the idea of compulsory service.

An army of labor trained in the work of reforestation, of irrigation, of building great highways, instructed in methods of camp sanitation and effective cooperation; from which every man would come out a more useful member of society and a more productive economic unit, would make a far different appeal to American young men than the standing army on [sic] the present system, or even a national guard of the socially elite.

This, however, was best achieved through competitive wages and voluntarism.

With this employment in useful production should go adequate compensation, just as there goes adequate compensation for police work, for the work of firemen and life-savers. Under a really democratic system of social service, such as this, there will be no difficulty in finding all the men that are needed, without resort to conscription.[9]

War and Selective Service

When the United States eventually entered the war in 1917, however, the Wilson administration chose none of these ideas, but instead, a selective military draft. (Wilson himself seems to have been the principal architect of the wartime strategy.) Still, Wilson couched the draft in rhetoric designed to appease everyone. This draft was "in no sense a conscription of the unwilling," he said; "it is rather, selection from a nation which has volunteered in mass." "Those who feel that we are turning away altogether from the voluntary principle seem to forget that some 600,000 men will be needed to fill the ranks of the Regular Army and the National Guard and that a very great field of individual enthusiasm lies there wide open." For those who sought a universal military obligation, Wilson had something to offer as well.

The principle of the selective draft, in short, has at its heart this idea, that there is a universal obligation to serve and that a public authority should choose those upon which the obligation of military service shall rest, and also in a sense choose those who shall do the rest of the nation's work.

And for those who argued for greater emphasis on national service, the administration published a *National Service Handbook* extolling the virtues of supporting the war effort through child care and other social work.

The argument was monumental dissembling, but it seemed to work. The 1917 measure was enacted within six weeks of the American declaration of war. The violence of the 1860s did not recur; fewer than 5,000 were imprisoned for draft resistance in the course of the war. By the new draft's terms (echoing Oakes) selections were by local draft boards; substitution and the commutation fee were eliminated. Failure to report for induction, however, was still a military offense punishable by court martial.

The wartime draft's deferment policies were intended to shift men from unessential to essential occupations. Skilled workers in industries essential to war production were deferred; a work-or-fight order forced idlers and those engaged in nonproductive employment to switch to essential jobs or be drafted.

The measure also increased the national power over that of the states. The president was authorized to appoint all officers, including those of the state National Guard (formerly the state militia). He could use any state official in carrying out the draft, a provision which further diluted the powers of the states.

In 1918, voluntary military enlistments were totally barred as inefficient, and the draft took over as the only device for military manpower procurement. Of the 3.7 million doughboys who entered service in 1917 and 1918, 72 percent were conscripts.

Still, the World War I draft did have elements of Jamesian national service and of UMT. The 1917 law provided that conscientious objectors (COs) (only members of the historic peace churches) could elect noncombatant military service as soldiers. Those who objected to military service itself, however, faced imprisonment. Confronted with the noisy trials of nonreligious objectors, Wilson relaxed these terms in two respects. In March 1918 he ordered that those who objected to war solely because of "conscientious scruples" be allowed to claim the privilege of noncombatancy, without regard to their religious affiliations. (Some 4,000 quickly made the claim.) Also, a way was established to furlough many COs out of military duty and into agricultural work and service with the American Friends Reconstruction Units in France. Technically, furloughed objectors remained under military jurisdiction, but a Jamesian form of alternative pacifist service had come about in fact.

At the same time, a variation of UMT occurred on the nation's campuses. In 1918 the Congress lowered the minimum draft age from 21 to 18, and nearly every able-bodied male college student — some 150,000 in 500 colleges — found himself suddenly conscripted in a new Student's Army Training Corps (SATC). SATC conscripts were not inducted into the regular forces; instead, they were trained as officers, noncommissioned officers, and specialists. It was the most massive federal intervention in higher education in the nation's history. It was also the closest the nation was to come to a draft for military training tied wholly to reserve service.

The 1917 measure provided the first occasion for the U.S. Supreme Court to rule on the constitutionality of national military conscription, and it did so with forceful conclusion but paltry explanation. Echoing Monroe's contention a century earlier, the Court observed that "as the mind cannot conceive an army without the men to compose it, on the face of the Constitution the objection that it does not give power to provide for such men would seem to be too frivolous for further notice." Military conscription was a quite appropriate exercise of congressional power.

PEACE, PROSPERITY, AND DEPRESSION

With the end of hostilities in 1919, American armed forces became once again voluntary, and once again small. The wartime navy was sharply reduced in a multilateral naval demobilization, and the army fell from over 2.3 million in 1918 to just under 205,000 in 1920. Talk of national service largely disappeared. The predominant intellectual issue became how to avert future wars, and conscription was discussed in this light.

In one of history's curious turnabouts, Woodrow Wilson, the man most responsible for the wartime draft, now proposed in the first draft of the League of Nations covenant that all signatories ban the use of conscription as a means to prevent future wars. The idea got nowhere, but in 1926, 71 prominent figures from 15 nations — among them, Albert Einstein, M. K. Gandhi, H. G. Wells, and Bertrand Russell — signed a manifesto for the universal abolition of military conscription. "It is our belief that conscript armies . . . are a grave menace to peace. Conscription involves the degradation of human personality and the destruction of liberty."

A few argued the opposite. In 1926 labor leader Samuel Gompers called for a national commission to study the desirability of universal peacetime conscription as a deterrent to future war. For Gompers, conscription meant not only the impressment of men to military service, but the conscription of goods and wealth as well, the latter to preclude wartime profiteering.

Still, it was an obscure debate, arousing no great popular sentiment. With the collapse of the economy beginning in 1929, the nation turned to other matters. In 1932 newly elected President Franklin D. Roosevelt promised a "New Deal," and the administration set about an unprecedented centralization of power in the national government. James' Army against Nature became a reality in 1933 with the establishment of a voluntary Civilian Conservation Corps (CCC) to provide short-term employment for young men from families on public assistance.[10] Some 1.5 million passed through the CCC's rolls in less than a decade. The CCC also provided the army a new peacetime role: processing and supervising CCC enrollees and managing CCC camps. Unemployed army reserve officers were appointed as CCC camp commanders.

The program enjoyed enormous popularity from its inception, and all manner of social benefits was attributed to it. Reforestation and camp life built character. "Civilian Conservation Corps Squelches Crime," said the *New York Times* in 1933 and the *Washington Star* in 1936. A poll in July 1936 found 82 percent of the public in favor of continuing the CCC. Favorable viewpoints cut across partisan lines: the CCC was supported by 92 percent of the polled Democrats, 79 percent of the Socialists, and 67 percent of the Republicans.

The CCC was essentially a short-term work relief program, and, before

1941, military drill had been prohibited. There was nevertheless considerable popular sentiment for transforming the program into a limited version of UMT. A 1936 Gallup poll reported 77 percent in favor of military training in CCC camps; a follow-up poll in 1939 reported 90 percent in favor. "Give Military Training to Civilian Conservation Corps," said the *Washington Post* in October 1939. In August 1941, military drill, without weapons, became a camp requirement. Five hundred CCC enrollees were dispatched to sea duty. Erosion control and reforestation were increasingly replaced by the building of fortifications and military installations. The program eventually gave way to the war effort and was terminated in 1942.

American military forces remained modestly sized throughout the twenties and thirties. The regular army totaled 140,000 in 1930. By the end of 1939, it numbered slightly under 190,000, and ranked seventeenth in size in the world.

THE DEBATES OF 1940

By mid-1940, the American Navy was in an undeclared shooting war with German U-boats in the North Atlantic. War with Japan seemed inevitable to some. Roosevelt had already placed U.S. forces on alert. Despite vocal opposition in both houses, America's first "peacetime" draft was passed in 1940 by comfortable margins: 58 to 31 in the Senate; 263–149 in the House. The issue had been removed from the 1940 presidential contest when Republican candidate Wendell Willkie declared that "some form of selective service is the only democratic way in which to secure the competent and trained manpower we need for national defense."

The 1940 measure was a limited draft, not more than 900,000 men could be enrolled at any time; the term of military service was limited to one year; conscripts were prohibited from service outside U.S. possessions and the Western Hemisphere. In an early version the measure had called for lower pay for conscripts ($5 per month) than for volunteers ($21 per month), but, as enacted, conscripts were to enjoy all the benefits of volunteers of similar rank and length of service.

Opposition to the measure came from pacifists, Socialists, Republican isolationists, and religious groups. Norman Thomas viewed the 1940 act as "the first essential to the totalitarian state." Senator Robert Taft of Ohio, a leading isolationist, echoed the theme.

The theory behind it leads directly to totalitarianism. It is absolutely opposed to the principles of individual liberty which have always been considered a part of American democracy.

Taft favored an army capable of home defense but not designed for overseas expeditions. To Taft, a draft was not only wrong, it was unnecessary. "It is only a question of making the service sufficiently attractive," and to do this he was prepared to double entry-level military pay. An all-volunteer force could adequately meet "the present emergency."

National service had its advocates as well. In August 1940, California Congressman Jerry Voorhis introduced a bill "to create a national service and training program in the United States." Unlike James' earlier pacifist nostrums, the Voorhis plan was intended to support military service. By its terms, *all* of the nation's youth would be obligated to serve in one of four categories: (1) active military duty in the army or navy; (2) a uniformed but behind-the-lines corps of communications and aviation specialists; (3) a nonuniformed, noncombatant group that would serve in defense industry, and (4) an agricultural group to work in conservation of natural resources.

WAR YEARS

In the early fall of 1941, the Congress (by a one-vote margin in the House) voted to keep the one-year draftees in service beyond their term. After Pearl Harbor, the draft was for the duration. Geographical restrictions on draftees were lifted. In late 1942, voluntary enlistments were barred. Men could join the service only by requesting early induction.

Roosevelt, however, wanted to go further. In early 1944 he proposed to the Congress a "national service law" which would have prohibited labor strikes and put every man and woman at the service of the government to be assigned to jobs of the government's choosing. A watered-down version, applicable only to males, passed the House by a vote of 246 to 167, but languished in the Senate through V-E day.

By May 1945, America had close to 12 million men and women in uniform. Ten million men had been drafted; 5.4 million had been deployed overseas. Over 300,000 women had been recruited to ease the crunch in manpower supply.[11] The nation had seriously entertained conscripting the civilian labor force for national service as well.

The World War II draft was different from its 1917 precursor in several key respects. Draft evasion and resistance, and failure to report for induction were no longer military offenses, but instead, crimes to be tried in civilian courts with imprisonment in civilian penitentiaries. Provisions for conscientious objection were liberalized. A CO no longer had to be a member of a historic peace church (although his objection still had to be based on religious training and belief). A new CO category, opposition to military service itself, was now available. COs could avoid induction by performing alternative national service under government direction at approved work camps sponsored variously by the historic peace churches, other religious groups, and the government. Twelve thousand COs joined these Civilian Public Service camps to do CCC-like conservation work for the war's duration; 70 percent stuck it out through demobilization. Another 5,000 uncooperative COs were imprisoned.

Also, the 1940 measure prohibited consideration of race in draft selections,[12] and the military services absorbed a new kind of soldier—the "limited service man"—who could perform some, but not all of the physical requirements of service. (In November 1943, fully 10 percent of the army's strength was comprised of these limited duty personnel.) Minimum mental standards were set at a fourth grade level of literacy, but the services began to provide remedial help to illiterates in 1943, and a new "aptitude test" was developed by wartime psychologists to improve upon merely assessing individuals' reading skills.

Apart from these, World War II manpower policy largely mirrored the policy of 1917. A work-or-fight order was promulgated; occupational and dependency deferments were allowed;[13] local draft boards decided who was to serve.

POSTWAR DEBATES

Over the opposition of Selective Service (but virtually no one else), Truman lifted the wartime ban on voluntary enlistments in 1945. The wartime draft was given two one-year renewals in 1945 and 1946, but congressional pressure to increase voluntary enlistments was intense. Proposals to recruit more aliens, raise military pay, and lower physical fitness standards were regularly offered. By January 1, 1946, the army had close to 10,000 men in recruiting activities. At the same time, demobilization was in full swing: the regular army of 8.2 million in 1945 stood at 1.9 million in 1946 and at 991,000 in 1947.

The late forties were dominated by four developments: (1) America tried, and then abandoned, its first postwar all-volunteer force; (2) the second peacetime draft in the nation's history was enacted; (3) UMT was resurrected and fiercely debated; and (4) an entirely new concept—a GI Bill of postservice financial assistance—was launched on a grand scale.

The First All-Volunteer Force (AVF)

In the Republican-dominated Eightieth Congress in 1947, the Truman administration faced a body even more hostile to the draft's continuation than its predecessor a year earlier. Doubtful that it had the votes, and with army enlistments somewhat optimistic in early 1947, the administration decided against seeking a third one-year renewal of the draft. According to Truman in March 1947, "this appears to be the logical time to shoulder the risks involved." One year later—with total active forces of 1,384,500, then the largest number of volunteers in peacetime history—Truman was back before the Congress to call for "the temporary reenactment of Selective Service legislation in order to maintain our armed forces at their authorized strength."

The conjunction of three distinct, but complementary, factors seemed to account for the turnabout. In February 1948 Czechoslovakia fell to the Communists in a coup d'état. At the same time, the first, tentative steps at a blockade of Berlin were taken by the Soviets in early March, when four allied trains were stopped.[14] These came on the heels of the loss of Eastern Europe to Soviet hegemony. Noting "specific, aggressive and dangerous actions on the part of the Government of the Soviet Union," the House Armed Services Committee applauded Truman's call as a necessary matter of precaution and resolve. "It is in order to deter any . . . rash decision on the part of the Soviet Government that it is now imperative for the United States to transform a reasonable measure of its armed strength from potential to actual."

Also, in the administration's view, demobilization had gone too far. Defense Secretary Forrestal and the Joint Chiefs of Staff produced a new manpower requirement in March 1947: overall strength had to be raised from 1,384,500 to 2,005,882. This could only be done, they reasoned, by a temporary reinstatement of conscription.

At the same time, a dispute over quantity versus quality had developed around the fledgling all-volunteer force. In 1947 the army raised the minimum qualifying score on its entrance examination by 15 points. In early 1948, it raised the minimum score another 12 points. Enlistments sagged. Between July 1947 and March 1948 monthly gains in the army averaged less than 14,000, while losses ran in excess of 29,000 a month. The *New York Times* estimated that 50 percent of the volunteers previously eligible for military service were now being turned away. Skeptics suggested that the army was out to sabotage the AVF in order to bring back the draft. One congressman characterized the new standard as one which "only a classical scholar in Greek or Latin or a Philadelphia lawyer could pass." The army rejoined that only 13 percent were being turned away because of the higher standards, that these standards would apply to draftees as well, and that heightened mental standards had been accompanied by a relaxation of physical standards.

In any event, the first AVF was through.

Temporary Conscription

Viewed against the sentiment in the Congress only a year earlier, the new draft measure passed with remarkable ease. Three months after Truman's

March 1948 request, the Senate enacted a peacetime draft by a vote of 70 to 10. The House quickly followed suit. On June 24, Truman signed the restoration of Selective Service into law. On July 20, he ordered the draft registration of 9.5 million men. The first inductions took place in November.

Truman's "temporary" 1948 draft would go on, through successive renewals, for a quarter-century. Curiously, the restoration of conscription was accompanied by a huge upsurge in volunteering. Also, the administration developed second thoughts about the budgetary implications of its planned buildup and began to scale back. Only 30,000 were inducted in the late months of 1948. With ample volunteers, draft calls were stopped in January 1949; the 30,000 already drafted were to be released after serving 12 months. There were no inductions in late 1949 and 1950. The Congress extended the temporary draft law to July 9, 1950, with little prospect that it would be further renewed. On June 24, 1950, however, North Korean troops crossed the 38th Parallel. With Truman's commitment of U.S. forces, a two-year extension passed easily.

The 1948 draft differed from its predecessors in two key respects. First, it was the first true peacetime draft in U.S. history. Second, it was to permanently coexist with volunteering. Unlike the war years, conscription was not to be a device for directly providing all military manpower. Instead, it was merely to encourage the maximum numbers of voluntary enlistments with the fewest numbers of inductions, and to make up for any shortfalls left by volunteering. The draft's subsequent terms—eight years of liability, an order of call that took the oldest first, a premium on extended uncertainty for those subject to call—evolved from and made sense within the context of this new posture. Peacetime conscription was to induce, much more so than to induct, for military service.

UMT Resurrected

While it had ushered in a new selective draft, the Truman administration was still no fan of selective service. A small, highly specialized and wholly volunteer active force, backed by a massive reserve composed of graduates of UMT, was Truman's postwar preference. The navy and the newly created air force were cool to the idea, but Truman and the army pressed the case for nearly six years before finally giving up. UMT, they argued, would permit rapid mobilization in time of war, something the nation had done poorly in the early forties.[15]

Critics lambasted the military arguments for UMT. Future wars would be decided by deep penetration bombing and atomic weapons, not by a mass conscript army of minimally trained young men. "Six months in training camp do not a soldier make." UMT also failed to provide manpower for the occupation forces in Japan, Korea, and Europe. These forces looked increasingly like permanently stationed, forward deployed units.

Truman eventually shifted from a military justification to a line of argument reminiscent of Charles Eliot: UMT was good for those who did it. According to Truman:

This was not a military training program in the conventional sense. The military phase was incidental to what I had in mind. While the training was to offer every qualified young man a chance to perfect himself for the service of his country in some military capacity, I envisioned a program that would at the same time provide ample opportunity for self-improvement. Part of that training was calculated to raise the physical standards of the nation's manpower, to lower the illiteracy rate, to develop citizenship responsibilities, and to foster the moral and spiritual welfare of our young people.

A GI Bill

A draft and the losing campaign for UMT were not the only postwar preoccupations. The likely effects of postwar demobilization on the employment market had been a matter of concern as early as 1943. General Lewis Hershey of Selective Service had that year proposed that the army hold men until jobs for them became available, even after peace. "We can keep people in the Army about as cheaply as we could create an agency for them when they are not."[16]

However, it was not a large postwar army that Roosevelt and the Congress settled on. Rather, a program of housing, unemployment, and educational assistance for returning vets was enacted in 1944. The educational assistance provided by the GI Bill would not only reward past military service, it would also encourage returning veterans to seek schooling instead of an immediate job. This it did. In its first 12 years the GI Bill assisted 7.8 million veterans (half of the 15.6 million who were eligible) at a cost of $4.5 billion. The impact on universities was substantial. In 1939 to 1940, American colleges and universities awarded 216,521 degrees; in 1949 to 1950, the number was more than double: 496,661.

COLD WAR

The GI Bill was terminated in 1956.[17] U.S. force levels were kept high following Korea. In 1954, combined active and reserve forces numbered more than 6 million; in 1959, more than 7 million.[18] An all-volunteer force did not factor in the Cold War debates over military service. Proposals focused instead on incremental reforms of a draft that was laden with special deferments and exemptions. (House Armed Services Committee chairman Carl Vinson spoke of the draft in 1951 as written "almost like members of a state assembly [writing] a sales tax before the election.")

Race, Sex, and Fitness

With Truman's postwar order to desegregate the armed forces, the draft at last began to take blacks without racial quotas. Conscription, however, remained a peculiarly male burden.

In anticipation of recruitment shortfalls in the first AVF, the Women's Armed Services Integration Act of 1948 had been enacted, and plans were made to recruit women as an alternative source of manpower. (The draft's resumption eliminated the pressure and the plans.) A spate of articles favoring conscription of women appeared in the popular press in 1951. Some, like anthropologist Margaret Mead, argued into the late sixties that women should be drafted but not assigned to offensive combat,[19] but it was not until the second AVF that the numbers of women in the ranks substantially increased.

Fitness standards provoked little debate, even though they seemed manipulable, and manipulated, by draft registrants and the system itself. In 1951 a commentator, Stanley Frank, argued in *Nation's Business* for conscription of the physically encumbered on the twin grounds of fairness to the fit and humaneness toward the not-fit, but standards seemed, if anything, to get higher. Congress set the standards to be used in wartime as those in effect in 1945, but authorized the president to fix higher criteria in peacetime. Volunteers and conscripts alike were rejected for such things as imbecility, dullness, criminality, urinary incontinence, stuttering or stammering, clubfoot, color blindness, high blood pressure, ongoing orthodontistry, various allergies, homosexuality, venereal disease, and abnormal weight, height, and shoe-size. Feigning of disqualifying ailments was not unknown. Standards themselves seemed at times quite elastic. In mid-1961, for instance, before John F. Kennedy enlarged the force by 300,000, induction rejections ran as high as 43 percent (and in two no-draft months actually topped 70 percent); at year's end, during the Berlin crisis buildup, the rejection rate was down to 14 percent.

Fitness standards were also manipulated to achieve social goals. "Project 100,000," launched in 1966, was an attempt to bring to military service young men who were otherwise ineligible. According to Lyndon Johnson:

> With intensive instruction, practical on-the-job training and corrective medical measures, these young men can become good soldiers. Moreover, the remedial training they receive can enable them to live fuller and more productive lives.

Reserve Forces

The early days of Korea precipitated the largest reserve callup of the postwar era: some 806,000 reservists from a base of 2.5 million (32 percent activated) augmented the 1.5 million active force. Yet, it was a haphazard callup. The army was required to activate the organized reserves (the regular reserves and the state National Guard) in entire units only. The army's critical need, however, was not for entire units but for individual replacements, fillers, and trainers, an incongruity that led to the callup of individual nondrilling reservists while entire units sat out the war at home. Nondrilling World War II veterans went before drilling nonveterans. Moreover, there was no good mesh between provisions for induction and provisions for reserve callup. As a result, reservists who were fathers, students, and skilled technicians were activated, while draftees were deferred on these very same grounds. Also, the 1948 draft law deferred from induction men who had joined the National Guard between the ages of 17 and 18½.[20] According to Eisenhower's Secretary of Defense, the provision was "really sort of a scandal. . . . It was a draft-dodging business. A boy could enlist in the National Guard and not be drafted and sent to Korea and fight."

The Korea reserve callup was short-lived. The draft soon took over as the principal source of manpower; reservists who had not been called in 1950 were spared; some 100,000 activated reservists were released by December 1951.

In 1952, the Congress reorganized the reserves, and among other things provided for an eight-year military service obligation. Years not spent on active duty were to be satisfied by a residual obligation in a new "ready" reserve. Participation in reserve drill was voluntary, however.

Still, problems remained. The 1952 act created a reserve made up chiefly of veterans (i.e., those with residual obligations). A future callup, then, would be a repetition of 1950: veterans going before nonveterans. At the same time, few veterans participated in unit drills: only 30 percent in 1953, a third of these in National Guard units. Thus, a cardinal principle of reserve utilization, that reserve forces would be ready because they trained as units in peacetime, was largely unmet. Also, the National Guard still received no active training. And men aged 17 to 18½ could still escape induction by joining the guard, but no similar escape was available for regular reserve service. Thus, there was little inducement for young men to join the already-heavy-with-veteran regular reserves.

The Reserve Forces Act of 1955, and administrative refinements by the Eisenhower administration in 1957, corrected these deficiencies by substituting a different kind of problem. The military service obligation was reduced to six years. A special, draft-deferred reserve program (six months active training and 5½ years ready reserve) was opened in 1957 to draft-aged men, 18 to 26. In 1958, guard personnel were required to serve in a federal status for six months' training in order to qualify for a draft deferment.

The changes were effective. With the draft deferment, the nation now had a device to induce large numbers of men to join the reserves directly from civilian life, and to diminish the reserves' historical overreliance on active service veterans. The ready reserve swelled. By 1962, 620,570 additional individuals with no prior service were in the reserves. Eisenhower, however, was appalled at the program's "success," and spent his last year in office inveighing against excessive reserve strength that was of no military value and that cost an additional $80 million a year.

The problem, however, was merely passed on. In 1967 a presidential commission (the Marshall Commission) reported widespread favoritism in securing reserve enlistments, observed that professional football teams were preserved intact within reserve units, and protested that blacks were disproportionately underrepresented in reserve ranks. Not only were the reserves overwhelmingly white, they were ludicrously well educated as well. By 1970, 54 percent of reserve enlistments were either college graduates or had some college; 94 percent were high-school graduates.

Kennedy called up 150,000 reservists in the Berlin crisis of 1961–62, but it was not an entirely smooth affair. Army Secretary Stahr reported that some reservists "were not cognizant of the responsibilities which they incurred as obligated reservists" and "there had been defects in the distribution of equipment, troop housing, unavailability of medical care at many installations." Lyndon Johnson ordered a token reserve activation in 1968 (a total of 36,972 reservists), but otherwise the reserves sat out the Vietnam War.

Also, the problem which Upton had decried a century earlier still lingered: the individual states retained their own reserve forces. While these could be activated for federal service, they contributed to inefficiencies in reserve manpower management, since both the army and the air force had two reserve components: regulars and the National Guard. Several proposals were made by Defense Secretary McNamara in the 1960s to either merge the two or eliminate one entirely, but nothing came of these.

Channeling and Drainage

In the mid-1950s, about 80 percent of the eligible young males were required for active and reserve service. By the early 1960s, the requirement had dropped to 60 percent; by the late 1960s, it was about 30 percent. Overabundance of manpower supply was the problem. "Channeling," said Selective Service, was the answer. Deferments were expanded, and registrants were encouraged (channeled) to enter draft-protected schooling and occupations.[21] Channeling happily married the nation's civilian and military manpower aspirations by inducing men to education and socially important work.

Channeling, however, also served a more pedestrian purpose. It was a way to drain off the manpower supply. The last thing Selective Service wanted was too many men falling into the category of "available for service" (I-A) and then reaching age 26 without being drafted. Channeling accomplished this with deferments. In 1965, there were close to 7 million more registrants than in 1957, yet Selective Service had a "qualified and available" pool that was 1 million men smaller. Though selective, the draft took most who were "eligible," Selective Service reasoned.

VIETNAM, DRAFT REFORM, AND
A CAMPAIGN PROMISE

With Vietnam, force size increased; close to 4 million were in active service in 1968, compared with less than 2 million in 1957. The idea of an all-volunteer force was resurrected, as were a number of proposals for national service, either as a universal obligation or as grounds for a draft deferment similar to the occupational deferment.

Little and Late

Inequities in the workings of the draft prompted a host of reform proposals: a random lottery to replace draft board decisions; an end to student, occupational, and fatherhood deferments; a youngest-first order of call and a one-year period of draft liability to replace the uncertainty and personal disruptions of the oldest-first-until-age-26 order of call. All were eventually enacted, but only after Richard Nixon had already committed the nation to an end to the draft entirely. Abolition of the reservists' draft deferment was proposed by the Marshall Commission, but got nowhere.

Conscientious Objection

At the same time, the courts took an increasingly active role in shaping the draft's terms. Various procedural refinements were judicially imposed on the system. More and more, local draft boards were forced to take account of due process and to record, not only selection decisions, but the reasons for them. And conscientious objection, once reserved for traditional religious pacifists, was expanded in terms that would baffle ordinary men.

The Supreme Court had had no difficulty with parcelling out CO status on the basis of religious beliefs in its 1917 ruling. "We pass without anything but statement the proposition that an establishment of a religion or an interference with the free exercise thereof repugnant to the First Amendment resulted from the exemption clauses of the act . . . , because we think its unsoundness is too apparent to require us to do more."

The Court of the sixties was much less confident, but it avoided an outright holding of unconstitutionality by simply interpreting the statutory language "religious training and belief" to include nonreligious beliefs as well. It was a strenuous intellectual exercise, but it did preserve the CO's status (albeit, at a cost of considerable confusion). Atheism was now acceptable. The proper test, the Court said in 1965, is that "a sincere and meaningful belief which occupies in the life of its possessor a place parallel to that filled by the God of those admittedly qualifying for the exemption comes within the statutory definition [of religious training and belief]." Draft boards and lower courts wrestled gamely with how this was to be applied in practice.

The Court struck another blow for obscurantism in a 1970 holding. The conscription statute excluded from CO status beliefs that were "essentially political, sociological, or philosophical views or a merely personal moral code." Nevertheless, said the Court, "if an individual deeply and sincerely holds beliefs that are purely ethical or moral in source and content, but that nevertheless impose on him a duty of conscience to refrain from participating in any war at any time, those beliefs certainly occupy in the life of the individual 'a place parallel to that filled by . . . God.'"

From a constitutionally suspicious but reasonably intelligible set of criteria in 1917, the court had moved the nation to a test so ethereal that it seemed beyond the ability of ordinary people to apply. Selective Service bravely issued new instructions to draft boards—these were about as lucid as the Court decision that prompted them.

Unlike their World War II counterparts, COs in the postwar years were not dispatched to remote work camps. Instead, they were to find on their own acceptable social work (in hospitals, educational systems, environmental work, and the like) and to do this at no cost to the federal government for the same period as inducted military service: two years. The CO's sponsoring employer paid and supervised him.

Compensation and Enforcement

The 1940 measure had firmly established the policy that draftees and volunteers would be paid the same. Both, in a sense, became captives of conscription, since incentives to pay them well were clearly lacking. When the Congress enacted military pay increases in the fifties and sixties, these were skewed toward retaining members in the career force. Steadily the disparity grew between junior enlisted pay on the one hand, and career military and civilian pay on the other. By 1963, civilian pay approximated 163 percent of its 1950 level; career military pay, 154 percent; the pay of first-term personnel, a mere 104 percent. By 1971, the margins of separation were even greater: civilian pay equaled 254 percent of the 1950 level; career military pay, 256 percent; recruit pay, 169 percent.

A few spoke bravely of the inequities of low first-term wages (the draft need not be miserly as well as obligatory), but substantial pay increases were not to come about until the nation was already committed to abandoning the draft entirely.

The 1940 and subsequent draft laws had brought some improvement over the sometimes bullyish enforcement mechanisms of World War I.[22] In the fifties and sixties, Selective Service relied on three devices.

First, there was the draft card, and the law's requirement that it be carried at all times. (How often this provision was actually enforced by federal and local police is not known.) The card was evidence of draft registration. It was also evidence of age for young men wishing to enjoy the fruits of adulthood, a fact which itself seemed to encourage men to register.

Second, there was criminal prosecution itself. Selective Service sought relatively few indictments, but complained nevertheless of light penalties.[23] Enforcement increased during the Vietnam conflict, but the conviction rate was not substantial.[24]

It was the third device that was most consistently effective. As Selective Service put it, the "basic philosophy was to try securing rather than compelling obedience to the law in recalcitrant cases." "The mission of the System," wrote Hershey with monotonous regularity, "is to put men into the Armed Forces, not to have them imprisoned." Delinquents were encouraged to choose military service over criminal prosecution. At the same time, delinquency was discouraged by the simple device of accelerated induction: the delinquent could lose his deferment and be placed before all others in the order of call.[25]

Still, Vietnam placed an enormous strain on the system. Between 1965 and 1968 there were more than 1,000 antiwar demonstrations. Not all were targeted on the draft, but many involved draft card burnings. In 1966, *Newsweek* reported that, for the first time since the Civil War, avoidance of military service in time of armed conflict had become socially acceptable.

The Second All-Volunteer Force

In the fifties and sixties, the incumbent administration favored the draft's preservation. Adlai Stevenson, making the draft an issue in the 1956 presidential campaign by raising the possibility of its eventual abolition, was roundly denounced by the Eisenhower administration. Vice-President Nixon labeled doing away with the draft "the easy way" but "not the right way." Eisenhower sniffed, "We cannot, in short, face the future simply by walking into the past backwards." In the 1964 campaign, Barry Goldwater, not discernibly receptive to Stevenson's proposal eight years earlier, promised that "Republicans will end the draft altogether, and as soon as possible." Vice-President Humphrey, quickly announcing new and comprehensive studies of the matter, rejoined that it was premature to talk of ending the draft without first studying all possible alternatives. In 1968, the shoe was on another foot. Conceding that "for the many years since World War II, I believed that, even in peacetime, only through the draft could we get enough servicemen to defend our nation," candidate Nixon offered a new belief: "once our involvement in the Vietnam War is behind us, we move toward an all-volunteer armed force."

Nixon appointed a commission (the Gates Commission), in 1969, to study the costs and practicability of an AVF. Not surprising given its mandate, the commission reported favorably on the idea. Conscription was a fundamentally bad idea — a selectively imposed tax on young men. Compensation could replace compulsion in force-manning. An army of the poor and the black would not result. Black enlistments in an AVF would be only a percentage point higher than in a draft. Military preparedness depends on forces in being, not on the ability to draft untrained men. The reserves, not the draft, would provide force augmentation. Reserve forces could do what they had never before done: provide a rapid and reliable support to active forces. A standby draft should be retained in peacetime, but activated in wartime only should there be the need to mobilize large numbers of men.

In a nation in which presidential commission reports are more commonly ignored than revered, the Gates' findings enjoyed remarkable political success. Military pay increases for junior enlisted personnel were enacted in 1970 and 1971. The last general draft call was issued in December 1972. The last induction was in June 1973.

Still, there were several ambiguities in the Gates Commission's reasoning. While the commission made cost projections for a volunteer active force of up to 3 million members, its working hypothesis was that the post-Vietnam AVF would be about the size of the pre-Vietnam draft force. (This was, in fact, the Nixon administration's assumption as well.) Yet, the pre-Vietnam force had the benefit of the draft for relatively quick (and certainly steady) force expansion in circumstances short of a full mobilization; the AVF presumably would have no such capability. Would not a shift to draft-free armed forces argue for a larger standing force in peacetime? The commission seemed to say "no," contending that the reserves were available for force augmentation. But this only begged other questions: how large a reserve force? And how would sufficient reserves be maintained absent a draft and the reserve deferment?

Also, the commission assumed that, with proper compensation, enlistments could be maintained in a steady state, but it took no account of the likely effects on enlistments of threatening international circumstances. In a period of international tension or limited emergency, would not the attractions of military service diminish at precisely the time when a sure supply of manpower is most critical? The commission had provided for manpower only at the bipolar extremes. In a short warning, short duration conflict, forces in being would be all that mattered. In a conflict of longer duration entailing a major mobilization of manpower, a standby draft could be reactivated. But absent conscription, there seemed little capability to expand or sustain force size in circumstances in between.

The standby draft was itself an anomaly. Its purposes were not clear, nor were the circumstances which might trigger its invocation and insure its prompt execution. And it was conceptually confusing. If, as the commission reasoned, a draft was an odious and unfair tax on the young in peacetime (when the tax would at most amount to inconvenience for those upon whom it is levied), it was not evident what transformed it into something less obnoxious in time of armed conflict (when the consequences of being drafted were presumably more severe).

Last, there was a lot of history that had to be ignored in order to find the commission's plan credible. The political difficulties of fairly distributing the burdens of a reserve callup contributed to the historical reluctance to use reservists; presumably such difficulties would remain. Truman's urgent 1948 draft reinstatement took six months to produce its first inductee. Early casualties had always had a way of drying up voluntary enlistments.

Still, the Gates Commission had probably made the best case that could be made for an AVF in the postwar era. A "total force" policy was announced. The regular reserves and the national guard would henceforth be the primary source of wartime force augmentation. The draft went into standby, and between 1975 and 1977, most of its peacetime machinery (draft boards, registration, classification, examination) was scuttled.

National Service

National service had been recommended in the sixties chiefly as a way to compensate for the inequities of the draft. The idea was to either require some public service of all draft-age men (and, in some formulations, of women as well) or allow those subject to induction the option of a civilian way to satisfy their military obligation. (Some, of course, had long proposed voluntary national service as a good in itself—something that should not in any way be tied to a draft exemption—and cited the Peace Corps as a sterling example.)

Proponents of "universal" service included persons such as anthropologist Margaret Mead, Labor Secretary Willard Wirtz, and military sociologist Morris Janowitz. All youth would be obligated to serve the nation for some period of time in either a civilian or a military capacity. This would not only compensate for the selectivity of the draft; in addition, unmet social needs would be satisfied, and the young would profit personally from performing a public good for some reason other than dollar compensation. How this universal obligation would be enforced was not spelled out (Mead, for instance, sometimes characterized the obligation as a legal requirement, other times merely as a moral imperative), but this was only one of several hazy spots. The magnitude of such an undertaking troubled some. A few studies suggested that over one million participants could be *absorbed* annually (a different proposition than suggesting that this number was actually *needed*), but these were casual in both their assumptions and their calculus.

Other proposals were less expansive. The National Student Association proposed to an unreceptive Congress in 1959 that certain limited forms of public service (teaching, social work, work in foreign missions) be allowed as substitutions for drafted military service. Candidate John F. Kennedy originally proposed such a draft exemption for the Peace Corps, but backed off under heavy attack from candidate Richard M. Nixon, who claimed such a scheme would only encourage draft-dodging. In the mid-sixties several groups proposed similar schemes. In 1971, Congressman Jonathan Bingham and others argued to expand the CO's traditional status to any who would be willing to perform rigorous alternative service.

The end of the draft took some of the impetus out of these proposals, but national service did enjoy a resurgence beginning in the late 1970s: proposed as either a supplement to or a substitute for the AVF, or as a means to return to conscription without resuming merely a selective draft. Whether national service should be universal or selective, voluntary or compulsory, tied to or wholly divorced from military manpower recruitment differed with the proposal. For some, national service would simply be a new kind of occupational deferment in a resumed draft. For others, worried that the Supreme Court's conscientious objector rulings risked crippling a future draft, national service was a way to make COs of any who would apply. Others, still, saw national service, not as assisting a draft, but the reverse. Reinstitution of a selective draft could be used as a way to "channel" large numbers to do national service in lieu of induction. Congressmen McCloskey and Cavanaugh offered different plans along this line. And there were some who believed that purely voluntary national service would supplement the AVF by imbuing in the youthful population a public spirit to serve.

Underlying all such proposals were several assumptions: (1) there are important unmet social and environmental needs beyond the reach of the market economy and the resources of existing social institutions; (2) these are sufficiently labor-intensive such that relatively unskilled youth can satisfy them by personal service of limited duration; and (3) participating youth need not be compensated at market wages and will presumably benefit personally from the emphasis on public service over compensation. Still, these proposals came with little specificity concerning what participants would actually do, how they would be organized and supervised, how long they would serve, and at what levels of compensation. Potential job displacement effects on others and opportunity costs for participants were rarely acknowledged. The existence of unmet social needs was assumed more often than demonstrated. For some, like Mead, service itself was not very important: the remedial and educational value of participation was the animating objective.

THE VOLUME OF LOGIC

The second AVF experience and contemporary draft and national service proposals are treated more fully elsewhere in this volume. The past adds several things to the logic of current choices.

First, of course, America has been at this juncture before. The details change, but the essential choices have been enduring. This may dismay as well as reassure, but it does offer some useful perspective on the evolution of current alternatives. Americans of great character and intellect have divided on these matters before; it is a stubborn but characteristically American debate. Past generations have somehow managed to muddle through, occasionally with critical and eloquent result. At the same time, past American experience amply underscores the value of some healthy detachment and good humor in viewing these issues. The nation has rarely been as clever, duplicitous, inspired, noble, venal, passionate, or absurd as in the act of inducing its citizens to military service. Past pitfalls lie as much in faulty logic as in faulty programs.

Second, military manpower procurement policy is a political issue as much as a military concern. The point may be obvious to some, but it profits from underscoring. The politics of military manpower are not simply matters of political ideology (although both history and current debates provide much of this). They are also the business of practical political accommodation. The postwar GI Bill had as much to do with concerns about massive unemployment as with expressing a nation's gratitude. Struggles over the National Guard in the 1950s concerned states' rights as much as military preparedness. A nation which has steadfastly refused to draft women for a host of lofty reasons, seemed consistently capable of turning to them to supplement men in voluntary forces. The second AVF may have been the right thing to do (on this there are different viewpoints), but it may, as well, have been the only practical alternative at the time. A resumed draft or national service program may be similarly animated.

Third, the debate is often about symbolism as much as about concrete issues. The 1948 draft was viewed, at least in part, as a visible manifestation of national resolve. So, too, was Kennedy's increase of draft calls and call-up of reservists in 1961-62. Woodrow Wilson demonstrated that what things are called may be as important as what they are in fact.

Fourth, while there is an ideological divide between and among choices of military manpower policy, the alternatives have no particular partisan ownership. Democrats uniformly voted against Mr. Lincoln's draft; Republicans led the campaign to derail Mr. Wilson's and Mr. Roosevelt's offerings. Adlai Stevenson and Barry Goldwater stood on one side of the issue; Dwight D. Eisenhower and John Kennedy and Lyndon Johnson on the other. Even national service, more commonly associated with Democrats than with Republicans, has enjoyed periods of roughly bipartisan support.

Fifth, there is a legal, constitutional dimension to these choices which must be reckoned with. No future Supreme Court is likely to be as pliant or presumptive as that headed by Chief Justice White in 1917. Judicial rulings can clarify, but as the Court amply demonstrated in dealing with conscientious objection in 1965 and 1970, judicial intervention can sometimes transform serious policy choices into intellectual gibberish.

Sixth, the debate has always been about "quality" as well as about quantity in the ranks. The first postwar AVF in part stumbled over contretemps about fitness standards. Some of the postwar draft's glaring inequities were similarly derived. In this context, "quality" is a political statement as well as a military standard—a way of expressing the distribution of the burdens and benefits of the common defense.

Seventh, while the current debate is commonly characterized as AVF-versus-draft, this seems a wrong-headed level of generality on several counts. America has had many different AVFs and different drafts; history is a legacy of versions. The AVFs of 1939, 1948, and 1980 had little in common. The draft of 1965 looked quite different than that of 1955; the last draft in 1972 bore little resemblance to its postwar forebears. Without ample specificity concerning what kind of AVF or draft, the issues are difficult to join. At the same time, national service looms uncertainly as a conceivable third choice. It is not a new idea, not a single idea, and, some suggest, not a particularly good idea, but history, if not logic, suggests that it will invariably occupy a place on the debate agenda. It, too, however, is unmanageable without much greater particularity.

Eighth, it is prudent to be cautious in projections about force capabilities, especially as they concern the nonactive-duty components. The Truman administration had on paper the capability to rapidly mobilize for the early days of Korea, but all the well-thought mobilization plans did not prevent a very clumsy and costly early American response. U.S. reserve forces have rarely been used and when used the experience was not reassuring. The nation may be more sophisticated in its planning now; it may not necessarily be wiser.

Last, military service recurringly has been thought of as serving more than strictly national defense concerns. Woven throughout concepts, from William James' Army against Nature, to Lyndon Johnson's Project 100,000, to the second AVF's sometimes emphasis on being the ultimate equal opportunity employer, are social concerns about the nation's youth and about its disadvantaged. These may not properly belong in the equation, but they seem to be doggedly present anyway. The relationship of military service to the employment market is equally resilient. An AVF has to compete in that market; a draft and national service intervene in it in ways that must be modulated. Whether allowing occupational deferments for such traditional enterprises as die-setting and railway brake inspection or for such national service ideas as tending to the very young, very old, rundown buildings, and denuded forests conscripted service must take account of job displacement of others and opportunity costs for participants. Equity—a difficult notion conceptually and in practice, and one that did not factor much until after World War II—colors both the argument and the choices. An equitable manpower procurement policy may be meaningless in terms of the fighting capability of the armed forces, but it seems essential to the political acceptability of any defense manpower policy.

NOTES

1. In colonial Massachusetts, for instance, at first (in 1631) only magistrates and ministers were excused from militia duty. By 1642, physicians, scholars, and surgeons had been added. By 1647, the exempted class included additionally all members of the general court; officers, fellows, and students of Harvard College; elders and deacons; schoolmasters; the treasurer and surveyor general; public notaries; masters of vessels above twenty-tons burden; fishermen who were employed at all fishing seasons; millers; constant herdsmen; all others who "from bodily infirmity or other just cause" were excused by any county court.

2. In what may have been the nation's first draft riot, citizens of Fredericksburg, Virginia, irate over inequities in the militia draft that sent men to fight the French in the Ohio Valley, stormed the jail in 1755 to release draftees who had been imprisoned as deserters.

3. Military compensation was also modest. Wages were not designed to attract the best and the brightest to the enlisted ranks. A private's pay was $6 a month in 1833, and $8 a month by the Mexican War. A whiskey ration supplemented wages (75,537 gallons were consumed in 1830 alone). There was no retirement system. Attrition was high, in 1823 desertions equaled 25 percent of the year's enlistments, and the volunteer force drew increasingly on Irish and German immigrants, who accounted for nearly half the recruits in the 1840s. Persistent complaints about the enlisted man's low intelligence, vagrant morals, and constant drunkenness led to replacement of the whiskey ration with a coffee and sugar ration in 1838, but this seems to have had little consequence for the character of the force.

4. The irony was not lost on then Georgia Governor Joseph E. Brown, who pronounced the measure "at war with all the principles for the support of which Georgia entered into this revolution."

5. Had the court been presented with the issue, it may well have found military conscription unconstitutional. Chief Justice Roger Taney, anticipating the issue, wrote his opinion beforehand. For Taney, conscription could not be reconciled with the federal constitution.

6. Substitution had been a feature of colonial militia service as well. John Adams extolled its virtues thusly in 1777: "Draughts in the Massachusetts, as they have been there managed, have not been very unpopular, for the Persons draughted are commonly the wealthiest, who become obliged to give large Premiums, to their poorer neighbors, to take their places. . . ."

7. Upton's work was not published, however, until 1904, 23 years after his suicide.

8. Unlike other UMT advocates, who focused chiefly on its military purposes, Eliot saw in UMT the need to include young women as well. "The soldier needs much more training of his senses than is given in American schools today; but so does the industrial worker, and the homemaker." Indeed, Eliot saw no need to confine UMT to military training. Boys would be encouraged as well to master hunting, fishing, carpentry, and the like; girls would be trained in cooking, nursing, sewing, climbing, and walking; both sexes would be instructed in swimming and dancing.

9. Yet another voluntary "national service" scheme was proposed by a pamphleteer named Richard Henry Adams. "Because the college is dedicated to the service of society, the sons of the college are keepers of a sacred trust to be fulfilled by service." It was for Adams the moral duty of the educated young to employ their talents in the service of the less fortunate.

10. Historians are divided as to whether Roosevelt drew the idea from William James. One school has it that FDR was influenced by James' essay while he was a student at Harvard. The more credible view is that FDR had always been interested in forest conservation (on his own land, he had been one of the first to demonstrate that Christmas trees could be grown for profit), and earlier, as governor of New York, had put 10,000 unemployed to work in refor estation projects.

11. Wartime military studies had concluded that many times this number of women could be utilized, but it was evident early-on that the desired numbers would not materialize without a draft of women, something the Congress was decidedly loathe to enact. At one point the Congress did come close to authorizing the conscription of nurses who were in critically short supply, but the wartime draft remained an exclusively male burden.

12. The provision was meaningless in practice, however, since army and navy units re mained racially segregated, and blacks could only be drafted in numbers fitting military re quirements by race.

13. The original 1940 measure deferred fathers, whether or not their children depended on them financially. Initially reluctant to go to the Congress for a change in the legislation, but concerned about the prospect of a post-Pearl Harbor "baby boom," Selective Service took mat ters in its own hands. The congressional intent was to defer fathers, it reasoned, but Congress had not defined "child." Selective Service simply used its own definition: for purposes of the act, a child was only an individual who had been conceived prior to December 7, 1941. (In 1942, Congress eliminated the deferment, except for hardship dependency cases.)

14. The eventual Berlin blockade took time to develop and the final measures were not im posed until August, months after Truman's call for the draft.

15. Once past the worst of the depression, and particularly after Roosevelt's decision to ex pand the army modestly in 1939, the prewar army had difficulties in meeting its limited man power requirements. War Secretary Stimson later characterized the early years of wartime mobilization as a time of "breathless haste and improvization . . . necessarily wasteful and ex orbitantly expensive."

16. Picking up Hershey's remarks, Republican presidential candidate Dewey made the mat ter an uncomfortable one for Roosevelt in 1944, charging the administration with planning for a massive postwar army as a means to hold down unemployment.

17. Those who had already qualified for its benefits, however, continued to receive them. While there were various proposals to reinstate the bill, these were resisted by the Department of Defense on several grounds. Defense worried that the bill lured people out of service and thus hurt retention. Also, the bill had been a reward for veterans of armed conflict (World War II and Korea) and accordingly, should not be available for peacetime service. A "Cold War GI Bill" was nevertheless enacted in 1966. It was terminated in 1976.

18. Active forces alone were 3.3 million in 1954 and 2.5 million in 1959.

19. Mead had no such reservation about employing women in defensive combat on Ameri-

can soil. Nor did she think biological facts complicated military personnel management. Pregnancy, she said, could be treated as a severe breach of contract, comparable to males going AWOL.

20. While the guard and reserves were now theoretically part of the single national reserve establishment, the guard was treated differently in several respects, among them: it was not subject to federal training standards or to a stint of active duty for training; state governors had some say in whether guard members would be activated; and, in deference to states' rights, guard units did not have to be racially desegregated.

21. The fatherhood deferment also channeled individuals toward early parenthood. Student deferments rose significantly in the early sixties. In two years (1963 and 1965) these leaped from 6 to 22 percent of all draft excusals. In 1965, Selective Service's Hershey told a Harvard Law School audience: "We deferred practically everybody. If they had a reason, we preferred it, but if they didn't, we made them hunt one."

22. One such First World War device abandoned in the 1940s was the "slacker raid," which had been conducted in several American cities beginning in Pittsburgh in March 1918. On a chosen day, federal agents, local police, and patriotic citizens would stop at random males who appeared to be of draft age and ask to be shown their draft cards. If the halted individual did not produce a card, he was taken to a local draft board, or "detained in some other place," until verification of his draft status could be made. In one such raid in New York City, all males entering the city by way of ferries were stopped at the exits and challenged as to their draft status.

23. Selective Service's Hershey wrote the Congress in 1962 of his concern "about the light punishment, or in numerous cases no punishment, for the out-and-out violator type of delinquent—the registrant who will not comply at all. . . . There is a tendency in some Federal courts of the land to impose very short sentences or grant probation to such men."

24. Approximately 192,000 registrants failed to appear for induction in the Vietnam years. Most subsequently agreed to enter the armed forces, but 19,153 were prosecuted, resulting in 10,035 dismissals, 1,186 acquittals, and 7,932 convictions.

25. So effective was the tool that its use was expanded in the Vietnam years. In 1965, the Congress provided for accelerated induction for anyone destroying or mutilating his draft card. In 1967, Hershey established a policy of punitive reclassification of antidraft demonstrators. Henceforth the demonstrator would be deprived of his deferment if he had one. The Supreme Court, however, looked with keen disfavor on punitive reclassifications, and in 1970 called a halt to the practice. "If federal or state laws are violated by registrants, they can be prosecuted. If induction is to be substituted for these prosecutions, a vast rewriting of the Act is needed."

SELECTED BIBLIOGRAPHY

While there is no single historical source that adequately accounts for over two centuries of military manpower policy and practice in America, there are numerous reference materials covering different periods and different aspects. The CCC's and Selective Service's annual reports are pertinent, as is a multivolume history of American conscription prepared by Selective Service after World War II. Among the secondary sources are several quite superb volumes that are commended to the reader.

Documentary Histories

Three excellent compendiums of original documents, letters, Congressional debates, newspaper articles, and the like are the following:

Chambers, John Whiteclay, ed. *Draftees or Volunteers: A Documentary History of the Debate Over Military Conscription in the United States, 1787–1973.* New York: Garland Publishing, Inc., 1975.

O'Sullivan, John, and Meckler, Alan M., eds. *The Draft and Its Enemies: A Documentary History.* Chicago: University of Illinois Press, 1974.

Schlissel, Lillian, ed. *Conscience in America: A Documentary History of Conscientious Objection in America, 1757–1967.* New York: E. P. Dutton & Co., 1963.

Historical Accounts

Perhaps the best account of nineteenth-century conscription is Leach, John Franklin. *Conscription in the United States: Historical Background.* Rutland, Vt.: Charles E. Tuttle, 1952.

A useful compendium on the CCC is U.S. Library of Congress, Legislative Reference Service. *Civilian Conservation Corps,* Letter and accompanying monograph from the Director of the Legislative Reference Service. Senate Doc. 216, 77th Cong., 2d sess., 1942.

A good account of the politics and sociology of the years immediately following World War II is Goulden, Joseph C. *The Best Years: 1945-1950.* New York: Atheneum, 1976.

The best rendering of postwar military manpower policy from UMT through Vietnam, with particular emphasis on congressional debates, is Gerhardt, James M. *The Draft and Public Policy: Issues in Military Manpower Procurement, 1945-1970.* Columbus: Ohio State University Press, 1971.

And the classic work on the United States Army is Weigley, Russell F. *History of the United States Army.* New York: Macmillan Publishing Co., 1967.

3

U.S. Security Requirements: Missions, Manpower, Readiness, Mobilization, and Projection of Forces

William J. Taylor, Jr.

WILLIAM J. TAYLOR, JR., is Director of Political/Military Studies at the Center for Strategic and International Studies, Georgetown University, and former Professor of Social Sciences and Director of National Security Studies, U.S. Military Academy. In this chapter, he examines current and evolving concepts of U.S. security requirements and finds significant discrepancies between the tasks assigned to U.S. armed forces and the means to carry them out.

INTRODUCTION

The first chapter addressed the broad range of U.S. security interests in an increasingly interdependent world and the growing number and variety of threats challenging those interests. A central question for the decade ahead concerns the military capabilities required as a backdrop for diplomacy and for purposes of deterrence, warfighting, and special operations.

The chapter is about military forces—not the theory of war, not strategy, not engagements, not the conduct of war, not war plans. We take our lead from Clausewitz in discussing "those aspects of the armed forces that must be regarded as *conditions necessary to military action.*"[1] We are talking about the next five years and:

- MISSIONS—the military tasks, together with their purposes, which clearly indicate the actions to be taken and the reasons therefor.

- MANPOWER—the human resources, required and available to the services, needed to accomplish specified missions.
- READINESS—the capability of military units to perform assigned missions (but with a focus on people, not hardware).
- MANPOWER MOBILIZATION—the capability and act of preparing for war or other emergencies through assembling and organizing people.
- PROJECTION OF FORCES—the capability for movement of military units and supporting bases to locations beyond our shores to accomplish assigned missions.

With the exception of the last term, these definitions parallel those of the Department of Defense *Dictionary of Military and Associated Terms.*

MISSIONS

Although the analysis which follows will address some of the features unique to each of the major components in the structure of the U.S. armed forces, it is important to keep in mind the "Total Force" concept which continues to guide formulation of defense policy. Except for relatively isolated military operations in which the Soviet Union is not directly involved, the total force structure of the 2 million Americans in the active-duty forces backed up by understrength reserve forces in 1982 might not suffice for the remainder of the 1980s. It is possible to argue that the total force structure has been inadequate to serve U.S./allied security interests for at least the past decade. But this line of analysis depends upon one's assumptions about Soviet intentions over that period. For example, it is possible to suggest that force structure has been adequate; the proof is in the fact that the Soviet Union has been deterred from military attack in Europe or in other areas where U.S./NATO vital national interests are involved. However, one might suggest that the Soviets have recognized U.S./NATO conventional force weaknesses, have been deterred from conventional military attack by the risks inherent in U.S. strategic nuclear capabilities, and have decided not to move directly against U.S. vital national interests until Soviet strategic nuclear superiority has been achieved. In the meantime, the argument might continue, the Soviets have chosen to use Soviet military forces directly only in areas where U.S. vital national interests are not involved (e.g., Afghanistan) and to rely on proxy forces to achieve strategic gains elsewhere (e.g., Angola, Ethiopia, the Yemens) without high risks of direct military confrontation with the United States. Simultaneously, one might continue, the Soviets have launched a major political-military campaign to erode the foundations of NATO. Given the mounting evidence of Soviet acquisition of at least strategic nuclear parity, conventional and nuclear warfighting capabilities in Europe, and capabilities to project military power abroad, the first argument supporting the adequacy of deterrence in Europe in the 1970s appears increasingly suspect for the 1980s.

During the 1970s U.S. strategy evolved through "2½ wars" and "1½ wars" to "swing" based on continuing reassessments of U.S./allied capabilities. In every case, it has been assumed that forces designated for the major contingency in Europe could be "earmarked" for other contingencies. This assumption probably is no longer valid. Conventional forces committed to the crucial role of deterring a Soviet attack in central Europe must remain in place in Europe, in the United States, and elsewhere and available, if necessary, for commitment to land, sea, and air warfare in Europe. A major lesson from Vietnam, even when we relied on the draft to expand U.S. armed forces, is that active forces in being will not suffice. With a Vietnam War high of 3.5 million people in uniform, U.S. policymakers were forced to draw down to dangerous levels the personnel and equipment committed to or designated for reinforcement of combat in central Europe, and even to use Europe as a rotation base for Vietnam.

Times changed rather dramatically from 1977 to 1981 in the ways U.S. national security decision makers perceived threats to U.S. national security interests. The change in perceptions began in the latter years of the Carter administration; the evidence is found in the real increases in U.S. defense budgets and in the ways the United States sought to motivate allies to pick up larger shares of the defense burden. However, it is clear, too, that the Reagan administration has an expanded and sharper perception of the threat from the Soviet Union and its allies and proxies around the world. The evidence was in three areas, the *initial* FY 82 defense budget request for $222 billion, the FY 83 request for $258 billion, and the rhetoric used by the president and his top advisors in relation to challenges to U.S. interests worldwide.

In October 1981 Secretary of Defense Weinberger prefaced a major report on *Soviet Military Power* in these terms:

> The Soviet Armed Forces today number more than 4.8 million men. For the past quarter century, we have witnessed the continuing growth of Soviet military power at a pace that shows no signs of slackening in the future.
> All elements of the Soviet Armed Forces—the Strategic Rocket Forces, the Ground Forces of the Army, the Air Forces, the Navy and the Air Defense Forces—continue to modernize with an unending flow of new weapons systems, tanks, missiles, ships, artillery and aircraft. The Soviet defense budget continues to grow to fund this force buildup, to fund the projection of Soviet power far from Soviet shores and to fund Soviet use of proxy forces to support revolutionary factions and conflict in an increasing threat to international stability.[2]

The nature and number of perceived challenges to the security of the U.S. and its allies' national security into the mid-1980s clearly have been expanded, and the missions assigned to American armed forces are to be expanded also. Whether or not the U.S. military force structure should or will be expanded is another matter.

The requirements to meet the most important threat over the next five years—Soviet strategic nuclear superiority which would enable the USSR to coerce the West, or which would lead to a preemptive nuclear first-strike or conventional attack in Europe—certainly are to be expanded, although the means for doing so (e.g., missiles, basing-modes, and ballistic missile defense) remain debatable issues. More to the point of this chapter, the deterrent and warfighting missions of the U.S. armed forces are being expanded significantly with implications not only for conventional force strategy and doctrine, but also for the size of the "total force" defense manpower effort required for the future.

More germane to our study is the growing U.S. perception of Soviet military expansionism worldwide which may entail enhancement of U.S. conventional force capabilities in: (1) the structure of the U.S. armed forces; (2) augmentation of U.S. capability to deploy military forces rapidly to disparate locations around the world and sustain them in combat; and (3) expansion in the number and types of roles that U.S. armed forces must be prepared to execute in the foreseeable future. A relatively new strategic concept involves acquisition of the capability for "horizontal escalation" (as opposed to "vertical" escalation with higher risks of tactical nuclear exchange) of any conflict initiated by the Soviet Union.[3] This is not to say that nuclear escalation has been ruled out. Clearly, Secretary of Defense Weinberger reaffirmed in his Senate confirmation testimony that the United States retains that option. Horizontal escalation appears to mean that, if the Soviets initiate military conflict in a theater where they hold a military strategic advantage, the United States will have the option of rapidly deploying military forces to other theaters where the United States, in tandem with its allies, holds comparative military strategic advantage. Such a strategic concept has two added theoretical advantages. First, the United States might be able to do damage to Soviet vital interests without becoming involved in a direct military confrontation with the Soviet Union. Second, if U.S. armed forces can be placed rapidly in another theater where the Soviets have vital national interests, but where they have not deployed military forces, the awful psychological burden of a decision for a direct military confrontation between the superpowers will be placed on the shoulders of the Soviet leadership. This concept provides supplementary rationale for forward basing in the Indian Ocean/Persian Gulf region as well as prepositioning equipment (but not "basing" of U.S. military personnel) in central Norway. Having base infrastructure (e.g., airfields, ports, storage, and equipment handling facilities) in place, or military equipment prepositioned, permits more rapid deployment of U.S. forces.

Beyond a capability for horizontal escalation, there appears to be a shift away from the older concepts underlying "1½ war strategy" and "swing strategy," which fundamentally imply short war scenarios. The direction appears to be toward developing a capability for rapid deployment anywhere derogating to the least extent possible central war deterrence or conventional warfighting capabilities in NATO Europe. This would be a significant change. U.S. forces currently comprise more than 25 percent of NATO's wartime, conventional combat power. Assuming that conventional force deterrence remains central to NATO planning, either U.S. conventional forces will have to be expanded to acquire capabilities for non-NATO contingencies, or European nations must expand their military force structure, releasing U.S. units for other missions.

The expanded mission requirements are especially crucial for the army to back up the Reagan administration's "more global approach toward employment of the force."[4] The Army Chief of Staff indicated that this will require manpower levels which he doubts can be acquired without a return to the draft. Clearly, given current (fall 1981) strategic assumptions, the army mission will require more active units for expanded missions. The navy appears to be moving from sea denial to sea control missions with emphasis on protecting sea lines of communication. It is possible to overstate the significance of this change; however, the thrust of the change is crucial in numbers of new ships required. This is especially important in the light of: (1) sealift requirements for providing reinforcement and sustaining supply in longer-war scenarios; (2) greater numbers of scenarios which would involve support for amphibious landings in defended or undefended areas, e.g., Marines in the Persian Gulf; and (3) local land combat operations in far-flung regions of the world. The fundamental aspect of these expanded missions is a significant increase in the number of ships required and the skilled personnel to operate them.

The expanded missions of the army and navy mean greater requirements for the air force both to project forces and to support combat operations in far-flung areas. In addition to expanded capabilities for counterair, air superiority, and battlefield interdiction operations geared primarily to the central European theater, the new emphasis on rapid deployment of army and marine forces implies greater responsibilities for airlift and air defense of Lines of Communication (LOC), as well as for rapid air support for over-the-shore joint force operations. We are talking about more aircraft and more skilled personnel to operate and maintain them. All these new mission requirements add up to lots of Americans in uniform who are not now there.

The central question is the strategic design or "grand strategy" the United States ought to develop. Such a strategy should include not only measures to counter an expanded Soviet political-military threat but also to restore strategic initiative worldwide. Although not the subject of this chapter, the centerpiece for future U.S. strategy would be a stable strategic nuclear balance sufficient to deter first-use by the Soviet Union. This means continuation of at least current programs to shore up the strategic triad. Although the optimal programs for curing near-term vulnerabilities in U.S. land-based missiles and strategic bombers remained hotly debated issues in the spring 1982, the Reagan administration made decisions which appeared to recognize these vulnerabilities and sought to place in motion modest programs to close the window of vulnerability and ensure nuclear parity without engaging in a wasteful and, over the long run, counterproductive race for numerical superiority.

Assuming these programs maintain strategic nuclear balance, the key to U.S. military strategy for the future will reside in the adequacy of conventional forces to counter expanding Soviet military capabilities. "Adequacy" must be based on assumptions about the nature of the Soviet conventional threat and the number and intensity of military engagements the United States must be prepared to fight simultaneously. Different defense planners can and do view these threats differently.

The Carter administration developed a five-year defense program based upon traditional assumptions that the Soviets would be able to launch only a single major attack at a given time. Presumably, in conjunction with NATO allies, the United States should be prepared to meet that attack principally in Europe and with the added insurance of Rapid Deployment Forces focused on Southwest Asia, but with a capability for deployment to meet a minor nonnuclear contingency elsewhere. The Carter program called for substantial modernization of conventional forces and augmentation of capabilities to deploy them rapidly and sustain them in combat. But no significant increases in general purpose force structure or personnel were envisioned.

The Reagan administration amended the five-year defense budget for FY 1982–86 significantly calling for: (1) $32.6 billion in surge spending to accelerate force modernization and sustainability which would not have been reached until 1984 under the Carter budget, and (2) an annual increase in defense appropriations at a rate of 7 percent, rather than the 5 percent proposed by the Carter program.

There were early indications that assumptions concerning Soviet capabilities and threats had been revised by the Reagan transition teams and that there was a recognition of a need to be prepared for major, multiple, long-war contingencies in Western Europe, Northeast Asia, Southwest Asia, and for lesser contingencies based on insurgency and terrorism elsewhere.

The problem centers on the combat force structure program adequate to meet expanded threats to U.S. interests worldwide. This depends on a number of assumptions, e.g., warning time of Soviet attack, how quickly Soviet units can be mobilized and brought to Category I (combat ready) status, how long they can sustain units in combat, and how NATO uses the warning time available. One might assume in the worst case that any calculated Soviet attack in central Europe would not be a geographically isolated event. Understanding current inadequacies in U.S. air and sealift and manpower mobilization capabilities, Soviet planners might seek to capitalize on interior lines by escalating ground conflict geographically in Europe and Asia through the employment of more than 126 motorized rifle divisions and 47 tank divisions, and by the use of Soviet advisors and proxy military forces armed with Soviet weapons in the Caribbean, Africa, and the Middle East. Any U.S.-Soviet military confrontation might quickly become a worst-case, fast breaking high-conventional-threat situation where shortfalls in U.S. force structure and manpower quickly would be realized. In such a high-threat scenario, army problems would be the most significant by far. It would take months to mobilize U.S. Army Reserve units. The shortfall in army requirements would be substantial (see table 3.1).

For the army alone the differences in immediate manpower requirements would be at least 750,000 people and some analysts would add another 235,000 total for the navy, Marine Corps, and air force in a high threat scenario.[5]

On the other hand, one might assume a long period of international crisis and longer warning times, that the Soviets require several months to mobilize units, that they will be unable to overcome logistical problems in the foreseeable future, that they will be unable to coordinate proxy forces, that war will be slow in developing and will be sustained over a long period. In such a scenario, U.S. reserves could be mobilized, additional trained strength could be provided through induction, and the picture changed significantly (see table 3.2).

In this scenario, the additional army manpower requirements would total at least 250,000, but could run to 500,000, depending on the extent to which the current shortfall in the pretrained manpower pool had been overcome.

Table 3.1. Shortfall in Army Requirements.

	Active Divisions Available	National Guard Divisions Available	Divisions Required	Shortfall
Caribbean	—	—	1	1
Central Europe	15	2	23	6
Korea	1	—	2	1
Middle East	—	—	1	1
Persian Gulf	—	—	4	4
TOTAL	16	2	31	13

Note: Assumed 1 Marine Division in Norway and 1 Marine Division in Korea.

Table 3.2. Shortfall in Army Requirements.

	Active Divisions Available	National Guard Divisions Available	Divisions Required	Shortfall
Caribbean	—	—	—	—
Central Europe	13	5	23	5
Korea	1	1	2	—
Middle East	—	—	—	—
Persian Gulf	2	2	4	—
TOTAL	16	8	29	5

Note: Assumed 1 Marine Division in Norway, 1 in Korea, and 1 in the Persian Gulf.

A final scenario would be close to the second but would assume different Soviet objectives (Western Europe only) and greater limitations on Soviet military conventional land force military capability (see table 3.3).

Reagan administration planning for the five-year defense program for 1982–87, envisioned an increase in active-duty manpower and strength by 1987 something above 200,000 (of which about 90,000 would be for the army). There appeared to be little doubt that all the armed services except the army would be able to meet their active-duty and reserve quotas by 1987. The Army Chief of Staff doubted that the army could meet a 90,000 increase without reviving the draft.[6] It seemed clear that, unless extraordinary manpower spending were approved by Congress, the army would continue to have a serious shortfall in both active-duty forces and the reserves.

Beyond the issues of the manpower numbers involved, which have been covered by press reports, one assumes modified training missions of considerable import, for example, in Joint Special Forces Operations.[7] All the services have been involved in a massive effort to rethink strategy, doctrine, training, and weapons acquisition. For example, the army is in the midst of a major overhaul of its "How to Fight" manual (Army Field Manual 100-5),

Table 3.3. Shortfall in Army Requirements.

	Active Divisions Available	National Guard Divisions Available	Divisions Required	Shortfall
Caribbean	—	—	—	—
Central Europe	14	7	23	2
Korea	1	1	2	—
Middle East	—	—	—	—
Persian Gulf	1	—	1	—
TOTAL	16	8	26	2

partly at army initiative, partly under the assaults of Robert W. Komer (former Under Secretary of Defense for Plans), and in part following the initiatives of the "Reform Movements" led by analysts such as James Woolsey, Edward Luttwak, Jeffrey Record, Steven Canby, Pierre Sprey, and John Boyd, joined now by the expanding Congressional Reform Caucus and by strategists in uniform who routinely remain nameless.[8]

Whatever the future results of current *plans* to change strategy and doctrine, one can be relatively certain that, given bureaucratic process, there will be a long lag-time between studies, proposals, and *decisions* on training requirements and the *implementation* of training changes reflecting those decisions in the professional military education system, at training facilities and in active-duty unit training programs worldwide. The lag-time for training implementation in National Guard and Selected Reserve (SR) units will be even greater.

MISSIONS AND MANPOWER

Subsequent chapters in this volume will examine defense manpower requirements in detail. One need not hear only that definition of U.S. interests, assessments of threats to those interests, and development of defense strategy and military mission requirements are crucial for the determination of future military manpower needs. For example, during the Carter administration, studies of Soviet defense spending, rapid development and deployment of strategic and theater nuclear weapons, increased deployments of Soviet conventional forces, use of proxy forces in the Indian Ocean region, and expansion of Soviet naval capabilities for force projection led not only to decisions mentioned above for real increases in the U.S. defense budget, but also to pressures on U.S. allies for annual real increases in their defense spending. The Soviet attack into Afghanistan in December 1979 was a major variable in Carter's decision to declare the Persian Gulf region and its oil resources as a vital U.S. interest (by definition, an interest the United States will fight to protect). In turn, ongoing development of a Rapid Deployment Joint Task Force (RDJTF) involves new and expanded missions. However, in 1980 and 1981 RDJTF contingency planning involved forces-in-being, many of which were earmarked for NATO reinforcement and other missions. The Reagan administration decided that, given current assumptions about Soviet threats, U.S. military manpower must be augmented significantly over the next five years and three new manpower budget initiatives were submitted to Congress for the FY 1982 Defense Manpower Requirements Report.

The baseline force level has not been altered significantly since the end of the Vietnam War (see table 3.4). Since its worst recruiting and retention year in 1979, there have been modest increases in the number of people in

Table 3.4. Defense Manpower: the Baseline Force.
(in thousands)

	1964	1968	1975	1980	1981	1982
Active Military						
Army	972	1,570	784	777	775	786
Navy	667	765	535	517	540	555
Marine Corps	190	307	196	188	191	192
Air Force	856	905	613	558	569	587
	2,685	3,547	2,128	2,050	2,075	2,120
Selected Reserve						
Reserve Personnel						
Army	269	244	225	207	217	237
Navy	123	124	98	87	87	88
Marine Corps	46	47	32	35	37	39
Air Force	61	43	51	59	61	64
National Guard						
Army	382	389	395	367	386	398
Air Force	73	75	95	96	98	98
	954	922	896	851	886	924
Civilians						
Army	453	542	401	361	371	382
Navy/Marine Corps	346	433	326	309	317	313
Air Force	338	357	278	244	243	247
Defense Agencies	37	74	73	77	82	83
	1,174	1,406	1,078	991	1,013	1,025

Source: Adapted from William W. Kaufman, "U.S. Defense Needs in The 1980's," Lt. Gen. Brent C. Scowcroft, ed., *Military Service in the United States* (New York: The American Assembly, 1981), p. I.4.

the total force. In FY 81, all the services showed improvement in recruiting and retention goals. There has been no intellectually satisfactory explanation of the army's success. The factors involved could have been the following: (1) hopes for a new 14.3 percent pay raise, G.I. bill, and other incentives packages impacted favorably on active-duty and SR recruitment and retention; (2) given higher unemployment, mass experiences or expectations about civilian employment opportunities for young Americans have been negative; (3) the concept of military service has been increasingly legitimized by a conservative swing in America; (4) recruiting programs have improved; (5) leadership in the services has improved; or (6) for one reason or another, the army lowered its FY 81 recruiting and retention quotas. How long this relative good fortune will prevail is problematic. In the short run quantitative success in recruiting and retention will be contingent in large part on congressional passage of very costly, key manpower legislation.

With current proposals for active-duty end strength increases of between 200,000 and 250,000 (perhaps around 11 percent) over the next five years (given favorable congressional action), all services except the army probably will be able to achieve active-duty goals. The army especially must contend with the hard facts that by 1987, the prime recruiting pool will be 15 percent smaller than its 1978 level and, by 1992, will be 20 percent smaller.[9]

The most important aspect of the proposed increases in active-duty forces probably does not reside in capabilities to increase force structure, for it is possible to argue that the army is simply overstructured now. More important is the capability to bring existing active-duty units to full strength and keep them there. It is positively debilitating for training and morale to maintain units which do not have adequate personnel and in which personnel turnover is high. This is a major reason for Army Chief of Staff Edward C. Meyer's concern in 1980 about a "hollow Army." Yet, to bring more existing units to full strength, army plans in 1981 called for reducing the 7th Division at Fort Ord, California, from its authorized strength of 14,000 to a cadre, or "skeleton" strength of 5,000.

But, the real problems will occur in the reserves. The reserves, at 877,000 people (slightly above authorized strength), are 17 percent short of wartime mobilization requirements of approximately one million. The current IRR shortfall is at least 200,000 and perhaps 400,000 of wartime requirements, with the biggest shortfall in the army. The large difference in IRR shortfall estimates is explained by differing estimates of requirements for trained replacements for the killed and incapacitated in a NATO/Warsaw Pact war. These estimates have fluctuated between 400,000 and 750,000. Projections of the availability rates of IRR personnel also have varied widely. A full explanation appears in Robert B. Pirie's contribution to this volume.[10]

It is important to recall that 50 percent of American combat strength and two-thirds of army support units for Europe in wartime reside in the National Guard and reserve. The most telling commentary in this regard came in October 1981 from General Bernard D. Rogers, Supreme Allied Commander, Europe: "My major concern with respect to the U.S. manpower is that the U.S. Army does not have an adequate manpower base from which to mobilize."[11] Expanded Reagan administration missions and manpower increases may make current manpower problems worse in the long run, assuming continuation of the All-Volunteer Force (AVF). It was the realization that these manpower problems are on the near-term horizon that led to the Reagan administration's July 1981 decision to form a National Manpower Task Force which may or may not consider alternatives to the AVF.

READINESS

Readiness clearly must be measured in the context of the Total Force concept considering both active forces and all categories of reserve forces. And, it is crucial to understand that although "readiness" involves *numbers* of weapons and support systems and *numbers* of people in active and reserve units, it involves much more than numbers. There are levels of readiness regularly reported from military units to the highest levels of the National Command Authority.[12] As noted above, in terms of wartime manpower requirements, the United States military is not "ready" now on the basis of SR and IRR quantity requirements alone. However, there are other critical aspects of measuring operational readiness which are not well understood and for which we have no adequate bases of measurement. It is important to highlight this aspect of readiness.

Operational readiness is the foundation of both warfighting capability and deterrence. The test of warfighting capability is the preparedness of weapons systems and personnel to carry out their assigned missions. The test of deterrence is what the Soviet leadership believes about the operational readiness of U.S. and allied armed forces. For U.S. forces, readiness reports quantify variables which indicate whether weapons systems and personnel *can* carry out assigned missions. Measuring unit proficiency is a complex task replete with problems too numerous to document here.[13] Readiness reports do not and cannot measure whether American military personnel *will* carry out their assigned missions or the impact of their attitudes on *how well* they will perform assigned tasks. In neither the armed forces of the United States nor in the NATO Alliance is there a standard statistical indicator for operational readiness accepted as valid by all NATO members, much less a reliable means of measuring performance attitudes among military personnel. To a large extent, informed intuition remains the basis for evaluating U.S./NATO operational readiness. The same conditions may prevail in the Soviet military, and the Soviets may have serious morale problems. Nevertheless, whether or not the Soviets are better able than we to assess these aspects of U.S./NATO operational readiness, for the purposes of deterrence what the Soviets perceive is important.

Deterrence has any number of definitions. As used here it means simply the ability "to hinder or prevent action by fear of consequence, or by difficulty, risk, unpleasantness, etc."[14] Deterrence is, therefore, at base a psychological phenomenon. Its object is to master the expectations of rational opponents, to convince them that attempts to gain their objectives would cost more than it is worth, and that the cost to the deterrer of applying the deterrent would be less than conceding the objective. To make a deterrent credible the adversary must believe one will do, or is likely to do what one says and, crucially, that one has the capability to do it. Capability is normally measured in terms of the relative balance of quality and quantity of weapons systems and units relative to those of one's adversary. Routinely, these balances assume "perfect systems," i.e., weapons and units that will perform according to design or mission. The obvious fallacy is the assumption that the people involved will perform "as ordered."

Deterrence theory based upon perfect operation of units or weapons systems cannot be totally reliable. The state of "weapons systems" readiness obviously depends on both the expertise of the personnel who construct, maintain, and fire them (which can be measured) — and upon the willingness of personnel to operate and fire weapons (which cannot now be measured reliably). It is critical to understand that the circumstances under which deterrence fails can be most ambiguous. Nuclear weapons could be launched by the Soviets without warning. There are scenarios in which nuclear war starts without the development of an international crisis. Too, there are scenarios in which the Soviets attack Western Europe without an international crisis and with the preliminary maneuver assumed necessary for all-out invasion — for example, a limited "land grab" by the Soviets.

In order for existing U.S. and allied forces to accomplish their most important role of deterrence, the Soviets must believe not only that the United States and its allies possess weapons systems and personnel capable of inflicting "unacceptable damage" at both the nuclear and conventional levels, but also that American and allied military personnel have the *will* to obey orders immediately to accomplish their assigned missions well. It should be noted here that mere *uncertainty* by the Soviets concerning the operational readiness of U.S. forces (as opposed to uncertainty concerning U.S. intentions) undermines credibility in U.S. military deterrence in the most fundamental way.

From the analytical viewpoint here, one must understand the high degree of importance the Soviets attach to the morale factor in operational readiness. Fortunately, we do not have to guess about this; rather, we can turn to Soviet military literature which abounds with documentation.[15] Although the Soviets employ the political commission system in part to insure morale, one cannot assume that their system "works" or that their own assessments are reliable.

Morale and Operational Readiness

The most fundamental aspect of military operational readiness is the ability of the unit commander to issue orders and directives and to establish standing operating procedures with high confidence that they will be obeyed to the letter and in the spirit given. Whether or not and how well American military personnel at each level of the chain of command will obey orders rests in part on their perceptions of the competence of their leaders and of the competence of their unit to accomplish its mission. The habit of obedience taught and reinforced through repetitive drill and training and supported by military law is important also.

One series of attempts to measure these perceptions in the army active-duty force in Europe is to be found in the Human Readiness Reports instituted in the late 1970s by the army. Human Readiness Report Number 5, submitted to the secretary of the army in 1980, casts considerable doubt on the state of morale in the AVF and, thus, operational readiness of the army. The secretary rejected the report and quietly dismantled the attempt to develop a system for measuring human readiness.[16]

In military organizations, that which links obedience to duly constituted authority with willing response to an order is organizational esprit which is, in essence, the manifestation of organizational morale. S. L. A. Marshall defined esprit as "the product of thriving mutual confidence between the leader and the led, founded on the faith that together they possess a superior quality and capability."[17] Unit esprit in the military is founded on a number of intangibles. They are the following: trust in, identity with, and dependence on the chain of command; individual and subunit knowledge that they have the resources needed to accomplish assigned missions and confidence in their abilities to do their assigned tasks well; camaraderie within the unit and the respect and support of others outside the unit. Analysts outside the defense establishment who have published work on these matters in relation to the contemporary U.S. armed forces give us cause to doubt that unit esprit and unit cohesion are sound in the U.S. armed forces.[18]

Military units with a high level of esprit or morale are units which obey lawful orders immediately and carry out their missions willingly to the best of the coordinated abilities of the individuals in the unit. Such units are operationally "ready." Sadly, although we claim to be able to measure all other aspects of operational readiness today, we do not have in the nation's defense establishment any measures accepted as valid to measure individual or unit morale. This is the missing link in determining operational readiness and, thus, the blind spot in military strategy. Relative to new requirements for U.S. armed forces over the next five years, we may or may not be ready in terms of Five-Year Defense Program requirements for conventional weapons systems, support systems, or people in uniform. There are indications that we are not ready in the area of *morale*. The problem is that we have no way of knowing, even if we were to get "ready."

MANPOWER MOBILIZATION

In June 1980, Under Secretary of Defense for Policy Robert W. Komer published "An Evaluation Report of Mobilization and Deployment Capability Based on Exercise Nifty Nugget-78 and Rex-78."[19] These exercises were based on a short-warning, fast-breaking attack by the Warsaw Pact in Central Europe. Seldom does one encounter from the defense establishment such a candid appraisal of capability. In the area of mobilization plans the 1978 Nifty Nugget exercise "made salient the fact that existing mobilization plans were a hodgepodge of old and unconnected presidential emergency orders, policies, regulations and procedures." More to the point of this chapter were findings in the area of military and civilian manpower mobilization:[20]

- *Selective Service.* The active and reserve forces were never intended to fight without additional draftees in the event of a major national emergency. Since 1973, however, the Selective Service System (SSS) has been reduced to a planning and training organization of less than 100 full-time personnel supported by reservists. The ability of a standby SSS to process untrained manpower as part of a potential mobilization has been a source of concern. In NIFTY NUGGET, the system was assumed to be fully staffed in advance of M-Day, so as to be capable of producing inductees within days of a presidential decision to draft. In a scenario which does not mobilize the system before M-Day, the system must be able to provide manpower to meet DoD's articulated schedule; this would require rapid congressional approval for induction authority.
- *Selected Reserve Shortfall.* A NIFTY NUGGET scenario requires the activation and early deployment of many reserve units simultaneously with a request for induction authority. At current readiness levels, some selected reserve units would not be adequately manned at deployment.
- *Trained Military Manpower Pool.* In the post-Vietnam all-volunteer force, the combination of a smaller active force and longer enlistments has resulted in a drastically reduced pool of trained people with residual military obligations. This pool, the Individual Ready Reserve (IRR), is well below the level needed, at least by the army, to bring active and reserve units to wartime manning levels and to provide a reservoir of trained combat replacements during the early phases of a major intense conflict with little warning. This "pretrained" manpower is needed in the early months of mobilization and deployment, well before the military training establishment could furnish meaningful numbers of newly trained recruits. Even if the Selective Service System were able to provide draftees as soon as the military could absorb them, we would still require the pretrained personnel. During NIFTY NUGGET the lack of enough pretrained personnel forced the army to levy late-deploying units for combat-skilled personnel.

In May 1979, the General Accounting Office (GAO) studied manpower mobilization capabilities in wartime with a focus on the army training base. Working with an estimate that army training centers would have to receive and begin training approximately 550,000 people, about 450,000 of whom would have to be drafted in the first 180 days of mobilization, the GAO concluded that the army did not have:[21]

- adequate plans for mobilization
- enough housing for the training centers
- enough physicians to provide medical exams

- the number of active or reserve training centers required
- enough reserve trainers to do the training
- adequately skilled reserve trainers
- knowledge of training equipment available

Between 1977 and 1979, the inability of the Standby Selective Service System to meet induction planning schedules set by the Department of Defense was the subject of a number of critical reviews and reports. The director of Selective Service himself concluded in a March 1979 report to the Congress that the Selective Service did "not presently have the capability to meet the Department of Defense wartime manpower requirements from our 'deep standby' status."[22] These are only three of many reviews and reports which made it clear that, in 1979 the United States' capability to mobilize manpower in time of war was totally inadequate and that the army had the biggest problem of all.

The government did not stand still on these issues and, by the summer 1981, had learned many lessons and moved to remedy the problems:[23]

- Office of Scientific Development (OSD) established a Mobilization and Deployment Steering Group at the secretary's level to oversee the defense mobilization planning process.
- The Office of the Assistant Secretary of Defense (Manpower, Reserve Affairs, and Logistics) established a Mobilization and Deployment Planning Directorate to provide support for the steering group and develop and manage a defense mobilization plan.
- The army established a Mobilization Planning Group to evaluate and analyze its own capacity to rapidly expand its training base upon mobilization.
- OSD authorized and preassigned retired personnel with health professions (including physicians and administrative personnel) to Armed Forces Entrance Examination Stations (AFEES) to meet full mobilization manpower requirements.
- OSD developed AFEES mobilization guidance.
- The army identified steps needed to overcome its training base capacity shortfalls.
- President Carter called for and Congress approved in 1980 a resumption of draft registration and revitalization of the Selective Service System.

Specific actions were taken in 1980 and 1981 to address the critical problems of shortages in the SR and IRR:[24]

- Varied enlistment options for the Selected Reserve. New accessions may enlist for four or five years in the Selected Reserve and may serve the balance of their six-year obligation in the IRR. These options augment the standard six-year enlistment.
- Flexibility in scheduling initial periods of training.
- Enlistment and reenlistment bonuses, as well as educational benefits.

- A full-time Army Reserve recruiting force, under the control of the Army's Recruiting Command.
- Screening of all individuals who leave the army before the end of their enlistments to insure that those with mobilization potential are transferred to the IRR.
- Services encouragement of members who reach the end of their six-year service obligation to reenlist in the IRR.
- Female enlistees incur the same six-year military service obligation as their male counterparts.
- Enlistees no longer allowed to count toward fulfillment of the six-year obligation the time after enlistment but before entering.
- All enlistees incur a six-year obligation.
- An active forces' test of two-year active-duty enlistments and the Selected Reserves' use of three- and four-year enlistments to increase the strength of the IRR.
- Army members transferred from the active forces to the IRR, matched with mobilization assignments and given orders telling them where to report upon mobilization.

In the summer 1980, the Department of Defense (DoD) official expectation was that these programs would fill out SR unit strengths and fully eliminate the army's IRR mobilization manpower shortfall by the end of FY 1985. However, by the following summer (1981), there was reason to doubt that the army's SR end strength requirements for FY 1987 would be met and no one foresaw any realistic solution to the serious IRR shortfall in an AVF context, short of extending the military obligation from six to eight years.

Continuous registration for 18-year-olds was initiated in 1981 and, based on the experience of 90 percent compliance in the first wave of registration, the outlook was optimistic. However, by the fall 1981, the second wave had produced only 70 percent compliance and the Justice Department began to move against two lists of violators totaling 183.[25]

It is difficult to judge what the increasing rate of noncompliance with draft registration means. There has been no national leadership on the matter, although President Reagan has reversed his campaign statement that he was opposed to draft registration.

In November 1980, the Department of Defense conducted another national mobilization exercise, "Proud Spirit," in which the ability of the Selective Service to mobilize the nation's manpower was demonstrated. At their First Impressions Conference on the exercise, the Organization of the Joint Chiefs of Staff reported that:

> Exercise results indicate Selective Service successfully achieved its exercise objectives. Most important, Selective Service demonstrated that Selective Service

can provide DoD the required manpower under the most demanding DoD requirements.[26]

With less than two years special effort, U.S. capability to mobilize manpower in wartime appeared to have improved, but some remained skeptical. However, there remained the Achilles heel of army pretrained manpower, especially in the IRR.

Another aspect of mobilization capability and future potential centers on the matter of national morale. There appeared to be a resurgence (the dimensions, depth, and duration of which really are not known) of a willingness to sacrifice in the name of national security. Support for the past two defense budgets constitutes one measure. Another might be opinion surveys on American attitudes toward conscription. All the major polls indicate that over 80 percent of Americans over the age of 24 support a return to some form of conscription. And, even though draft age youth (18–24) remain opposed to draft, the margin of opposition appears to have declined slightly over the past 18 months. Some polls show that youth opposition has dropped to less than half.[27] Should the general concept of service to a higher calling resurge in America, even the problems of the IRR might be solved in the Volunteer Force context. More important, acceptances of the notion that young Americans have an *obligation* to serve could be the decisive factor for the morale component of operational readiness. Nevertheless, young middle-class Americans, whose family income level and educational background and potential provide real alternatives to military service, were generally missing from the ranks of the U.S. armed forces in 1981. There was every reason to believe this condition would continue in the AVF context.

FORCE PROJECTION

Even if we assume the availability of sufficient numbers of skilled and motivated people in uniform to meet the nation's military strategic requirements over the next five years, we are not so fortunate in other aspects of capability to project power abroad in the far-flung regions of the world for which the Reagan administration now expects the military to be prepared. Power projection capabilities are complex and we will mention only three aspects of such capability here — forward basing, prepositioning of military equipment and supplies, and mobility forces.

We have long experience in forward basing around the world. Our planners understand the strategic utility of basing ground units, ships, and aircraft in the regions of the world where threats are most likely. They recognize, too, the thorny political problems of securing and maintaining the required agreements and leases from host country governments in a world where a visible U.S. military presence is not always desired. In some cases there are bases with permanent or periodic stationing of U.S. troops and in other cases airfields, ports, and other facilities are prepared for the introduction of U.S. forces in time of crisis if a foreign, host government asks for or agrees to their use. Recent experience, for example, in the Persian Gulf region, indicates that the United States often is able to acquire only limited or contingent access. Over the past two years through patient and quiet negotiation, we have been able to get such access to 13 "facilities" in the Indian Ocean/Gulf region, in addition to a major base at Diego Garcia.

Facilities Agreements in Indian Ocean/Persian Gulf Region

Egypt:	Cairo West (airport)
	Ras Banas (port)
Saudi Arabia:	Riyadh (airport)
Bahrain:	Capital City (port)
Oman:	Muscat (airport, port)
	Thumrait (airport)
	Salalah (airport, port)
	Masirah (airport)
Somalia:	Berbera (airport, port)
	Mogadishu (airport, port)
Kenya:	Mombasa (airport, port)
	Nairobi (airport)
	Nanyuki (airport)

Forward basing units is a mixed blessing. It is often less expensive because host governments may offset costs. However, U.S. ground units, especially those with heavy equipment, lose flexibility. If the military engagement does not occur in the locale expected, the units must be moved.

Prepositioning extra sets of equipment abroad to which people can be moved reduces dramatically the airlift and sealift required early in a conflict. The vast majority of prepositioned stocks are in Europe. For a war in Europe more than 90 percent of Supreme Allied Commander, Europe's (SACEUR) out-of-theater ground and air reinforcement units committed to NATO would come from the United States.[28] Under an assumption of a two-week warning time, peacetime storage of U.S. equipment for *initial* reinforcing units have been deemed feasible, so that only troops and light equipment need be flown in.[29] The equipment, called POMCUS (Prepositioned Organizational Material Configured in Unit Sets), for U.S. Army divisions is exercised regularly in Reforger operations where troops are flown in from the United States to be issued and test the readiness of the people and the equipment. Current five-year defense budgets have called for a large expansion of POMCUS, perhaps to six division equivalents. However, current battles between the services for slices of the budget leave these figures in doubt. The navy's fight to find funds for 600 ships could lead to imposition of budget ceilings and obviate army plans. The contention evidently is that two additional POMCUS sets constitute the equivalent of two navy aircraft carriers.

In a 1980 memorandum of understanding with the government of Norway, the United States established a plan to preposition stocks for a marine brigade in central Norway. Norway has a firm "base and ban" policy (no foreign troops based on Norwegian soil and a ban on nuclear weapons in Norway), and prepositioning equipment in this vital area on NATO's northern flank is the best agreement NATO could possibly achieve. Based on the time it would take to move a marine brigade north to the most likely and critical avenues of Soviet approach, it is problematical whether much time would be saved.[30]

Given contingencies in the Indian Ocean, the United States has moved forward in maritime prepositioning. Supplies and equipment for two Marine Amphibious Brigades are to be prepositioned on Maritime Prepositioning ships in the region.

Airlift and sealift for mobility forces will constitute a critical constraint on power projection for the next five years. Depending on the scenarios, it is conceivable that mobility forces, the Rapid Deployment Joint Task Force (RDJTF), could be required to move to Europe up to six army divisions and several marine amphibious forces, and simultaneously move to the Persian Gulf region, or elsewhere, two army divisions, a marine division, and a marine amphibious force—and all this within two weeks.

Although only detailed planning can show how extensive the mobility forces shortfall will be over the next five years, it is clear that we do not have sufficient air and sea transports now and, given the long lead times needed to build ships and aircraft *after they are budgeted*, we will not have sufficient resources by 1987.

For sealift, the ships are founded in the Military Sealift Command Controlled Fleet, the National Defense Reserve Fleet (of the Navy Ready Reserve), and U.S. merchant ships committed to the Sealift Readiness Program. Altogether these ships add up to fewer than 400, including breakbulk ships (the vast majority) and smaller numbers of container ships, seabee ships, roll-on/roll-off ships and seatrain ships. Current airlift capacity is primarily in the 70 C-5 and 234 C-141 aircraft of the Military Airlift Command, although there are more than 100 wide-body cargo carriers and perhaps another 125 narrow-body cargo carriers in the Civilian Reserve Air Fleet which can be ordered into military service by the president in a time of national emergency. Current programs to improve airlift capability include purchasing an additional 50 C5A's and "stretching" C-141 aircraft to handle greater loads and "outsize" cargo. However, especially in consideration of RDJTF power projection capabilities, it is instructive to note that a C-5 can carry only one of the army's new M-1 tanks or, alternatively, six to seven attack helicopters. *Never* will all aircraft be available at the same time for reasons of maintenance and repair.

Force projection capabilities are further constrained by a woeful lack of surge capability for material-handling equipment at airports and seaports and by a lack of trained U.S. ammunition-handling companies, even in Europe. Force projection may be the single most critical problem confronting U.S. military capability over the next five years. The problem can be diminished significantly both by prepositioning military equipment abroad and by building new air and sea carriers, but both require long lead times beyond 1987.

CONCLUSION

The FY 82 budget at just under $200 billion and FY 83 budget proposal at over $256 billion might help to reestablish the military capability of the United States. But, simply more defense dollars do not necessarily provide greater capability. The army probably cannot sustain under the AVF an enlarged active force to successfully fulfill its expanded and far more varied missions over the next five years, but, in any case, the army IRR will be the Achilles heel of the AVF. Readiness is problematical; even if we acquire the requisite numbers of operational weapons and support systems and adequately trained people, we will not be able to measure accurately the crucial element — morale. Manpower mobilization planning and capability may be moving slowly in the right direction and draft registration may be underpinned by a national consensus, but force projection capabilities are inadequate for the foreseeable future security needs for simultaneous rapid deployment in Europe and a second theater of combat.

Fundamentally there are only three ways to maintain manpower levels under the status quo, i.e., the All-Volunteer Force. First, one can continue the effort at increasingly high money costs to provide incentives for people to join and remain in the active and reserve components, keeping the current system of Selective Service registration as a means of mobilizing manpower under a state of national emergency, and relying on the president's authority to call up active and reserve forces in a national emergency. Second, one might make some different assumptions about the nature and extent of threats to national security, adopt different strategies to counter threats—and opt for a smaller conventional military force. Third, one might continue the search for increasing numbers of "military" functions that can be performed by civilians, eventually achieving a "fighting military force" and a "military support force."

Beyond the status quo, and perhaps for reasons other than strategic requirements for the right number of quality people in uniform (e.g., national cohesion and morale), the options extend from variants of a military draft to various forms of compulsory or voluntary national service.

Whether or not the current thin veneer of public support for defense resources remains will depend on *national morale*—the key variable to be addressed by the nation's leadership. This is primarily a matter of explaining the political purpose of preparations for war. As Clausewitz told us, "means can never be considered in isolation from their purpose."[31] And, "if policy is directed only toward minor objectives, the emotions of the masses will be little stirred and they will have to be stimulated rather than held back."[32] It remains to be seen whether the American public has been persuaded that the political purpose of our new emphasis on means makes the light worth the candle.

NOTES

1. Carl Von Clausewitz, *On War*, eds. and trans. Michael Howard and Peter Paret (Princeton: Princeton University Press, 1976), p. 279.

2. Caspar W. Weinberger, *Soviet Military Power* (Washington, D.C.: Government Printing Office, 1981), p. 1.

3. See Caspar W. Weinberger, *Annual Report To The Congress, Fiscal Year 1983* (Washington, D.C.: Government Printing Office, 1982), pp. I 15–17.

4. General Edward C. Meyer, quoted in Charles W. Corddry, "Army Seeks to Move East in Germany," *Baltimore Sun*, August 16, 1981, p. A2.

5. The army general planning figure for the total personnel to support an army division of 16–18,000 is approximately 50,000, although this figure varies by theater to which divisions are deployed. The figure for the navy, Marine Corps, and air force is from William W. Kaufman, "U.S. Defense Needs in the 1980's," in *Military Service in the United States*, ed. Lt. Gen. Brent C. Scowcroft (New York: The American Assembly, 1981), p. I-31.

6. In addition to a 750,000 shortfall in required division strength, one must add a shortfall of 250,000 in reserve strength and at least another 100,000 for overhead. Charles W. Corddry, "Army Seeks to Move East in Germany," *Baltimore Sun*, September 28, 1981, p. A2.

7. The latter in the light of the failed rescue mission in Iran.

8. For the reasons why military strategists remain "nameless," see William Taylor, "'Clearance' Muzzles Military Strategists," *Washington Star*, July 14, 1981, p. A-9.

9. See Robin B. Pirie, Jr., "Military Manpower into the 1980s: An Overview," in William J. Taylor, Jr. et al., *Defense Manpower Planning: Issues for the 1980s* (Elmsford, N.Y.: Pergamon Press, 1981), p. xv.

10. For another explanation of the wide variances in such estimates, see Robert L. Goldich,

"Recruiting, Retention, and Quality in the All Volunteer Force," *CRS Report No. 81-106F* (Washington, D.C.: Congressional Research Service, June 8, 1981), pp. 18–19.

11. Rick Maze, "Rogers: Draft Necessary for Mobilization," *Army Times*, October 21, 1981, p. 10.

12. Readiness ratings are based on many variables such as unit strength, number of weapons authorized and on hand, numbers of vehicles and weapons operational or requiring maintenance or spare parts, etc. The ratings are:

> C1 — Ready
> C2 — Ready with minor deficiencies
> C3 — Ready with major deficiencies
> C4 — Not Ready
> C5 — Not Ready, by directive of higher
>   headquarters (e.g., the unit is being
>   reorganized).

Readiness ratings are classified and not releasable to the public.

13. See Colonel Irving Heymont, "Measuring Unit Proficiency," *Military Review*, LVII, no. 6 (June 1977): 28–35.

14. Sometimes, in the wrangle of academic definitions in the literature on national security affairs, it is not a bad idea to see what a term means in the English language; see *Webster's Third International Dictionary of the English Language*, 2nd ed., unabridged p. 711.

15. For example, see V. D. Sokolovsky, *Soviet Military Strategy*, 3rd ed., with analysis and commentary by Harriet Fast Scott (New York: Crane, Russak & Company, Inc., 1975), p. 33; Ibid., 2nd ed., translated with an analytical introduction, annotations, and supplementary materials by Herbert S. Dinnerstein et al. (Englewood Cliffs, New Jersey: Prentice-Hall, Inc., 1963), pp. 127–29; and Colonel A. M. Danchenko and Colonel I. F. Vydrin, eds., *Military Pedagogy: A Soviet View*, translated and published under the auspices of the U.S. Air Force (Moscow, 1973), pp. 192–235.

16. See John Fialka, "The Report No One Wants to Talk About," *Washington Star*, December 15, 1981, p. 1.

17. See S.L.A. Marshall, *Men Against Fire* (New York: William Morrow, 1947), pp. 50–57 and S.L.A. Marshall, *The Officer as a Leader* (Harrisburg, Pennsylvania: Stackpole, 1966), p. 151.

18. See, for example, Stephen D. Westbrook, "Sociopolitical Alienation and Military Efficiency," *Armed Forces and Society*, 6, no. 2 (Winter 1980); Melvin R. Laird, "People Not Hardware: The Highest Defense Priority," in William J. Taylor, Jr. et al., *Defense Manpower Planning: Issues for the 1980's*; Paul L. Savage and Richard A. Gabriel, "Cohesion and Disintegration in the American Army," *Armed Forces and Society*, (Spring 1976), and Alan Ned Sabrosky, "Defense Manpower Policy: A Critical Reappraisal," Foreign Policy Research Institute Monograph no. 22, 1978.

19. Office of the Secretary of Defense, "An Evaluation Report of Mobilization and Deployment Capability Based on Exercises Nifty Nugget-78 and Rex-78," June 30, 1980, p. 8.

20. Comptroller General Report to the Congress, "Manpower Effectiveness of the All-Volunteer Force," July 15, 1981, p. 16.

21. Ibid., p. 13.

22. See Bernard D. Rostker, in Taylor et al., *Defense Manpower Planning*, pp. 180–181.

23. Comptroller General, "Manpower Effectiveness," p. 17.

24. Office of the Secretary of Defense, "Mobilization and Deployment," pp. 14–15.

25. See *Washington Post*, November 3, 1981, p. A1.

26. Rostker, in Taylor et al., *Defense Manpower Planning*, p. 192.

27. See Louis Harris, "Support for Reinstatement of the Draft Growing," *ABC News—Harris Survey* 2, no. 102 (August 18, 1980): p. 1.

28. See General W. Y. Smith, "Reinforcing NATO Rapidly," *Defense 80* (Washington, D.C.: U.S. Government Printing Office, August 1980), p. 2.

29. Ibid.

30. See William J. Taylor, Jr. and Richard D. Hooker, "Soviet Foreign Policy Toward The Northern Theatre" (Paper presented at the 22nd Annual Convention of the International Studies Association, Philadelphia, Pennsylvania, February 3–March 28, 1981), pp. 29–31 and Appendix.

31. Carl Von Clausewitz, *On War*, p. 87.

32. Ibid., p. 88.

4

The All-Volunteer Force: Status and Prospects of the Active Forces

Richard V. L. Cooper

RICHARD V. L. COOPER, Partner, Coopers and Lybrand, and formerly Director, Defense Manpower Studies, Rand Corporation, writes that attracting some 450,000 new recruits each year and sustaining an active military force of more than 2 million without a draft during the past nine years was an accomplishment of major proportions. The military services as a whole essentially met their objectives as to strength, quality, and retention, although manpower requirements had been reduced by some 200,000, and the army fared less well than the other services. The declining size of the manpower pool, combined with a prospective decline in unemployment, as the author indicates, make it far from clear that the All-Volunteer Force can do as well in the rest of the 1980s, especially if manpower requirements are increased.

INTRODUCTION

March 1980 marked the tenth anniversary of the Report of the President's Commission on an All-Volunteer Armed Force. November 1981 marked the tenth anniversary of the military pay raise that made the volunteer force possible. And, in all likelihood, January 1983 will mark the tenth anniversary of the beginning of the All-Volunteer Force (AVF) itself.

What have we learned from this experience? And what does this experience tell us about the future? The purpose of this chapter is to shed some light on these questions. Although a complete analysis of the volunteer force is obviously beyond the scope of any single paper, or even any single volume, this chapter examines some of the key issues that have emerged during the course of the debate about the All-Volunteer Force.

The tone of this chapter is factual in nature. There is a wide variety of philosophical and moral issues that must necessarily be a part of the debate, but they are not included here. It is not that these issues are unimportant, but rather they are simply beyond the scope of this chapter. There are also many nonquantifiable issues that directly concern the performance of the volunteer force, such as esprit de corps and unit cohesion, which likewise could not be included here. Again, these are also important issues, but they too are beyond the boundaries of the present effort.

This chapter thus takes on the relatively easier task of describing some of the key quantitative factors regarding the volunteer force. The importance of this task should not be underestimated, however, since the AVF debate often has lost sight of much of the factual evidence. It is thus hoped that this chapter will serve as a factual base for the eventual consideration of a much broader set of issues concerning the All-Volunteer Force.

The next section of this chapter provides a brief review of the reasons underlying the termination of the draft in 1973. The third section reviews the experience from the first eight years of the volunteer force. This discussion is keyed to five main issues: the numbers of new recruits, the quality of new recruits, representation, retention, and cost. The last section examines the reasons the evidence presented here differs from much of what has appeared during the course of the AVF debate, and then considers the future prospects for the volunteer force.

ORIGINS OF THE ALL-VOLUNTEER FORCE

It is useful to begin a review of the status and prospects for the All-Volunteer Force with a consideration of why the draft was terminated. Not only does such a consideration provide the historical context, but more important, it helps to put into perspective the problems and tradeoffs that must be faced today when evaluating military manpower procurement policy. The reason for this is simply that many of the factors that led to the removal of the draft are likely to persist throughout the remainder of this century.

In retrospect, the demise of the draft can be attributed primarily to two factors: the Vietnam War and the growing inequity of the Selective Service draft. In turn, the latter was the result of some simple population changes. The role of the Vietnam War is readily acknowledged, if not overstated, by most observers. To be sure, the Vietnam War clearly dramatized the draft issue and indeed acted as a catalyst for the draft debate. Moreover, many liberal members of Congress were moved to oppose the draft on the grounds that terminating the draft would force the United States to withdraw from Vietnam.

Despite the common public perception that the AVF was the result of the Vietnam War, demographic changes probably played a larger role in the termination of the draft. Simply stated, the numbers of young men reaching military age each year increased substantially during the course of the 1960s, to a much larger level than required to man a peacetime military. The European nations, confronted by similar demographic trends, largely chose to reduce the length of the military obligation, to as little as 9 to 12 months in some countries, thereby increasing the numbers of young men that could be inducted each year. The United States rejected this option, on the grounds that such drastic reductions in the minimum service commitment would seriously degrade force readiness. This meant that only a small proportion of the population had to serve, but increased the inequity of the draft.

There are two parts to the equity issue: the burden of conscription and the selective way that the burden was applied. Those individuals subjected to the draft were forced to bear a burden that other members of society were able to avoid. The specific burdens were many: low pay, risk to life and limb, personal hardship, arduous working conditions, and disruption of personal and working lives.

The imposition of a burden does not in itself constitute an inequity, since society must frequently impose "burdens" on its citizenry, usually in the form of taxes. Rather, the issue of inequity arises when the burden is applied selectively.

In the case of the selective service draft, the issue of inequity arose because of the selective way that the burden of military service was applied to young men of military age. As shown in figure 4.1, the numbers of young men reaching military age increased substantially during the 1960s. At the beginning of that decade, there were less than 1.2 million young men reaching military age each year; by the mid-1970s, that number increased to more than 2 million each year. Combined with constant or decreasing force sizes, this increasing cohort of young men meant that the vast majority of military aged youth would never have to serve. For every young man forced to serve, figure 4.1 shows that three or four would not. Thus, no matter how fair or equitable the selection process could be made in an ex ante sense, such as using a random lottery, a selective service draft would be inequitable ex post to the small proportion unfortunate enough to be drafted.

The selective service draft turned out to be even more inequitable since "Who serves when most do not?" very often turned out to be those least able to spend the resources required to avoid induction—namely, the poor and the black. A large part of the reason for this was that the available draft deferments and exemptions, such as student and occupational deferments, served mainly to benefit the middle and upper classes.

It is important to remember that many of these draft deferments and exemptions were implemented for one of two purposes, if not both. First, some were designed to "channel" youth into so-called approved pursuits,

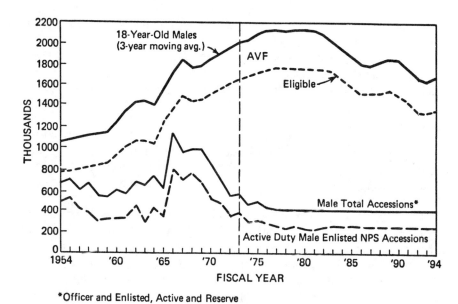

*Officer and Enlisted, Active and Reserve

Fig. 4.1. Military manpower procurement and male youth population.
Source: Richard V. L. Cooper, *Military Manpower and the All-Volunteer Force*, Rand Corporation, 1977.

such as attending college. Second, the effect of all deferments and exemptions, and the purpose of some, was to reduce the size of the Classification I-A draft pool (available for induction) so that it would more closely match the military's need for recruits. That is, given that the manpower pool was much larger than the military's manpower requirements, the Classification I-A pool was reduced to make the process of selecting draftees more manageable. As the military aged manpower began to grow rapidly in the early 1960s, more deferments and exemptions were added. Graduate students were eligible for deferment. And, deferments or exemptions became available, first, for fatherhood and later for marriage.

In the last half of the 1960s, two things occurred. First, the increasing manpower demands resulting from the Vietnam War made it necessary to increase the size of the Classification I-A draft pool, which led to the elimination of the marriage and fatherhood deferments. Second, the inequities of the Selective Service deferment and selection policies became more apparent. Student and occupational deferments, for instance, discriminated against the poor and minorities. Second, the oldest-first draft policy served to maximize the personal inconvenience and uncertainty of being drafted.

Draft policy was changed accordingly with a series of draft reforms in the late 1960s. These included the elimination of graduate school deferments, curtailment of many undergraduate and occupational deferments, and implementation of a youngest-first lottery draft.

Even after the draft reforms of the late 1960s, youth from less-affluent backgrounds stood a much greater chance not only of serving, but also of being inducted, than their more affluent counterparts. The reason for this was that there were still ways of avoiding active military service, such as joining the reserves and being disqualified for medical reasons. (Indeed, more than 50 percent of reserve accessions in the early 1970s were college educated!) Thus, not only did the selective service draft distribute the burden of military service to just a small proportion of military aged youth, it also shifted the burden disproportionately to the less-advantaged members of American society.

The final element leading to the removal of the draft was presidential politics. Recognizing the dissatisfaction with the draft, including the fact that it was symbolically tied to the Vietnam War, Richard Nixon announced his opposition to it in a radio speech during the 1968 presidential campaign. It is noteworthy that George McGovern also announced his opposition to the draft during his belated attempt for the 1969 Democratic presidential nomination, as had Barry Goldwater in his run for the presidency in 1964 and Adlai Stevenson during his run in 1956.

Following his campaign pledge, Nixon announced the formation of the President's Commission on an All-Volunteer Armed Force in March 1969 (also known as the Gates Commission for its Chairman, former Secretary of Defense Thomas Gates, Jr.) to study the feasibility and desirability of ending the draft. Recognizing the problems of having to draft only a few from the eligible population, the Gates Commission concluded in 1970 that, at a minimum, those serving in their nation's military should not have to pay a large financial penalty in addition to the other burdens of service. The commission thus recommended that the pay for junior military personnel be raised from the then low amount to a level commensurate with that earned by their peers in civilian employment. A volunteer military would not require a large pay premium, but merely the comparable wage due for equity reasons alone. Thus was born the All-Volunteer Force.

Many factors had a role in the decision to end the draft. Some have concluded that the Vietnam War played the dominant role, while others have claimed that the draft actually would have ended sooner in the absence of the Vietnam War. It seems clear that, at a minimum, demographic trends would have forced a change in draft policy as it had existed in the 1950s and early 1960s. The draft reforms of the late 1960s solved some of the most egregious problems, but others remained. So, more changes would likely have taken place, such as raising the pay for junior military personnel. The All-Volunteer Force was one solution to the problems that remained and was the solution ultimately adopted.

PERFORMANCE OF THE ALL-VOLUNTEER FORCE

Would an all-volunteer military work in fact as well as in theory or, in the view of its skeptics, be doomed to failure? It remained for the draft actually to end to determine the answer to this question. Regretfully, the AVF experience does not provide a clear-cut answer, as the issues continue to be widely debated. Critics charge that the AVF has already proved itself a failure, while advocates view the AVF as a success. In truth, the answer probably lies somewhere between these extremes. The volunteer force has probably not done as well as indicated by some of its most ardent proponents, but it has also probably done much better than indicated by its severest critics.

This divergence of opinion regarding the performance of the volunteer force is in a large part attributable to the fact that there are so many dimensions to the AVF issue. In some areas, the AVF has done quite well; in others, it has been less successful. As a result, how one views the overall performance of the volunteer force depends somewhat on which particular aspects are judged as being the most important. On net, however, this chapter will argue that the volunteer force appears to have done reasonably well. There have been problems—some of them significant. But, it will be argued here that the AVF has accomplished much of what was originally intended.

The discussion below examines the active forces' experience during the first eight years of the All-Volunteer Force; the reserves' experience is examined in chapter 5.

Military Capability

Of the various criteria that could be used to assess the volunteer force, military capability must be viewed as one of the most important. Specifically, how has the conversion to a volunteer force affected U.S. capability? After all, the purpose of maintaining an armed force is to provide an effective military deterrent and warfighting capability.

For two reasons, though, it is difficult to make such an assessment. First, we do not have very good measures of overall military effectiveness. Second, even if we did, it would be difficult to relate these to the method of military manpower procurement, since military capability depends on so many other factors as well, including weapons systems, matériel, leadership, and organization.

Because there is no ready measure of national defense capability, military planners and analysts are forced to use various proxy measures, some output oriented and some input oriented. The more formal output proxies include assessments, such as the performance of units in military maneuvers and exercises. Less formal proxies, such as commanders' appraisals of their troops, can also be useful indicators of performance. The advantage of these kinds of formal and informal measures is that they provide some indication of capability; the disadvantage is that they are not as amenable to rigorous analysis, in terms of comparison with either some absolute standard or previous experience.

Viewed from this perspective, it would be difficult to judge the AVF as either an overwhelming success or failure. For example, U.S. scores in NATO exercises during the mid- to late 1970s were lower than those of many of our European allies, although there appears to have been recent improvement in U.S. performance. Some returning commanders have been very laudatory about the performance of their troops; however, perhaps a larger number have bemoaned such performance. In short, there does not appear to be a consensus regarding how the AVF has affected U.S. military capability.

Because of the difficulties in using and interpreting these types of output measures, analysts and planners have come to rely more on input oriented proxies such as the quantity and quality of new recruits. The rationale for this approach is twofold. First, even though the measures of inputs are far from perfect, they are better than the available measures of output. Second, it is easier to determine the extent to which the volunteer force is responsible for changes in manpower inputs than it is to determine the extent to which the volunteer force is responsible for changes in military capability. The remainder of this chapter accordingly focuses on these input measures, especially recruiting and retention.

Enlisted Recruiting: Quantity

Generally, it was agreed at the outset of the AVF-draft debate in the 1960s that recruiting enough volunteers to fill the enlisted ranks in the active forces would be the most difficult problem to confront the military in the absence of a draft. The removal of the draft would of course pose other problems for the military, such as manning the reserves or recruiting enough physicians. But, in terms of sheer volume, manning the enlisted ranks of the active forces would be the largest problem, and the most important.

Table 4.1 shows that the services, in general, have met the challenge successfully. With the exception of some modest recruiting problems during the first year without the draft and again in 1979, the military services have done quite well in meeting their quantitative recruiting objectives for the active forces during the first nine years of the volunteer force.

More important, table 4.2 shows that the services have also been successful in maintaining their manpower strength requirements during this period. Again, with the exception of 1979 when the 25,000 strength shortfall left the military about 1.5 percent below its targeted level, the services have been

Table 4.1. Recruiting Performance: Enlistments versus Objectives.
(in thousands)

		Fiscal Year									
		73/2*	74	75	76	TQ**	77	78	79	80	81
Army:	Enlistments	71	200	209	192	57	181	134	142	173	138
	Objective	83	212	205	191	59	182	137	159	170	137
Navy:	Enlistments	37	88	110	102	33	110	87	86	98	104
	Objective	44	85	109	104	35	114	93	92	98	102
USMC:	Enlistments	25	50	60	53	15	47	41	42	44	44
	Objective	25	56	59	53	15	49	41	43	44	43
USAF:	Enlistments	45	76	77	74	21	74	69	68	75	81
	Objective	45	75	75	73	21	74	69	69	75	81
DoD:	Enlistments***	179	413	456	421	194	411	332	338	390	367
	Objective***	191	418	450	421	198	420	340	362	386	362

*Second half of fiscal 1973 (i.e., January–June 1973)
**Transition quarter (summer 1976)
***Totals may not add due to rounding

Table 4.2. Enlisted End Strengths: Actual versus Programmed. (in thousands)

		Fiscal Year										
		72	73	74	75	76	TQ	77	78	79	80	81
Army:	Actual	687	682	675	678	678	680	680	670	657	674	675
	Programmed	735	703	672	680	681	688	686	673	673	671	671
Navy:	Actual	512	491	476	466	458	460	462	463	455	460	470
	Programmed	525	499	479	466	457	463	468	465	456	460	468
USMC:	Actual	178	177	170	177	174	171	173	172	167	170	172
	Programmed	178	178	177	178	177	177	173	173	172	167	170
USAF:	Actual	600	572	529	503	481	480	470	470	459	456	467
	Programmed	605	573	530	503	480	481	470	471	462	456	461
DoD:	Actual	1977	1922	1850	1825	1790	1791	1785	1775	1738	1760	1784
	Programmed	2043	1953	1858	1826	1795	1809	1799	1782	1763	1755	1770

within 1 percent of their strength objectives since the draft was ended. They finished fiscal 1980 5,000 personnel above the targeted level, and fiscal 1981 nearly 15,000 above the targeted level. (This was done in anticipation of the strength increases called for in the president's 1982–1987 defense program.) Interestingly, table 4.2 also shows that the largest strength shortfall in the 1970s occurred in 1972, the last year of the draft, when the services collectively fell more than 60,000 short of their programmed strength objectives — more than twice the size of the fiscal 1979 strength shortfall under the AVF.

The magnitude of the services' achievement under the volunteer force should not be underestimated. Recruiting 350,000 to 450,000 new recruits each year and sustaining an active military force of more than 2 million personnel without a draft, as the military has done since 1972, is clearly an accomplishment of major proportions that has not been duplicated elsewhere.

One final note regarding the services' quantitative performance deserves mention. Clearly, the military's ability to provide sufficient numbers of personnel without a draft was eased by the fact that the required numbers of personnel in uniform are now smaller than was the case, say, in the 1960s. As shown in table 4.3, uniformed personnel strengths declined from nearly 2.7 million in 1964 to a little more than 2 million after the Vietnam drawdown. However, table 4.2 shows that the services have been able to increase their strengths modestly when called upon to do so, between 1979 and 1981 enlisted strengths were increased by 50,000, and present plans call for another 50,000 increase between 1981 and 1983.

Table 4.3 also shows that total defense personnel in 1980 were only about 100,000 less than they were in 1973, and 10 percent less than they were in 1964. The reason for this is that the defense establishment has apparently come to rely much more heavily on contractor supplied civilian manpower to perform many routine maintenance and support jobs formerly done by

Table 4.3. Total Defense Personnel.
(in thousands)

	Fiscal Year			
	64	73	76	80
Active Duty Military[a]	2687	2253	2084	2051
Civilian: Direct Hire[a]	1030	1031	998	960
Indirect Hire[a]	140	102	84	75
Contract Hire[b]	219	428	455	623
Total	4076	3814	3621	3709

Sources: a. *Selected Manpower Statistics*, Department of Defense.
   b. *Contract-Hire Personnel in the Department of Defense*, Rand Corporation, 1977. (1980 estimates based on methodology used for 1973 and 1976.)

uniformed personnel, as was recommended by the Gates Commission.[1] Moreover, the Department of Defense (DoD) has reduced the numbers of personnel in nonreadiness activities, such as trainees, trainers, and transients. The result is that a larger proportion of the force is available for actual unit assignments. Total defense manpower strengths have declined nowhere near as much as a simple comparison of military personnel strengths would seem to imply.

Enlisted Recruiting: Quality

Whereas there appears to be general agreement that the AVF has met its quantitative recruiting objectives for the active forces, there is no such consensus regarding the quality of enlistees since the removal of the draft. Because it is difficult to even define quality, let alone measure it, debate about the quality of new volunteers has been more rampant, and more anecdotal in nature. Indeed, quality is one of the two most controversial AVF issues. (The other concerns the racial composition of the military, which is discussed later in this chapter.) To many critics, quality—or, rather, the lack of it—is seen to be the most crucial shortcoming of the volunteer force.

A large part of the reason for this debate is that, unlike the quantitative performance of recruiting, where reliable numerical evidence exists, there is no universally accepted measure of quality. As a result, observers are often forced to rely more on anecdotes and personal experiences, which are less verifiable and more subject to personal coloration than numerical evidence. This is not to deny the importance of nonnumerical evidence, but rather is to emphasize the difficulties in assessing the qualitative performance of the AVF.

The problem of assessing the quality of recruits under the AVF was compounded, and the controversy exacerbated, by the discovery in 1978 that the written tests used to screen applicants for enlistment had been misnormed—individuals previously thought to be of average mental aptitude according to the norming standards were instead found to be below the average in terms of mental aptitude.[2] Although the studies identifying this problem focused on the mental aptitude tests that had been in use since 1976, it appears that this misnorming problem existed, though perhaps to a lesser extent, even in the 1960s.

The above problems notwithstanding, there are two bodies of evidence that enable us to gauge in broad terms, how the volunteer force has performed with regard to quality: statistical data and vignettes. With respect to statistical data, the services use two main indicators to determine an applicant's acceptability: educational attainment and mental aptitude. Educational attainment, specifically, whether the individual possesses a high-school diploma, is used more as a measure of the individual's adaptability to the military environment and "stick-to-itiveness" than it is an absolute measure of capability or intelligence. The empirical evidence strongly supports the use of the high-school diploma as a screening device, as high-school dropouts show attrition rates that are about double those for high-school graduates.

To test for mental aptitude, applicants for enlistment are given a battery of written tests, known as the Armed Services Vocational Aptitude Battery (ASVAB). The ASVAB is used to test for both general mental aptitude and certain specific aptitude areas, such as mechanical and electrical aptitude. The applicant's raw test score is converted through a norming algorithm to a percentile score.[3] (It was this norming algorithm that was discovered to be in error.) The percentile scores are then grouped into one of five so-called mental categories, Category I through Category V, with Categories III and IV being divided into subcategories as well. Applicants falling in the top 7 percent of the mental aptitude spectrum are classified in Category I, while those in the bottom 10 percent fall into Category V. The complete list of mental categories and subcategories is given below:

Category	Percentile
I	93–100
II	65–92
IIIA	50–64
IIIB	31–49
IVA	21–30
IVB	16–20
IVC	10–15
V	0–9

Category V personnel are legally ineligible to serve. The services typically accept all or most Category I–III high-school graduate applicants who also meet the medical and moral fitness requirements.

The services, however, try to limit the numbers of Category IV and non-high-school graduate recruits. For example, they typically do not accept Category IV high-school dropouts. Moreover, applicants scoring below the thirty-first percentile on the overall ASVAB may be required to score average or above average on one or more portions of the exam to be deemed acceptable.

With this background, the two most frequently used descriptors of quality are the percentages of new recruits who are Category IV or who are not high-school graduates. In this regard, table 4.4 shows that the non-high-school graduate intake of the AVF is roughly comparable to what it was during the last 12 years of the draft. About one-third of the volunteers since

Table 4.4. Quality of Enlisted Accessions.
(percentage)

	Draft				AVF		
	53–59	60–64	65–69	70–72	73–76	77–80	81
Non-High-School Graduates							
All DoD	n.a.	35	25	33	35	28	19
Army	n.a.	36	28	37	43	38	20
Category IV							
All DoD: reported	24	14	21	22	6	6	n.a.
revised[a]	24	17	30	35	19	29	18
Army: reported	n.a.	19	26	23	11	9	n.a.
revised[a]	n.a.	23	37	36	36	45	31

n.a. Not available
a. See the Appendix

the removal of the draft have been high-school dropouts, as opposed to about 30 percent during the draft.

Table 4.4 also shows the impact of the misnorming problem. Whereas about 6 percent of AVF enlistments were thought to have been Category IV before the misnorming problem was discovered, correcting for the error suggests that the actual number for all of DoD was about 32 percent. However, if one similarly tries to correct for the misnorming that presumably existed prior to the AVF, then we see that this 32 percent Category IVs is about the same as the Category IV intake between 1965 and 1972. (Test scores have not been formally renormed for recruits entering before 1976. Therefore, the results shown in table 4.4 for years earlier than 1976 have not been subjected to psychometric validation. Rather, these results were derived through the statistical procedures described in the Appendix.) This 32 percent is appreciably greater than the 17 percent or so evidenced during the early 1960s, but is also considerably less than the 45 percent or so that the services took in immediately following the Korean War.

Turning to the other end of the mental aptitude spectrum, the volunteer force does not in the aggregate appear to differ too much from the experience under the draft. Category Is and IIs together comprised about 35 percent of enlisted accessions during the lottery draft, as opposed to 33 percent during the first eight years of the volunteer force. Even at the very top of the mental aptitude spectrum, there does not appear to have been much change, as about 4 percent of all AVF recruits were classified as Category Is, compared with 5 percent for the lottery draft.

The story is not quite the same for the upper end of the educational spectrum. Although college graduates have never served in large numbers in the enlisted ranks (about 3 percent during the last dozen years of the draft) nearly 15 percent of all recruits during the draft era had at least some college education. The corresponding numbers for the volunteer force, 1 percent (actually a little less) and 5 percent, respectively, show a marked decline. Proponents of the volunteer force discount the importance of this decline by noting that most enlisted occupations do not need college educated recruits. On the other hand, critics refer to the leavening effect that the introduction of college educated youth has on enlisted units.

One further point should be kept in mind with regard to college educated recruits. The numbers of college educated enlisted accessions were as large as they were under the draft—and even then only 3 percent were college graduates—because of the oldest-first draft policy that was used prior to the draft reforms of the late 1960s. With those reforms the oldest-first draft policy was changed to a youngest-first policy in order to reduce the inequities of selective service. However, a youngest-first policy also reduced the number of college educated recruits, simply because individuals had not had a chance to complete college by the time they are drafted. Since a youngest-first policy would likely be retained in the event that this nation returns to a draft (indeed, that policy is currently written in the law) a return to conscription by itself would be unlikely to produce a large numerical increase in college educated enlisted accessions.

Overall, the statistical evidence available suggests that the quality of recruits under the volunteer force is not very different from that experienced during the draft years. The major exception to this generally optimistic assessment concerns the army. According to most measures, the army has experienced a decline in quality since the removal of the draft, especially during the 1977 to 1980 period. For example, the proportion of army recruits with a high-school diploma fell from 67 percent under the draft to 57 percent under the volunteer force. Similarly, given the renormed test results, the army's Category IV intake is estimated to have been more than 40 percent during the late 1970s, and reached a high of 52 percent in fiscal 1980. This was at least 5 to 10 percentage points above what the army experienced during the lottery draft. Equally striking, although the army managed to maintain its combined Category I and II intake at about 30 percent of enlistments during the first four years of the volunteer force (which was near the rate experienced during the draft era), this rate declined substantially during the second four years of the AVF. In 1977, it dropped to 20 percent; in 1979, to 17 percent; in 1980, it fell to a low of 15 percent.

However, this generally negative trend in the measured quality of army recruits during the late 1970s showed a marked turnaround in 1981. For a variety of reasons, including congressionally imposed quality constraints, improved pay and benefits, difficult economic conditions, increased public support for the military, and what appeared to be generally improved recruiting practices, the army achieved a significant improvement in the various measures of quality. Its high-school graduate intake increased to 80 percent in 1981, the best single year percentage ever recorded for the army; its Category IV intake dropped from 52 percent in 1980 to 31 percent in 1981; its Category I and II intake increased to 24 percent in 1981 from 15 percent in 1980.

This one year certainly does not necessarily establish a trend. However, there is some reason to view these results as more than a one- or two-year aberration. At least some of the factors responsible for this improvement, increased pay and greater public support for the military, likely will continue to aid the military during the next several years. Moreover, a large part of this recent success is attributable to the dramatic gains in reenlistment (discussed later in this chapter) that have enabled the army to reduce its annual accession requirements, thereby permitting the army also to be more selective in recruiting.

As noted earlier, these statistical data provide one source of information regarding the quality of recruits under the volunteer force; anecdotes and vignettes from commanders in the field and other observers is another source. In general, this source of information is less complimentary about the volunteer force, for although some commanders have extolled their volunteer troops as "the best that they have ever seen," a larger number seem to view the 1970s volunteers as less capable than the draft-era soldiers. This information obviously is less measurable and less analytic than the statistical data, but it can provide important insights. For example, during the late 1970s, the statistical data were still showing the Category IV percentages to be at an all-time low. Yet, reports from the field suggested that the soldiers who joined during that period were not nearly as capable as their test scores indicated. It turned out, of course, that the reports from the field were largely correct; because of the norming error, the statistical data were wrong. Once the statistical data were corrected, they seemed to conform with the perceptions and reports from the field.

Interpreting information such as reports from the field is obviously an art, but two general themes emerge. First, the statistical data (as corrected after the renorming) and the more informal evidence reported in the popular literature do seem to conform, at least in the direction of change. For example, the press was probably most critical of AVF quality in 1979 and 1980, about the time that the statistical evidence also suggests quality was the worst. Since then, the literature has been less critical. In fact, several articles have appeared recently that are much more complimentary to the volunteer force.[4]

Second, it is important to realize that the press generally tends to be more critical than laudatory with respect to existing policies. The AVF has been the existing policy since 1973, and thus has been the target for these critical appraisals, just as the draft was during the 1960s. This is not to dismiss the importance of such criticisms, but rather to suggest that vignettes, anecdotes, and the popular press, just like the statistical data, need to be interpreted with caution.

To summarize, the quality of new recruits under the AVF appears to be broadly similar to what it was under the draft. The other services generally seem to have at least maintained, if not actually improved somewhat, the quality of enlisted accessions under the volunteer force as opposed to the draft, but this performance to some extent appears to have come at the expense of the army. Although the quality of army recruits during the first four years of the volunteer force does not appear to have been too much below that experienced during the draft, it did drop significantly during the 1977 to 1980 period. However, the results for 1981 provide some basis for cautious optimism.

One final note with respect to quality is warranted. The preceding discussion has been couched in terms of the available measures of quality and how the AVF and earlier draft compare in this regard, not in terms of what quality ought to be. The rationale for this approach is twofold. First, and regretfully, we do not have the required knowledge to determine what quality ought to be and are thus forced to rely to a great extent on the kinds of comparisons used here. Second, the previous experience with the draft provides some measure of what quality likely would be in the event that the nation returned to conscription at some time in the future. Although it is possible to think of combining a return to the draft with caps on the numbers of, say, Category IV accessions, as the Congress has done under the AVF, it is unrealistic to think that a return to conscription would dramatically increase the quality of enlisted manpower. To illustrate, the Selective Service System has estimated that drafting 50,000 young men would result in an increase in the Category I intake from 3.0 percent of enlisted accessions to 3.1 percent—hardly a significant difference.

Representation

Certainly one of the most controversial issues to emerge during the AVF concerns social representation, in general, and the racial composition of the forces, in particular. In a sense, this concern is ironic, for the historically unrepresentative nature of the draft was one of the principal causes for its termination. Nevertheless, representation has been a major issue since the end of the draft and likely will continue to be in the future.

The source of this concern can be found in some simple statistics. By 1980, minorities accounted for 41 percent of all army enlisted personnel; 33 percent of army enlisted personnel were black, 4 percent Hispanic, and 4 percent other minorities. Moreover, some specific units in the army are over

50 percent black. Thus, since blacks comprise about 13 percent of all male youth, their representation in the army is more than 2½ times their representation in the relevant age group.

It is useful, however, to put these figures into a broader perspective, first, by comparing these figures with the other services and, second, by examining the trends over time. In this regard, figure 4.2 shows that blacks accounted for about 22 percent of enlisted personnel for all of the DoD in 1980, which was about double the rate experienced during the 1960s. The army had the highest proportion of minorities and blacks, and the navy the lowest.

Second, figure 4.2 shows that the trend toward greater minority participation in the armed forces was under way well before the onset of the volunteer force. Between 1969 and 1973, just before the volunteer force, black participation in the army was increasing at the rate of 13 percent per year.

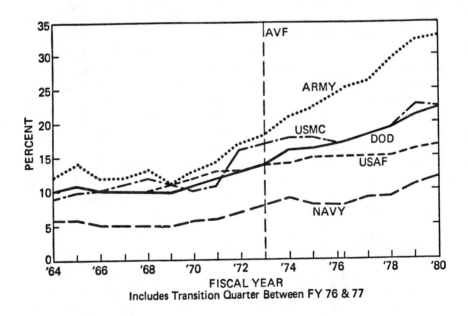

Fig. 4.2. Blacks as a percentage of active-duty enlisted end strengths.
Source: Richard W. Hunter and Gary R. Nelson, "Eight Years with the All-Volunteer Armed Forces," The Sixtieth American Assembly, September 17-20, 1981, Seven Springs Center, Mt. Kisco, NY.

Between 1973 and 1980, this rate of increase dropped to 9 percent per year. It will be argued below that this trend of increased minority participation, which began before the volunteer force, was merely the manifestation of factors far more fundamental than the method of manpower procurement and, thus, the increased minority participation itself is largely unrelated to the volunteer force.

To understand the reasons for the changing racial composition of the military, we need to examine both enlistments and reenlistments. Figure 4.3 shows that blacks have represented an increasing share of enlisted accessions over the last 20 years. Whereas blacks comprised about 10 percent of enlisted accessions in the early 1960s, they represented nearly 15 percent during the last year of the draft. And, during the volunteer force, this rate grew to a high of about 26 percent in 1979, although it dropped back to about 22 percent in 1980 and 19 percent in 1981. For the army, the rate

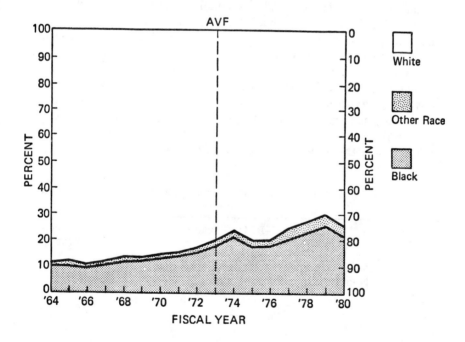

Fig. 4.3. Distribution of enlisted accessions according to race.
Source: Hunter and Nelson, "Eight Years with the All-Volunteer Armed Forces," The Sixtieth American Assembly, September 17–20, 1981, Seven Springs Center, Mt. Kisco, NY.

peaked at about 35 percent in 1979, but dropped to 30 percent in 1980 and 27 percent in 1981.

As stated earlier, the increased numbers of black enlistments is largely unrelated to the volunteer force. Rather, table 4.5 shows that this increase can be explained mostly by the increased numbers of blacks now qualified for military service. For example, in the mid-1950s, only about 13 percent of all young blacks fell into mental categories I–III; by the mid-1970s, this figure had grown to more than 40 percent. As a result, whereas blacks comprised only a little more than 2 percent of the Category I–III recruiting pool in the mid 1950s, they made up nearly 7 percent of the pool by the mid 1970s. (Some of this increase may have been attributable to the misnorming problem described earlier. However, blacks made up a larger proportion of the population that was declared as qualified to enlist.) Because the number of young blacks eligible to enter the military increased substantially relative to young nonblacks during the last 20 years, the number of young blacks actually entering also increased substantially relative to nonblacks.

Table 4.5 shows further that blacks have historically served in much larger numbers relative to their eligible population than have nonblacks. Indeed, the participation rate (defined as the number of Category I–III accessions relative to the Category I–III population base) has been roughly twice as high for blacks as for nonblacks throughout the past 20 years. The reasons for this are largely economic: blacks have historically faced less-attractive employment opportunities in the civilian job market than whites, and, thus, in proportionately larger numbers, turned to the military. Whereas some compare the 10 percent or so black representation in the military dur-

Table 4.5. Qualification and Participation Rates for Category I–III Males: by Race.
(percentage)

	Category I–III Qualification			Participation Rates[c]	
	Nonblack[a]	Black[a]	Blacks As A Percentage Of Cat. I–III Pool[b]	Nonblack	Black
1953–57	69	13	2.2	n.a.	n.a.
1958–1963	73	18	2.9	43	83
1964–68	79	25	3.6	44	73
1969–1970	82	29	4.5	34	54
1971–72	83	33	5.0	24	53
1973–75	84	43	6.8	18	49

n.a. not available

Source: Richard V. L. Cooper, *Military Manpower and the All-Volunteer Force*, Rand Corporation, 1977.

a. Proportion of nonblack and black male youth falling in mental categories I–III

b. Black category I–III males as a percent of all category I–III males

c. Number of category I–III enlisted accessions divided by number of Category I–III male 18-year-olds.

ing the draft years with the 10 percent or so black representation in society, table 4.5 shows that the only reason that blacks were not overrepresented during the draft era was because the majority of black youths were not classified then as qualified to serve.

A second reason for the increased black participation in the military during the 1970s can be traced to the particularly bad unemployment situation for black youth during this period. Table 4.6 shows that the 1970s hit black youth proportionately harder than white youth in terms of unemployment. Whereas black teen-age unemployment rates averaged 10 to 12 percentage points above those for white teen-agers during the 1960s, they soared to more than 18 percentage points above white teen-age unemployment rates during the 1970s.

Thus, a large part of the reason for increased numbers of blacks in the volunteer military can be found in the fact that increased numbers of young blacks volunteered for enlistment. Again, the reasons for this are that increased numbers were classified as qualified to enlist and that black youth faced particularly poor economic opportunities during the 1970s, both of which are unrelated to the AVF.

The other reason for the greater than proportional representation of blacks is equally unrelated to the volunteer force. Specifically, blacks have historically reenlisted at much higher rates than have whites—about 1.6 times higher, during both the draft and the volunteer years. Again, the reason for this is largely related to job opportunities: blacks as a whole are likely to have less-attractive opportunities outside the military than whites. This means that irrespective of what method of military manpower procurement is used, blacks will make up a greater share of the career force.

Although most attention has been focused on the enlisted ranks, it is important to note the progress that the services have made with respect to recruiting larger numbers of black officers. As recently as 1970, blacks comprised only about 1 percent of new officer accessions; by the mid-1970s, the services increased this to about 7 percent by making a conscious effort to recruit more young blacks into the officer corps.

Although the debate about representation has concentrated mostly on the racial composition of the volunteer force, similar concerns have been raised with respect to the numbers of middle- and upper-class youth serving in to-

Table 4.6. Unemployment Rates for Male 16- to 19-Year-Olds by Race.

	1960–64	1965–69	1970–72	1973–1980
Black—% unemployed	24.9	22.4	27.8	33.2
White—% unemployed	14.8	10.8	14.3	15.0
Difference—Black less white	10.1	11.6	13.5	18.2
Ratio: Black–White	1.7	2.1	2.0	2.2

day's military. The charge most frequently levied against the volunteer force in this regard is that "the American middle class has deserted the military." It will be argued below that this view is not necessarily correct for two reasons: first, significant numbers of young men and women from middle-income families continue to serve in the volunteer force; second, the term "deserted" implies that large numbers of middle- and upper-income youth served during the draft years, an assumption that simply is not borne out by fact.

Table 4.7 shows the distribution of male enlisted accessions according to ZIP codes ranked according to average family income. First, ZIP codes were ranked according to average family income as reported in the 1970 census. Second, using the individual's home address ZIP code, the distribution of enlisted accession was then calculated. Thus, table 4.7 shows, for instance, that 0.3 percent of enlistees during the first three years of the volunteer force came from families who lived in the top 1 percent of ZIP codes ranked according to average family income.

Perhaps the most striking feature of table 4.7 is the strong similarity between the last two years of the draft (which, because most deferments had been eliminated, was probably the most socially representative period of the Vietnam era draft) and the first three years of the volunteer force. For the most part, the differences in the two distributions can be measured only in tenths of a percent. For example, 3.2 percent of all enlisted accessions during the last two years of the draft came from families living in the top 5 percent of all ZIP codes, as opposed to 3.0 percent during the first three years of the volunteer force. (Unfortunately, the estimates shown in table 4.7 have not been updated beyond fiscal 1976. The distributions are likely to have dropped somewhat since then for the same reasons that indicators of quality also dropped during the 1977 to 1980 period. (At the same time, some recent unpublished statistics from the National Longitudinal Survey suggest only minimal changes.)

Second, table 4.7 shows that youth from middle- and upper-income families have been somewhat underrepresented under the draft and the volunteer force. Even draftees did not constitute a random sample of American youth, and this was after most draft deferments had been eliminated. This should not be viewed with surprise since middle- and upper-income youth have historically been underrepresented in the enlisted ranks. To the extent that they have served in the active forces, they have been more likely to do so as officers; but, more often than not, they either served in the reserves, or not at all.

In this regard, it is important to distinguish the draft of the mid- to late 1960s and the volunteer force of the 1970s from the draft of the 1950s. Large force sizes and a relatively small manpower pool meant that a large

Table 4.7. Distribution of Male Enlisted Accessions by SMSA ZIP Codes
Ranked according to Average Family Income[a].
(percentage)

| | Distribution of Enlisted Accessions[c] | | | Distribution of 16- to 21-Year-Old Male Population[d] | |
Percentile[b]	Draftees	Draft Enlistees	AVF	All	Not in School
99	0.3	0.4	0.3	1.1	0.4
95–99	2.5	2.8	2.7	5.1	2.6
90–95	4.9	5.1	4.9	7.4	4.6
75–90	20.0	19.3	19.0	20.8	16.7
50–75	32.4	29.9	29.7	28.6	28.0
25–50	23.9	25.2	25.2	22.6	27.7
10–25	10.0	13.2	14.0	12.1	16.7
5–10	2.5	2.9	3.0	2.1	2.9
5	3.5	1.2	1.2	0.2	0.4
Total	100.0	100.0	100.0	100.0	100.0

a. Reports the percentage distributions for total DoD enlisted accessions (inductions and enlistments) by percentile rankings of five-digit ZIP codes located in Standard Metropolitan Statistical Areas. SMSA five-digit ZIP codes were ranked according to average family income within the ZIP code, and then grouped into percentile groupings. Accessions were then matched with these percentile groupings by using the home address ZIP code for each enlistee or inductee. Sources: U.S. Census and Manpower Research and Data Analysis Center, OASD (M&RA), provided the data tapes.
b. Percentile rankings, based on within ZIP code average family income, for five-digit SMSA ZIP codes. Based on 10,708 five-digit ZIP codes out of 11,972 ZIP codes located in SMSAs (data on either population or income were not available for the remaining 1,264 ZIP codes).
c. Percentage distributions for DoD enlisted accessions (see note above). Time periods draft, 1/71 through 12/72; AVF, 1/73 through 6/75.
d. Percentage distributions for all 16- to 21-year-old males residing in these ZIP codes and those not enrolled in school.

proportion of military aged youth served in the military during the 1950s. As a result, the draft of that era was almost, by definition, more representative than the one of the 1960s. By the mid-1960s, the population had grown sufficiently that the draft began to lose its representativeness. Thus, it is in this sense that the volunteer force of the 1970s does not appear all that different from its draft predecessor.

To summarize, although the thought that blacks, or other less-advantaged Americans, might comprise 40 or 50 percent of casualties in the initial stages of a war may be cause for concern, the numbers of blacks serving in the military would probably be about the same whether or not the draft had ended, unless blacks were explicitly or implicitly discriminated against and not allowed to join.

The main difference between the draft and the volunteer force is not in the numbers of blacks or poor serving, but rather, by paying a fair wage, the AVF has not discriminated against these young men the way the draft did.

Retention

Improved retention was one of the principal arguments that proponents of the volunteer force used in their initial advocacy of the AVF. It was argued that by bringing in individuals who wanted to be there, rather than those who were forced to be there, the military would evidence much higher retention. Not only would higher retention result in lower personnel turnover rates, which would, in turn, reduce the numbers of new recruits to man a given sized force, it also would lead to a more capable, cost-effective, and highly motivated force.

With one notable exception, the prediction of higher retention rates under a volunteer force has proved correct. The major exception concerns first-term enlisted attrition—that is, the failure of enlisted recruits to complete their first tour of duty. The discussion following reviews the AVF experience with retention, focusing first on enlisted attrition, then on reenlistment, and, finally, personnel turnover rates.

Attrition. Proponents of the volunteer force apparently failed to recognize that first-term enlisted attrition rates would almost certainly increase in the absence of a draft. During the draft, the services were forced to hold down enlisted attrition rates, lest attrition become too much of an "easy out" for those serving involuntarily. Units were forced to carry their malcontents or, in extreme cases, have them incarcerated.

Once the draft was ended, the pressure to hold down attrition rates was lessened correspondingly. Indeed, the services actually encouraged their unit commanders to "weed out" early those individuals not deemed suitable for military service. A number of specific programs, such as the Trainee Discharge Program and the Expeditious Discharge Program, were actually developed with the express purpose of aiding unit commanders in this regard. The intent of these programs was to identify and separate, early in their service careers, those individuals found not suited to the military, thereby improving the overall readiness and morale of the forces. By most accounts, these programs were at least partially successful in reaching this goal, as the numbers of malcontents and various measures of indiscipline, such as rates of incarceration, seem to have generally declined following the removal of the draft.

But the price was high, as first-term enlisted attrition rates soared, from 26 percent for the fiscal 1971 cohort to 37 percent for the fiscal 1974 cohort of young men entering the military. Recognizing the magnitude of the problem, the Department of Defense began to focus its efforts in the late 1970s on reducing enlisted attrition, for example, by levying attrition goals on the services. These efforts appear to have been quite successful, as attrition rates for the 1979 cohort are projected to drop to about 29 percent, only three percentage points above the fiscal 1971 rate and only one percentage point above the fiscal 1972 rate.*

Reenlistment. Reenlistment is the other main part of the retention picture — that is, those enlisted personnel eligible to separate from the service who decide to reenlist for another term. Analytically, it is useful to think of reenlistment in two components: first-term reenlistments and career reenlistments. First-term reenlistments are those individuals who reenlist upon the completion of their first term of duty, whereas career reenlistments are those individuals who reenlist and have completed at least two terms of duty. Career reenlistment rates typically are much higher than first-term reenlistment rates, since those individuals who have already reenlisted at least once are, on average, likely to be more favorably disposed toward military service — that is, they have already demonstrated this by reenlisting at least once.

It is further useful to distinguish between reenlistment rates and retention rates. In this regard, reenlistment rates are calculated as the number of reenlistments divided by the number eligible to reenlist. However, not all individuals reaching the end of their term of duty are in fact eligible to reenlist, and this gives rise to the second definition of use; retention rates. Retention rates are calculated as the number of reenlistments divided by the total number eligible to separate. The denominator for calculating retention rates thus includes both those eligible to reenlist and those not eligible. Noneligibility can occur for a variety of reasons, including reaching retirement, dishonorable discharge, and failing to meet certain specific criteria for reenlistment. For example, except under certain circumstances, the army does not allow those without a high-school degree or its equivalent to reenlist. Reenlistment eligibility rates for first termers have averaged about 50 percent during the 1970s and for careerists about 70 percent.

With this as background, we turn to first-term reenlistment. In this regard, the volunteer force has lived up to expectations, as reenlistment rates have improved substantially relative to the draft era, up from about 18 percent during the 1965 to 1972 period to 33 percent under the first eight years of the volunteer force. (Unfortunately, we do not have reliable reenlist-

---

*Attrition is measured as the proportion of those entering in a given year who fail to complete their obligated term of service. Thus, one typically needs to look out three to four years to determine the attrition rate for a particular cohort.

ment figures prior to 1965.) It is difficult to calculate retention rates before 1972, but it should be noted that first-term retention rates almost doubled between 1972 and 1980, from 11 percent to 21 percent for DoD as a whole. First-term reenlistment rates have improved the most dramatically in the army, from 10 percent in 1972 to 53 percent in 1980, but this is not surprising, given that the army had the highest proportion of draftees and draft-motivated enlistments before the volunteer force—i.e., those individuals least likely to reenlist.

Figure 4.4 helps to explain some of the controversy about career reenlistment rates that has emerged during the past few years. In particular, figure 4.4 shows that career reenlistment rates evidenced a gradual decline during most of the 1970s, from more than 80 percent in 1973 to a little less than 70 percent in 1979. However, figure 4.4 also shows that career retention rates held fairly stable through most of the 1970s, and then showed a gradual increase toward the end of that decade. Moreover, the number of career reenlistments also showed a modest increase over the course of the 1970s, from

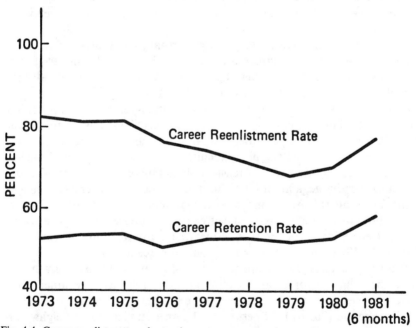

Fig. 4.4. Career reenlistment and retention.
Source: Nelson and Hunter, "Eight Years with the All Volunteer Armed Forces," The Sixtieth American Assembly, September 17–20, 1981, Seven Springs Center, Mt. Kisco, NY.

114,000 in 1972, to 116,000 in 1976, to 125,000 in 1980. Thus, career reenlistments have done considerably better than a casual examination of career reenlistment rates by themselves would seem to imply.[5]

The one important exception to this generally optimistic assessment of career reenlistment concerns the navy, since the navy has experienced a decline during the 1970s in all three measures of career reenlistment: reenlistment rates, retention rates, and actual number of reenlistments. For example, the navy had close to 30,000 career reenlistments per year in the early 1970s, but this fell to a little more than 20,000 per year by the end of the decade. This decline in navy career reenlistments has little to do with the volunteer force, however, as a return to the draft would likely worsen the problem. Rather, the problem seems to center much more on the extensive sea duty requirements that navy career enlisted personnel must undergo. Using this as a rationale, the navy successfully argued for a substantial increase in sea pay, which, when combined with the other pays and bonuses available, can earn a first class petty officer, for instance, between $25,000 and $30,000 per year. The experience from the first half of fiscal 1981 indicates that these improvements in pay have had the desired effect, as navy reenlistment rates exhibited a marked upturn.

Turnover rates. Although it is useful for analytical purposes to break the retention problem down into its component parts, i.e., attrition, first-term reenlistment, and career reenlistment, enlisted personnel turnover rates provide a useful summary measure of the combined effect of these various components of the problem. Turnover rates show the number of new personnel needed each year, expressed as a proportion of force size, to replace losses from all sources: attrition, ineligible to reenlist, failure to reenlist, and retirement.

Table 4.8 shows that, after the turbulence of the first few years of the volunteer force had subsided, the volunteer force has experienced lower enlisted personnel turnover rates than was the case during the pre-Vietnam draft. (As would be expected, the Vietnam era turnover rates of about 30 percent for DoD as a whole were substantially higher than either the pre-Vietnam or AVF periods.) Indeed, excluding the Marine Corps, aggregate turnover rates for DoD dropped by nearly 4 percentage points, from 23 percent during the 1955 to 1965 period to 19 percent during the 1978 to 1980 period. The marines present an anomaly, since in the mid- to late 1960s they apparently revised their enlisted manning philosophy so as to rely on a much more junior enlisted force than was the case in the 1950s and early 1960s.

Table 4.8 also shows that even these improved rates are greater than the Gates Commission had originally projected, a difference that is largely attributable to the fact that the Gates Commission failed to take adequate account of the increased enlisted attrition rates that a volunteer force would

Table 4.8. Enlisted Personnel Turnover Rates[a].
(percentage)

	Draft 1955–1965	AVF		Gates Rec.[b]	Cost-Effective[c]
		1974–77	1978–1980		
Army	28	29	22	17	20
Navy	23	22	20	n.a.	18
USMC	20	30	25	n.a.	21
USAF	16	15	15	n.a.	13
DoD	22	23	20	15	18
DoD less USMC	23	23	19	n.a.	18

n.a. not available
a. Turnover rates defined as enlisted accessions in year t divided by enlisted end strength in year t-1
b. Gates Commission recommendations
c. "Cost-effective" rates as described in Richard V. L. Cooper, *Military Manpower and the All-Volunteer Force* (Rand Corporation, 1977), p. 181, Table 9-5.

experience. The 1978 to 1980 rates are not, however, too much above the "cost-effective" rates (as noted in table 4.8). Thus, overall the volunteer force has in fact demonstrated considerable improvement in enlisted retention.

Cost

At one time, cost was an important issue in the AVF debate. The importance of this as a key issue in the AVF-draft debate has subsided in recent years, however, as people came to realize that the cost-savings from a return to conscription would likely be only minimal.

Looking retrospectively, there are four main categories of costs that might be thought of as related to the volunteer force: the pay raise for junior military personnel in 1971, increased recruiting costs, enlistment bonuses, and bonuses for health professionals. The pay raise for junior military personnel really should not be viewed as an AVF cost, since, as noted previously, the Gates Commission argued vigorously that the pay for junior military personnel ought to be raised for the equity reason alone. Similarly, although the services certainly expanded their recruiting efforts significantly in moving to the volunteer force, it should be noted that they maintained a sizeable recruiting establishment during the draft years as well and would still need some recruiting effort in the event of a return to conscription. Not only are the costs associated with the volunteer force less than were sometimes alleged during the early AVF period, the volunteer force has also resulted in certain cost-savings. For example, the costs of the Selective Service System in its standby capacity are at least $100 million less than they would have been had the structure of the 1960s been continued today.

Longer enlistment tours have resulted in significant cost reductions in training, estimated by the DoD to be $500 million per year or more.

Looking prospectively, what would be the cost impact of a return to the draft? Probably the biggest single savings outside of recruiting would result from reducing the size of the recruiting budget, which is projected at more than $800 million for fiscal 1982. At least half, but probably not much more, of this could be saved. Another $60 to $80 million in enlistment bonuses could be saved, as well as a like amount for health professional special pays and bonuses. On the other hand, there would be cost increases, such as the training and Selective Service System costs just noted. In addition, reenlistment bonuses would likely have to increase, to help offset the depressing effect that a draft would have on first-term reenlistment rates.

Although it has been argued earlier that the pay for first-term personnel ought to be maintained for equity reasons alone, even if conscription is reinstated, the greatest potential for budgetary cost-savings under a draft would clearly occur by cutting the pay for recruits. Should such a decision be made, one could measure the cost-savings not in tens of millions or hundreds of millions of dollars, as would be the case for the other cost items mentioned earlier, but rather in terms of billions of dollars.

Even this, however, would be a relatively small proportion of total manpower spending or total defense spending. The reason, as shown in table 4.9, is that the pay for those in their first two years of service, i.e., those whose pay could be cut under a return to the draft, accounts for less than 10 percent of total manpower costs and only a little more than 5 percent of total defense costs. Defense manpower costs are indeed very large, but they are large, not because first-term military personnel are paid a competitive wage, but rather because of the large costs for career personnel, retired military personnel, civilian employees of the DoD, training base support, and so forth. In other words, a draft provides limited leverage over costs that collectively make up less than 10 percent of the defense manpower budget, and no leverage at all over the remaining 90 percent.

Other Issues

The volunteer force is clearly more than recruiting, retention, representation, and cost, the issues that this chapter has focused on. Also key are such important, but hard to measure, issues as combat effectiveness, esprit de corps, cohesion, military-civil relations, and so forth. This chapter has focused on the quantifiable issues such as recruiting and retention, not because the other issues are unimportant, but rather to provide a baseline for the AVF-draft debate that is already underway. Although one must be very careful not to become lost in the statistical evidence, one must be equally careful not to lose sight of this evidence altogether.

Table 4.9. Defense Manpower Costs by Source.
($ billions)

Fiscal Year	Active Military			Reserve	Retired	Civilian	Other[a]	Total Manpower[b]	Total Defense
	First-term		Career						
	0-1 YOS	2-3 YOS							
1956	$2.1	$2.0	$ 6.8	$0.2	$ 0.5	$ 5.3	$ 2.4	$19.3	$ 35.8
1964	2.3	2.4	7.6	0.7	1.2	7.6	3.7	25.6	49.5
1976	5.2	4.6	13.5	1.8	7.3	16.6	10.9	59.9	87.9
1981	7.4	6.6	19.6	3.0	13.7	23.9	21.7	95.9	66.1

a. Includes costs of family housing as reported in the budget, personnel support as reported in the annual report of the Secretary of Defense, and contract hires as reported in V. L. Cooper, *Contract-Hire.*

b. Total manpower costs as shown here are larger than traditionally stated because of the inclusion of (an estimate of) the costs for contract-hires.

PERCEPTIONS AND PROSPECTS

The all-volunteer force has, from its inception, been the subject of an often heated public debate. Indeed, scarcely one week after the authority to draft had expired in 1973, former Army Chief of Staff General William Westmoreland declared that "As a nation we moved too fast in eliminating the draft." During the period since then, the volunteer force has been criticized, among other things, for being too costly, producing low quality recruits, leading to a force that is unrepresentative of the American public, destroying the unique character of the military, and, in general, providing a military force that is not capable of meeting U.S. defense needs.

The results presented in this chapter thus stand in considerable contrast to the often grim assessment put forth by AVF critics, since, for the most part, it has been argued earlier that the volunteer force generally has accomplished much of what originally was intended by its architects. The military services, for example, have met or come close to their quantitative targets throughout the AVF period. The quality of new recruits appears broadly similar to that experienced during the draft era. And the volunteer force seems to have evidenced clear improvements relative to the draft in terms of such factors as retention and indiscipline.

Racial composition is one of the few areas where the AVF has differed significantly from what originally was predicted, since minority participation in the armed forces is substantially higher than initially estimated by proponents of the volunteer force. The reasons for this change, however, largely are unrelated to the volunteer force per se, but rather concern economic and demographic factors that would have had a similar impact whether or not the draft had been ended.

The above should not be taken to mean that the volunteer force has been without problems, for that is clearly not the case. The army, for instance, has fared less well than the other services. The services have also had difficulty recruiting adequate numbers of physicians. Attrition was likewise a major problem during the first few years of the AVF. Perhaps most important, however, the military services will face a very difficult recruiting environment beginning in the mid-1980s, when the numbers of military aged youth begin to decrease significantly.

Perceptions: Why?

Given this favorable optimistic assessment, the previously mentioned problems notwithstanding, why then has so much of the AVF debate come to a different conclusion? There are several reasons.

The first is that AVF critics have tended to focus particularly, and perhaps disproportionately, on certain specific aspects of the army, such as recruit quality, rather than on the military as a whole, or even on the army in total. For example, whereas the other services generally seem to have at least maintained, if not improved upon the quality of recruits they enjoyed during the draft, a number of measures indicate that the army has not fared as well under the volunteer force—especially during the 1977 to 1980 period —as it did under the draft. This only presents a very partial picture, however, even for the army. For instance, although army recruit quality indeed suffered during the 1977 to 1980 period, the army was also the largest beneficiary of the improved reenlistment afforded by the volunteer force. Thus, even in the case of the army, the picture is not as bleak as has sometimes been portrayed. In fact, given the army's dramatic gains in reenlistment, we can expect the future to brighten for the army, since improved reenlistment means that the army can be more selective in recruiting.

Second, many criticisms of the volunteer force are based on comparisons that either are not really relevant to the policy environment of the 1980s or that reflect an overly optimistic appraisal of the past. To illustrate, the volunteer force is frequently compared to a draft where Harvard and Princeton graduates, for instance, served alongside youth from less affluent backgrounds. This phenomenom, which did occur on occasion during the 1950s, was, however, the result of both force sizes that were large relative to the then small youth population cohorts and of the oldest-first draft. Neither of these conditions would be likely to prevail in the 1980s.

Third, the AVF debate has often confused general manpower problems with the volunteer force—that is, critics of the AVF have often blamed the volunteer force for problems that are largely unrelated to military manpower procurement policy. The frequent references by AVF critics to the large exodus of skilled manpower from the military is one of the more striking examples, since, if anything, retention would likely be worsened by a return to conscription. Cost is another example, since rising manpower costs are mainly a result of the increased costs of civilian personnel, retired personnel, and career military personnel, not the volunteer force.

Finally, and perhaps most significantly, general defense problems are often confused with AVF problems. In this respect, it is not one, but rather two parallel debates that have been taking place for the past five to ten years: one concerning military manpower procurement policy and the other concerning U.S. defense posture in general. Concerns about the United States having a "hollow army," as voiced by the Army Chief of Staff in 1980, are much more a question of "How much is enough?" than of what military manpower procurement policy to use. Although the two issues are not entirely separable, it is important to keep these two debates in perspective. One cannot blame the AVF for all supposed inadequacies of U.S. defense posture, just as all the ills of the Vietnam–era military cannot be attributed to the draft.

The point is not to make excuses for the volunteer force, but rather to emphasize that simply returning to a draft would do little by itself to solve most of the problems that have been raised during the course of the AVF debate. In many ways, the AVF debate has served as a watershed for a whole array of defense and manpower issues and concerns. This in fact was part of the rationale for the volunteer force—namely, to make manpower issues and problems more visible so that they might be identified and dealt with more quickly and effectively. To the extent that this has helped focus attention on the broader problems confronting the U.S. military, the debate has served a useful purpose. Unfortunately, by dwelling so exclusively on the AVF in the narrow sense, the debate may have done more to focus attention away from the important issues than toward them. As a result, the more fundamental problems of the military manpower system have gone largely unaddressed.

In this regard, the AVF debate of the 1970s and 1980s almost seems to be a replay of the draft debate of the 1960s. Just as many then draft critics saw a volunteer force as the solution to most military manpower problems, too many AVF critics see the draft as the solution to today's manpower problems. Both groups are almost necessarily destined to be wrong. Although military manpower procurement policy clearly has effects beyond the narrow confines of recruitment, military manpower procurement policy cannot by itself solve the myriad of manpower and personnel problems that confront any large organization, let alone one as unique in character and mission as the American military.

Prospects

The discussion presented here, although far from a complete analysis of the volunteer force in its entirety, nevertheless highlights some of the key issues, problems, and successes experienced by the active forces since the removal of the draft in 1973. In the aggregate, the discussion presented here suggests that the active forces have fared reasonably well in the absence of a draft. They have almost certainly done better than the most pessimistic forecasts of the late 1960s and early 1970s, though perhaps not as well as the most optimistic projections of that period.

What does the experience to date tell us about the prospects for the AVF in the 1980s and beyond? The answer to this question depends critically upon force size requirements. So long as force sizes are to remain near their present levels, i.e., 2 to 2.3 million uniformed personnel in the active forces, the volunteer force would appear to stand a reasonable chance. If, on the other hand, manpower requirements increase substantially beyond these levels—by 500,000 or more—the future of AVF would at best be problematic.

Assuming for the moment that manpower requirements do not change appreciably, the overriding problem to be faced by the volunteer force clearly concerns how the military can recruit enough young men (and women?) without seriously degrading quality from a manpower pool that will decrease some 15 percent between 1980 and 1985, and by another 10 percent between 1985 and the mid-1990s. During much of the early AVF period, the volunteer force muddled through on a more or less "business as usual" basis. Some of this the military did to itself, but much of it was done to the military, by the administration and the Congress. The demographics just cited tell us, however, that "business as usual" will not work as well as for the next eight years. The services struggled to meet their recruiting quotas during the last part of the 1970s, when the size of the recruiting pool was at an all-time high. What will happen when there is a much smaller manpower pool from which to recruit? And what will happen when youth unemployment rates drop from their present very high levels?

From a technical viewpoint, the answer rests in both the supply side and the demand side. With regard to manpower supply, military pay was allowed to fall somewhere between 5 and 15 percent relative to civilian wages and salaries from 1973 to 1980, depending on what index is used to reflect potential civilian earnings. The services were forced to cut their recruiting effort in the late 1970s. And the GI Bill was eliminated, while educational assistance for those not serving in the military was simultaneously increased, thus giving rise to the phrase, "The GI Bill without the GI."

There has recently been or promises to be improvement with respect to all these problems, thus giving rise to increased optimism regarding manpower supply. The October 1980 and October 1981 military pay raises have helped to close the gap created during the preceding eight years. Perhaps more important than the dollar amount of the pay increases themselves, they have signaled a reversal from the downward slide in military pay relative to the civilian sector. The services' recruiting resources have been restored. And, there is the promise of some improvement in military educational benefits, while educational assistance for those not serving in the military has been cut substantially. In short, although the military may not be entirely in a "buyers" market, its position should be substantially improved relative to what it was in the late 1970s.

On the demand side—that is, reducing enlisted personnel turnover, thereby reducing the need for new recruits—the services have more themselves to blame, although they have made considerable progress during the late 1970s. They must continue to hold down turnover rates, and improve them, if they are to have a real chance at meeting strength objectives in the 1980s, especially if force sizes are increased along the lines suggested in the Reagan defense budget. This, in turn, can be accomplished by increasing the career content of the force, and holding down first-term enlisted attrition.

Perhaps more important than these technical solutions, is the need to revitalize the American military and the general public's attitude toward its armed forces. This is something that neither a volunteer force nor a draft can accomplish by itself. Yet, it is critical to the ultimate success of either policy.

APPENDIX: METHODOLOGY FOR CALCULATING REVISED CATEGORY IV PERCENTAGES

The Defense Department discovered in 1980 that there was an error in the norming algorithm used to translate individuals' raw test scores to a percentile basis. Although the studies that identified the current problem focused only on the ASVAB, in use since 1976, there is good reason to believe that the misnorming problem was not the result of a single test, but rather can be traced back, well into the 1960s.

To understand why this misnorming probably goes back a number of years, consider the following: First, an increasing proportion of the youth population has been classified into Categories I-III, when in fact there is no a priori reason to indicate why this should have been the case; second, the proportion of applicants for enlistment so classified did not change much during the 1970s, when the new tests were introduced. These two issues are discussed below in more detail.

With respect to the first issue, column (1) of table A-4.1 shows that there was a substantial increase in the proportion of white preinductees classified into Categories I-III, beginning in the mid-1950s. (Whites are used here since there is good reason to believe that the proportion of blacks classified into Categories I-III should have increased appreciably over the past 30 years. These reasons include increased high-school graduation and generally improved schooling opportunities.) Preinductees were presumably a random cross section of American youth, and thus provide a reasonable basis for determining the proportion of the youth population classified into mental categories I-III. Since there is no reason to believe that the proportion of white youth classified into Categories I-III should have increased appreciably over time, the 20 percent increase in the proportion of white preinductees so classified between the mid-1950s and the early 1970s may thus have been more an artifact of the norming algorithms used than of a genuine change in the mental aptitude of youth. (If anything, we might actually have expected to see the proportion of preinductees classified into Categories I-III decrease over time, since to the extent that preinductees did

Table A-4.1. Percentages of White Preinductees and All Army Applicants for Enlistment Classified as Category I–III.

Fiscal Year	Test[a]	White Preinductees (1)	All Army Applicants (2)
1953–57	AFQT	68.2	–
1958–63	AFQT	69.7	–
1964–68	AFQT	77.2	–
1969–1970	AFQT	81.1	–
1971–72	AFQT	81.4	64.0
1973	AFQT	–	65.3
1974	ACB	–	65.7
1975	ACB	–	68.7
1976 (Oct.–Dec.)	ACB	–	63.2
1976 (Jan.–Sept.)	ASVAB	–	60.7
1977	ASVAB	–	64.7
1978	ASVAB	–	65.4

a. AFQT, Armed Forces Qualification Test; ACB, Army Classification Battery; ASVAB, Armed Services Vocational Aptitude Battery.

not constitute a representative sample of youth, the growth of the youth population in the 1960s would have meant it becoming less representative over time.)

Turning to the second issue, column (2) of table A-4.1 suggests that the misnorming problem discovered in 1980 cannot be attributed solely to the introduction of the ASVAB in 1976. As shown in table A-4.1, the military has used three main batteries of tests over the past 25 years or so: the Armed Forces Qualifying Test (AFQT) until June 1973; the Services' own test from July 1973 through December 1975 (in the army's case, the Army Classification Battery [ACB]); and the ASVAB since January 1976. Note from column (2) that there were not marked changes in the proportion of army applicants for enlistment classified as Category I–III in either 1973 or 1976 —that is, when the new tests were introduced. It is thus unlikely that the new tests themselves were responsible for the misnorming problem. (If the new test itself was responsible, then we should see a marked increase in the Category I–III classification rate immediately following the introduction of the new tests, either in 1973 or 1976, or both. But, no such increase can be found in column (2) of table A-4.1.)

Together, columns (1) and (2) of table A-4.1 suggest either one of two hypotheses. If the misnorming problem discovered in 1980 is in fact real, then it has probably existed well back into the 1960s. Alternatively, there may have been less of a misnorming problem in 1980 than the studies conducted for the Department of Defense have indicated. The following discussion is based on the assumption that the first hypothesis is the correct one, and shows how the earlier reported test results can be corrected to reflect the misnorming that presumably was present before 1976.

The methodology for making these corrections is presented in table A-4.2. Line (1) shows the percentage of white males that the then existing tests classified into Categories I–III over time. Line (2) shows the "true" proportion of white male youth falling in Categories I–III, assuming that the true proportion remained constant over time at the rate experienced during the 1953 to 1959 period. Line (3) is simply the ratio of line (1) to line (2).

Line (4) is the proportion of male enlisted accessions that were reported to have been Category III. Line (5) is an estimate of what the "true" proportion of enlisted accessions was and is calculated as line (4) divided by line (3). That is, line (5) is calculated under the assumption that the proportion of actual Category IV accessions mistakenly classified as Category III was the same as the proportion of the white male Category IV population mistakenly classified as Category III. Line (6) is simply the difference between lines (4) and (5).

Line (7) shows the percentage of enlisted accessions that were reported as Category IV. Line (8) shows the "true" Category IV percentage, assuming that all mistakenly classified Category IIIs were in fact Category IVs and is thus calculated as line (7) plus line (6).

Table A-4.2. Methodology for Calculating Revised Category IVs.

Line			1955–59	1960–64	1965–69	1969–1972	1975	1979
(1) Population:	Measured	III	33	35	42	46	49a	53a
(2)	"True"	IV	33	33	33	33	33	33
(3)	Ratio		1.0	1.06	1.27	1.39	1.48	1.61
(4) Accessions:	Measured	III		49	41	45	58	68
(5)	"True"	III		46	32	32	39	42
(6)	Difference			3	9	13	19	26
(7)	Measured	IV	24	14	21	22	6	6
(8)	"True"	IV	24	17	30	35	25	32

a. Estimates of what preinductee Category I–III classifications would have been if preinduction tests were still conducted.

NOTES

1. It should be noted that there are no official numbers regarding contract hires. Rather, the numbers presented here are estimates derived from expenditures for contracts, as presented in the defense budget. Thus, conclusions regarding contract hires should be viewed with caution. For a description of the methodology used to derive these estimates, see, Richard V. L. Cooper, *Contract-Hire Personnel in the Department of Defense*, Rand Corporation, 1977.

2. The misnorming problem was first discovered in 1978. DoD then commissioned several studies to analyze the problem. By 1980, these studies were completed, and the results used to renorm the ASVAB.

3. The reference population for this norming is the 1945 mobilization population, officer and enlisted.

4. See, for example, Thomas Doherty, "Don't Sell the Army Short," *Newsweek*, February 1, 1982; and H. Joachim Maitre, "American Troop Quality and the Tank Olympics," *Wall Street Journal*, September 2, 1981.

5. The decline in career reenlistment rates during the mid-1970s was also the result of the changing years-of-service mix of enlisted careerists. In the early 1970s, there were large numbers of enlisted careerists with 15 to 19 years of service who, because of the military retirement lure, exhibit very high retention and reenlistment rates. As these individuals reached retirement age, they were replaced by younger "careerists," who exhibit lower reenlistment rates. Thus, aggregate reenlistment rates for careerists—i.e., the reenlistment rates for the combination of younger and older "careerists"—declined somewhat.

5

The All-Volunteer Force Today: Mobilization Manpower

Robert B. Pirie, Jr.

ROBERT B. PIRIE, JR., Director, Naval Strategy Group, Center for Naval Analyses, and former Assistant Secretary of Defense for Manpower, Reserve Affairs and Logistics, evaluates the experience and prospects of the military reserves and the standby Selective Service System in the all-volunteer era. Since the advent of the "total force" policy in the early 1970s, he writes, military planning has placed "unprecedented demands" on the reserves for augmenting and supporting the active forces in a mobilization emergency. Yet, the reserves, particularly in the army, have developed major manpower shortfalls and a decline in quality that new Department of Defense programs have only recently begun to correct.

INTRODUCTION

The purpose of this chapter is to give the reader some sense of how well present military manpower policies serve the needs of the armed services for mobilization manpower, what alternative policies might be, and how effective they might be. It should be read with two main qualifications in mind. First, needs or requirements by military organizations for people or matériel or anything else are not hard-and-fast calculations, but are estimates based upon a host of assumptions and calculations. They tend to be very conservatively done. For the sake of discussion, in this chapter the author has generally accepted the requirements statements of the services at face value, but the reader should be alert to the uncertainty involved. Second, the military effectiveness of reserve units depends on a large number of factors, which include the amount and state of repair of their equipment and their state of training, as well as the quantity and quality of manpower assigned. It is of course important that the reserves be fully manned. But it is very important in sifting arguments about problems in reserve forces, to discriminate those that depend upon manpower policy from those that arise from other causes.

Requirements for reserves are calculated to meet the needs of a worldwide war between NATO and the Warsaw Pact that breaks out suddenly in Europe. Thus it is immediately clear that reserve callup is expected to take place in the context of full mobilization. In mobilization, manpower is deployed in several echelons. First, the active forces, which are expected to hold the line until reinforced. Then come the reserves, which augment and support the active forces. Finally, come the people inducted and trained after the mobilization begins. Some of these will be volunteers, but most will be conscripts, delivered by the Selective Service System.

The reserve forces are an indispensable part of the nation's ability to support national security policy with armed force. Not only do they supply reinforcement and follow-on echelons, but, since the advent of the "Total Force" policy in the early 1970s, the reserves have been assigned tasks integral to large active force units, and essential to their operation. For example, nine of the sixteen active army divisions depend upon augmentation by affiliated reserve units, from battalion to brigade size, to reach deployment strength. Both the Strategic Air Command and the Military Airlift Command depend on Air Force Guard and reserve tankers to complete their wartime missions. Thus present U.S. military planning makes unprecedented demands upon the reserve forces, as a matter of necessity, since we clearly cannot pay the cost of maintaining active forces of the size needed if we did not have reserves.

The reserve forces consist of two main parts. The Selected Reserves are those organized into units. They have equipment, train regularly, and are scheduled in mobilization plans for specific roles. Some selected reserve units, for example, will deploy to Europe within 30 days of the beginning of hostilities.

The Individual Ready Reserves (IRR) are people who have served less than six years in the active or selected reserve forces, have residual military obligation, but who are not organized into units. In theory, they are liable for immediate callup and may be deployed to the combat zone without further training. In fact, it may be difficult to locate some members of the IRR, and they are likely to require some refresher training. The IRR is needed to fill out the active and selected reserve units being deployed, and to replace casualties after the fighting begins. Because the IRR and the Selected Reserve may be deployed immediately, they are usually grouped under the term "pretrained manpower," to distinguish them from conscripts, or "untrained manpower" to be delivered after mobilization begins.

Untrained manpower will be delivered by the Selective Service System (SSS) to the training base at some time after the draft is reinstated. By law, no individual may be sent to a combat zone with less than three months' military training. Thus, the stream of untrained manpower does not represent a useful source of augmentation to the active and reserve forces until at best 100 days or so after the decision to start the draft. The worst-case planning scenario is generally taken to be one in which the war breaks out suddenly, requiring mobilization to take place while the fighting is going on. In such a case, then, the active and reserve forces cannot look for augmentation until the war has gone on for some time. Many believe that the critical stages of the war would be over well before that time. In any case, there is strong pressure to ensure that the combined active and reserve forces are deep enough to last until conscripts can be inducted, trained, and deployed.

In many ways, the reserves have been the stepchildren of the All-Volunteer Force (AVF). The Gates Commission, which was formed by President Nixon in March 1969 to consider the entire military manpower question, recognized that a volunteer regime would change fundamentally the way the reserves obtained manpower. During the pre-Vietnam draft era, and especially during the Vietnam War, the reserves had no trouble in filling their ranks, and had the pick of America's youth. Since reserve duty offered automatic deferral from being drafted into the active forces, and since without such a deferral there was a high probability of being drafted, membership in selected reserve units was much sought after. The problem in managing the reserves was not how to recruit people, but how to screen out all but the most desirable. Similarly, the problem with the IRR was not too few people, but too many—far more than could be justified by any reasonable statement of requirements. The IRR is created by the residual obligation of people who flow through the active forces and Selected Reserve leaving before six years' service. Under the draft, a great many people on active duty are short-term conscripts, which tends to create a very large IRR.

In spite of some concern over the effect of the all-volunteer environment on reserve recruiting, the Gates Commission decided that the problem would most likely be manageable if requirements for reserve forces remained at about the levels stated in 1970.

The bulk of attention in managing the AVF was focused from the beginning on the active forces, which were thought to pose the most serious challenge. The result of the benign neglect of reserve forces was a startling decline in reserve strength and was, in itself, cause for many responsible people to call for the resumption of the draft. From 1973 to 1978, the total number of individuals in the reserves (Selected Reserve and IRR) fell from 2.2 million to just over 1 million.

Beginning in 1977, the Department of Defense (DoD) began a series of actions aimed at rebuilding reserve strength. Recruiting for the Selected Reserves was put in the hands of full-time recruiters. Additional full-time administrative and technical manpower was allocated to reserve units. A system of enlistment and reenlistment bonuses was set up, first for units scheduled for early deployment, and then more broadly. Educational assistance was made available in 1978, and substantially increased in 1981.

For the IRR, management actions were taken to reduce losses through early transfers to inactive reserve status, and through failure to earmark all eligible personnel leaving active and selected reserve duty.[1] The result of these actions was a reversal in the downward trends of the preceding five years and a slight but significant increase in numbers. The Department of Defense has been projecting that the positive trends will continue, and that by the end of this decade all reserve forces will be numerically equal to the stated requirements.

The key issue is whether the DoD projections are credible. Even if they are, in terms of quantity, will the quality of the reserves be adequate?

If the decline in reserve strength was bad, the Selective Service System fell on even worse days. The Gates Commission had specifically provided that its AVF should be backed by a standby draft that could be activated rapidly. However, in 1975 the Ford administration, partly as a budgetary measure, terminated registration and placed SSS in deep standby. This meant that time to reactivate the system, estimated variously at six months to a year, would have to be added to the mandatory three months' training period in calculating when new recruits would be available to augment forces in battle. If a policy of having adequate active and reserve forces to fight effectively until conscript armies could be raised were applied to this situation, the forces implied would be of staggering size and expense. Given the decline in reserve forces generally, it was doubtful if such an expansion could be achieved. But, in fact, the issue was never addressed in these terms. The Department of Defense continued to articulate requirements for delivery of conscripts that the Selective Service System had no prospect of filling.

The situation with respect to Selective Service changed quite dramatically on January 23, 1980. On that date President Carter, primarily impelled by the Soviet invasion of Afghanistan, announced a decision to resume registration of draft-eligible young people. In spite of some resistance in the Congress, funds were made available to expand and revitalize the Selective Service to accomplish this task. Between July 21 and August 2, 1980, men born in 1960 and 1961 were registered. On September 4, the director of Selective Service announced that registration was complete, with a 91 percent response rate, or about 3½ million young men registered.

Important uncertainties remain about how rapidly the SSS could deliver conscripts to the training base. The system of local draft boards, needed to adjudicate claims to conscientious objector status, and the like, has not yet been fully established or tested. There is some concern about the vulnerability of the system to legal challenge and consequent obstruction when mobilization is ordered. However, in principle the system is now capable of responding adequately. A large scale test of the mobilization system conducted in November 1980, exercise Proud Spirit, confirmed that callup and direction of conscripts to induction stations can meet DoD requirements.[2]

SELECTED RESERVES: STATUS AND PROSPECTS

Each of the armed services has different needs for selected reserve units, different histories of manning and training such units in peacetime, and different modes of mobilizing them for war. Thus, for clarity, the selected reserve must be analyzed service-by-service.

Figure 5.1 indicates trends in selected reserve strengths, DoD-wide and by individual service, since 1958.

The air force appears to be the success story of the Selected Reserves. Table 5.1 shows USAF selected reserve strength for selected years.

Fiscal Year 1964 is selected as characteristic of the peacetime draft before the Vietnam buildup. Fiscal Year 1973 was the first year of the AVF—essentially the end of the Vietnam and draft eras. The year 1978 was the low point in AVF reserve force strength.

Along with evident capability to maintain strength, even in adverse years, the air force also appears able to attract and retain people of high potential. Over 95 percent of the people in the Air Force Reserve (AFR) and Air Na-

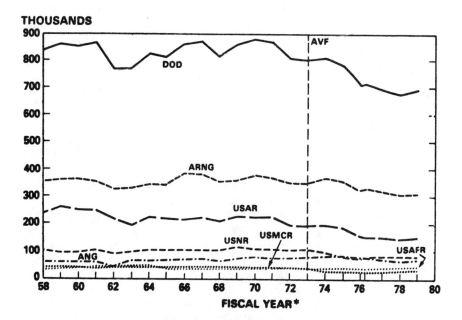

Fig. 5.1. Selected reserve enlisted end strengths.
*Includes transition quarter between FY76 and 77.
Source: Manpower Requirement Report for FY 1981, Department of Defense.

Table 5.1. United States Air Force Selected Reserve Strength.
(End Strength, in thousands)
(Wartime requirements in parentheses)

	FY64	FY73	FY78	FY80
Air National Guard (ANG)	73(NA)	90(88)	92(101)	96(101)
Air Force Reserve (AFR)	61(NA)	44(50)	54(57)	59(69)
Total	134(NA)	134(138)	146(158)	155(170)

tional Guard (ANG) are high-school graduates, compared with about 78 percent for all DoD reserve forces. About 55 percent of AFR and ANG personnel score in the upper two entrance test categories (above average to well-above average) compared with about 40 percent for all DoD reserve forces.

The success of the USAF reserve forces appears to arise from the very good recruiting image the air force enjoys generally, from the traditionally high level of full-time manning of the units, but perhaps, above all from the fact that reserve units are closely integrated with the active forces and indeed support the active forces on a day-to-day basis. The realistic training and sense of mission involvement appear to be very strong positive factors in recruiting and retention.

Next to the air force, the marines appear to have been most successful in meeting reserve requirements in the AVF era. Table 5.2 shows their history.

The stated requirement was 46,000 in 1973 and has declined to about 42,000 today. Anticipated strength at end FY82 is 38,500, and it appears that the Marine Corps believes this to be a manageable shortfall from requirements. (Indeed, most services do not plan to meet requirements fully in peacetime, depending on the Individual Ready Reserves (IRR) to provide fillers on mobilization.) As in the case of the air force, a good regime of peacetime training exercises appears to help the USMCR maintain strength.

The situation of the Navy's Selected Reserve presents a different picture. The strength numbers are shown in table 5.3.

Part of the decline between FY73 and FY78 can be attributed to the very sharp decline in the size of the navy. But that is only part of the story. Be-

Table 5.2. Marine Reserve Requirements.
(End Strength, in thousands)
(Wartime requirements in parentheses)

	FY64	FY73	FY78	FY80
USMCR	46(46)	38(46)	33(37)	35(42)

Table 5.3. Navy Reserve Requirements.
(End Strengths, in thousands)
(Wartime requirements in parentheses)

	FY64	FY73	FY78	FY80
USNR	123(170)	126(129)	83(57)*	87(49)*

*These requirements are anomalous. See the explanation in the text.

tween 1976 and 1979, there was waged an acrimonious battle between the Office of the Secretary of Defense (OSD) on the one hand and the navy and Congress on the other, regarding the appropriate size of the Naval Reserve. OSD had questioned the need to retain naval reservists whose mobilization duties were to augment existing operational staffs and shore support units in the Selected Reserve. The argument was that they could be transferred to the IRR and maintain their skills adequately with two weeks' training per year. This would entail sizable savings, because they would not be paid for 48 drill periods per year as selected reservists. The resultant requirement for the Naval Reserve was then 51,400.

The navy, the reserve community, and the Congress did not view this plan with favor. They cited several studies, including one done by OSD itself, that concluded that about 100,000 was the true naval reserve requirement. They characterized the OSD action as "cutting the Naval reserve in half."

This dispute went on until late 1979, when yet another navy study, involving extensive OSD participation, concluded that the requirement was not likely to be fewer than 87,500 (the number, not coincidentally, that Congress had directed the administration to maintain). The surprising thing, given this background of turmoil and uncertainty, is that naval reserve strength did not decline more sharply than it did. It appears that the navy has no difficulty maintaining or somewhat exceeding 87,000 selected reservists. It also appears that the 87,000 limit is policy driven, and is not necessarily related to shortages of available manpower or to the AVF environment.

While it is probably safe to conclude that the AVF-related problems raised for the selected reserve components of the navy, Marine Corps, and air force are not insuperable, that conclusion is not so easy to reach in the case of the army. Table 5.4 shows the army manning history.

This manning must be compared with a FY 1982 wartime requirement of 446,000 for the ARNG, and 286,000 for the Army Reserve, a sizable and incontrovertible shortfall, even in allowing for the practice of manning the reserves below wartime authorization (which was followed even in draft years). This shortfall could absorb virtually the entire Army IRR, leaving no fillers for active forces or replacements for combat casualties. Thus, its seriousness is clear.

Table 5.4. Army Manning History.
(End Strengths, in thousands)
(Wartime requirements in parentheses)

	FY64	FY73	FY78	FY80
Army National Guard	382(400)	386(400)	341(431)	367(436)
Army Reserve	269(300)	235(260)	186(267)	207(266)
Total	651(700)	621(660)	527(698)	574(702)

Perhaps somewhat belatedly the army took action to reverse the declines in selected reserve strength. In addition to recruiting improvements and measures to fit initial reserve training better into the time available to students and part-time workers, a substantial program of bonuses and educational benefits was developed. The history of that program is summarized below:

1978 — Reenlistment bonuses of $900 for three years and $1800 for six years.
  — Educational assistance of up to $500 per year to a total of $2000 in six years.
1979 — Enlistment bonus of up to $1500 for six years.
1981 — Enlistment bonuses increased maximum of $2000 for six years.
  — Educational assistance increased to $1000 per year to a total of $4000 for six years.
  — Affiliation bonus of $25 per month for those leaving active duty for each month of the six-year obligation remaining at the time of joining the Selected Reserve.
  — Loan forgiveness for those with education loans insured under the Higher Education Act, at a rate of 15 percent or $500, whichever is greater, for each year of satisfactory Selected Reserve service.

These efforts have been successful to some extent. Since they were instituted, ARNG strength has increased by 26,000 and Army Reserve strength by 21,000. These are substantial improvements. DoD projects that by the end of fiscal year 1982 the ARNG will be at 398,000, and the army at 252,000. By 1985 the guard and reserve shortfall against requirements is expected to be reduced to near zero. DoD admits that these projections are done on the basis of limited experience. The recruiting incentives and improvements have been in operation only two to four years. However, recent increases in military pay, substantially increased recruiting and retention funding, and the success of the program so far lend credence to the projections. In terms of quantity, even lacking the motivation of the draft, the Army Selected Reserve can, in all probability, come close to its stated requirements for numbers.

With respect to quality, education levels, and entrance test score data, which are generally taken as indications of individual potential to be trained and to perform well in military occupations, have declined in all selected reserve forces since the beginning of the AVF. Figures 5.2 and 5.3 indicate the trends.

These trends are primarily due to the changes in motivation of people enlisting in the reserves. During the draft era, the reserves were able to recruit the best educated and highest scoring from amongst large numbers of draft-motivated volunteers. That is not the case today.

The Army Selected Reserves have shared in this general decline. Tables 5.5 and 5.6 show the present status.

By way of comparison, the active army recruiting in 1981 has so far brought in about 69 percent high-school graduates. For FY 80 this figure was 48.5 percent. Comparisons of test score categories indicate that the guard and reserve are significantly better off than the active army.

It is important to bear in mind the reasons the armed services are concerned with educational status and test scores. They are screening devices used to predict, in a rough way, whether candidates will succeed in military

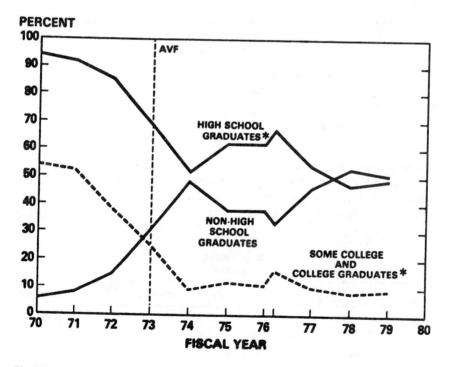

Fig. 5.2. Educational attainment of Selected Reserve NPS accessions.
*High-school graduate line includes those with some college and college graduates.
Source: Manpower Requirements Report for FY 1981, Department of Defense.

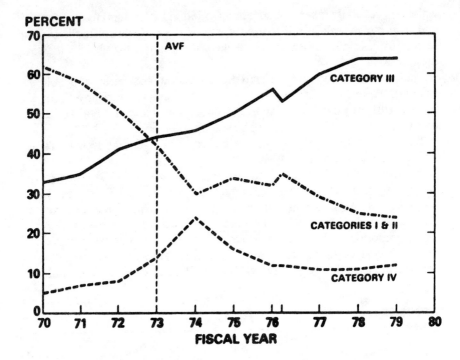

Fig. 5.3. Selected Reserve NPS accessions by mental category*.

*There are five mental categories related to scores on the Armed Forces Qualification Test, an aptitude test given to candidates as part of initial screening. The categories are: I — Well Above Average; II — Above Average; III — Average; IV — Below Average; and, V — Well Below Average. Individuals scoring in category V are not eligible for enlistment.

Source: Manpower Requirements Report for FY 1981, Department of Defense.

training and then in military jobs. High-school graduates, for example, are twice as likely to last through initial training and the first enlistment than nongraduates. The services have long used test scores, like the Armed Forces Qualification Test (AFQT), to screen for assignment to initial skill

Table 5.5. Educational Status.
(percentage)

	High-School Graduate*	Nongraduate**
Army National Guard	69.9	30.1
Army Reserve	78.7	21.3
DoD	77.9	22.1

*Includes GED

**Includes those still attending high school

Source: Reserve Forces Manpower Charts, Office, Deputy Assistant Secretary of Defense (Reserve Affairs), September 30, 1980.

Table 5.6. Test Score Categories.
(percentage)

	Cat. I	Cat. II	Cat. III	Cat. IV	UNK.
Army National Guard	6.0	29.0	55.0	10.0	—
Army Reserve	8.1	28.7	49.9	11.1	2.2
DoD	8.0	32.9	51.2	7.9	—
Army Active	3.0	20.0	43.0	35.0	—

Source: Reserve Forces Policy Board, "Readiness Assessment of the Reserve Components—Fiscal Year 1981."

training for various kinds of jobs. The important thing to remember is that these are initial measures. The services retain ample ability to screen out poor performers at any stage in their military careers. And it is evident that this is being done: for example, attrition, or people leaving the service before completing their initial enlistments, has been running about 35 percent. During the draft era it ran about 26 percent. Thus there is no reason to suppose that the services are putting up with people who can't do their jobs.

There is still too little known about the relationship between entrance test scores and later performance. The little work that has been done suggests that people with lower test scores do less well in conventional measures such as likelihood of attrition or promotion and scores in skill tests. But people in test category IV do only slightly less well, on the average, than people in category III, and many people in category IV do acceptably well. Thus it is not evident that the army cannot function with substantial numbers of category IV individuals. In any case, the numbers shown in table 5.6 appear to show a very tolerable proportion of category IVs in the Army Selected Reserve.

Some believe that, because of the increase in experience level of the reserves, and the increase in prior service accessions, the general level of individual performance may be higher.[3] Others point out that a reserve filled substantially by people who have chosen it as a means to avoid active service may not show good fighting qualities if called up. But it is a plain fact that there are significantly fewer high-school graduates and high test scorers in the reserves under the AVF. DoD has stated that determining what this means is a priority goal. That answer must play a key role in determining future force-manning policies.

Two major concerns with respect to the active army are reflected also in the guard and reserve. They are the percentage of blacks and other minorities, and the percentage of women in the forces.

Concern about minority representation in the armed forces arises from the notion that the burden of defending the country should be shared equally by all socioeconomic groups. Since minority citizens tend to come from poorer groups, they are disproportionately attracted to the opportunities represented by military service. This is particularly the case when minority youth unemployment is running, as it is now, at appallingly high levels. Thus for the active army, the percentage of blacks presently being recruited is somewhat over twice the proportion of black youths in the population (30 percent versus 14 percent). Some who are very concerned about this situation have called it "conscription by poverty."

The reserves present a somewhat different picture in this area than the active forces. Just as the draft era made the reserves very attractive to college graduates and others, it made entry into the reserves quite difficult for minorities. Table 5.7 shows the trend in black representation in the guard and reserve since FY74.

From being substantially underrepresented at the end of the draft era, blacks have come to be slightly to moderately overrepresented. Whether this presents a problem of equity is not clear. The reserves, being a part-time occupation, does not have the drawing power of the active forces. But it does represent some economic attraction and some opportunities for self-improvement. It seems reasonable to conclude that the minority representation in the reserves is a subset of, and dominated by, the general problem of balance and equity in the armed forces, particularly the active forces.

The issue of women in the military is also one of primary interest with respect to the active forces rather than the reserves. The percentages of women in the guard and reserve have increased sharply since the beginning of the AVF. Women now are 4.6 percent of the Army National Guard, up from 0.7 percent in 1974, and 14.2 percent of the Army Reserve, up from 2.0 percent in 1974. The percentage in the Army Reserve is interesting, since it is higher than the 10–11 percent that the active army will have by the mid-80s. It is true that the reserve is mainly composed of support units, and thus can probably use more women without encountering problems with respect to women in combat. However, the entire question of the use of women in the armed forces is under review at present. Major decisions, if any, will be taken primarily on the basis of active force considerations. It is unlikely that they will affect either the viability of the Selected Reserve or its place in force planning.

Table 5.7. **Black Representation.**
(percentage)

	FY74	FY75	FY76	FY77	FY78	FY79	FY80
Army National Guard	5.6	7.2	10.6	14.5	16.6	17.0	16.7
Army Reserve	7.2	11.1	14.8	19.7	21.7	23.3	23.7

THE INDIVIDUAL READY RESERVE: STATUS AND PROSPECTS

The IRR is an artifact of force-manning policies for the active and selected reserve forces. These policies are not directly concerned with the size or quality of the IRR, and it is not surprising that what results is the kind of history shown in figure 5.4.

The very sharp drop in IRR size during the first years of the AVF era, though disconcerting, was only to be expected. In fact, the drop started in 1972 as the result of the Vietnam War phase-down actions. New policy initiatives for the active and Selected Reserves exacerbated the drop. Congress showed little interest in DoD proposals to ameliorate the trend.[4] Increased active-duty enlistments, from two to three or four years, increased length of time spent in the delayed entry pool (a recruiting device), and increased emphasis on prior service accessions for the Selected Reserves all reduced the size of the IRR pool.

The cumulative effects of reduced force size, increased enlistment terms,

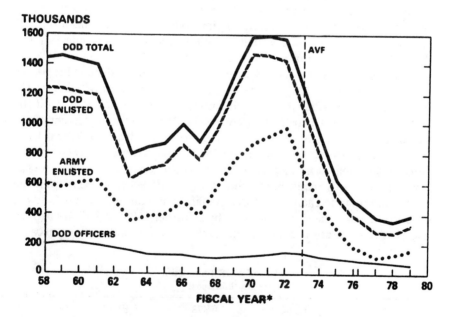

Fig. 5.4. Strength trends in the Individual Ready Reserve.
*Includes transition quarter between FY 76 & 77.
Source: Manpower Requirement Report for FY 1981, Department of Defense.

and the like appear to have reached a plateau in 1978, by which time the IRR bottomed out at about 356,000. Table 5.8 shows the trends in IRR size.

It can be seen from table 5.8 that the Navy and Marine Corps IRRs are larger than their selected reserve components. The air force is a little less than one-third the size of the ANG and AFR combined. The Army IRR is 30 percent of the wartime selected reserve requirement, and only 54,000 over the shortfall between Army Selected Reserve manning in FY80 and the wartime requirement.

Evidently, Navy and Marine Corps IRR manning is adequate for the purpose of augmenting active and selected reserve forces, and replacing casualties. The Air Force IRR, while it is not as large when compared to the forces it must augment, is probably more than adequate when we consider the excellent recruiting and retention experience in those forces. There remains, then, the army, where the picture is not as encouraging.

Determining a requirement for the Army IRR has been a very difficult process for the Defense Department. Statements of the requirement have fluctuated between 400,000 and 750,000, and the shortfall has been held to be anything from zero to 350,000.[5] Three main issues drive these differences. The first is the percentage of the IRR on the books that could be located and brought back into service in time to be useful in mobilization. The second is the rate at which casualties would be suffered and replaced. The third is the need to form new units out of the IRR.

In the first case, the standard estimate of IRR yield of deployable people has been 70 percent. This number has had the sanction of official use for some years, but has not been tested empirically. Nevertheless, using it the army has calculated a "true requirement" for IRR that is 143 percent of the stated requirement (i.e., the stated requirements divided by 0.7). It is from this calculus that requirements in the 750,000 range arise. The response of DoD civilian managers to this is that it would make more sense to take whatever action is required to achieve a yield of 90–95 percent from the IRR, rather than to change the force management policies of other forces in order to increase the size of the IRR by a further 150,000–200,000 people.

Casualty rates are exceedingly difficult to understand, in part because

Table 5.8. IRR Strengths.
(in thousands)

	FY64	FY73	FY78	FY80
Army	461	759	177	212
Navy	211	217	93	97
Marine Corps	57	116	40	57
Air Force	116	137	46	47
DoD	846	1,229	356	413

much of the work underpinning the estimates is classified. It is worth noting that estimates of the casualties the United States might suffer in a European war were revised considerably upward on the basis of analysis of the October War. Some analysts believe that the dissimilarity between the desert and the central European landscape makes extrapolations of that sort uncertain at best. Further, and more puzzling, the estimates continue to grow. For example, the need for casualty replacements 90 days after mobilization has been stated to be 225,000 in FY 1982 growing to 392,000 in FY 1987.[6] The cause of this dramatic growth has not been explained.

It must also be noted that the casualties predominantly occur in the combat arms. Only about 29 percent of the Army IRR is in the combat arms. This means, among other things, that to use the IRR most effectively the army should emphasize coming to full strength in the combat arms in the active forces and Selected Reserves. It also suggests that larger numbers of soldiers should be trained with secondary job codes in combat skills.

The third salient difference in calculating requirements is whether additional support units should be formed from the IRR. The army does not have equipment or an organizational framework for such units in peacetime. It has not, since 1964, accorded them priority adequate to warrant equipment or manning. Nevertheless, the army insists that such units are part of the required mobilization support base.

While these issues have not been, and may never be, fully resolved, a compromise was reached in 1979 between the army and the Office of the Secretary of Defense that pegged the IRR requirement at about 480,000 and the shortfall at about 270,000. Even if that number is not quite so unsettling as the 500,000 shortfall talked about by some commentators, it is bad enough. And it is not immediately apparent how it is to be made up, since the means of affecting the number, other than conscription for the IRR, are at best indirect.

As in the case of the Selected Reserve, the Department of Defense has, since 1977, tried a number of initiatives to improve manning. These have included such steps as eliminating automatic transfer from IRR to inactive reserve status in the fifth year of obligated service, closer attention to the need to place people leaving the active forces or the Selected Reserve in the IRR — even if the separation was administrative and for the convenience of the government, and transferring women with residual service obligation to the IRR, instead of simply discharging them at the end of active service. These measures probably account for at least some of the turnaround seen in IRR strengths between 1978 and 1980. Further measures, such as a program of direct enlistments to the IRR and a reenlistment bonus for the IRR, have been tried on a small scale with reasonable success in the past few years. The direct enlistment program was tried in 1979, but without cash incentives. Some in DoD believe that a modest cash incentive could result in direct enlistment of some 15,000 soldiers for the IRR each year. The 1981 reenlistment bonus program was terminated by Congress at the end of FY 1981, apparently on the basis of less than six months experience. DoD believes the program showed enough promise (1,000 per month in the Army IRR in September 1981) that it should be reinstated in FY 1983, with a bonus of $900 for an extension of obligation of three years. The combination of all these things has led DoD to project a total IRR strength of about 400,000 in FY85. This number is 80,000 short of requirements, but can be augmented by return of military retirees to active duty in support jobs.

The forces draining the Army IRR of people seem to have reached an equilibrium state. New initiatives have turned around the strength numbers, but the turnaround has been slight with respect to shortfalls (35,000 in the Army IRR against a shortfall of 270,000), and the initiatives were in some cases one-shot fixes that have run their course. On the other hand, some initiatives, notably the enlistment bonus, have not really been given an adequate trial. Previously untapped sources, such as retirees, may provide substantial relief. The army now anticipates using as many as 120,000 by the end of the decade. Finally, to the extent that programs aimed at manning the Selected Reserve are successful, they will directly reduce requirements for the IRR.

One measure that has not yet been tried, but which is under serious consideration by DoD is extension of the military service obligation (MSO) incurred by volunteers for the active or selected reserve forces from six to eight years. This would, if applied to people entering the forces now, start increasing the size of the IRR six years from now, and, by 1990, increase the Army IRR by about 150,000.

Taken together, the potential for increasing supply or reducing the demand for Army IRR is quite impressive. Table 5.9 shows a range of estimates.

The numbers in table 5.9 suggest that at least there is considerable potential for solving the IRR problem within the framework of present military manpower policies. Certainly that potential should be thoroughly evaluated before coming to the conclusion that we must either scale down our requirements, or resort to some form of conscription.

SELECTIVE SERVICE: STATUS AND PROSPECTS

DoD stated requirements for draftees are for 100,000 to be delivered in the first 30 days after mobilization starts, and 650,000 within the first six months. At present about 7,000,000 young men are registered, and about 2,000,000 will be added each year. Evidently there are adequate numbers available.

Table 5.9. Potential for Army IRR Demand.

Action	Result	
	Optimistic	Pessimistic
Fill Selected Reserve Shortages	186,000	93,000
Direct Enlistment Program	75,000	0
Reenlistment Bonus	75,000	30,000
Use Retirees	120,000	60,000
Increase MSO	150,000	150,000
Total	606,000	333,000

Problems for the Selective Service System now focus on reconstitution of local boards as avenues of appeal, and on meshing the system of calling draftees with the Military Enlisted Processing Command, which will receive, induct, examine, and deliver draftees to the training base. While these tasks are neither easy nor unimportant, they are minor in comparison to that of reconstituting the Selective Service System and compiling the registration lists themselves. And there is no reason to think that they cannot be accomplished on the schedule laid out by the SSS.

In retrospect, the notion of a mass registration after mobilization appears to be unwarrantedly risky. Registration has proved to be an unexceptionable, relatively inexpensive, and reasonably prudential step toward preparation for mobilization if that is ever required. The range of uncertainty about when the training bases would start being filled to capacity has been narrowed from a matter of months to a matter of days.

In spite of the excellent start, it may be that Selective Service will not be able to perform adequately in the long run, and will be abandoned. There have as yet been no complete tests of sanctions against violators of the Selective Service order. And there appears to be a growing propensity for eligible young men not to register. If sanctions should prove ineffective, and noncompliance widespread, equity would appear to demand change or abandonment of the system. We have not reached that crossroads yet, however. Past experience with registration indicates that year groups often lag by as much as 25 percent in the year they are required to sign up, but ultimately register 95 percent or better.

BALANCE SHEET AND PROJECTIONS

During the first five years of the AVF, mobilization manpower was neglected, and U.S. capabilities declined sharply. The decline was most serious for the army. Present shortfalls in the army stand at 130,000 in the Selected Reserve and 270,000 in the IRR. Measures to reverse the trends and restore reserve manning have begun to take effect. Since 1978 the army has gained 47,000 in the Selected Reserve and 35,000 in the IRR. DoD projections are that these trends will continue, and that the shortfalls will be decreased by the end of the decade. While there is some uncertainty about this, the wide variety of measures available and the large recent increases in military pay support an optimistic view. Assuming that the present bonus and educational incentive programs are pursued in the Selected Reserve, and that reenlistment bonuses and an increase in the MOS to eight years are instituted for the IRR, it is reasonable to accept the DoD projections.

With respect to the issues of quality, balance, and equity the reserve forces appear quite similar to the active forces. If recruit quality for the active forces is adequate, it should be so for the reserves. More important, measures to redress active force problems will subsume solutions to reserve force problems in these areas. Reserve force quality would appear to be bound up far more in the issues of training and equipment than in marginal changes to their manpower supply.

The Selective Service System has been shown by Joint Chiefs of Staff (JCS) exercise Proud Spirit, and independently judged by the General Accounting Office (GAO), as presently capable of meeting DoD mobilization manpower requirements. Continued revitalization of the system, especially the local boards, and determined administration support for peacetime registration will provide a high degree of assurance that the system will work, as designed, in support of a general mobilization in the face of a national emergency.

NOTES

1. Harold Brown, "Department of Defense Annual Report, Fiscal Year 1979," pp. 333–4.

2. Statement of Mr. Robert A. Stone, Acting Assistant Secretary of Defense for Manpower, Reserve Affairs and Logistics—Hearings before the Manpower and Personnel Subcommittee of the Senate Armed Services Committee, February 24, 1981.

3. See Richard V. L. Cooper, "Military Manpower and the All-Volunteer Force," RAND Report R-1450-ARPA (September 1977).

4. For example, the Fiscal Year 1977 Defense Report of Secretary of Defense Donald Rumsfeld (Washington, D.C., January 27, 1976), p. 295.

5. For an excellent discussion of this problem see, Robert L. Goldich, "Recruiting, Retention and Quality in the All-Volunteer Force," Congressional Research Service Report No. 81-106F (June 8, 1981).

6. "Readiness Assessment of the Reserve Components—Fiscal Year 1981," Reserve Forces Policy Board, Office of the Secretary of Defense, Washington, D.C. 20301.

6

Beyond the Marketplace:
National Service and the AVF

Charles C. Moskos and John H. Faris

CHARLES C. MOSKOS, Professor of Sociology at Northwestern University, and JOHN H. FARIS, Professor of Sociology at Towson State University, argue that the emphasis of the All-Volunteer system on monetary incentives has eroded the "institutional" character of the armed forces—a development reflected in the changing social composition of recruits, a high level of attrition, an erosion of barracks life, a high incidence of moonlighting, and widespread attitudes of alienation and disaffection. To correct this without resuming the draft, they propose, in part, a program of student aid incentives designed to attract larger numbers of upwardly mobile young people to volunteer some service to the nation. Many, they believe, would opt for short, low-paid terms of enlistment in the military; others would have the option of performing brief periods of unpaid civilian service.

Discussion of the All-Volunteer Force (AVF) often takes the easy path of focusing on end-strength figures. We do not want to be so bedeviled with rival sets of numbers that the key policy choices are hardly understood, much less addressed. The real choice is not between tinkering with the AVF, on the one hand, or bringing back the draft, on the other. The difficulties of the AVF do not stem from the absence of conscription; the crucial flaw is to view military service primarily as a job to be filled by monetary incentives. The attempt to manage military manpower with econometric analytic techniques and the operation of the marketplace can be seen as part of a more general outlook which tends to ignore organizational outcomes and to cloud values of citizenship responsibility. This chapter offers an alternative perspective. Specifically, we will present a rationale and policy that would provide for a functional equivalent to conscription, that is, achieve what would be expected of a draft without resorting to a draft. This can be accomplished by increasing the volume of middle-class entrants for short-term enlistments whose service would be more an expression of the values of civic obligation rather than a response to cash inducements.

We first review the institutional-occupational framework as it applies to the military. The consequences of recent "occupational" manpower policies are examined within this framework. This analysis is then placed within the perspective of both military effectiveness and long-term organizational change. Finally, the types of policies which are required to achieve appropriate organizational adaptations are presented, with particular attention to a national service concept which would link governmental support for higher education to civilian service to the country and would establish GI Bill educational benefits for short-term and modestly remunerated soldiers. The focus will be on the army, the largest of the services, the one which most relied on the draft, and the one most often regarded as the bellwether of the AVF. While the analysis is centered on the army, we consider that it has relevance for all four services, recognizing the particular circumstances and requirements of each.

THE ALL-VOLUNTEER FORCE: INSTITUTION OR OCCUPATION?

The military can be understood as an organization which maintains levels of autonomy while refracting broader societal trends. It is from this standpoint that two models—institution versus occupation—can describe alternative conceptions of the military. The contrast between institution and occupation can, of course, be overdrawn. Both elements have been and always will be present in the military system. Our concern is to describe significant trends within the military and society which bear upon central issues of military manpower.

An *institution* is legitimated in terms of values and norms, i.e., a purpose transcending individual self-interest in favor of a presumed higher good. Members of an institution are often seen as following a calling. They are commonly viewed and regard themselves as being different or apart from the broader society. The standard is that one's primary role identification corresponds with one's organizational membership. An *occupation* is defined in terms of the marketplace, i.e., prevailing monetary rewards for equivalent competencies and skills. Supply and demand rather than normative considerations are paramount. The cash-work nexus emphasizes a contractual relationship between individual and organizational needs.

The military has traditionally sought to avoid the organizational outcomes of the occupational model. Despite certain exceptions, the conventional system of military compensation has been a function of rank, seniority, and need. It also has reflected, not only in the so-called X-factor, the unusual demands of service life—but the corporate whole of military life. Further, and more fundamentally, the military has traditionally placed paramount importance on institutional values—captured in words like "duty," "honor," "country"—rather than on the utilitarian matrices of compensation.

The military institution is organized "vertically," whereas an occupation is organized "horizontally." To put it in as unpretentious a manner as possible, people in an occupation tend to feel a sense of identity with others who do the same sort of work, and who receive about the same pay. In an institution, it is the organization in which people live and work that creates the sense of identity that binds them together. Vertical identification means that one acquires a sense of responsibility for the performance of the organization as a whole. In the armed forces the very fact of being part of the service has traditionally been more important than the fact that military members do different jobs. The organization one belongs to creates the feeling of shared interest, not the other way around.

The end of the draft, coupled with the dominant market-oriented premises of the All-Volunteer Force, can be seen as a major thrust to move the military toward the occupational model. The Selective Service System was based on the notion of citizen obligation—a "calling" in the almost literal sense of being summoned by a draft board—with concomitant low salaries for junior enlisted personnel. Even though the termination of the draft in 1973 has been one of the most visible changes in the contemporary military system, it must be stressed that the AVF in and of itself not be correlated with an occupational model. It is only that the architects of the present AVF have chosen the occupational model as their paradigm.

The 1970 Gates Commission Report, which established the basis for the current AVF, was underpinned by a marketplace philosophy. A pattern was set and adopted by which primary reliance for manning the AVF was to be placed upon supply and demand variables in the labor force. This implied a redefinition of military service away from an institutional format to one more and more resembling that of an occupation.

Such a redefinition of military service must necessarily be based on a set of core assumptions. First, there is no analytical distinction between military systems and other systems—in particular, no difference between cost-effectiveness of civilian labor force members and military members. Second, that military compensation as much as possible should be in cash, rather than in kind, or deferred (thereby allowing for a more efficient operation of the marketplace). Third, that military compensation should be linked as much as possible to skill differences in the occupational assignments of individual service members. Implicit within these assumptions is the emphasis on end-strength targets, with notions of citizen obligation and social representativeness being incidental. When such issues are raised, the response is typically that social cohesion and goal commitment are essentially unmeasurable and are therefore inappropriate objects of analysis.

THE CONSEQUENCES OF OCCUPATIONAL MILITARY MANPOWER POLICIES

The consequences of occupational military manpower policies may be seen in both the first-term enlisted ranks and in the career force. Within the first-term enlisted ranks the effects of the occupational trends are manifested in the changing social composition of recruits, the high level of attrition, the erosion of barracks life, the high incidence of moonlighting, and in the widespread attitudes of alienation and disaffection.

Social Composition of Recruits to the AVF. The evidence is conclusive that the enlisted ranks of the active-duty army at present include a lower proportion of middle-class, college-oriented males than did the military of the peacetime draft:

- Since the end of the draft through FY 1981, 65 percent of male black recruits and 57 percent of male white recruits possessed a high-school diploma. In contrast, for the same period and age group, 55 percent of blacks and 78 percent of whites in the male civilian population were high-school graduates.
- Recruits with some college made up one in four army entrants in 1960 compared with less than one in twenty since the end of the draft. In light of the increasing percentage of military age youth enrolling in college during this period, this is a dramatic reduction.
- In the five-year period before the war in Vietnam, 33 percent of army entrants placed in mental categories I and II. In the five-year period since 1977, the corresponding figure has been 19 percent.
- Thirty-eight percent of E-4s — the modal junior enlisted grade — were married in 1980, a figure double that of the draft period. Since E-4s during the draft era, on the average, were older than present E-4s, the comparison understates the increasing incidence of married junior enlisted personnel. This increase runs counter to national patterns where the clear trend is toward later marriage.
- From World War II through the Vietnam War, military veterans have composed a much smaller share of the jail and prison population than their proportion in the general population. This historical pattern is reversed for those under 24 years of age. "The age group that showed an overrepresentation of veterans in jail was composed largely of those who joined the armed forces as volunteers *after* the end of the draft and the end of U.S. military involvement in Vietnam. Black inmates were less likely to be veterans."[1]

Attrition. In the pre-Vietnam military it was considered aberrant for an enlisted man not to complete his initial tour of duty. Since 1973, over 800,000 young people have been prematurely discharged from the military for reasons of indiscipline, personality disorders, job inaptitude, and the like. The attrition phenomenon reflects changing policies of military separation—the "easy-out" system of the AVF—as well as changes in the quality of the entering enlisted force. Put in another way, the AVF, like industrial organizations, is witnessing the common occurrence of its members "quitting" or being "fired." In all but name, the AVF has moved a long way down the road toward indeterminate enlistments.

The high rate of attrition can be attributed in part to the shifting social composition of recruits. High-school dropouts are twice as likely as high-school graduates to fail to complete their initial term of enlistment. To the extent that most attrition reflects insufficient motivation rather than inability, this consistent differential may be seen as an indicator of the insufficiency of marketplace incentives. That is, those who are most attracted by the monetary incentives—high-school dropouts and marginal high-school graduates, who have the fewest opportunities for civilian employment—are least likely to have the motivation to sustain themselves through a complete term of service.

The careful research of Manning and Ingraham suggests that attrition is not a unitary phenomenon. They identified two major groups of attriters from the U.S. Army in Europe. One group had entered the army with extremely unrealistic expectations and were happy to leave the army. The other and larger group was composed of soldiers who "had expected and wanted challenge, discipline and hard work, but generally found soldiering easier than anticipated."[2] The researchers attributed the attrition of this latter group to "the system," particularly in terms of leadership deficiencies and a very pronounced vertical segregation between junior enlisted, noncommissioned officers (NCOs), and officers, rather than to the characteristics of the individual soldiers. Our understanding of these findings is that the first group reflects the direct effects of occupational policies, i.e., recruits enlisting for the wrong reasons with false expectations. The second group also reflects the effects of occupational policies—the failure of "the system" to foster unit cohesion—as will be discussed below.

Work and Residence Separation. As recently as the late 1960s, it was practically unheard of for a bachelor enlisted man to live off base. Not only was it against regulations, but few could afford a private rental on junior enlisted pay. By 1981, although precise data are unavailable, a reasonable estimate would be that about one out of four single enlisted members in stateside bases lived away from the military installation. To the increasing number of single enlisted personnel living off base, one must add the growing proportion of junior enlisted marrieds, nearly all of whom also live on the civilian economy—along with single parents. One of the outcomes of the large salary raises for junior enlisted personnel used to recruit an All-Volunteer Army has been the ebbing of barracks life. What barracks life remains tends to be vulnerable to social fragmentation.

Moonlighting. One striking manifestation of the occupational model is the growing number of military personnel who hold outside employment. According to military surveys, one-quarter of enlisted personnel in the United States report themselves as holding a second job. Moonlighting is often attributed to the service member's need for additional income in an inflationary economy. Yet the anomaly exists that moonlighting is also increasing within the enlisted force even though current buying power far exceeds that of the pre-all-volunteer era.

Attitudes of Junior Enlisted Personnel. Underlying many of the difficulties of the All-Volunteer Army is a source of enlisted discontent that had no real counterpart in the peacetime draft era. This is postentry disillusionment, resulting from unrealistic expectations as to what the military would offer, generated by advertising and recruitment appeals. The peacetime draftee never held high expectations about what he would encounter, and therefore was not unpleasantly surprised; indeed, he might often, at least in hindsight, find the army favorable on its own terms. Significant percentages of officers and NCOs currently in the career force have indicated on surveys that they would never have joined the military had there been no draft; many of these were actually conscripted.

Recruitment for the AVF, by contrast, has stressed the self-serving and occupational aspects of military life—that is, what the service can do for the recruit in the way of pay and training in skills which are transferable to civilian jobs. Postentry disillusionment speaks directly to the excessive attrition rate. The reality of military service is that many assignments—by no means exclusively in the combat arms—do not have transferability to civilian jobs.[3]

Another fundamental source of disillusionment is the difficulty that many soldiers have in understanding the role of the military and in finding their military service to be sufficiently interesting and challenging. The 1976 Department of Defense Personnel Survey found that 30.2 percent of army E4s did not agree that "doing the job the military does is both necessary and important."[4] The findings from the survey data are supported by the results of a variety of field studies. Gottlieb's interviews with soldiers at Fort Sill in 1978 indicated that few seemed to have given any serious thought to the possibilities of actually going into combat, most did not feel ready for combat, many found their work to be monotonous and boring and saw no clear relationship between their job assignment and the mission of the military organization.[5] Significant numbers of soldiers reported a need for improving the quality of recruits.

THE EFFECT OF OCCUPATIONAL POLICIES ON THE CAREER FORCE

The effects of occupational manpower policies on the career force are more subtle. There is strong evidence that most members of the career force resist conceptualizing military service in occupational terms and are motivated at least as much by noneconomic factors as by pay and benefits. This is not to say, however, that the career force has been unaffected by occupational manpower policies.

One study shows a significant decline, between 1971 and 1975, in the percentage of army officers who believe that civilians have sufficient respect for officers and in the percentage of officers who believe the military is treated fairly by civilian leaders.[6] Wood's study of air force junior officers found that an increasing use of salary as a significant indicator of job performance has resulted in feelings of relative deprivation in comparison with civilians.[7] This observation suggests that the pay factor must be considered not only in narrow economic terms, but also in terms of its symbolic meaning. There is, for example, some evidence that much of the resentment over the "erosion of benefits" issue of the 1970s was a result of the perception that reduced benefits represented an insufficient appreciation, by Congress and civilians in general, for the efforts and sacrifices of military personnel, rather than simply an economic loss.

Another consequence of occupational policies is the creation of widespread cynicism in the career force, particularly with regard to what is often called "the numbers game." The emphasis on meeting end-strength goals is explicitly manifested in recruiting quotas and is implicitly manifested in pressures to keep informal ceilings on attrition in training. Sorley has shown that a superficially quantitative system of assessing combat readiness can corrode the integrity of the reporting system and the officer corps.[8]

Similarly, soldiers in the career force are often disillusioned with the quality of junior enlisted personnel being recruited into the AVF. Dissatisfaction with subordinates depresses retention. In a comparison of factors relating to retention among mid-level NCOs and junior officers, "the people I work with" was the second most important, behind "chance for interesting and challenging work," and well ahead of "wages and salaries" and "retirement benefits."[9]

The various outcomes of occupational manpower policies are interactive — disillusioned NCOs and officers do not perform well as leaders, degraded leadership depresses the performance of junior enlisted personnel, large numbers of potentially capable soldiers separate early or decline to reenlist, and those who do reenlist are not always the ones best prepared to assume positions of authority and responsibility. Within this context, it is accurate to say that any particular personnel problem, such as attrition, is a symptom, rather than the problem in and of itself.

IMPLICATIONS OF OCCUPATIONAL POLICIES FOR MILITARY EFFECTIVENESS

The effects of the various phenomena associated with the occupational policies of the AVF on military effectiveness, particularly in the ultimate test of combat, cannot be precisely calculated. The necessity for experienced professional judgments is inescapable. There is historical evidence to support the views of most military professionals that increasing the number of better-educated, more intelligent soldiers would improve combat effectiveness. Studies of combat soldiers in World War II and the Korean War showed that soldiers with higher education and mental scores were rated as better fighters by peers and immediate superiors.[10] Whatever scholarly debates may occur over performance indicators, judgments by members within combat groups of other members is probably the most valid performance measure possible.

AVF soldiers have not been put to the ultimate test of combat, but the findings of survey researchers are discomforting. A comparison of survey data collected from AVF soldiers and various groups serving in World War II is revealing. AVF soldiers in peacetime were more disaffected than combat soldiers in World War II (who were more disaffected than the support troops of that war) and came closest to the most disaffected group in the World War II samples—a military prisoners unit.[11] An extensive 1979 survey of youth in America found the alienation levels of army enlisted men exceeded, by a significant margin, that of all other comparison groups, including unemployed youth.[12] Yet another survey concluded that the AVF was drawing soldiers from the most socially alienated segments of the youth population, thereby raising questions of soldierly effectiveness in the event of hostilities.[13]

By no means does being middle class or educated make one braver or more able. There are many outstanding members in the AVF who come from impoverished backgrounds. But our concern must also be with the chemistry of unit cohesion which requires a blend of talents and backgrounds. Research evidence serves to confirm the observations of commanders and NCOs who remember the draft period; middle-class and upwardly mobile youth enriched the skill level and commitment of military units in peace as well as in war.

The military has always recruited large numbers of youth who had no real alternative job prospects. It will always continue to do so. But present trends toward labeling the army as a recourse for America's underclasses are self-defeating for the youth involved, because they directly contradict the premise that military participation is one of broadly based national service. Whatever successes the military once had as a remedial organization for deprived youth derived largely from its association with positive ideals, such as national defense, patriotism, citizenship obligation, even manly honor. In other words, those very characteristics of military service that serve to resocialize poverty youth toward productive ends depend upon public perception of the armed forces as other than a welfare agency or an employer of last resort. Short-term gains in recruit quality arising out of the depressed economic scene of the early 1980s are not to be viewed as solid ground for maintaining a viable AVF. This is not to argue that the makeup of the enlisted ranks be perfectly calibrated to the social composition of the larger society, but it is to ask what kind of society excuses its privileged from serving in its military.

There can be no serious dispute that improved unit cohesiveness and a stronger attachment to the importance of the military mission would improve military effectiveness.[14] The most salient aspect of low cohesion is the personnel turbulence caused by the high rates of attrition. Less obvious, but perhaps as important, are the possibilities for contextual effects, i.e., that one of the important though unquantifiable contributions of better-educated and more mature junior enlisted personnel is to facilitate the formation of effective peer networks which compose the cohesiveness of military units. A barracks world of fragmented and, sometimes, hostile interpersonal relations reflects the relative scarcity of such persons. The effectiveness of current initiatives to improve cohesion, therefore, will be constrained by the continuation of occupational manpower policies for recruiting an AVF.

THE CONTEXT OF LONG-TERM ORGANIZATIONAL ADAPTATION

The analysis of the AVF within the institution-occupation framework does not imply that it is either possible or desirable to turn the clock back to 1960. An examination of the direction of organizational adaptation made at that time suggests the possibility that the contemporary dilemmas of the AVF should be viewed within this longer perspective. Before the AVF and before the war in Vietnam the U.S. military was involved in a process of adjusting and adapting to "the problems of managing the instruments of violence when national policy is designed to avoid general war, and manage limited war so as to avoid general war."[15] This adaptation includes the decline of the mass army, changing patterns of military authority, an increasing but limited convergence with civilian styles of organization, and an accommodation of traditional conceptions of combat readiness to new requirements of a posture of deterrence.

This process of adaptation is not limited to the internal organization of the military, but is shaped by more general processes of societal change and patterns of civil-military relations. The advent of the AVF, based on marketplace principles has resulted in an attenuation of the connection between military service and societal definitions of citizenship. This has occurred at the same time as the emergence of a necessity for a greater degree of voluntaristic compliance to authority within the military. Thus, one of the directions of necessary adaptation of the military is to reinvigorate the dimension of citizenship in military service. This is desirable for its direct impact on military effectiveness as well as in terms of broader national values.

The fundamental premise of this chapter is that organizational adaptation is evolutionary. No program or policy, no matter how carefully planned and tested, will be implemented precisely as planned, nor will it have precisely the expected consequences. From this perspective, consensus on the efficacy of general principles is more important than precision-engineered cost estimates. (One cannot help note that the present AVF is not exactly the one that was planned.) Accordingly, we present in general terms a set of interconnected policy options which could make a substantial contribution to improving the effectiveness of the AVF, with the central thrust being a revitalization of a national service ethic.

The framework advanced here departs from the econometric and labor substitution approaches to the AVF. The starting point is not how empty spaces are to be filled, but rather how substantial and representative numbers of American youth can serve their country. Our proposal is premised not only on a moral preference for a socially representative junior enlisted force—the functional equivalent of the draftee, but also on the practical desirability of a recruitment system which reaches beyond the one-dimensional incentives of the marketplace.

We take a long-term view of the AVF and place little stock in analyses based on atypical "good" or "bad" recruitment years. To view the improved recruitment of the early 1980s as somehow independent of the state of the economy—as does the Department of Defense—stretches credulity. At the same time, we believe a return to the draft is unlikely. A bungled draft, moreover, could leave us in even worse straits than the undesirable status quo. Rather than looking backward toward conscription, we ought to look forward to a state of affairs where the model of the citizen-soldier can be subsumed within a practical concept of voluntary national service.

We propose a renewed set of educational benefits similar to the old "GI Bill," a new, two-track personnel and compensation system within the military, and a voluntary civilian service program for youth linked to federal educational benefits. A national service AVF could be expected to address all of the major manpower difficulties which now confront our armed forces, and to do so within the limits of current spending. Most important, it would replace the occupational paradigm of military manpower with one that would emphasize citizenship responsibility and strengthen the institutional dimensions of military service.

PROVISIONS OF A GI BILL FOR THE AVF

We should immediately introduce postservice educational benefits for certain members of the AVF along the lines of the GI Bill following World War II. An AVF GI Bill must be specially designed to attract the functional equivalent of the draftee, that is, the kind of recruit whom proponents of conscription expect a draft to bring into the military.

Cost estimates of a GI Bill vary widely, depending upon entitlement levels and other assumptions. In 1982, the Congressional Budget Office computed the costs of an across-the-board GI Bill by looking at the costs of attracting high-quality entrants who otherwise would not join the services, i.e., additive recruits. Estimates were that the costs would be upward of $120,000 for each of these additive recruits![16]

Any across-the-board GI Bill suffers from extravagant costs because it would apply to great numbers who would have joined the military in any event. More telling, in order to rationalize such costs, across-the-board GI Bill proposals typically offer low levels of individual benefits and require minimum enlistments of three years or longer—an almost sure-fire guarantee that such proposals will not have widespread appeal among those youth presently not joining the military. A GI Bill to be truly cost-effective and to insure really "new" recruits enter the armed services must be linked with a lower-paid and short-enlistment option as detailed in the next section of this chapter. The rationale is that linking GI Bill eligibility with a short-term enlistment will maximize the likelihood of attracting those youth for whom high recruit pay or enlistment bonuses are not inducements; that the low-pay-no-bonus feature will minimize siphoning off those already inclined to join the military.

Let us posit a generous AVF GI Bill which offers $3,000 tuition per academic year and $300 per academic month under various enlistment options. Under one option, the "Reserve GI Bill," a young person who enlists in an army reserve component (five months of active-duty training followed by five years in a reserve unit) will be eligible for two academic years of educational benefits. Under another option, "the functional equivalent of the draftee," a recruit who joins the army for two years will be eligible for four

academic years of GI Bill eligibility. An 18-month enlistment offering three
years of educational benefits might also be considered.

The estimated costs of such an attractive and meaningful GI Bill, including savings in lower active-duty pay (computed at $250 less per month than
prevailing rates), would be under $10,000 per recruit as shown in the com-
putations given in table 6.1. Even if costs are double (or triple, for that matter) of the given estimates, they are only a small fraction of the per additive
recruit costs found in other GI Bill proposals. There would, of course, be
added costs in GI Bill administration and training outlays, fewer absences
and desertions, and no dependency allowances. Also, the estimates err on
the high side inasmuch as the maximum tuition benefit of $3,000 per aca-
demic year will not be utilized by those recipients who attend public institutions of higher learning.

At present it is a virtual article of faith among manpower analysts that
bonuses are a more cost-effective enlistment tool than educational benefits.
Yet estimates are that one billion dollars annually would be required in enlistment bonuses to meet manpower quality standards set by Congress.[17]
This represents an extreme form of reaching out for recruits for whom immediate and short-term economic incentives are paramount. Whereas a GI
Bill carries with it the positive symbolism of one of America's most success-

Table 6.1. GI Bill Cost Estimates with Citizen-Soldier Track.
($3,000 tuition per academic year; $300 stipend per academic month)

Reserve GI Bill (5 months active-duty training; 5 years reserve duty)

	$6,000	($3,000 @ year; 2 years)
	5,400	($300 @ month; 18 months)
Maximum Entitlement	11,400	
	× .81	(assume 90 percent use 90 percent of benefits)
	9,234	
Minus Salary Savings	− 1,250	($250 @ month; 5 months)
Per Recruit Costs	$7,984	

24-Month Enlistment ("functional equivalent of the draftee")

	$12,000	($3,000 @ year; 4 years)
	10,800	($300 @ month; 36 months)
Maximum Entitlement	22,800	
	× .68	(assume 90 percent use 75 percent of benefits)
	15,504	
Minus Salary Savings	− 6,000	($250 @ month; 24 months)
Per Recruit Costs	$9,504	

ful social programs, enlistment bonuses are inextricably linked with the strategy of recruiting at the margin; a GI Bill, in theory certainly, in practice to be determined, seeks to attract youths heretofore not in the recruitment pool. One way out of the conundrum of enlistment bonuses versus the GI Bill may simply be to offer enlistees an either/or choice.

A GI Bill, in and of itself, cannot simultaneously serve the purposes of both recruitment and retention. These goals should be separated lest we end up with a convoluted bill that serves neither. Recruitment must be the over-riding intent of a GI Bill. It may help clarify matters to think of an AVF GI Bill as the functional equivalent of conscription. For even with a draft, re-tention problems would persist, especially in the technical branches, and have to be dealt with on their own terms; namely, by well-constructed career compensation and entitlement packages along with a public recognition of the service ethic in the armed forces. A GI Bill is not a cure-all for what ails the AVF. But it is a necessary step in the right direction.

Two general principles should always be kept in mind when appraising recruitment and retention proposals. First, incentives for initial recruitment must be kept as simple as possible (almost as much for the recruiter's sake as for the recruit); "flexibility" in GI Bill proposals also means increased com-plexity for potential enlistees. Second, reenlistment incentives may be fairly involved with many choice points. One will never go wrong overestimating the grasp career service members have of compensation packages.

CITIZEN-SOLDIER AND PROFESSIONAL SOLDIER: COMPLEMENTARY ROLES

The definition of military service in the AVF needs overhauling as much as does the machinery of recruitment.[18] There must be a recognition of the dif-ferences in motivation between those who might enter the military as a short hiatus in their life, and those who might make a longer commitment. The army can set up a two-track personnel and compensation system recogniz-ing a distinction between a "citizen-soldier" and a "professional soldier."

The professional soldier would initially enlist for a minimum of four years. He or she would receive entitlements and compensation in the man-ner of the prevailing system, but there would be significant pay increases at the time of the first reenlistment and throughout the senior NCO grades. This would help rectify the compression of enlisted salaries resulting from the "front-loading" of compensation toward the recruit level, an outcome of the marketplace AVF. Many career members would be trained in technical skills, though others would make up the future cadre in a variety of military specialties. In certain skill areas with extreme shortages, special reenlistment bonuses will be required (and even, perhaps, off-scale pay). Unlike enlistment bonuses, reenlistment bonuses are proper career incentives because they reflect demonstrated capabilities and past service. Present contributory educational assistance programs could be continued with options of transferability to family members. Strong consideration must be given to allow career NCOs to take a "sabbatical" involving an engineering curriculum for future technical work in the military. The professional career force must also be given improved housing, medical care for family members, and adequate reimbursement for reassignments that involve family moves. Steps such as these would go a long way toward the retention of the experienced and trained personnel required for a complex and technical military force.

The citizen-soldier would enlist for two years of active duty (the term of the old draftee) and be assigned to the combat arms and other labor-intensive tasks. These are the kinds of assignments in today's military where recruitment shortfalls, attrition, and desertion are most likely to occur. Active-duty pay for the citizen-soldier would be lower—say, by one-third— than that received by the professional soldier of the same rank. And, other than the GI Bill, the citizen-soldier would receive no entitlements, such as off-base housing or food allowances. This would reduce the frequency of marriage and single parenthood at junior enlisted levels and help restore unit cohesion in the barracks. With no presumption of acquiring civilian skills in the military, the terms of such service would be honest and unambiguous, thus alleviating a major source of postentry discontent in the AVF. At the same time, this could only add to the integrity of military professionalism.

An undergraduate or graduate education, or vocational training, in exchange for two years of active duty, or a five-year reserve commitment, would be the means to attract highly qualified soldiers who can learn quickly, serve effectively, and then be replaced by similarly qualified recruits. There is also the consideration that a lower paid track might make a meaningful GI Bill more politically acceptable to the public and to the Congress. Another consideration, that vexing question of how to "grandfather" an AVF GI Bill, would be resolved by focusing it on new recruits entering the citizen-soldier track. A lower paid citizen-soldier, moreover, would measurably increase the probability that those joining for the GI Bill would not be drawn from the same pool of those who would have joined the service in any event. There is also the important, though difficult to quantify, feature that the absence of college-educated young people in the junior enlisted ranks makes service life particularly unattractive to middle-class youth. Recruits of whatever background, but, perhaps, especially college-oriented youth, need to know that they will find others like themselves once in the military. The AVF, if it is to survive, must attract upwardly mobile youth who would find a temporary diversion from the world of school or work tolerable, and perhaps even welcome.

A concern raised by some analysts of military manpower is that a mix of differentially paid soldiers in the lower enlisted ranks would cause invidious comparisons. (Though these same analysts have no trouble with differential pay based on skill levels.) Obviously, because of the higher active-duty compensation in the longer enlistment track, some of the two-year joiners will opt for the higher paid track once in the service. But the overwhelming number of citizen-soldiers will undoubtedly leave the military after their initial obligation. Most likely, the citizen-soldier will adopt the attitude of his peacetime drafted counterpart; namely, to accept the military on its own terms because military life is viewed as a hiatus in one's life. We do have the peacetime draft experience in which many young men accepted a short tour in the combat arms over the technical training advantages of a long enlistment; and even accepted a short tour as a lowly enlisted man over the compensation and privileges of a longer term officer.[19]

Another concern regarding the two-track system is its impact on retention. It is asserted that a GI Bill induces recruits not to reenlist. However, there is no basis for assuming such an adverse effect (assuming for the moment it is adverse), if the GI Bill is limited to the citizen-soldier track, as such recruits would otherwise not be in the service at all. In fact, as satisfaction with subordinates increases, we could probably expect improved retention, both in quality and quantity, in the professional soldier track. The experience of the draft suggests, moreover, that some numbers of those who enter the military with no intention of staying beyond their initial two years will change their minds and eventually join the career force. We argue that the two-track option, because it leaves current AVF recruiting mechanisms intact, is in many ways a risk-free innovation. If no one selects the lower paid track, nothing has been lost.

The dominant econometric model of the AVF relies on the mistaken notion that long initial enlistments are always to be preferred over short enlistments. Thirty-six percent of all enlisted entrants in 1964 signed on for four or more years, compared with 61 percent in 1980. Yet with the high attrition rate, the personnel turnover in the AVF has been about the same as it was during the peacetime draft era. The attrition rate, it is important to remember, is higher by far in the combat arms and labor-intensive positions, precisely the areas where short enlistments would be directed. Indeed, it is probable that personnel turnover would *decrease* in high attrition positions with the introduction of a citizen-soldier track.[20]

Most important, the focus of DoD manpower analysts on aggregate turnover rates obscures the fundamental differences between those who leave as regular separations and those who are prematurely discharged. The differences between these two types of turnover have tremendous implications for military effectiveness and command climate. The citizen-soldier concept is in direct opposition to the occupational premise of the marketplace AVF that *every* member of the military deserves a decent wage comparable to what he or she would expect in civilian life. Rather, the principle set forth here is that short-term enlistees are explicitly performing a duty that neither in purpose nor in life style has civilian equivalency.

The two-track system outlined here has advantages beyond immediate manpower considerations. It would be a beginning toward resolving the "benefits/burdens" issue of military service. Broadly speaking, the burdens — service at low pay in combat units and in tasks with low civilian transferability — would become much more of a middle-class responsibility than at present. The benefits, career progression, technical training, and decent compensation, would still be most attractive to youth with limited oportunities in civilian life. Rotating participation of middle-class youth would leaven the enlisted ranks and help reinvigorate the notion of military service as a widely shared citizen's role. A growing expectation of voluntary service among youth generally will improve the climate of military recruitment without resort to ever-higher pay and enlistment bonuses for recruits. At the same time, more of a national cross section in the lower enlisted ranks can only raise the regard in which military service is held by civilian society and can only help to enhance the self-image of the professional force.

A PROGRAM FOR CIVILIAN NATIONAL SERVICE

The process of recruiting youth to serve in the military is necessarily cm bedded in a larger societal context. Two major barriers to more effective recruitment in the AVF have been the elimination of the GI Bill in 1976 and concurrent expansion of federal assistance to college students. Under the Veterans Educational Assistance Program (VEAP), a contributory scheme which replaced the GI Bill, it is estimated that governmental expenditures will be around $130 million annually. In comparison, federal aid to college students exceeded $5 billion in 1980 and $6 billion in 1981. In effect, we have a GI Bill without the GI.

It is surprising that no public figure thought to tie such student aid to any service obligation on the part of the youths who benefit. On the contrary, the effect of present provisions for federal aid to college students runs in the opposite direction and this effect, as of this writing, has not been significantly changed by the altered qualifications of the Reagan budget. Students from families earning up to $30,000 a year ($70,000 if attending a high-tuition private university) would still qualify for federally guaranteed loans. To relate student aid at the college level to a service obligation is sound national policy, and indeed the higher educational establishment should take the lead in proposing such a linkage in order to protect and legitimate student aid programs. The abolishment or severe curtailment of these programs would be devastating to colleges and universities and would immeasurably set back equal access to higher education.

From the viewpoint of the national server, the educational benefits would be substantial. Let us assume an annual outlay of $5 billion (approximately the 1980 federal expenditures for college student aid) and one million national servers (a figure most likely too high). This would mean $5,000 in educational benefits for each recipient per year. (In 1980, some 2.2 million college students received federal aid for an average of about $2,500 each.)

Obviously, the program of voluntary national service proposed here would be a far-reaching step. A detailed plan is not the province of this chapter; rather, a commitment to make subsidies of higher education consistent with voluntary national service is urged.[21] The preferred conditions of such national service should be broad but light, rather than narrow but heavy. The aim is for inclusiveness of youth participation, but with maximum decentralization and minimum costs. The following is set forth as one way to meet these standards.

To be eligible for federal postsecondary educational aid, a young man or woman would be required to serve a short period—perhaps six nonconsecutive months—in an unpaid capacity. Recruitment would be handled by voluntary associations, welfare agencies, local governments, nonprofit institutions, schools, recreational facilities, and the like. The range of tasks involved could include grooming care for the aged in nursing homes, day care for the elderly, serving in hospices, monitoring safety on public transit systems, and library and museum cataloguing. Neither conventional bureaucratic governments nor the private sector can fill these kinds of needs. Local institutions must become the organizers and beneficiaries of national service.

Inasmuch as recruitment and monitoring would be the primary responsibility of local agencies and associations, it would be such local units that would determine the need for short-term servers. If such local units concluded volunteers were not useful, the national service program should quickly be phased out. The criterion of national service tasks is services not otherwise performed, not finding positions to place youth or to displace the gainfully employed. The initial procedure would be a listing of such services, relying especially on the needs defined by local units. The avenue of what conscientious objectors would do in the event of a draft would be a productive way to explore needed services.

It has been estimated that the Comprehensive Employment and Training Act (CETA) produced 150,000 to 200,000 jobs, which were neither make-work nor involved replacement of regular workers (e.g., playground supervisors, help for elderly shut-ins, record keeping for the police). That is, many CETA workers did not simply substitute for regular public employees. The General Accounting Office has established that between 125,000 and 300,000 of the elderly now living in nursing homes could live in a normal community if special homemaker and transportation services were available to them.[22] A national service program must be built around precisely these kind of tasks.

Determination as to whether or not a specific task would meet service criteria would be the responsibility of local national service boards, whose members would be volunteers (albeit not youth). Salaries would be received only by clerical help at local, regional, and national levels, and staffers at regional levels and at a headquarters office. The total annual costs of such an administrative setup would probably be less than $50 million. If national service determination were made part of the responsibilities of the selective service boards, now coming into place, costs would be somewhat lower.

Costs of a semisubsidized national service would be higher, though not excessively so. Assume a per capita cost of $250 monthly for out-of-pocket expenses for six months of service, or $1,500 per server. For each 100,000 servers outlays would be $150 million plus additional administrative costs. Expenditures for a residential national service would, of course, be substantially higher. Assume a per capita cost of $650 monthly (to include board, barrackslike accommodations, and spending money) for six months of service, or approximately $4,000 per server. For each 100,000 servers in a residential program, outlays would be close to $.4 billion plus additional administrative and supervisory costs of perhaps $.1 billion. Such residential national service — seen here only as a long-range possibility — would be directed primarily toward conservation work. Considering the subsistence wages of the servers, it is possible that outlays would more than pay for themselves in the long-term preservation of our country's natural resources.

Putting the necessary machinery in place should not be attempted on a full-scale basis. Rather, the program should be introduced step by step over, perhaps, the next five years. In the interim, those youth who already are performing national service should have priority for federal aid to college students. This would include the numbers who presently perform volunteer work in hospitals and hospices as well as those in more formal programs such as VISTA. Military reserve duty would be a clear example of national service. At an easily administered level, blood donors could be considered as meeting national service criteria in the interim period. At the very least, males who have not registered for the draft should be denied federal college aid.

Initial attention should be directed toward the Guaranteed Student Loan program, the largest of the student aid programs and the one most beneficial to middle-class youth. In time, it might be desirable to combine all student aid into one package linked to national service, perhaps a low-interest loan coupled with a basic grant. Vocational training in technical schools should be included in any federal aid program tied to national service. As for implementation in the first phase, it may be most practical to make incremental changes in student aid eligibility favoring national servers along the lines of lower-interest loans and higher levels of benefits.[23] If these prove feasible, then we can move on to a more comprehensive linkage of federal student aid with national service. In time, participation in some form of national service would become a prerequisite for federal postsecondary school assistance.

To go a step further, sanctions might be employed to encourage national service. One can imagine the effect if national servers were selected over otherwise equally qualified applicants for admission to competitive professional schools. The same standards could be used in corporate hiring. National service could become a requirement for public employment or eligibility for government and foundation grants. At the least, persons who complete national service ought to have a priority in federal or other public employment. In time, one can envision a state of affairs in which national service, an earned attribute, would replace ascribed characteristics, such as race or sex, as the basis for affirmative action.

In terms of priorities, we would rank order our policy proposals as follows: (1) a GI Bill for reserve components linked to a lower-paid reservist while on active-duty training; (2) an AVF GI Bill linked to short-term and lower-paid enlistments in the active-duty force; and (3) bringing into public discussion, aided by the higher educational establishment, the desirability of connecting voluntary civilian service with federal aid for postsecondary school education (to include vocational training). We must acknowledge that the actual outcomes of any military personnel policy changes, much less a national service program, cannot be foreseen with exactitude. What most likely will happen is that modifications will be made as we adapt to unanticipated developments.

Yet, the costs of a citizen-soldier option are so minimal that little can be lost by introducing it. If it fails to attract youth presently unwilling to join the military, then we remain where we are. If it works, we will have accomplished a major restructuring of the AVF away from an occupational model. Reliance on the cash-work nexus for recruitment will in a major degree be replaced by the ideal that the defense of the country is properly a widely shared citizen experience. Such developments would also clarify the military's role by emphasizing the larger calling of national service.

NOTES

1. U.S. Department of Justice, Bureau of Justice Statistics, *Profile of Jail Inmates*, National Prisoners Statistics Report SD-NPS-J-6, Washington: GPO, October, 1980. See also, Bureau of Justice Statistics, *News Feature*, November 8, 1981.

2. Frederick J. Manning and Larry H. Ingraham, "Personnel Attrition in the U.S. Army in Europe," *Armed Forces and Society*, 7 (1981), p. 266.

3. For a discussion of the contradictions between occupational recruitment appeals and actual military service, see David R. Segal et al., "Institutional and Occupational Values in the U.S. Military," in *Changing Military Manpower Realities*, eds. James Brown et al., (Boulder, Colo.: Westview Press, 1982), in press.

4. John H. Faris, "Leadership and Enlisted Attitudes," in *Military Leadership*, James H. Buck and Lawrence J. Korb, eds. (Beverly Hills, Calif.: Sage, 1981), p. 155.

5. David Gottlieb, *Babes in Arms* (Beverly Hills, Calif.: Sage, 1980). See also, Larry H. Ingraham, "The Boys in the Barracks," unpublished manuscript, 1979.

6. B. Guy Peters and James Clotfelter, "The Military Profession and Its Task Environment," in *The Changing World of the American Military*, Franklin D. Margiotta, ed. (Boulder, Colo.: Westview Press, 1978), pp. 57–68.

7. Frank R. Wood, "Air Force Junior Officers: Changing Prestige and Civilianization," *Armed Forces and Society* 6 (1980): 483–506.

8. Lewis Sorley, "Prevailing Criteria: A Critique," in *Combat Effectiveness: Cohesion, Stress, and the Volunteer Military*, Sam Sarkesian, ed. (Beverly Hills, Calif.: Sage, 1980), pp. 57–93.

9. John H. Faris, "The Military Occupational Environment and the All-Volunteer Force," in *Manning the American Armed Forces*, Allan R. Millett and Anne F. Trupp, eds. (Columbus: Mershon Center of Ohio State University, 1981), pp. 31–42. An excellent summary of surveys pertaining to enlistment attitudes in the AVF is David R. Segal, "Military Service in the 1970s," ibid., pp. 43–63. A survey of army officers reported that "dissatisfaction with soldier quality became stronger with decreasing rank and increasing proximity to troops." *U.S. Army War College Study on Officer Professionalism* (Carlisle Barracks, Pa.: U.S. Army War College, 1979), p. 12.

10. For the World War II data, see Samuel A. Stouffer et al., *The American Soldier: Combat and Its Aftermath* (Princeton, N.J.: Princeton University Press, 1949), pp. 36–41. On the Korean War, see Roger L. Egbert et al., *Fighter 1: An Analysis of Combat Fighters and Non-Fighters* (Washington, D.C.: HumRRO, 1957), Technical Report 44. A good summary on the literature dealing with "quality/performance" in the military is Juri Toomepuu, *Soldier Capability–Army Combat Effectiveness–SCACE* (Ft. Benjamin Harrison, Ind.: U.S. Army Soldier Support Center, Feb., 1981). The evidence also indicates that on measures of enlisted productivity, higher educated and higher scoring soldiers do better in low skill jobs as well as in high skill jobs. See David J. Armor, *Mental Ability and Army Job Performance*, working draft (Santa Monica, Cal.: Rand, June, 1981).

11. David R. Segal, Barbara Ann Lynch, and John D. Blair, "The Changing American Soldier: Work-Related Attitudes of U.S. Army Personnel in World War II and the 1970s," *American Journal of Sociology* 85 (1979): 95–108.

12. Separate data run adapted from Choongsoo Kim et al., *The All-Volunteer Force: An Analysis of Youth Participation, Attrition, and Reenlistment* (Columbus, Ohio: Ohio State University, Center for Human Resource Research, 1980).

13. Stephen D. Wesbrook, "Sociopolitical Alienation and Military Efficiency," *Armed Forces and Society* 6 (1980): 170–189.

14. A good and recent collection of studies dealing with this issue is Sarkesian, ed., *Combat Effectiveness*.

15. Morris Janowitz, "Organizing Multiple Goals: War Making and Arms Control," in *The New Military*, ed. M. Janowitz, (N.Y.: Russell Sage Foundation, 1964), p. 12.

16. Congressional Budget Office, *Improving Military Educational Benefits: Effects on Costs, Recruiting, and Retention* (Washington, D.C.: CBO, 1982), p. 50.

17. Congressional Budget Office, *Resources for Defense* (Washington, D.C.: CBO, 1981), p. 87.

18. A seminal formulation of this issue is Morris Janowitz, "The Citizen Soldier and National Service," *Air University Review* (Nov.–Dec., 1979), pp. 2–16.

19. It is relevant to note that two highly regarded NATO armies utilize differential compensation tracks in their enlisted ranks. The Bundeswehr operates under a two-track system (15-month draftees receive one-third of the pay of a two-year volunteer); only 9 percent of German draftees opt for the higher-pay track once in the service. The British army pegs pay rates to enlistment lengths.

20. Inasmuch as the short-enlistment option, the functional equivalent of the draftee, seems most suitable to the army, the question can be raised as to its impact on the more technologically oriented air force and navy. It is to be repeated that the rationale is that the lower-paid citizen-soldier would be one who presently would not join any service. Because of the greater reliance on technicians, the proportion of career-oriented personnel in the air force and navy will necessarily be higher than in the ground forces. Looking ahead, however, if the citizen-soldier track was successful in the army, the air force and navy might consider a short-enlistment option as well. In the Air Force, recruitment and attrition problems are most pronounced in labor-intensive tasks, e.g., aircraft security guards, munition loaders. The same is true in the navy, e.g., first division crew members, nonrated personnel. The general rule should be kept in mind, however, that the greater the proportion of citizen-soldiers, the more compensation and institutional benefits can be directed toward the professional force.

21. Comprehensive studies of the feasibility of national service are found in Potomac Institute, *National Youth Service: What's at Stake* (Washington, D.C.: Potomac Institute, 1980); and Michael W. Sherraden and Donald J. Eberle, eds., *National Service: Social, Economic, and Military Impacts* (N.Y.: Pergamon Press, 1982).

22. Anne Woodward, "Housing the Elderly," *Society* 19 (Jan.–Feb., 1982): 53.

23. In 1981 Brown University announced a path-breaking program called the National Service Scholarship Program. Funded by a $1 million gift from the C.V. Starr Foundation, Brown University will offer scholarships to students who have completed at least one year of full-time civilian or military service. The Brown University program could serve as a model for a federal program whereby a portion of present student aid funds are set aside for scholarships for national servers. It is estimated that an endowment of $1.4 billion would be needed to finance all institutions of higher education with the same level of national service scholarship aid that is expected at Brown University. *National Service Newsletter*, no. 39 (October, 1981).

7

Peacetime Voluntary Options*

William K. Brehm

WILLIAM K. BREHM, Chairman, Systems Research and Applications, and former Assistant Secretary of Defense for Manpower, Reserve Affairs and Logistics, discusses current U.S. manpower trends and unresolved basic issues and proposes criteria — relating, for example, to quantity, quality, and representativeness — by which, he argues, any U.S. peacetime military system should be judged. He then outlines a series of enlistment options based on increased educational incentives for both active and reserve forces which the armed services might offer with the prospect of more nearly satisfying the proposed criteria.

INTRODUCTION

As with beauty, the viability of America's Peacetime Military Volunteer Force (PMVF) is largely in the eye of the beholder. Each one who judges the PMVF seems to have his own standards and favorite issues. Often these are not clearly defined, sometimes because they are controversial. Differences in viewpoint are then hard to understand, much less reconcile.

Recent improvements in some of the standard recruiting indicators have given comfort to proponents of the PMVF, and muted the cries of critics, who in 1981, pointed to recruiting results that even most proponents found disturbing. However, despite these improvements, quality and quantity trends are not yet acceptable for all of the services, and there are other factors that have been improved hardly at all, notably representation. Moreover, the active and reserve forces are now enjoying an extraordinary recruiting climate, brought about by the confluence of these factors: temporarily low annual accession requirements; very high unemployment (which helps both recruiting and retention); recent generous compensation

---

*The author is indebted to Brigadier General Paul D. Phillips, U.S.A. (Ret), for his counsel in the development of this paper, and for his preparation of the Appendix.

increases for the military rank and file; and a large age-cohort for potential recruits. This climate will change—as annual accession requirements increase, as the economy improves, and as the youth population shrinks.

If America continues with the voluntary option as it now seems inclined to do, the PMVF must be designed properly, supported fully, and managed well. So far the PMVF has been managed reasonably well with the resources available. However, it has design flaws, and it has not been supported well in all aspects. As a result, it has serious problems, even now in the best of recruiting environments. In addition to a major shortfall in army reserve manpower, other issues confront the peacetime military manpower program that involve its fundamental objectives and character. Their resolution is essential, but will not come easily. Proponents of any scheme—draft or nondraft—should press for their resolution and foster a national consensus formed around clear objectives for the kind of military manpower program the nation really wants.

This chapter has four objectives: First, to examine the long-term military manpower trends caused by the policy decisions of the last 15 years; second, to describe three unresolved, fundamental issues regarding military service today; third, to set forth criteria for a peacetime military force, applicable to either a PMVF or a draft-induced force; fourth, to explore some new enlistment options for the army—options aimed at improving quality, representation, personnel management, and mobilization preparedness as regards trained manpower availability.

Most of what is written here focuses on one service—the army. This is because the public tends to think of the army as it ponders its "all-volunteer force," and because the services cannot be aggregated if one is to understand the true texture of the PMVF. Using Department of Defense (DoD)-wide statistics frequently obscures the real issues. And the army tends to have the greatest number of them.

LONG-TERM TRENDS

The character of the military manpower program today has been affected by much more than the decision to phase out peacetime conscription at the end of 1972. Indeed, there have been seven policy decisions of major importance:

1. The 1967 decision by the Congress to make military careerist pay comparable to federal civilian pay (which in turn was to be pegged to civilian pay in the private sector).
2. The 1970 revisions to peacetime conscription policy that abolished college deferments, set up the lottery selection process, and required the youngest rather than the eldest to be called first.

3. The 1971 decision to raise junior enlisted pay to competitive levels.
4. The 1971 decision to place heavy dependence on the reserves for, not only a deliberate augmentation of the active forces, but also for rapid augmentation requiring both a combat-ready force structure and a pool of pretrained individuals.
5. The liberalization of conscientious objector criteria, accomplished largely through court decisions during the 1960s and early 1970s.
6. The 1972 ending of draft calls.

A seventh major policy decision was made by Congress in 1976 when it elected *not* to take action to increase the six-year military service obligation, even though it was clear at that time that, by 1980, the reserve manpower program would be severely understrength without such an increase.

The overall effect of these policy decisions on the military manpower program has been dramatic, particularly for the army. Specific trends are highlighted below, and then analyzed in more detail later.

Educational Level of Army Accessions

In the 1960s, about 25 percent of army nonprior-service enlisted accessions (enlistees and draftees) had some college education. About 5 percent actually were college graduates. As a result of the 1970 changes in draft policy, the percentage of enlistees with college training started to drop. The numerical trends are shown graphically in figure 7.1. Today less than 5 percent have some college. Less than 1 percent have degrees. To put these numbers in perspective: In the early 1960s, the army had at any given time 20 to 30 thousand college graduates in its enlisted ranks, and over 100 thousand enlistees with some college. That pool of older, better-educated youth was a great asset and stands in stark contrast to the low numbers of enlistees today who have a college background. Indeed, today the interest focuses on how many enlistees are high-school graduates, not on how many are college graduates. Ironically, the army today is much more demanding in its technical and managerial chores. One should note that these trends would have occurred even if peacetime conscription had been continued.

Upper-Level Mental Categories

Figure 7.2 shows that the army, during 1977–80, obtained only about two-thirds as many upper-level Category I and II mental group accessions (Category III is "average") as it did during the draft years and the earlier years of the PMVF. While there has been an improvement in the last 12 months, the remarkable recruiting climate that exists now is very likely responsible and may not persist.

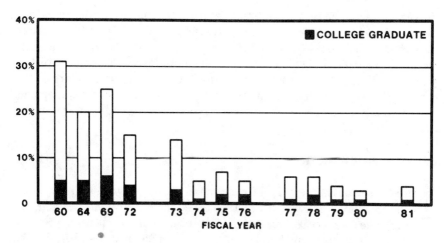

Fig. 7.1. Army accessions with some college. (Percent of nonprior service.)

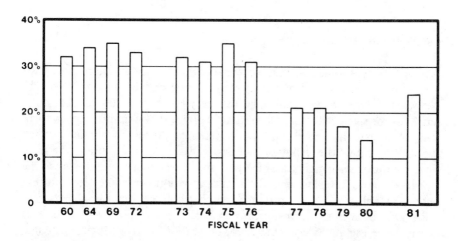

Fig. 7.2. Army Cat. I and Cat. II accessions. (Percent of nonprior service.)

Lower-Level Mental Categories

Those who score below average on the entrance examination comprise Category IIIB (the lower half of Category III) and Category IV (the lowest group accepted for enlistment). Below-average army enlisted accessions actually reached 75 percent in 1980, and even in the more favorable climate of 1981, did not fall back to the levels of the draft era or the earlier years of the PMVF when (as a matter of interest) army annual accession requirements were actually much higher than they are today. The trend is shown in figure 7.3.

Black Representation

Figure 7.4 shows the trend in the proportion of the army enlisted force that is black. Starting from a figure in 1960 of 12 percent (roughly the national average), the number has climbed to 33 percent. Clearly, blacks are finding opportunities in the army that they cannot find in the private sector. But the question must be asked as to whether a major social group within American society—particularly one deprived for 200 years of rights to equal opportunity including the right to a quality education—should be asked to shoulder such a disproportionate share of the burden and the risk of military service.

First-Term Attrition

As the draft was phased out, it was inevitable that the "attrition" policy for first-term enlistees would gradually change from one designed to keep people in, to one under which it is relatively easy for them to get out. The challenge for the services has been to develop a policy that minimizes costly turnover while assuring that misfits are not retained. As most who have studied the subject know, the strongest predictors of success or failure in the first-term are the educational attainment, the mental category, and the sex of the enlistee. Figure 7.5 illustrates the army's attrition experience for a recent cohort of enlistees. In general, male high-school diploma graduates fare quite well, even in the lowest mental group. Women, however, experience nearly twice the attrition rate as men; even above-average female diploma graduates suffer 40 percent attrition. Nongraduates of either sex fare much less well, with 50 percent attrition for male Category IVs, and 60 percent or above for women regardless of test score. In the current favorable recruiting climate, accompanied by a cyclic downturn in the absolute number of enlistees needed, the active army has stopped enlisting nongraduate and Category IV females. It has also stopped taking nongraduate Category IIIB and IV males. Indeed, the army now has a remarkable opportunity not only to

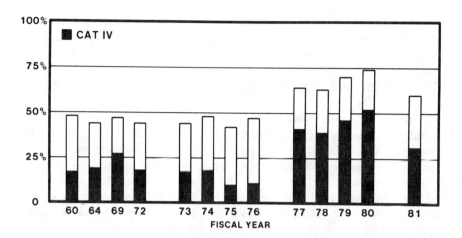

Fig. 7.3. Army below-average accessions. (Percentage of nonprior service.)

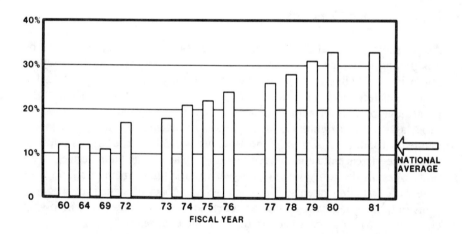

Fig. 7.4. Black representation in the army enlisted force.

lower attrition but to "stockpile" quality, and judging from the very tight rein they are putting on reenlistments and prior-service enlistments, they are doing just that. The army's perceptive management of the situation will pay dividends for years to come, since later they will draw heavily upon these higher quality first-termers to add quality to the enlisted career force.

The Attack on Fringe Benefits

The elevation of military pay to competitive levels for careerists in 1967 inevitably has brought a broad-based attack on traditional military fringe benefits—from subsidized commissaries to retirement compensation. This has been and still is painful for many service members and their families. It has had a major impact on morale, since many careerists see the actions as attempts to break commitments and promises. While the constant search for manpower cost-savings assures continued pressure on these benefits, oddly the attempts to reduce them have seldom been handled with sensitivity by any administration. It is as though the military is somehow "ripping off" the taxpayer, when in fact, the military had little to do with the creation or modification of these policies, but mostly would like to have a coherent explanation of what the government really intends.

Enlistees with Dependents

At the same time that in the general population young people seem to be postponing marriage, the tendency for first-term enlistees in the army to marry is sharply higher. One could guess that the competitive pay scales for junior enlistees have encouraged that trend. Army surveys suggest that the percentage of first-termers who are married has increased 50 percent since 1964, as shown in figure 7.6. That means an increase of 50 percent in dependents for that group, with an obvious impact on the army's support base. The increase must also have had an impact on the team concept—on unit cohesion the army would say—with more squad members living off base with their dependents. There is also an impact of significant proportions on personnel management activities at the small unit level, involving everything from day-care centers to marriage counseling.

Dependence on the Reserve Components

It is now academic whether it was a budget imperative that reduced the active army in 1971 to its smallest size since the Korean War or simply a desire to make the active army small enough to ensure that its manpower needs could be met by the volunteer force. Whatever the reason, the active army—

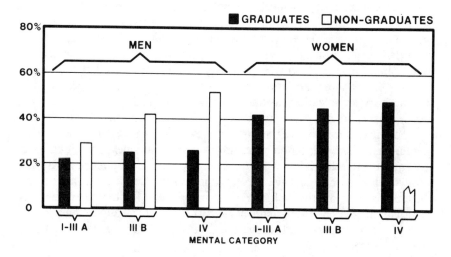

Fig. 7.5. Army first-term attrition rates. (Percent of nonprior service.)

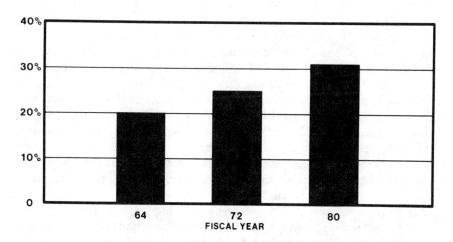

Fig. 7.6. Army first-term enlistees—percentage married. (Survey Data)

smaller by nearly 200,000 compared to 1964 but still with 16 combat divisions—is now heavily dependent on a rapid mobilization of reserve and National Guard units to meet the nation's military objectives for rapid deployment of large-scale land forces. Those objectives are implicit in the emphasis on such defense programs as greatly enhanced airlift and sealift, expanded prepositioning of equipment in Europe and in ships, the acquisition of modern and expensive army weapons clearly intended to contend with the Soviet threat and its quick-strike capability, and the formation of such military organizations as the Rapid Deployment Joint Task Force. The problem is—and has been for at least 20 years—that the Army Reserve Components do not receive the support they need to meet their readiness requirements. Their manpower programs are habitually neglected, and modern equipment seldom reaches them. Thus, they are undermanned, and what equipment they do have is often not compatible with that held by active units with whom they might have to operate and fight, side by side. The result is a mismatch among national security objectives and commitments, actual force readiness, and resource allocation priorities as revealed in the defense budget.

The Individual Ready Reserve

Most Americans think of the active army first when they think of army manpower. Some also recognize that there is an organized force of Army Reserve and National Guard units that rivals the active army in size and that has a critical role to play in any extensive deployment of army forces. But far fewer are aware of the third "component" of trained and experienced personnel—the Individual Ready Reserve (IRR). This is a pool of people who have served on active duty or in a reserve unit and have a residual military obligation. They would be the individuals called in an emergency to bring active and reserve units to wartime strength (few units are manned at wartime strength in peacetime, for reasons of economy) and to replace combat casualties in the early stages of a fast-breaking war before new recruits could be acquired, trained, and deployed. Largely due to the dynamics of the army manpower program, the IRR, once very large, is now far too small to meet the army's needs. The IRR is just as important to the army manpower program—at least to its readiness for mobilization and deployment—as are the active army and the Army Reserve and National Guard. But the IRR has largely been ignored by the Department of Defense and the Congress. As a result, the "volunteer force" comes up short by a *quarter of a million* trained personnel. (Had the Congress extended the military service obligation suggested by the Department of Defense in 1976, there would be no shortfall today.)

The "Voluntary" Draft

As a result of case law developed during the 1960s and early 1970s, if the draft were reinstituted today in an emergency, compliance would be largely voluntary. The criteria for conscientious objection have been so liberalized as to transform the draft into a voluntary program, as far as military service is concerned, and to create the need for an enormous program of alternate service for those who choose not to put on a uniform. Apparently only a new draft law, carefully thought through, can change this situation. In the meantime, the country has an unreliable mechanism for conscripting manpower in a national emergency.

Summary

Thus, the seven policy decisions just described, beginning with the pay comparability statute passed in 1967 for military careerists, have had major and enduring impacts on the military services and the army in particular. Most would agree that some of them have been beneficial. But others are controversial, and some represent significant problems.

THREE UNRESOLVED ISSUES

Three PMVF issues produced by the confrontation of strongly traditional — even constitutional — tenets are in need of resolution. The first sets the principle of equal opportunity against the principle of a representative military. The second involves viewing the military as an occupation rather than as an institution, a situation already described by Professor Charles C. Moskos. The third is a struggle between the right of individual choice regarding military service based on conscience, and the constitutional right of the Congress to raise armies and navies.

Equal Opportunity versus Equal Representation

Equal opportunity is firmly established as a desired principle in American life. The military scores high in its application, having been a pioneer among major employers. President Harry S. Truman ordered the end to segregated units in 1948. Under the leadership of Defense Secretary Robert S. McNamara, DoD broke the back of segregated off-base housing in the 1960s, and later opened the military to large numbers of disadvantaged youths through Project 100,000. Virtually all noncombat positions have now been opened to women. While no large organization is totally free of racial or sexual biases, it would be hard to find one more progressive than the U.S. military in righting the accumulated wrongs of two centuries.

But one of the results of the military's success in being an equal opportunity employer is that the army—the largest service and the one most closely associated with the volunteer versus conscription issue—has not been recruiting a representative cross section of the American populace:

> During the first eight years of the PMVF (1973–80), black enlistments averaged 29% of all Army non-prior-service recruits, over twice the national population average, and in one year (1979) reached 37%. Moreover, black first-termers have been re-enlisting at a rate 1.6 times that of whites (though a smaller percentage of blacks than whites are judged eligible to reenlist). The active Army enlisted force is now about 33% black, or about two-and-one-half times the national average.

> The Army's male white enlistees include few college-educated or college-bound young people and a high proportion of high school dropouts; indeed, in Fiscal Year 1980 only 48% of white male Army enlistees entered the Army with a high-school diploma. While the percentage was up sharply to 76% in FY 1981, the total number of recruits taken was down about one-quarter which, together with the increases in youth unemployment, makes the improvement somewhat less impressive and possibly temporary.

> During the period 1977–80, two-thirds of the Army's enlistees were of below-average mental capacity. Even in 1981, considered a "good" recruiting year, the percentage of below-average enlistees was still 60%. By contrast, during the draft years and in the first four years of the PMVF (1973–76), the below-average group was consistently below 50% each year, even though annual recruiting requirements were actually much higher than they have been in the last five years.

Some Americans see these trends as acceptable. They are grateful that opportunities are being afforded the disadvantaged and less capable among the nation's youth who cannot find jobs elsewhere. They also note that through history the poor and the less capable have played a prominent role in the American military. However, others believe that now, regardless of the past, the foundation of the U.S. military should be a citizen army with wide representation from American society. The latter suggest that an enlisted army skewed significantly from being representative runs the risk eventually of becoming isolated from the nonrepresented segments, and that this is undesirable.

Still others go even further and say that a military force grossly disproportionate in its representation might be less viable than a representative force, simply because a commander in chief might be reluctant to commit it to combat if the expectation were that casualty lists would likewise be grossly disproportionate.

The administration and the Congress recently have taken aggressive steps that should broaden the appeal of the PMVF. Among the steps are large pay increases differentially applied to specific skill areas. Postservice educational benefits have been expanded in an attempt to draw upon the youth population interested in advanced education or training. In a forthright move, the army has been given authority to use certain of these incentives to improve significantly the relative attractiveness of enlistment in the army as opposed to the other services. (The army historically has operated at a competitive disadvantage because of both its size and its high concentration of land combat positions.) But, the racial balance has not been affected much, and so far it appears that certain social groups, college-bound youths particularly, still are not being attracted to military service.

The issue thus remains: Does America prefer its army to represent a reasonable cross section of the American racial and social fabric, or will it be content to accept major departures from a representative force as a consequence of applying the principle of equal opportunity to a PMVF recruited largely through economic incentives? How long can the PMVF endure with this issue unresolved? Should not the Congress, representing the people, deal with it openly, with the aim of reaching a national consensus?

Institution versus Occupation

Professor Moskos, with characteristic insight and candor, has written that the military services are undergoing a transition away from the institutional concept to an occupational approach based on marketplace economics, a transition in which the services bid for their manpower and (some say) are now gaining their first real appreciation for the actual value of labor and skills. He points out that an "occupational model" is a natural consequence of the recommendations of the Gates Commission appointed by the first Nixon administration.

The pay comparability concept (adjusting federal pay levels to match private sector pay for comparable jobs), adopted by the Congress in 1967, actually initiated the transition to an economic model almost inadvertently, well before plans were laid to phase out the draft. In fact, adoption of the comparability concept was driven by the Congress' desire to correct *civilian* pay inequities; the pay scales of military careerists were adjusted almost as an afterthought under protective initiatives of the Armed Services Committees. (Corresponding pay improvements for junior enlisted personnel were authorized in 1971, but as a specific part of the transition to the PMVF.)

Inevitably, after the comparability pay raises, the vast array of institutional "fringe" benefits for the military person and his family — subsidized commissaries, housing, recreation facilities, generous retirement annuities — that had accumulated over the space of 200 years in lieu of direct compen-

sation began to come under attack. In retrospect, it might have been better
to have given the military an explicit choice between higher pay and loss of
traditional benefits; the value placed by military families on many of those
"institutional" benefits far exceeds their actual cost. Many in the military
now feel shortchanged. And the move away from the institutional concept
may be making the army seem less attractive to some who have other alternatives open to them.

The removal of traditional benefits and the emphasis on using market
forces to attract and retain people for the military has eroded the concept of
a paternalistic, we're-all-in-this-together-and-we'll-be-cared-for institution.
Many more junior enlisted personnel have dependents and live off base. The
squad that lives and trains together is no longer taken for granted as the
norm. Some say that is good and long overdue. Others disagree. However,
it is quite possible that when the country asks some of its citizens to endure
the frequent hardships and dangers of military life, a needed dimension
called tradition (or perhaps patriotism) is more likely to be found in association with the concept of institution than of occupation.

Does America want its military forces to have the institutional flavor or
the occupational flavor? We should choose deliberately. We should not
simply accept the occupational model by default.

Freedom of Individual Choice verses the Right of the Congress to Raise Armies and Navies

This issue at first seems peripheral to the PMVF, yet its resolution is fundamental to the viability of the military manpower program from the standpoint of mobilization preparedness. It is directly related to the subject of
willingness to serve. In World War I, for a draftee to declare himself to be a
conscientious objector (CO) was to take an unpopular stance indeed, and
the criteria for granting CO status were narrow. These were less narrow in
World War II when the concept of alternate service was introduced, and
even less so during the Korean War. By the time the draft was phased out at
the end of 1972, the criteria had been broadened by court decisions resulting
from the Vietnam War resistance movement. The procedures for gaining
CO status became relatively straightforward. CO status had gained respect-
ability. However, the real implications of what was, in reality, a rapidly
growing tide of CO applications were never faced because of the rapid reduction in the size of the active forces and the ending of the draft.

Today the CO "movement" is well prepared for the next test, in whatever
form it comes. (The revived process of peacetime registration does not involve classification and thus does not explicitly invite CO declarations or
applications.) The Constitution says that Congress shall raise the military
forces needed for the common defense. However, massive resistance to an

emergency draft (not to mention to a reinstatement of peacetime conscription), as permitted and even encouraged under recent case law, could bring the military manpower program to its knees in direct defiance of the Congress. In fact, one could take the view that the draft law has come to contain a definite component of voluntary compliance, almost a contradiction in terms.

This kind of confrontation could occur, particularly under an ambiguous ("unpopular") emergency scenario. Should it occur, which tenet will govern: The Congress' right to raise military forces, or the individual's right to deny the country his service under arms? We must choose in peacetime, before the matter is put to the test. Resolution may be difficult, but it is necessary to the framework of the peacetime military manpower posture, since a smooth, predictable, rapid mobilization capability is one of its essential attributes. A new permanent emergency draft law is needed, with a new (presumably narrower) definition of conscientious objection that is acceptable to the courts. The administration, the Congress, and the courts have an obligation to settle this matter while there is time to address it thoughtfully, with due regard for individual rights of conscience and the imperatives of mobilization preparedness.

Summary

The American people need to resolve these three issues and reach a consensus tied to a broad base of public support. Only then are actions aimed at correcting specific peacetime and mobilization problems in military manpower meaningful. Only then will such actions be seen as clearly consistent with a set of underlying national objectives.

CRITERIA FOR THE VOLUNTARY OPTION

The following criteria may be used for measuring the effectiveness of a peacetime military force. The criteria are applicable either to a volunteer or a draft-induced concept, but here are applied to the PMVF.

Quantity Requirements

The PMVF must meet the first-term and career strength needs of *all* components of *all*[1] uniformed services. The strength needs must be those dictated by the military force structure levels authorized to support a clearly articulated national defense strategy; they must neither be revised downward in anticipation of supply or budgetary problems nor fail to account for all manpower categories, nor can deficiencies be hidden within the halo of a fuzzy notion of what it is the military establishment must be prepared to do. Total strength requirements include, not only the various active and reserve needs by grade and skill, but also the DoD civilian workforce; when the latter is significantly understrength, military personnel inevitably are diverted at great cost in readiness and morale to do the civilian jobs left uncovered.

Quality Requirements (New Entrants)

The enlisted personnel recruited into the services must be mentally, physically, and attitudinally equipped to serve effectively as first-termers, i.e., to meet the basic entry skill and junior leadership needs of the services, and to generate an adequate pool of experienced people from which to draw candidates for further service.

Quality Requirements (Career Force)

Enlisted personnel retained for the career force must have the qualities necessary to meet the leadership and specialist requirements of each succeeding level of responsibility.

Personnel Management

Enlistment terms, first-term attrition (unplanned or unscheduled early discharges), assignment flexibility, first-term reenlistment rates, careerist retention rates, and administrative workload in the field must be controllable within limits that provide a reasonable balance among such basic factors as force readiness, management burden and complexity, and cost.

Quality of Life

The PMVF should provide its members not only challenging and meaningful jobs but also a total military experience that is both satisfying to those involved (including military families) and generally consistent with their reasonable expectations.

Representation

No particular group or segment of American society should bear a grossly disproportionate (high or low) share of the burden of meeting America's peacetime or wartime military needs (within the obvious limits set by physical capability requirements [accent on youth and physical fitness], mental capability and physical dexterity requirements, and limits that may be set by Congress [e.g., no women in "front-line" combat positions]), where such a disproportion is perceived either as unfair (particularly in regard to casualty rates in combat) or as contributing to a potentially harmful isolation of segments of society from the military.

Mobilization

A concomitant part of a viable peacetime military manpower posture is a structured, reliable, workable, and tested means for mobilizing the manpower needed to support a major military contingency. That includes a viable emergency draft law.

ANALYSIS OF CRITERIA

Strength

Even among military manpower professionals, there is confusion about the precise strength needs of the military forces, because of inconsistent assumptions and imprecise national objectives. There is clearly a tendency in our government to confuse uncertainty about the specific requirements of a specific military contingency with an implicit lack of consensus on what our military strategy and preparedness objectives should be. Debates about the viability of the PMVF are often—if carefully analyzed—really debates about what our forces are expected to do in a given contingency. There are, for example, apparent differences of opinion about the viability of (or need for) our army reserve forces—but these differing views are seldom made explicit. A continuing shortfall of 250,000 trained reservists is a clear manifestation of the problems cited here.

As noted, the PMVF must meet the manpower needs of *all* the uniformed services, active and reserve. The manpower needs, in turn, must be derived explicitly and reproducibly from a set of precise military preparedness objectives. That there is inevitably some uncertainty about the correctness of any particular set of requirements calculations is obvious. And one must cover a wide variety of contingencies, among other variables. However, there is no excuse for failure to have a single set of military objectives and requirements to which all defense planning and management actions are tied. Consistency is absolutely essential to efficient management and use of resources, and to public credibility. The fact is, however, that we do not have consistency—not from year to year, not even among officials within the government at one particular time.

Under the Total Force policy military plans appear to require the early deployment of Reserve Component units and a substantial drawdown on the trained personnel assets of the Individual Ready Reserve (IRR). As noted,[2] there are now substantial reserve manpower shortfalls. While there may be a lack of agreement on precisely how large these reserve needs really are, few argue that the trained manpower shortfall is under 250,000. The current PMVF can hardly be called a success with a shortfall that large.

The greatest source of uncertainty regarding the IRR requirement is actually the projected casualty rate in the early weeks and months of a major conflict in Europe. A shortfall figure of this size, in addition to Mr. Pirie's reference, was also cited by Mr. Robert A. Stone, Acting Assistant Secretary of Defense (Manpower, Reserve Affairs, and Logistics) before the Senate Armed Services Committee, February 24, 1981. It is also cited in the army 1981–82 "Green Book," dated October, 1981, in an article by Major General William R. Berkman, Chief, Army Reserve. An army calculation of the shortfall projected for 1982 is shown in table 7.1 at M-Day plus 120 days. If this shortfall were to be made up solely through additions to the IRR, the add-on would have to exceed 360,000 to allow for a "no-show" rate of, for example, 30 percent.

In this chapter (in the later exploration of new voluntary options) it is assumed that this shortfall is real and must be eliminated if the PMVF is to be judged acceptable. If the shortfall is not real, then the design, size, complexity, preparedness objectives, and cost of U.S. conventional active and reserve forces can be scaled back.

It is also assumed that overall peacetime strength requirements (all services, all components) will not be less than they are today if we are to hope to meet national security needs, but on the other hand will increase at most only modestly (less than 10 percent) in the next several years owing to budgetary constraints.

Quality — New Entrants

Selecting quality standards for the PMVF requires deciding what the standards should be in relation to military job performance requirements, how

Table 7.1. Army Trained Manpower Requirements versus Assets.

Requirements:	
Force structure manning	1,464,000
Added mobilization support structure	40,000
Equipped but unmanned force structure	70,000
Personnel pipeline allowance increase	27,000
Casualty replacements	218,000
Total requirements	1,819,000
Projected assets:	1,562,000
Shortfall	257,000

to express them, and then how to measure the aptitude of potential volunteers and the performance of serving members. This is a difficult and imprecise, if not subjective, process. However, common sense suggests that a reasonable spread of quality (intelligence, aptitude, motivation) is required, and in particular that the quality spectrum must not be severely truncated at the higher levels.

As noted earlier in figures 7.1 to 7.6, in recent years the army's quality spread among accessions has been truncated, by almost any measure. Table 7.2 shows in detail the quality spread of the army's nonprior service (NPS) enlisted accessions at selected points over the past two decades. Table 7.2 reveals several interesting trends. First, in regard to the spread among mental categories shown in the upper part of the chart:

1. In the draft years, 1960–72, about one-third of all new army enlistees (including draftees) were in the high mental Categories I and II, and just over half were above average (Categories I, II, and IIIA).
2. In the same period, Category IV enlistees (the lowest mental group accepted) were under 20 percent, except during 1969 when *Project 100,000* was an active program specifically aimed at increasing the intake of Category IVs.
3. In the first four years without the draft, 1973–76, the army maintained the same ratio of Category I–II and total above-average enlistees they had obtained with the draft operating. Category IV intake was somewhat less, and Category IIIB—the portion of Category III that is just below average—was correspondingly increased. Overall, the army was doing slightly better without the draft than it had done with it.
4. But then, during the following four-year period, 1977–80, there was a dramatic change: The Category I–II intake fell immediately from one-third to just over 20 percent, and then to 14 percent in 1980. The total above-average intake likewise fell, from well over half to about one-third, and then to one-quarter in 1980. These changes were taking place at the same time that annual accession requirements were substantially lower than in 1973–76. And while total army non-prior service accessions increased in 1980 compared with 1978–79, they were still below the levels of 1973–77 when much higher above-average percentages were obtained. (Educational benefits under the GI Bill were phased out after 1976, a factor that must explain at least part of this sudden change, though no one can be sure how much. But, even if these postservice benefits had been continued, the rapid growth of other educational support programs that require no military or public service to earn them—reaching $8 billion in 1981—would have reduced their utility as a recruiting incentive.)
5. Correspondingly, during 1977–80 the below-average group increased to three-quarters by 1980. Moreover, the Category IVs reached one-half of

Table 7.2. Active Army Enlisted Nonprior Service Recruit Quality Distribution as Measured by Mental Groupings and Educational Level. (Percentages)[1]

	Pre-War Draft		War Peak	Post-War Draft	Fiscal Years PMVF								
	(1960) 60	(1964) 64	(1969) 69	(1972) 72	73[2]	74	75	76	77	78	79	80	81
Mental Categories													
I & II (highest)	32	34	35	33	32	31	35	31	21	21	17	14	24
IIIA (just above avg.)	20	22	18	23	24	21	23	22	15	16	13	12	16
Subtotal (above avg.)	52	56	53	56	56	52	58	53	36	37	30	26	40
IIIB (just below avg.)	31	25	20	26	27	30	31	36	24	23	24	22	29
IV (lowest accepted)	17	19	27	18	17	18	10	11	41	39	46	52	31
Educational Attainment													
College Degree	5	5	6	4	3	1	2	2	1	2	1	1	1
Some College	26	15	19	11	11	4	5	3	5	4	3	2	3
High-School Diploma	36	50	45	46	48	45	51	54	53	68	60	51	76
Subtotal (At least HSDG)	67	70	70	61	62	50	58	59	59	74	64	54	80
Nongraduate	33	30	30	39	38	50	42	41	41	26	36	46	20
Total NPS Accessions (000)	185	268	455	187	215	182	185	180	168	124	129	158	118
At least High-School Diploma Accessions (000)	124	187	319	114	133	91	107	106	100	91	83	86	95

[1]Numbers may not add to 100 percent due to rounding. U.S. Army data, current as of December, 1981.
[2]Year of transition to the Peacetime Military Volunteer Force.

all enlistees, squeezing the percentage in Category IIIB from roughly one-third to about one-fifth. Again, except for 1980 which was a moderately large accession year (but below 1973–76), this significant deterioration in quality took place while total accession requirements were falling by one-third, a phenomenon resulting from reduced turnover and more reenlistments. This should have made recruiting quality easier, not harder. (The very large increase in Category IV can be explained in part by the mis-norming of the revised standard enlistment test introduced in 1976; the mis-norming made it difficult to distinguish between the below-average Category IVs and Category IIIBs, and to a lesser extent between Category IIIBs and Category IIIAs. Thus the army recruiters thought they were getting higher quality recruits than they were.)

6. The downward trend was reversed in Fiscal Year 1981 when the above-average group moved back up to 40 percent. However, this is still well below the levels of 52–58 percent achieved in FY 1973–76 when total accession requirements were at least 50 percent greater.

Overall, the army's experience of FY 1977–80 cast a pall over the PMVF. The lower levels of quality obtained during that period no doubt have been the primary stimulant in raising concern about the viability of the PMVF for the army. Recent results are encouraging for now, but hold little promise for the future, given that the recruiting climate almost certainly will worsen by the mid-1980s.

Of course, as the army looks ahead it must consider changes in the demand for quality as well as in the potential supply. Indeed, the army now plans to acquire large numbers of complex aircraft, tanks, and other combat and support items that will place very great demands on the enlisted force. While technical complexity is hard to measure and to translate into skill requirements, one indication of complexity is procurement cost. Table 7.3 uses some rough estimates of cost to compare four basic army vehicles now in the inventory with their replacements. The table shows the approxi-

Table 7.3. Army High-Technology Trends as Indicated by Cost.

	Approximate Recurring Procurement Costs ($)		
	1970 Vintage		1982 Vintage
	Cost Then	Cost Now	Cost 1983
Squad Helicopter	250K	1.0M	7.6M
Armed Helicopter	500K	3.5M	15.0M
Main Battle Tank	250K	1.2M	2.6M
Personnel Carrier	60K	0.2M	1.5M

mate effect of a decade of inflation on the costs of the older equipment, and then a direct comparison of the old and new in today's dollars. Without doubt, the new generation of equipment is more capable than the old. No judgments are made here as to the wisdom of acquiring such high-value equipment for the army. But there can be little question that maintaining and operating such equipment will place special demands on the quality of army enlisted personnel. The new M-2 infantry fighting vehicle, for example, incorporates a turret, a device not found on the familiar M-113 armored personnel carrier. The M-1 tank is equipped with a turbine engine, and the AH-64 armed helicopter with millions of dollars worth of electro-optical and other electronic equipment. These devices, while promising in their capability, will present some headaches to G.I. Joe—and to G.I. Joe's bosses.

Little can be done to recreate the results of the 1960s when the army actually had substantial numbers of college graduates in its enlisted ranks. But something might be done about attracting more college and trade-school *bound* youth, which would be the next best thing, perhaps by offering shorter enlistments with educational benefits. An alternative might be considered also that would bring people into the army after they have completed a trade-school program or even a college degree with government financial support. To do so might require the army to pay a somewhat higher price in annual turnover, though the enlistees involved would almost certainly experience low attrition rates, offsetting somewhat the theoretical increase in turnover.

Leadership, problem solving, peer assistance, and especially the growing complexity of modern weapons require that the services have a reasonable number of higher level enlisted personnel, particularly those bound for post-high-school education either in technical trade schools or in college. The future voluntary option must provide for a sustained reversal of the army's trends of the past five years.

Quality—Careerists

Great care is needed in the selection and retention of those who become military careerists—the part of the force that is truly volunteer. This involves the complex equation that connects retention goals with career progression, promotion opportunity, grade distribution, and cost. The major concern in recent years has been the premature loss of technical specialists and seasoned leaders with eight to twelve years of experience. Recent pay increases for the middle enlisted grades and incentive pay for specialists (and no doubt high unemployment) apparently are solving the problem now at that level. Other options that could be explored to enhance careerist retention include improving quality of life for members and their families. Like recruiting, retention can encounter cyclical problems, and thus this aspect of quality must be watched carefully. However, monetary incentives are the key, and one can only assume that the Congress will be willing to pay what is needed.

Personnel Management

Attrition—Unprogrammed first-term losses. It was predicted by the Gates Commission that the PMVF would result in longer terms of service than would a conscription-based system, and thus that turnover would be reduced and stability increased. This was to provide a greater return on the training investment, and to increase average experience levels. In a determined effort to achieve these benefits the DoD decreed in 1975 that the minimum active duty PMVF first-enlistment term be increased from two to three years.

Not all of the predicted benefits in reduced turnover have been realized because of high first-term attrition rates. The high attrition rates are necessary to assure quality in the force. The rates are high largely as a result of lack of preparation and motivation and of incompatibility with military life on the part of many recruits. Since conscription is not involved there is no practical legal bar to early termination of an enlistment contract, by either party; the services are not eager to, nor should they have to retain misfits and malcontents. Thus, they pay a price for the high attrition in additional resources for recruiting, training, and counseling activities.

But, readiness also suffers because of unplanned personnel turnover. About one-quarter of the attrition in the army occurs during the initial training period of about three months; these losses can be treated statistically "in bulk" since no personnel assignments to actual unit billets are affected. But once assigned to units, early discharges are random losses that disrupt unit readiness and cohesion.

Table 7.4 shows the overall effect of early discharges on average active-duty terms of service for the army for those who entered service in FY 1978. Assuming that attrition were spread evenly within the years, the average term of service so far for the 1978 year group is only 2.4 years. (The 2.4 average will move up slightly as four-year enlistees in the FY 1978 cohort

Table 7.4. Army Attrition Losses.

Nonprior Service Enlistments	(000)	Percent Loss (Cumulative)
Number entering during FY78	124	—
Number remaining at end of 12 mos.	100	19
Number remaining at end of 24 mos.	88	29
Number remaining at end of 36 mos.	81	35

serve part or all of their fourth year.) And, as noted, fully one-third did not complete the three-year minimum enlistment, of which over half were random losses from units. High attrition is costly, whether it occurs during training or afterward. But large numbers of unprogrammed losses are particularly disruptive in units, where they affect unit training, cohesion, teamwork, and readiness. Personnel management then tends to be a chaotic rather than a predictable process.

Careerist Turnover. Turnover in the higher enlisted grades has been a problem, as noted earlier. The services have been losing their middle-management leaders and technical specialists at rates beyond their ability to produce them. The recent series of compensation improvements seems to be overcoming this problem. Unless there are other significant disincentives or unless pay is allowed to lag again, turnover among careerists should be manageable. That is the assumption of this chapter.

Married Members and Dependents. The army has experienced a 50 percent increase in the percentage of junior enlistees who are married. Dependent allowances, benefits, and relatively high pay for first-termers under the PMVF may be providing the incentives that are causing the trend. In addition, the army is finding that many single members have dependents. It estimates that there are now 25,000 such members. One-third of these are female, which means that one out of every eight females in the army's enlisted force is a single with a dependent.

The large increase in the number of enlistees with dependents has substantially changed the personnel management challenge and the character of the army. Fewer enlistees live in the barracks, which has an undesirable impact on unit cohesion and esprit de corps. Families have difficulty living "on the economy," both overseas and in high cost-of-living areas of the United States, e.g., Washington, D.C. Single members with dependents create requirements for day care. The resulting complications in personnel management are felt by unit commanders up and down the line, adding to their leadership burdens.

The army also estimates that there are about 27,000 in-service marriages, including 11,000 couples with children. The army is concerned whether those couples with children, and single members with dependents are really mobilization assets.

The Congress, in its concern about the growing number of dependents, has even legislated a limit on the total number of dependents in Europe, in an attempt to discourage the trends there. However, that approach doesn't deal with the fundamentals. Clearly the PMVF is providing incentives that encourage early marriages, in-service marriages, and singles with dependents. To the extent these trends work to the disadvantage of military effectiveness and readiness, the incentives should be modified.

Matching Enlistment Terms and Tours of Duty. The army sustains a force of over 200,000 enlisted personnel overseas, primarily in Europe and South Korea. Since attrition during the first term of enlistment is high, and average terms of service are effectively reduced well below the "minimum" term of three years, the army could consider developing new enlistment options of shorter length specifically matched to the tour lengths in the overseas areas. For example, an enlistee assigned to Europe in the combat arms, where the commanders apparently prefer an 18-month tour for junior enlisted personnel, could be enlisted for 21 months, including three months for training. After his/her European tour, the recruit and the army would be spared a bobtailed assignment in a Continental United States (CONUS) unit, and upon discharge, the recruit would become an early asset for the IRR. An even shorter option (15 months) could be developed for South Korea, where the nominal tour is 12 months. The army could enlist just enough in these special options to meet entry-level junior enlisted needs in those two theaters, thereby reducing the turbulence within CONUS combat forces. Shorter periods of enlistment probably would cut down substantially on random attrition losses. In effect, the early "attrition" would be built into the program through short enlistments but in a way that would be predictable and that would start building up the IRR. Of course, an important point also, is much shorter periods of enlistment might appeal to a wider spectrum of youth, particularly if coupled with educational benefits.

Summary. One must deal with the complicated and costly phenomena of high attrition, and the increased tendency for first-term enlistees to have or to acquire dependents, as one looks to the future of the voluntary option. The direction must be to find new initiatives to reduce attrition, to discourage dependency status for junior enlisted personnel, and to consider a system of shorter enlistment options (for the army particularly) that matches terms of service to tours of duty for first termers and might be more attractive to college bound and trade-school bound youth.[3]

Force effectiveness is reduced by anything that adds to the administrative burden of the unit commander. Higher attrition does so because of the amount of counseling and processing required, not to mention the need for added unit training. The higher incidence of married junior enlisted personnel and single members with dependents does so as well, particularly overseas. These also reduce flexibility in reassigning military personnel. Finally, without the enrichment of the force brought by reasonable numbers of upward-bound, better-educated enlistees, the small unit commander has a far greater leadership and administrative task on his hands. He simply has fewer people he can depend on to solve problems and assist the slower learners.

Quality of Life

In the minds of military members and their families, perhaps the three most important factors bearing on quality of life are adequate compensation, traditional fringe benefits, and adequate housing and living conditions. Compensation levels are now receiving the attention they deserve. Traditional benefits have given way as a sometimes painful trade-off for higher compensation (compared to the subsistence levels of 20 years ago). However, the situation concerning housing and living conditions, particularly for married and single junior enlisted personnel with dependents, is not satisfactory. The problem should not (and probably won't) be solved simply by building more housing or raising allowances; rather, the incentives now built into the system that appear to encourage junior enlisted personnel to acquire dependents should be changed.

Representation. In this country certain segments of our society have been systematically excluded from full enjoyment of privileges guaranteed by the Constitution, not the least of which are equal rights to education and employment. Young members of such groups often find that their only viable option for employment is the military, a phenomenon that, while ostensibly involving voluntary choices, could be described as a form of economic conscription. Inevitably, such groups become "overrepresented" in the PMVF precisely because they are "underrepresented" in the civilian sector of employment.

Simultaneously, segments of American society are passing up the opportunity to share in the volunteer military experience. To put it less euphemistically, better-educated, upward-bound white youths seem to be failing to carry their share of the load in supporting the volunteer program, particularly in the army.

Overrepresentation in the volunteer force is viewed by some as acceptable since it provides opportunity for groups that typically suffer high unemployment rates and have few if any other employment choices. But others take a different view. They question the basic fairness of having a military force of which the disadvantaged and less able have become a disproportionate part committed to preserve the institutions and freedom dear to *all* segments of our society.

The Defense Department can do little to change public attitudes regarding patriotism and the sense of duty to serve. It is the public that must resolve the representation issue. However, with the help and understanding of the

Congress, DoD *can* change its enlistment program to make it more attractive to a wider range of American youth. It should strive to do so.

Mobilization. The continuing debate about the PMVF tends to focus on the active forces. As noted, there are issues there that must be honestly addressed. However, they tend to obscure two structural deficiencies in the readiness posture of the military manpower program. One is the lack of a viable emergency draft law. The other is the major quantitative deficiency in the voluntary program; the IRR shortfall. Today, if the nation had to mobilize and deploy large-scale conventional forces into combat on short notice, the army would encounter a major shortage of reserve manpower available for recall. The current voluntary program simply is not configured to meet reserve manpower needs. There would also be major problems in reinstituting conscription if needed for a long-term crisis.

Enough has been said here about the draft law as modified by court decisions, but perhaps a full explanation of the IRR problem is needed.

Because thousands of active-duty support units were inactivated after the Vietnam War, the services now depend to an unprecedented degree upon the Ready Reserve to provide on Mobilization Day essential firepower and support units and a pool of pretrained replacements and augmentees. This is what former Secretary of Defense Melvin Laird aptly dubbed the Total Force concept—the meaningful and clear-cut dependence on the Reserve Components to help meet national military requirements. The Ready Reserve must be up to strength in peacetime or the nation's major war plans can't be implemented. (Indeed, there is some question as to whether the Army's Reserve Components can meet their current rapid mobilization and deployment requirements even under ideal circumstances.)

Today there are manpower shortages in many reserve units, particularly units of the Army National Guard and Army Reserve. However, the major quantitative military manpower shortfall is found not in the units, but in the IRR. As noted earlier, the Army IRR is a reserve pool of veterans of the active and reserve component forces who have a residual military obligation and are subject to recall. The general public knows very little about the IRR and its critical role in mobilization preparedness.

Few army tactical units, active or reserve, are manned in peacetime at 100 percent of wartime strength. About 10 percent of their wartime billets are not needed for peacetime training. To fill them in peacetime would be wasteful, and probably boring for soldiers assigned to such jobs. Thus when the army calculates its active and reserve peacetime manning requirements, it omits filling these spaces.

In a fast-breaking military emergency, however, these vacant positions must be filled so that the units can deploy at wartime strength. Augmentees to fill these vacancies can only come from an *existing* supply of trained and experienced soldiers. There will be no time to train new volunteers or draftees before the units deploy. The draft mechanism and the training apparatus cannot deliver large numbers of newly trained personnel for several months.

Moreover, in addition to the individuals needed to bring units to wartime strength, the army needs still more pretrained personnel to replace combat casualties in the early months of a conflict. These replacements also would be needed — in a fast-breaking war — well before large numbers of newly inducted or enlisted recruits could be assembled and trained. This, to a degree, is a "new" requirement, dictated by the assumed need for rapid deployment capability of large-scale forces and the possible early engagement of these forces in intense combat.

Another requirement for individuals from a pool would be generated by an increase in the personnel pipeline, a requirement that is hard to predict but inevitable because of the travel and delays associated with a rapid mobilization, or, indeed, with any major enlargements of the force. And any units suffering manpower shortages against desired peacetime manning levels must be filled up as well.

The pool that nominally should supply these needs for trained individuals — the IRR — comprises men (and now women) who, having served on active duty or in a reserve unit, are inactive[4] but still have a portion of their statutory military obligation remaining from their original voluntary enlistments. The length of this military obligation, established in the draft era, is six years. Significantly, it was *not* set as a parameter specifically tailored to the dynamics of the PMVF begun in 1973. The demands of the PMVF are very different from the draft. The six-year obligation is thus an anachronism.

During the Vietnam War, the army's IRR pool was huge because there were many people coming out of the army each year. The active army itself was large (twice as large as now), turnover was high because draft calls were substantial, and many draftees served only 18 months on active duty. Upon being discharged they were in the IRR pool for four years or more.

But now, the large numbers of Vietnam veterans have completed their six-year military obligation. They are out of the IRR. And the number of people leaving the services each year is much smaller. The forces are smaller and, under the volunteer force, the services impose longer minimum terms of active-duty service for first enlistments, thereby reducing the average amount of time service people have left under the six-year blanket obligation when they complete their enlistments. (While there is also high turnover due to attrition losses, most of those discharged early during their first enlistment as a result of lack of aptitude or compatibility are also excused from their six-year obligation and thus are not assigned to the IRR.) Consequently, the IRR pool has shrunk dramatically.

As early as 1975 it was known that corrective action was needed then to prevent an IRR shortfall from developing that would reach alarming proportions by 1980. In fact, defense officials, testifying before the House Armed Services Committee in January 1976, predicted that a trained manpower shortfall of 250,000 would develop by 1980[5] if action were not taken soon to initiate policies to augment the IRR. No action was taken, and the prediction proved all too accurate; as noted earlier, the army is now short about 250,000 trained individuals who can only be furnished by the IRR. The additional number needed in the IRR to provide the 250,000 could be as high as 360,000, assuming, for example, a 70 percent show rate.

The Defense Department recently began some modest administrative actions to expand the IRR pool, among them broadening the six-year obligation to include women, and terminating the practice of allowing obligated veterans to transfer from the IRR to the Standby Reserve (a less accessible category of obligated veterans). However, neither of these actions really has helped significantly in meeting requirements. The greatest need for trained individuals is in combat jobs. Women do not qualify, and obligated individuals in the Standby Reserve are available for recall under emergency conditions anyway and are already counted as assets. DoD has also tried with a bonus plan to induce IRR obligers to "reenlist" in the IRR when their obligations expire, and has offered some new enlistees the option of entering the IRR directly after completing active-duty training. Neither program has been marked with success or complete support.

Without an adequate reservoir of trained individuals available for recall, the army simply is not ready to meet the very contingencies that are used to justify the size, composition, hardware programs, and budgetary cost of our conventional forces—those elements that account for the vast majority of our expenditures on defense (with the cost now approaching $250 billion annually) and around which our major war plans are built. Thus, effective initiatives are needed to replenish the IRR or in some other way to meet mobilization needs for pretrained manpower.

ENLISTMENT OPTIONS

Introduction

It was noted in the previous section on criteria that it might be possible to increase the attractiveness of military service to college and trade-school bound youth by considering a series of shorter-term enlistment options. If successful, this alternative would improve quality, simplify personnel management by matching terms of active service to tours of duty, and improve representation by drawing on part of the youth population not being reached now. It was also noted that initiatives were needed to replenish and sustain the IRR, both now and in the long term. The following paragraphs offer some specific possibilities.

The options deal first with the major quantitative problem in the IRR, and then with the basic enlistment program for active and reserve forces. The army is again chosen as an example, both for the reasons mentioned at the outset, and also because the army probably requires the greatest array of options. It appears that the other services, if interested, could adopt the options laid out for the army, with no interservice compatibility problems. However, those interested in (and possessing) stability and satisfied with their current programs (e.g., the air force) might not opt for them.

Mobilization Needs: The IRR

A permanent (though long-term) solution to the IRR problem is available that costs virtually nothing. It is to increase the statutory military obligation for new enlistees from the current period of six years to ten years. The change would be in keeping with the volunteer concept, and, indeed, was suggested as long ago as 1976. It is not logical to depend on volunteers to meet only *some* categories of military manpower needs; the "all-volunteer" concept must meet *all* needs, including those of the IRR pool of trained and experienced veterans. A six-year total obligation doesn't "fit" the PMVF concept because it doesn't meet all of the needs. A ten-year obligation would. It would produce an additional input to the army's IRR of about 80,000 per year after the sixth year, and by the end of the tenth year would have added at least 320,000, substantially erasing the deficit. The steady-state size of the IRR would then approach 500,000, apparently the size needed. Thus, the selection of ten years for the new obligation is directly related to the trained manpower pool requirement. If the pool requirement was smaller, the obligation could be made shorter. If the pool requirement was larger, then ten years would not be enough.

Most major countries (and many small ones) impose a much longer military obligation than does the United States, extending even beyond age 40. The ten-year obligation proposed here would be over by age 28–30 for most enlistees. No combat veterans would be involved—only veterans of the peacetime volunteer force, active or reserve, and only new enlistees.

Some have said that to lengthen the period of obligation might inhibit volunteer enlistments and thus endanger the viability of the PMVF. That concern not only has little validity, it is wrong-headed. First, the recall of IRR obligers would occur *only* under a dire national emergency. Most potential enlistees would assign that a low probability and would heavily discount it in a decision to enlist. Indeed, their near-term employment prospects are likely to be a much weightier matter. Second, the volunteer force is not a success unless it meets *all* needs, not just active-duty needs. The

PMVF is not meeting the needs of the reserve program, and if it can't be made to do so, it should be replaced by something that will. Indeed, *not* to deal with the IRR problem effectively is the real threat to the PMVF, not an increase in the military obligation.

Is a soldier who has been out of uniform for five years or more a viable mobilization asset? Apparently he is in Europe. Why not in the United States? And what is the alternative?

The volunteer concept we have today is clearly deficient in meeting our needs for reserve manpower and is rightly subject to hard criticism for that reason. Volunteer force advocates should be proposing legislation today to lengthen the obligations for new enlistees. Moreover, those who favor a return to peacetime conscription also should favor an increase in the military obligation, since even peacetime conscription would not cure the IRR problem unless draft calls were large and terms of service short.

In the near term, the army should be authorized to pay current IRR obligers a substantial bonus to reenlist in the IRR. Even though the same result could have been achieved for free if action had been taken six years ago to lengthen the obligation, a bonus now appears to be the only practical short-term fix. An alternative — direct enlistment in the IRR — is extremely costly and merely stockpiles training-base graduates who have never served in military units and trained as team members.

The final plea for extending the military obligation for future enlistees is based on a sense of fair play. Obviously, a large pool of inactive, trained, and experienced recent veterans of the peacetime force exists, whether or not such individuals are in the IRR with a formal, residual military obligation to complete. In a dire emergency under which the nation's vital interests were at stake — a massive surprise attack on NATO forces in Western Europe, for example — the president and the Congress would have no alternative but to make up any IRR deficit by recalling unobligated veterans *involuntarily* through special legislation passed at the time of the crisis. Because action was not taken by Congress in 1976, that is the alternative we now face, and veterans should be told as much. In the near term, IRR members vulnerable to involuntary recall should have the voluntary option of obligating themselves for an additional four years in exchange for a bonus. But, for the future it would seem only fair to inform prospective active and reserve enlistees ahead of time — when they first sign on the dotted line — of the possibility of being recalled from inactive status for as many years as security requirements dictate, following their completion of an active-duty or reserve enlistment. That can be done most fairly by increasing the military obligation now to ten years for new enlistees — ten years being the best guess at what the obligation needs to be if the manpower requirement is to be met. Then each enlistee would know exactly what he or she may expect *before* making the commitment to military service.

Once the IRR is on the road to recovery in quantitative terms, the army must manage it just as they manage the active manpower program. Requirements by skill must be determined, and compared with assets. Availability criteria must be established and enforced. This is no small undertaking, but it is a logical extension of the military objectives set for America's conventional forces.

First-Term Enlistment Quantity, Quality, Representation, and Personnel Management

To attract higher quality and college or trade-school bound youth into the army to improve significantly the quality spread, and to reach those socio-economic groups not participating in the PMVF in proportional numbers requires significant changes in (or additions to) the enlistment conditions and incentives now being offered. There are two things that can be tried: Shorten active-duty enlistment terms, and increase educational benefits. At the same time, to reduce cost and to mitigate some significant personnel management problems, pay for new short-term enlistees could be reduced,[6] and enlistee skill and assignment options curtailed for the short enlistments. Active-duty enlistment terms could be matched to assignment tours as outlined earlier. Dependent allowances would not be authorized for enlistees on short enlistments, say those of less than three years.

Table 7.5 presents a series of illustrative enlistment options for the army. The series is designed to do several things:

1. Provide a limited-length active-duty enlistment option and a reserve enlistment option aimed at attracting college or trade-school bound youth. Assignment to skill and location would be at the convenience of the service.
2. Provide generous postservice educational benefits for the short active-duty enlistments in proportion to time served. Educational benefits for the reservists would be earned simultaneously with satisfactory performance in a National Guard or Reserve Unit, but would also require a year of active duty following completion of the education program. The educational benefits for both active and reserve options would include tuition support, fees, and subsistence for living expenses at the school of choice. Current educational benefits for the three- and four-year active enlistments would not be changed, i.e., the Veterans Educational Assistance Program (VEAP)[7] would remain as the incentive for the longer enlistment terms.
3. Match active-duty terms of service with the imperatives of personnel management, particularly those having to do with regulated tours overseas, such as the 12-month tour in South Korea or the desired 18-month (or even 24-month) tour in Europe for first-termers.

Table 7.5. Army PMVF Enlistment Options.

Enlistment Term	Total Obligation	Specialty Or Skill	Tour Assignment	Dependent Allowances	Educational Benefits[1]	Compensation	Housing
Active							
1. 12 mos. plus training	10 yrs.	Service convenience	12 mos., Korea	No	2 academic yrs. postservice	Subsistence level	Barracks
2. 18 mos. plus training	10 yrs.	Service convenience	18 mos., Europe	No	3 academic yrs. postservice	Subsistence level	Barracks
3. 24 mos. plus training	10 yrs.	Service convenience	12 mos., CONUS plus 12 mos., KOREA; or 24 mos., Europe or CONUS	No	4 academic yrs. postservice	Subsistence level	Barracks
4. 3 yrs.	10 yrs.	Limited options	Options	Yes	Current VEAP	Regular	Regular options
5. 4 yrs. or more	10 yrs.	Full options	Options	Yes	Current VEAP	Regular	Regular options
Reserve Components							
6. 6 yrs.	10 yrs.	Service convenience	4 yrs. in a unit near school, followed by 1 year on active duty	N/A	4 academic yrs. concurrent with satisfactory service in a unit	Subsistence level during drills and active duty	N/A
7. 6 yrs.	10 yrs.	Limited options	6 yrs. in a unit, less training time	N/A	None	Regular	N/A

[1]Tuition support, fees, and subsistence at school of choice.

4. Offset the cost of (somewhat) higher turnover and educational benefits by reducing the active-duty and drill-pay compensation level for those in the program, and by not authorizing the service members serving the short terms (less than three years) dependent allowances.

To meet these objectives, the active enlistment options would have to break with the long-standing, but outdated, tradition of keying enlistments to integral numbers of years. Instead, the training time, whatever its length, would be an additive to the basic active term, permitting the service to improve personnel rotation planning. The options would be open to both men and women, though quotas might be necessary to assure balance among the skills the army needs at any given time, particularly in regard to the combat arms.

Because the preponderance of those electing to enlist for the shorter periods would go into the combat arms — the skills that have the shortest training schedules — the training time would fit into the summer time frame. Thus, for the active-duty option, a high-school graduate could go immediately into a training program following graduation, complete training by the end of the summer, begin the effective period of active-duty service in a unit, and complete the ensuing 12-month, 18-month, or 24-month term and begin postservice education in the corresponding fall or spring semesters. This works to the convenience of both the service and the individual. Obviously, a short-term enlistee who wanted to shift to a longer period of enlistment could be given the option to do so at any time; however, in so doing, the enlistee would forego any additional educational benefits (other than VEAP) in exchange for the higher active-duty pay and other benefits associated with the "regular" enlistments.

A side-benefit of the short enlistments would be an earlier buildup in the IRR. For example, enlistees selecting the one-year (plus training time) option would enter the IRR as early as 15 months after enlistment. The buildup rate would of course depend on the mix of enlistment terms.

The reserve enlistee, like the active enlistee, would enter active-duty training upon graduation from high school. Upon completion of the training period (as short as three months for a combat specialty, or longer for a hard skill), he (or she) would enter school and also start serving in a nearby Reserve or National Guard unit. As long as his military performance was satisfactory, he would be paid the monthly educational benefits, and could go to school for as long as four years. He would then serve one year on active duty, and then serve out the remainder of his 10-year military obligation in the IRR. If the program were well subscribed, the army could exercise approval of his field of study at school to try to correlate it to his military specialty. This could be particularly helpful to the army in the hard skill areas and especially for trade-school students.

As noted, for these special enlistment options, active-duty and reserve-duty pay would be pegged at a subsistence level to offset educational costs and to discourage the acquisition of dependents for those on active duty. The reserve enlistment option would also have to be carefully designed to be compatible with the ROTC program. For example, a cross-over option from one to the other might be desirable.

The army's training base capacity (or at least, annual throughput) would have to be expanded to meet the somewhat higher training load associated with the shorter terms of service. Offsetting this need to some degree would be an expected reduction in failure rates during training as a result of faster-learning recruits. Also, because the higher load would occur during the summer months, a surge capability might be available using the Army Reserve Training Divisions more extensively during their summer training periods. In any case, a larger training throughput potential could be regarded as an important mobilization readiness asset.

The points below summarize the key quantitative effects of the new active-duty enlistment options in a steady-state situation, assuming that they were found sufficiently attractive to meet the army's annual needs for junior enlisted personnel in South Korea and Europe (about 39,000) who deploy directly from the training base:[8]

1. Army annual NPS enlistments would increase from 120,000 to about 140,000. Of the total, 41,000 would be in the new short-term options.
2. Army total strength would increase about 22,000 (including overhead).
3. The percentage of NPS enlistees who are above average (Category I, II, and IIIA) would increase to 55 percent, and there would be many more of them in the first-term force because annual accessions would be higher as well.
4. The percentage of NPS enlistees who have high-school diplomas would be maintained at 80 percent, much higher than the average achieved in recent years, and as in #3 there would be many more in the force.
5. The buildup in the army IRR would be faster and ultimately would top out at a level higher than would be obtained without the short-term enlistment program. Without an increase in the total military obligation, the IRR strength would settle out at 260,000, compared with 150,000 based on the current mix of three- and four-year enlistments (and assuming nothing else were done to keep people in the IRR). But with an increase to ten years in the military obligation, the total IRR would reach 570,000 and, importantly, would be richer in combat skills, the skills really needed.
6. The annual costs of the additional manpower, training, and educational benefits for the active force would total about $435 million. The savings in base pay and dependent allowances would total perhaps $320 million, assuming a subsistence pay level of $200/month (which compares with the regular compensation level of about $550/month for new army en-

listees). Thus, the cost impact is estimated at $115 million annually, far less than the sums normally associated with a "GI Bill".

7. The effects on quality of life would be positive since there would be less competition for on- and off-base housing and post facilities (clubs, commissaries, recreational activities). The number of dependents could be reduced by as many as 40,000, or about 20 percent of the army's current total of dependents. Most of this would occur in Europe, moreover, and thus could cause a major reduction in family problems with which the soldiers, NCOs, and officers must deal.

One unresolved issue regarding an initiative to increase turnover for the sake of improving quality is the impact it would have on the army's desire to emphasize unit cohesion and to return to the regimental concept – to move away from a personnel management system that emphasizes individual replacements, and to move toward unit replacements to support overseas deployments. At first, the two would seem to be antithetical. However, the army will always have a fair measure of turnover in the first-term enlisted force due to attrition (now one-third during the first-term). Thus, the idea of a unit replacement or rotation system will work best for careerists who are more stable as members of the force. Whether the use of large numbers of short-termers (those who enter the army to serve at low pay, earn their educational benefits, and leave) would be disruptive to the army's new goal or actually might fit quite well, requires careful study. The answer is not obvious. In any case, the army would benefit greatly from having many more higher quality enlistees, a point of great importance as it modernizes its forces with high-technology equipment.

Finally, one cannot predict the effect on representation other than in the dimension of quality. That impact would be determined largely by the economy, by the expansion of employment opportunities for blacks in the private sector, and by the national sense of duty to serve.

SPECIFIC RECOMMENDATIONS

Any reasonable assessment of the military manpower program suggests that several specific actions should be taken to strengthen the Peacetime Military Volunteer Force and to improve the mobilization preparedness of the manpower program:

1. The law regarding military enlistment terms should be changed to permit enlistments for periods other than an integral number of years.
2. The Military Service Obligation for new active and reserve enlistees should be increased to ten years.
3. The army should be authorized the use of a reenlistment bonus for members of the IRR.

4. The army should establish a management program for the IRR that assures a thorough knowledge of requirements by skill, inventory by skill, and member availability, and incorporates an extensive program of pre-assignment of IRR members to active and reserve units.
5. Emergency legislation should be drafted permitting the recall of recent but unobligated veterans to be used in case of a severe national emergency to meet any needs for pretrained individuals not met by the IRR.
6. A new emergency draft law should be enacted that in the eyes of the courts narrows the definition of conscientious objection and corrects other known defects to assure that the draft, if reinstituted (in a time of national emergency), would be effective in meeting the needs of the military forces.
7. The services should be authorized to offer a new active-duty enlistment program, to supplement regular options, that consists of an enlistment term of one to two years of active service preceded by as much active-duty time as is needed for basic and skill training. Legislation should be enacted to reward successful performers in this program with two to four academic years of postservice education (at a ratio of two years of education for each year of active duty served after completion of training) at an accredited institution, with the government paying tuition support (up to a maximum amount), fees, and modest subsistence allowance. Active-duty pay for these enlistees should be reduced by law to a miminum subsistence level, and dependent allowances should not be authorized for them. Such enlistees while on active duty should have the option, if qualified, of switching to regular longer-term enlistment options with regular pay and benefits, and to retain whatever educational benefits had been earned at the time of transfer.
8. The services should be authorized to offer a new Reserve Component enlistment program, to supplement regular options, that requires two to four years of effective service in a Reserve Component unit preceded by as much active-duty time as is needed for basic and skill training. Legislation should be enacted to reward successful performers in this program with two to four academic years of concurrent education or training at an accredited institution, with the government paying tuition support (up to a maximum amount), fees, and a modest subsistence allowance. Active-duty and drill pay for these Reserve Component enlistees should be reduced by law to a minimum subsistence level, and dependent allowances should not be authorized for them. The service should also have the option of approving the major field of study selected by the enlistee. Following completion of the educational program, the enlistee should serve one year on active duty at full pay and allowances, in whatever grade and specialty were earned in the Reserve Components. Such enlistees should have the option, if service needs

permit, of shifting to ROTC with a possible additional active-duty obligation.

9. The government should strive to end the piecemeal attacks on military fringe benefits by completing a comprehensive evaluation of these benefits and including their value in a new index of total military compensation. This is needed, not only to educate service members as to the real potential value of the military compensation program (including retirement), but also to permit reasonable comparisons with similarly constructed civilian pay indices, if civilian pay levels are to continue to be used as a basis for adjusting military pay.

10. The army's heavy dependence upon its Reserve Components should be examined to determine whether rapid mobilization and deployment goals can be met even under ideal circumstances, much less while faced with chronic lack of support, particularly in the area of logistics.

IN CONCLUSION

One must recognize that whatever "the analysis" says about the needs of the military manpower program and whatever steps are taken over the years to try to meet them, much of what will happen ultimately will depend on perceptions, particularly those held by American youth and their families. The government has a continuing obligation to report the facts without embellishment. There is a tendency for the executive branch (not just now but in the past as well), to give more emphasis to the *defense* of the military manpower program than to the *explanation* of it and its importance to readiness. The PMVF is *not* DoD's program or the administration's program. It is America's program. It is the public, informed by the government, who must defend and rationalize it. And it is then the public who ultimately must change it, and indeed *can* change it, if there are things about it they do not like.

APPENDIX: THE EFFECTS OF
SHORTER ACTIVE-DUTY TERMS OF SERVICE

A. *Objective.* To determine the effects that a two-track system of NPS accessions would have on the army.

B. *System Description.* Under the AVF, achieve an NPS mix which accepts a mix of short-term (ST) enlistments and long-term (LT) enlistments.

• Short-term enlistments will be for one year plus training time, limited to the number needed to fill the need for replacements to Korea directly from Advanced Individual Training (AIT)

and

For 18 months plus training time limited to the number needed to fill the need for replacements to Europe directly from AIT.

- LT enlistments of three and four years to make up remainder.
- Details of short-term enlistments:
  - Must be HSDG, Mental Category (MC) I–IIIA
  - Will be paid base pay of $200/month and no dependent or bachelor allowances
  - Will have no options as to skill or station
  - Eligible for two academic years postservice (college level) schooling (12-month plus training) or three academic years (18 months and training)
- Details of long-term enlistments: Same as today

C. *Effects to be Assessed.* All at Steady State

1. The resultant size of NPS accession requirements
2. The resultant size of the army
3. Cost
4. Change in quality of accessions
5. Study of IRR at alternative military obligated service (MOS)

D. *Computational Procedure.* We will attempt to make the analysis based on trained strength man-years as the prime tool for comparison.

1. *General*

Step 1 — Compute the trained strength man-years delivered by army NPS accessions in a typical future year.

Step 2 — Compute the trained strength man-years required in Korea and Europe from short-term enlistees and convert to short-term NPS accessions and man-years delivered.

Step 3 — Determine man-years to be delivered by long-term NPS accessions (1–2 above), and compute long-term NPS accession requirements.

Step 4 — Determine added NPS accessions needed by short-term/long-term mix of recruits/soldiers in the army and total NPS accessions required.

Step 5 — Determine added trainers required to handle added trainees and add Transients, Holdees, and Students to arrive at probable army end strength needed.

Step 6 — Cost the increases and savings likely.

Step 7 — Determine the change in educational level, mental category, and racial mix of typical NPS accession cohort.

Step 8 — Determine the effect on the IRR with current six year and possible eight and ten year MOS.

2. *Step 1* — Compute the trained strength man-years delivered by army NPS accessions in a typical future year.

a. Fact: Army NPS accessions over the next several years will run about 120,000 of which 103,000 will be males and 17,000 females.

b. Assumptions:
— ¼ of the enlistments will be for four years.
— ¾ of the enlistments will be for three years.
— The quality mix and racial mix will be as it was in the FY78 cohort so that losses will run the same.[9]

FY78 CUMULATIVE LOSSES (%)

TIME	LOSSES	
YEAR 0–1	17.6	
0–2	26.3	
0–3	31.6	
0–4	33.3	(ESTIMATED)

— Training will take an average of three months.
— Losses in training will equal 50 percent of first-year losses.

c. Computations[10] show that the three- and four-year first-termers will deliver 277,300 trained strength man-years. And that is what our mixed schedule of short-term/long term must deliver each year.

3. *Step 2*— Compute trained strength man-years required in Korea and Europe from short-term enlistees and convert to short-term NPS accessions required.

a. Fact: In the 12-month period ending September 30, 1981, the following first-termers were sent overseas to the places shown directly from AIT. This was a typical, not an unusual, year.

Europe	34,400	
Korea	4,500	
TOTAL	38,900	Trained Strength

b. Assumptions:
— Training will take 3 months.
— The Europe fill will be for 1½ years there.
— The Korea fill will be for one year there.
— All will be HSDG, MC I–IIIA
— Short-term enlistments will split by sex 86 percent male and 14 percent female.

c. Fact: Historical losses among HSDG, MC I–IIIA are as follows for first three years.

Male	22 percent
Female	42 percent

About one half of the losses occur the first year and one half of these occur in the first three months of training.

About 80 percent of the losses occur in the first two years.

d. Computations[11] show that we annually must bring in

Males	35,401
Females	6,085
	41,486

Total to cover training losses and to deliver 38,900 AIT graduates to Korea and Europe.

THUS: Short-t rm NPS annual accessions must be 41,486.

e. Computations[12] show that these 41,486 short-term enlistees will deliver 52,630 trained strength man-years at steady state.

4. *Step 3*: Determine MY to be delivered by LT enlistments and LT NPS accession requirements.

a. Computations
* From Step 1, we need annually 277,300 TS first-term MY
* From Step 2, the ST enlistees will produce 52,630 TS between MY
* We lack, therefore, 277.3K − 52.6K or 224.7K TS MY
* This 224,700 TS MY will be made up of three- & four-year enlistees.

b. Fact: From Step 1, 120,000 annual accessions deliver 277,300 TS MY or $\frac{277,300}{120,000}$ = 2.31083 MY per accession.

We will use this as a factor.

c. Computation:

$$\frac{224,700}{2.31083} = \frac{97,238}{} \text{ three- \& four-year NPS enlistments needed}$$

5. *Step 4*: Determine added NPS accessions required by ST/LT program.
* From Step 2, ST NPS REQ = 41,486 say   41,500
* From Step 3, LT NPS REQ = 97,238 say   97,200

ANNUAL NPS ST/LT NPS REQ TOTAL 138,700

* Added REQ = ST/LT REQ − Current REQ
  Added REQ = 138.7 − 120 = 18,700 extra accessions/year

6. *Step 5*: Determine added trainers required
  Add transients, holdees, and students (THS)
  Compute Army End Strength required

a. Assumptions: Each extra trainee requires $\frac{1}{20}$ of a trainer
  THS will add 10 percent to all new added strength

b. Computations:

Extra NPS Accessions		18,700
Extra trainers	18,700/20 =	935
	TOTAL	19,635
THS 10%	=	1,964
		21,599 (say 21,600 increase in end strength)

7. *Step 6.* Cost the increases and savings
  a. Training Cost Add-on
    (1) Trainer MY
       $18,700 \times {}^3/_{12} \times \$15,000$ (assumed cost per = $70.1 M trainee MY)
    (2) Trainer MY
       $935 \times \$1060.50^* \times 12 = \$11.9$ M
       *Base Pay E-6 w/8 yrs service $11.9 M
    (3) Trainer dependent and other allowances
       $\$3000/yr \times 935 = \$2.8$ M $ 2.8 M

                         TOTAL TRAINING $84.8 M

  b. Other MY, (THS) Add on
    (1) $\{1964 \times \$1060.50 \times 12\} +$
       $\{\$3000 \times 1964\} = \$30.9$ M $30.9 M
  c. Educational Program—Add on
    (1) Assumptions: Only those who finish the 12 months and training will be eligible to receive the benefit of two academic years and only those finishing the 18 months and training will be eligible for three academic years.
       —Half of all the eligible people will use the full benefit; ⅓ will use ½ the benefit; ⅙ will use none.
       —Academic Costs = $5,000/yr. for college average
    (2) Fact: From calculations at note 12, we find the following:

NUMBER SUCCESSFUL COMPLETIONS OF ST

TOUR	NUMBER			BENEFIT
	Male	Female	Total	(years)
18 mos. & Trg.	26,519	3,572	30,091	3
12 mos. & Trg.	3,605	510	4,115	2

(3) *Calculations*

Cost = {$5000 × 3 × ½ × 30091} + {$5000 × 3 × ⅓ × ½ × 30091} +
{$5000 × 2 × ½ × 4115} + {$5000 × 2 × ⅓ × ½ × 4115} =
$328 M

   d. Other Costs:

—Extra clothing bags, administrative, transportation for increased end strength of 21,600

—Possibly a need for more or higher first-term reenlistment bonuses, since about 30% of all NPS accessions will be (we hope) college bound after their short enlistment.

SAVINGS—Base Pay

   (1) Facts: Referring to Steps 1 & 3, we find the following:

      —We will pay 277,300 T.S. MY first-termers if accessions are 120,000 over some time. These will be 3 & 4 year volunteers.

      —Under the ST/LT program the 277,300 T.S. will be furnished by:

LT people	224,700 MY
ST people	52,600 MY

   (2) Assumptions:

Base Pay of avg LT = E-3 at 2 yrs Svc. = $677.70/mo.

Base Pay of avg St = $200/mo.

   (3) Cost Computations[13] show a base pay savings of $302 M

   e. Other Savings

   (1) Dependency (housing, medical, transport, etc.)

     (a) We will be paying (277,300 − 224,700) = 52,600 fewer three- and four-year enlistees.

     (b) Thirty-one percent of them, or 16,306 are married and have at least one dependent.

     (c) There are also a large number of single parents.

     (d) It is not unreasonable to presume, therefore, about 2 × 16,000 or 32,000 dependents now receiving benefits, would not receive them under a LT/ST plan.

     (e) At only $500/yr/dependent, cost savings is $500 × 32,000 = $16 M

   (2) Size of and, hence, longevity pay in career force

   (3) Retirement pay due to smaller career force

   f. *Cost Reconciliation*

COSTS ($M)		SAVINGS ($M)	
• Trainee MY	$ 70.1	• Base Pay	$302
• Trainer MY	11.9	• Dependent Allow.	16

- Trainer Allow.   2.8
- Other MY Add-ons   30.9
- Educational Program   328.0

      TOTALS $443.7 $318

E. *Change in Quality of NPS Accessions*
  1. Assumptions
    - All ST are MCI–IIIA and distributed normally
    - MCI & II will be $^{39}/_{56}$ of total ST
    - MC III A will be $^{17}/_{56}$ of total ST
    - And 56 percent will be I–III A
    - Balance of accessions will be distributed as in FY78
  2. Calculations[14] permit the following comparison.

QUALITY COMPARISONS (%)

	FY75	FY78	FY81	ST/LT at Steady State	Change (%) Over FY78
MC I & II	35	21	24	35.6	+70
MC IIIA	23	16	16	20.3	+27
Above Avg.	58	37	40	55.9	
III B	31	23	29	16.1	−30
IV	10	39	31	27.3	
At least HSDG	58	74	80	81.8	+10.5

F. The IRR. We will compute the IRR at Steady State with 6, 8, and 10 years MOS.
  1. Facts: Residual obligations under 6, 8, 10 year MOS are:

	MOS (YRS)		
TERM OF ENLISTMENT	6	8	10
12 MOS + 3 MOS TNG	4¾	6¾	8¾
18 MOS + 3 MOS TNG	4¼	6¼	8¼
3 YEAR	3	5	7
4 YEAR	2	4	6

    - Assuming no attrition losses are put into the IRR, we see in note 12 that 30,091 of 18 MOS. + TNG. and 4,115 12 MOS. + TNG. complete their term of service. These, therefore, join the IRR.
  2. Assumption:
    - Assume no losses (for simplicity) within the IRR.

- Assume no short-term people reenlist (probably about 95–98%
  accurate).
3. Computations[15] permit the following table:

MAXIMUM BUILDUP OF IRR (000)

	MOS. (YR.)		
	6	8	10
From LT NPS Accessions	121.4	209.6	297.9
From ST NPS Accessions	136.8	205.2	273.6
TOTAL	258.2*	414.8	571.5

*This improvement is greater than it appears. If NPS accessions remain in 120,000 range, the
IRR will drop to about 150.

NOTES

1. Army, Navy, Air Force, Marine Corps, Coast Guard, Public Health Service (Uniformed
Members), National Oceanic and Atmospheric Administration (Commissioned Corps); Active
Forces, Selected Reserve Forces, and the pretrained Individual Ready Reserve (IRR).

2. See Chapter 5, *The All Volunteer Force Today—Mobilization Manpower* by Robert B.
Pirie, Jr.

3. The army already offers a limited number of 24-month enlistments for diploma graduates
in Categories I, II, or IIIA, and generally sends these enlistees to Europe upon completion of
training, and then discharges them upon completion of their overseas tours. The concept outlined here is an extension of that approach, though the author believes that the "available" recruit population would be expanded significantly and would reach new segments of society if
even shorter terms of active service were offered.

4. A limited number may return to active duty for two weeks each year for refresher
training.

5. Statement of Assistant Secretary of Defense (Manpower and Reserve Affairs), Hearings
Before the Subcommittee on Investigations, House Armed Services Committee, January 21,
1976.

6. Charles C. Moskos has also advanced the idea of reducing pay levels in exchange for
postservice educational benefits, thereby creating a "two-track" system.

7. Veterans Educational Assistance Program—a program under which the enlistee deposits
part of his earnings to an educational fund, and additional funds are deposited by the government. The army has now been authorized to offer more generous versions of the VEAP that it
hopes will attract significant numbers of HSDGs in Categories I, II, and IIIA.

8. The Appendix presents the supporting calculations.

9. FY78 is the last year on which we have three years of data. It had better quality than did
any of the following years although years FY74–76 were better.

10.   Total and Trained Strength Man-Years Delivered Annually by
                           NPS Accessions of 120,000

ENLISTMENTS (000)			LOSSES (000)				REMAINDER (000)		
TIME	3 YR.	4 YR.	TOT	RATE	3 YR.	4 YR.	TOT	3 YR.	4 YR.	TOT
0	90	30	120	0	0	0	0	90	30	120
0–⅓				0.176/2	7.92	2.64	10.56	82.08	27.36	109.44
0–1				0.176	15.84	5.28	21.12	74.16	24.72	98.88
0–2				0.263	23.67	7.89	31.56	66.33	22.11	88.44
0–3				0.316	28.44	9.48	37.92	61.56	20.52	82.08
0–4				0.333	N/A	10.00	10.00	N/A	20.00	20.00

MAN-YEARS DELIVERED BY YEAR (000)

TIME (YRS.)	COMPUTATIONS	TRAINEE MY	TS MY	TOTAL
0–⅓	$\dfrac{120 + 109.44}{2} \times \dfrac{3}{12} =$	28.68		
⅓–1	$\dfrac{109.44 + 98.88}{2} \times \dfrac{9}{12} =$		78.12	
1–2	$\dfrac{98.88 + 88.44}{2} \times 1 \;=$		93.66	
2–3	$\dfrac{88.44 + 82.08}{2} \times 1 \;=$		85.26	
3–4	$\dfrac{20.52 + 20}{2} \times 1 \;=$		20.26	
	TOTAL	28.68	277.3	305.98

11. Computation of NPS accession requirements to provide 38,900 trained strength to
Europe and Korea.

• LOSS RATES TO BE APPLIED (%)

TIME PERIOD (YR)	MALE	FEMALE
0	0	0
0–⅓	$\dfrac{22}{2 \times 2} = 5.5$	$\dfrac{42}{2 \times 2} = 10.5$
0–1	$\dfrac{22}{2} = 11$	$\dfrac{42}{2} = 21$
0–1⅓	$11 + \dfrac{17.6 - 11}{4} = 12.65$	$21 + \dfrac{33.6 - 21}{4} = 24.15$
0–1¾	15.95	30.45
0–2	$22 \times 0.8 = 17.6$	$42 \times 0.8 = 33.6$

• Given need for 38,900 trained strength,

Male need   = 38,900 × .86 = 33,454
Female need = 38,900 × .14 = 5,446

• Let M = Number of Male NPS accessions required + F = number female NPS
accessions required. Then

M − 0.055* M = 33,454; M =   35,401
F − 0.105* F = 5,446 F =   6,085
                              ———————
                              41,486

12.

Trained Strength Man-Years Delivered at Steady State by 41,486 Short-Term Enlistees

Time Pd.	Enlistments 41,486				Losses				Remaining at End of Period			
	1½ yr. + 3 mos. Training (36,687)		12 mos. + 3 mos. Training (4,799)		1½ yr. + 3 mos. Training		12 mos. + Training		1½ yr. + 3 mos. Training		12 mos. + 3 mos. Training	
	Male (86%)	Female (14%)	Male (86%)	Female (14%)	Male	Female	Male	Female	Male	Female	Male	Female
0	31,551	5,136	4,127	672	0	0	0	0	31,551	5,136	4,127	672
0–⅓	31,551	5,136	4,127	672	1,735	539	227	71	29,816	4,597*	3,900	601
0–1⅓	31,551	5,136	4,127	672	3,991	1,240	522	162	27,560	3,896	3,605	510
0–1¾	31,551	5,136	N/A	N/A	5,032	1,564	N/A	N/A	26,519	3,572	N/A	N/A

*Computed as follows: 31,551 − (31,551) (0.055)
See above for loss rates by period of time.

Trainee and Trained Strength Man-Years

0–⅓ (Trainee MY):
$$\frac{31,155 + 29,816}{2} \times \frac{3}{12} + \frac{5,136 + 4,597}{2} \times \frac{3}{12} + \frac{4,127 + 3,900}{2} \times \frac{3}{12} + \frac{672 + 601}{2} \times \frac{3}{12} = 10,050 \text{ MY}$$

0–1⅓ (TS MY):
$$\frac{29,816 + 27,560}{2} + \frac{4,597 + 3,896}{2} + \frac{3,900 + 3,605}{2} + \frac{601 + 510}{2} = 37,243 \text{ TS MY}$$

1⅓ to 1¾ (TS MY):
$$\frac{27,560 + 26,519}{2} \times \frac{1}{2} + \frac{3,896 + 3,572}{2} \times \frac{1}{2} = 15,387 \text{ TS MY}$$

$$\text{TOTAL} \quad 52,630$$

(footnote 11 continued)

*Training loss rates

- Split between Europe & Korea

$$\text{Europe} = \frac{34,400}{38,900} \times 41,486 = 36,387$$

$$\text{Korea} = \frac{4,500}{38,900} = 41,486 = \frac{4,799}{41,486}$$

13. Base Pay Savings = (277,300 − 224,700) (12) ($677.70) − (52,600) (12) ($200) = $302 M

14.

	Nr.	%
MCI&II (41,500) (39/56) + (138,700 − 41,500) (0.21) =	49,314	35.6
MCIIIA (41,500) (17/56) + (138,700 − 41,500) (0.16) =	28,150	20.3
Above Avg.	77,464	55.9
MCIIIB (138,700 − 41,500) (0.23) =	22,356	16.1
MCIV (138,700 − 41,500) (0.39) =	37,908	27.3
TOTALS	137,728*	99.3*

*Does not add to 138,700 due to rounding to nearest percentage in FY 78 quality data.
HSDG = 41,500 + (138,700 − 41,500) (0.74) = 113,428 or 81.8%

15.   Contribution to IRR of ST Enlistments

	End Year* (000)									
MOS (YRS)	1	2	3	4	5	6	7	8	9	10
6										
From 12 MOS + TNG	4.1	8.2	12.3	16.4**	16.4				SAME	
From 18 MOS + TNG	0	30.1	60.2	90.3	120.4**				SAME	
	4.1	38.3	72.5	106.7	136.8					
8										
From 12 MOS + TNG					20.5	24.6	24.6			
From 18 MOS + TNG					120.4	150.5	180.6			
					140.9	175.1	205.2			
10										
From 12 MOS + TNG								28.7	32.8	32.8
From 18 MOS + TNG								180.6	210.7	240.8
								209.3	243.5	273.6

*(Years after program is in effect 15 months)
**(These numbers will increase in between years so that maximum under six-year MOS will occur toward end of sixth year.

- Contribution of long-term accessions to the IRR
  Facts: The IRR at end FY81 through FY78 was about 200,000
    The 200,000 comprised mainly enlistees of three- and four-years who enlisted from FY76 through FY78
    Enlisted inputs for those years were:

ENLISTEES (000)

FY 76	77	78	TOTAL
180	168	124	472

Assumption: Enlistments in FY 76–78 were ¼–4 year and ¾ for 3 years.
Computations

POTENTIAL INPUT TO IRR FROM FY76–78 COHORTS (000)

	FY 76	77	78	TOTALS
3 year @ 75%	135	126	93	354
4 year @ 25%	45	42	NONE	87
	180	168	93	441

of 441,000 potentials for the IRR, only 200,000 joined, or $\frac{200}{441} = \underline{45.4\%}$. We will use this

factor to compute the contribution of long-term enlistees.

FACTS: From Step 4, we see that annual long-term accessions will be 97,200. Of these ¼
or 24,300 will be for four years.
¾ or 72,900 will be for three years.

POTENTIAL AND ESTIMATED INPUT TO IRR FROM LT ENLISTMENTS (000)

MOS (YRS)
6 (3 × 3 year cohorts + 2 × 4 year cohorts) (0.454) = [(3 × 72,900) + (2 × 24,300)]
(0.454) = 121.4
8 (5 × 3 year cohorts + 4 × 4 year cohorts) (0.454) = [(5 × 72,900) + (4 × 24,300)]
(0.454) = 209.6
10 (7 × 3 year cohorts + 6 × 4 year cohorts) (0.454) = [(7 × 72,900) + (6 × 24,300)]
(0.454) = 297.9

8

Obligatory Service: The Fundamental and Secondary Choices

James L. Lacy

JAMES L. LACY, former Special Assistant to the Assistant Secretary of Defense for Manpower, Reserve Affairs and Logistics, and currently completing a history of U.S. naval strategy at the Center for Naval Analyses, as well as finishing a book on the details of resuming a military draft, examines the principal compulsory service options that the nation might consider if and when it concludes that the all-volunteer system no longer provides adequate security. These are universal or selective national service, universal or selective active-duty military service, conscription for the Selected Reserve components, and conscription for universal or selective military training. The author concludes that some form of selective active-duty service — different in important respects from the "permanent" draft law now on the books — would be the stronger policy choice.

INTRODUCTION

One alternative to the kinds of options examined in the preceding chapter, of course, is to institute some form of conscription. The United States has substituted compulsion for compensation in procuring military manpower in the past; the All-Volunteer Force (AVF) is still very much a recent departure from America's post-World War II military manpower policies. Moreover, with the limited exceptions of Canada and Great Britain, every principal ally (and virtually every conceivable military adversary) employs compulsory military service in one form or another. A modern defense capability tied to the whims of the labor marketplace is an idiosyncrasy by international standards. Some, within the United States and abroad, suggest that better security, more even recruit quality, lower costs, and greater heterogeneity in force composition would follow from the adoption of some kind of draft.

What kind of draft, however, is an essential question, since conscription is not a single or self-evident proposition. While simply resurrecting the last draft is certainly one option,[1] current proposals to replace the AVF tend to reach substantially beyond and move in several different directions. A draft confined to repairing shortfalls in the IRR would satisfy some; for others, conscription should replace all active-duty enlistments; for still others, nothing less than a sweeping program of universal compulsory service would be sufficient. The exact correspondences between these various obligatory "solutions" and the kinds of force-manning problems identified in earlier chapters are not always self-evident, but this is a product of three factors. First, these options tend to speak to broad and widely varied military and social objectives. (Indeed, in some, especially those that suggest universal conscription, military objectives are often incidental to the achievement of other social goals.) Second, resolving chronic problems in the AVF is not always the animating concern. Conscription brings its own problems, and some of the prominent choices represent little more than a debate about how to solve these. Third, the telling is often in details that have not been formulated in a manner that permits discrete analysis.

While the agenda of compulsory opportunities is abundant, the prominent proposals flow broadly from two sets of threshold choices. First, there is the matter of inclusiveness: whether conscription should be universal or selective, and whether it should be confined to military service, or alternatively, should be broadened to permit or require some to perform nonmilitary public service ("national service") as well. Second, as regards the military, there is the question of where in the total force structure conscription should be primarily aimed: the active forces, the Selected Reserve, or the IRR.

In these terms, the range admits seven major possibilities, each pitched to a different set of military and/or social concerns: national service, universal or selectively imposed;[2] active-duty military service, again universal or required only selectively; conscription for the Selected Reserve, almost always suggested only on a selective basis; and conscription for military training (but without regular reserve drills or active service in peacetime) — universal in the sense of a universal military training obligation (UMT), or selective, in the form simply of a draft limited to filling shortfalls in the Individual Ready Reserves (IRR). There is invariably some overlap among these (universal national service, for instance, both implies and subsumes a form of selective military service) — and in specific formulations the distinctiveness among them is occasionally dim — but by and large, these are the principal options advocates of a return to some form of draft seem to have in mind.

While all are rationalized, at least in part, by their putative contributions to improved manning of the armed forces, there are some threshold differences. Universal national service, for instance, overlays compulsory civilian service for many on compulsory military service for some. While it may thereby achieve other social goals, it adds little directly to defense manpower that would not be accomplished by a military draft alone. UMT is promoted as much for its perceived contributions to the healthiness, self-discipline, and remedial education of its trainees as for its military value, and in this sense the armed forces may be more the provider of services than the beneficiary of anything of great military utility. A draft for the active forces could fill both the Selected Reserve (by offering a draft deferment for reserve service) and the IRR (by requiring a follow-on period of IRR callup status); a draft for the Selected Reserve or the IRR would probably have much less corresponding effect on the quality and quantity of active-duty manpower.

Furthermore, there are broad differences in cost (although there are many uncertainties about specifics), in practicality (save for a selective active-duty draft and a limited form of national service allowed to conscientious objectors, none of these has ever been tried, and some seem particularly exotic), and in the detail in which they have been articulated.

Whether and what specifically, compulsory service adds to national security, then, is first, a matter of threshold sorting of several quite different visions and promises, and, second, a matter of developing a framework in which detail that is often currently lacking subsequently can be filled in. In this vein, the discussion that follows has four purposes.

The first is to describe the relevance to force-manning concerns of obligatory service generally. Why is it pertinent? Where lies the potential? What are the inherent limitations?

The second is to narrow the agenda to those options which offer some reasonable promise of contributing to defense manpower objectives at tolerable cost. Several prominent prospects—ones that look to a "universal" draft and those targeted only on the reserves—do not fare well when examined closely. It is useful to underscore why, and then to move on.

The third purpose is to develop a way of looking at the remaining choices, their principal variants, and the specific costs and benefits they likely entail. Here it is useful (albeit not without difficulty) to distinguish two overlapping questions: a draft for what? and, a draft of whom? While the answers to one influence the other (for such is the circularity of the underlying issues), each requires a different set of observations and considerations. As regards the first of these questions, conscription choices can be arrayed according to the extensiveness of compulsion involved. A draft can meet the same military manpower requirements by quite different combinations of inducements and inductions. With respect to the second, powerful political choices, more so than strictly military concerns, are dominant.

The final purpose is to describe the most reasonable contours that a re-sumed draft might take. Conscription can indeed offer redemption from at least some of the problems of the AVF, but this seems best assessed in the context of fairly specific documentation.[3]

TRIGGERS, PRECEPTS, AND PARADOXES

Obligatory service in any form diverges sharply from the prospects exam-ined in preceding chapters. An obvious question concerns its pertinence, potential, and limitations.

Before turning to specific alternatives, then, it is helpful to briefly set the context along three general lines. These correspond roughly to the following questions: is it timely or necessary to examine these non-AVF options at all? what might these offer that the AVF does not? what kinds of problems and ambiguities does obligatory service itself introduce to a discussion of mili-tary service?

Looking Beyond the AVF

The short answer to the first of these questions is that the AVF, for a host of reasons, may not be a prudently enduring national policy in the 1980s — this despite the many energies devoted to its maintenance. It is certainly not an incontrovertible policy. Far from being put to rest, doubts about the ef-ficacy of a wholly volunteer armed force seem to have intensified as the ex-periment has matured. Some have long argued that the AVF is a perilously mistaken idea; others, simply that the gap between its ruling assumptions and its everyday existence is its glaring pitfall.

Several facts are salient. After nearly a decade of the AVF, American force strength entering the 1980s was at its lowest ebb since June 1950 (table 8.1).[4] Few, but the most ardent advocates of volunteer forces, would assert that force size could be substantially increased (to, say, its pre-Vietnam level) through reliance on volunteers alone. At the same time, the conditions that favored the AVF in the 1970s (chief among them, auspicious demo-graphics and an optimistic climate of U.S.-Soviet relations) have largely eroded. And a ten-year trend toward greatly disproportionate concentra-tions of minority members in the ranks (especially in the army) seems be-yond the capability of the AVF to check — a circumstance severely worri-some to some.

Also, in times of tension or conflict, the active force of the AVF must rely on manpower reservoirs which have historically offered little reassurance: the Selected and Individual Ready Reserves; a standby draft comprised of

**Table 8.1. Active Duty and Ready Reserve Personnel
Strength,[a] Selected Years: 1950–1980.
(Numbers in thousands)**

Year	Active	Ready Reserve[b]	Year	Active	Ready Reserve[b]
1950	1,460	c	1968	3,548	3,195
1952	3,636	2,447	1971	2,715	4,150
1954	3,302	2,821	1973	2,253	3,598
1959	2,487	4,601	1975	2,127	2,816
1961	2,484	3,965	1977	2,074	2,400
1964	2,687	2,781	1979	2,024	1,161
			1980	2,050	1,264

a. Includes officers and enlisted
b. Includes Selected and Individual Ready Reserve
c. Current reserve categories were not established until the Armed Forces Reserve Act of 1952

an address directory of registrants and untested plans for their mobilization in unprecedented numbers in a crisis.[5]

In this light, any of a number of factors could tilt the equation away from retaining the AVF toward replacing it by mid-decade: a failure to maintain existing force levels with volunteers; an upward revision of military manpower requirements; an external provocation (including one short of a direct military attack on American interests, but one calling nevertheless for a manifestation of precaution and resolve); a critical public reassessment of the AVF's essential assumptions; a political weariness with the frustrating inconclusiveness of the AVF-draft debate itself. None is foreordained. None, as well, is especially remote or implausible. Indeed, decreasing manpower supply (by 1992, 20 percent fewer 18-year-olds than in 1978) seems to run counter to the Reagan administration's public commitment to enlarge forces and to the Congress' insistence, at the same time, on tougher enlistment standards. Even for those who do not view obligated service as the better national policy in its own right, some form of conscription may be simply unavoidable by mid-decade.[6]

Obligated Service and the AVF

At the same time, there should be little doubt that, depending on its terms, peacetime conscription has the potential to address several salient concerns attending the AVF.[7] Foremost among the attributes of obligated service is a certainty of military manpower supply in times of peace, escalating tensions, or armed conflict. In time of tension, force strength can be bolstered, as a manifestation of precaution and national resolve, with reasonable confidence through larger draft calls. National security and foreign policy judgments need not be tailored accordingly to account for the cyclical whims of the labor marketplace.[8] Less-perilous reliance on untested force augmentation schemes (such as reserve activation, recall of military retirees, the standby draft) can be realized. A better proportion of higher scoring recruits should follow from conscription. Racial imbalance in the ranks may or may not be dramatically reversed, but existing trends should certainly be slowed or arrested. Last, conscription may not be cheaper than an AVF (and in several obligatory schemes would be conspicuously costlier), but, in some formulations the escalating costs of defense manpower should be slowed. None of the foregoing is an insubstantial gain.

The Limitations

Still, obligatory service in any form brings to the equation its own ambiguities and paradoxes as well. These present no great obstacles when contemplating conscripted service as a general matter, but they do have considerable bearing on the choice of particular formulations.

The precepts by which an America resuming conscription would hold it accountable are not difficult to recite. The difficulty is that they are not easy to harmonize.

Most salient, perhaps, are two: *fairness* in distributing the draft's burdens, and *responsiveness* to military manpower needs. Beyond these, America would seek the following in a draft:

- flexibility: it should be able to provide the required manpower in a range of situations and circumstances, and to react promptly to changes in these requirements;
- economy: it should provide no more (and no less) manpower for military service than is needed—nor "types" of manpower that are incompatible with that "need"—and should be cognizant of the manpower demands of the civilian economy, especially in the context of a mobilization;
- representativeness: it should draw by race and socioeconomic situation in rough proportions to corresponding concentrations among youth qualified for military service;
- compassion: it should be capable of exonerating from its burdens individuals for whom conscription would cause a severe hardship or violate a strict moral scruple;
- certainty and minimalization of burden: as far as possible, it should allow persons subject to it to plan careers, start families, and otherwise take charge of their lives;
- procedural consistency and correctness: it should comport as much as possible with standards of due process and consistent treatment of like persons in like circumstances;
- sanctions: its burdens and requirements should be enforced rationally, and without fear or favor.

While these precepts may be singularly embraceable, they are enormously difficult to meld. A truly "fair" draft (a term that admits of no single vision) is not likely to be either flexible, economical, or responsive to military requirements, since it places strictures on "supply" that necessarily warp the manpower supply-demand relationship. Anything short of universal service seems essentially unfair, but economy in manpower use argues for heavy doses of selectivity, since the theoretical supply will likely exceed all but the grandest visions of demand. Flexibility and certainty are not ideal handmaidens, nor do compassion and consistency easily correspond.

Moreover, none of these aspirations evokes a single, simple vision. A truly "responsive" system would net the skills the armed forces needs without regard to their distribution in the civilian economy (in terms of age, race, sex, etc.), but by responsiveness we normally intend something other than a roaming conscription program, picking manpower at will. "Compassion" is elusive and has been fickle historically: at a given time orphans with no dependents have been exempted; the fathers of small children, inducted. Fairness would seem to require, if not equal service by all, then equal vulnerability to the call for service, but here, too, there tends to be something less than the precept implies: few would propose, for instance, that hospitals and prisons be emptied to round out the pool of eligibles.

Furthermore, which, among these various pulls, gets emphasis in wartime may be quite different than those that are most cherished in peacetime, but peacetime predilections may not be alterable quickly enough to meet wartime circumstances. In the face of a clear and present danger, responsiveness and flexibility would probably take on heightened value; in peacetime, fairness, procedural regularity, and certainty may command primacy. Yet, if this is so, it is not obvious how a nation converts a force conscripted according to peacetime norms into one that must respond to wartime exigencies without doing some violence to both standards. (This, in even more aggravated fashion, is a crucial shortcoming of the existing standby draft. Its "youngest-first" order of call, defensible in peacetime, presents the indefensible incongruity of fighting the major war for which it would be activated with a single year-of-birth group, and this composed of the younger registrants.)

In short, while it is wrong-headed to undervalue the contributions of obligated service to national security, it is equally wrong-headed to consider peacetime compulsory service an unblemished alternative. Trade-offs and balances of competing objectives are essential. Single-minded, cure-all draft (and national service) prescriptions should, accordingly and properly, be viewed with suspicion.

The difficulties posed by conscription vary widely according to the specific formulation. Examination of the principal choices follows.

FRAILTIES OF UNIVERSAL CONSCRIPTION

From the perspective of simple equity, easily the most defensible compulsory manpower policy is to draft everyone. Three options hold forth such promise: universal military service; universal conscription, but only for military training in peacetime; and universal national service, in which some would enter the armed forces but most would perform obligatory nonmilitary public service. From the perspective of plausibility, however, each is demonstrably fragile. Among other things, the basic arithmetic is crippling.

Certainly in the case of universally compelled active-duty military service, to raise the proposition is to dispose of it; the available manpower supply far exceeds the grandest visions of military utilization in virtually any equation short of Armageddon. The largest military force assembled in American history barely reached 12 million in 1945. Yet, in 1981, approximately 2 million males and 2 million females turned 18. Had each been required to give one year of military service, the first-term ranks of the active forces would have topped anything the nation has experienced since the Second World War; had each been required to serve two years, first-term ranks would have swelled to an unimaginable 8 million (or to 4 million were such a draft confined to males). Even if 50 percent were disqualified on physical or mental grounds (a circumstance which would render universal military service something other than "universal"), the arithmetic would still be staggering. (To train and supervise a first-term force of these dimensions would also require enormous additions, presumably volunteers, to the career force.) While projected declines in the youth population through the 1990s will change the details slightly, they will not subtract appreciably from the order of magnitude.

Proponents of universal conscription commonly concede the practical limitations when applied solely to the standing armed forces. They offer, instead, two alternative avenues to a universal obligation. First, all (or nearly all) youth (or only male youth) would be required to undergo basic military *training*, but in peacetime actual military *service* would be expected only of volunteers. Accordingly, a reasonably sized standing force might be maintained, a formidable IRR of trained manpower would be developed (and could be mobilized in a military emergency), and a near-universal distribution of a common military obligation would be achieved. Alternatively, compulsory national service would be added to conscripted military service, thereby enlarging the "demand" for manpower to approximate its supply without having to enlarge the armed forces to do so.

While notions of equity animate these visions, and while they are linked in some respect to military manpower needs, they are rationalized, as well, for their expected achievement of other social objectives. The dramatic self-improvement in city boys who volunteered for six months in army-managed Civilian Conservation Corps workcamps in the 1930s is cited as evidence that four to six months of military training would have great educational and maturing value for trainees, as well as provide for an abundant IRR.[9] Universal national service is premised on the assumption that there are great unmet social needs to be performed by relatively unskilled youth, and that the young benefit personally from being engaged in such enterprises. Unlike the purely military draft options examined in later pages, then, these propositions argue for assessment in terms that go beyond their direct contributions to military effectiveness.

Military Effectiveness

It is difficult to make the case for either on pure military grounds. "Not even the most fearful and extreme of our militarists pretend that an army of seven to ten million men, which the system of universal military [training] would give us after a few years of building up reserves who had passed through the military machine, would be necessary to repel an actual invasion on American soil," scoffed the American Union Against Militarism in 1917, and this has been a recurring difficulty: the inability of UMT proponents to make a convincing case for its military necessity. The idea has never quite shaken the impression that it is an enormously clumsy, costly, inefficient, extravagant, and ineffective way to provide defense manpower.

The reasons for doubting the military worth of UMT should be fairly evident. First, there is the very uncertain value of creating such large pools of reservists with limited training and no active-duty experience to begin with. Save for defending against a ground invasion of the United States—or, as Dwight D. Eisenhower once suggested, providing basically trained citizens who might be useful to their communities in the aftermath of a nuclear attack—the circumstances in which the training investment might be repaid by militarily useful service are difficult to imagine. Second, UMT would require an enormous military training base (compared with some 500,000 new active and Selected Reserve accessions in fiscal year 1980, UMT would require the training of somewhere between 1.2 and 2 million annually, depending on assumptions about how "universal" it would be in practice). This not only would require substantial dislocations of men and matériel from the "tooth" to the "tail" of the force structure; it would also require substantial additions to the career force for training and supervision. Third, unless UMT graduates were to be drafted selectively for peacetime active duty (which is not commonly proposed), the United States would still have to maintain and support a wholly volunteer active-duty force. UMT costs would be additions, not offsets, to current AVF manpower costs. Last, the only conceivable military beneficiary of UMT would be the Army IRR, but the bounty in numbers would come at a price: the current IRR is comprised entirely of members with some prior service; to these UMT would merely provide unmanageable numbers of individuals with no such experience.

Less sure are the contributions of universal national service to military effectiveness, since the only thing that distinguishes it from a selective military draft is that it compels those not entering military service to perform other public service. In this sense, its direct military costs and benefits should be roughly the same as those of the traditional military-only draft.

One argument is that universal national service "legitimizes" selective military conscription and thus makes the latter more palatable, but this rests on the fragile assumption that conscription is politically dismaying, not because it limits the freedom of those subject to it, but because it does not do so equally for every person. A second supposition is that, by manipulating the relative attractiveness of compulsory civilian service and compulsory military service, the better-qualified youth would choose the armed forces. In this way, current concerns about the "quality" of the force would be amply addressed. The prospect is not inconceivable, of course, but it does amount to an enormously costly and cumbersome device to influence these individual choices. A third proposition is that universal national service brings the best of both worlds: the compulsion of all produces a measure of certainty in manpower supply which is lacking in the AVF, but at the same time preserves voluntarism and free choice in the actual decision to join the armed forces. Unlike a selective military draft, then, the military is free of individuals who do not want to be in uniform. Still, apart from the confusion of forced choice and free choice, there is again the matter of over-kill; there are less costly and extravagant ways to shield the armed forces from unmanageable numbers of conscripted malcontents (one such device is examined subsequently in the context of "selective" national service).

Indeed, the counterarguments are equally persuasive: that far from legitimizing conscripted military service, a draft of great numbers for purposes that are not easily defined or related to national security would undermine the political legitimacy of all conscripted service (in the words of one critic, create a "gigantic Brook Farm, spurred by compulsion"[10]); that unless civilian service were reasonably attractive, and thus a lure to the better qualified, the obligation to do it would quickly become unenforceable; the increased expense of paying large numbers of individuals to perform service of no direct military value might soon amount to a funding drain-off that would itself impair military effectiveness.

Equity and Other Social Values

At the same time, the contributions of universal conscription to other perceived values are not self-evident. First, it is doubtful that either UMT or universal national service produces much beyond a veneer of increased equity. UMT might provide the same training obligation for all, but unless all UMT graduates were to be called to duty in a national emergency (an unlikely prospect given the numbers), actual military service in crisis would remain selective. National service produces different, and yet more stubborn, equity concerns. While a duty to serve may be imposed on all, it is unlikely that compulsory civilian service can be tailored to be an equal alternative to the risk, regimentation, and restrictions on personal freedom of military service. Nor is it likely that, within civilian service itself, burdensomeness can be fairly distributed across activities, given the large numbers that would have to be placed. And, if only three in ten or three in twenty are actually needed for a compelling national purpose, to induct all ten or twenty would itself not appear to be either economical or equitable with respect to the additional seven or seventeen.

Fundamentally, the social value of both alternatives is not readily persuasive. UMT might provide a necessary addition to the education and training of American youth, but only at the considerable price of an unprecedented federal intervention into basic education, of potentially enormous disruption of the normal educational process,[11] and with serious risks of excessive regimentation. Compulsory national service, at the same time, rests on assumptions which require great leaps of faith. The United States managed only to double its job base between 1945 and 1980. It is not readily apparent where jobs and service opportunities exist for some 3 to 6 million young conscripts; it is even less apparent why, if useful public service in such dimensions could be found to exist, the better social policy would be to fill these positions with conscripts rather than with wage earners.[12] Indeed, there is a debilitating haziness in most national service proposals concerning the types of nonmilitary work that would be done, supervisory requirements, length of obligated service, levels of pay, means of enforcement, and the like.[13]

As regards costs, different assumptions lead to widely different projections. Basic military training of three-months' duration for 2 million males would cost approximately $7.7 billion in additional manpower costs in 1981. One year of national service by 2.7 million participants at the minimum wage would have cost approximately $19 billion in wages alone in 1981; there might be some saving in military recruiting costs, but these would probably be offset were such a program to offer lures to the better-qualified to join the armed forces. Some estimates have placed the annual cost per national service participant as low as $3,000 (assuming no pay and a bare-bones stipend only); others, at $8,000 to $9,000 (assuming only living expenses and modest benefits).[14] Without much greater specification than has been formulated to date, however, all such estimates are whimsical. And, the costs associated with administering a public employment program of such unprecedented dimensions are incalculable—there is simply no analogous base of experience.

Last, while the courts have interpreted the federal constitution liberally with respect to the powers of the national government to conscript for military service, both UMT and compulsory national service step considerably beyond all past constitutional boundaries. The courts have held that the power of the national government to compel service reposes in the enumerated power to raise armies. No court speaking with constitutional authority has yet wed such a power to any other enumerated power of the Congress (the commerce power, for instance) or to any general provision (such as to promote the general welfare). At the same time, "involuntary servitude" is proscribed by the Thirteenth Amendment, a prohibition from which the Supreme Court rescued the military draft—and limited forms of obligatory civilian service for some citizens subject to the military draft—but nothing other. Widespread compulsion for nonmilitary service, or for UMT with only a highly attenuated relationship to military requirements, reaches substantially beyond what has been historically permitted and seems to clash quite quickly with what has been explicitly proscribed.

Legal scholars differ on the nuances—whether, for instance, "involuntary service" and "involuntary servitude" are the same thing for purposes of applying the Thirteenth Amendment—but, in practice, the courts have allowed very few historical exceptions—jury service, a few days' compulsory work each year on state roads—to an otherwise firm aversion to compelled service for the common good. And, while some have likened UMT and national service to compulsory education, the linkage slips in two respects. First, the power to compel basic education has historically reposed in the states, not in the central government. Second, that power has not extended to schooling after age 16, and the Supreme Court strongly suggested in 1972 that it could not be further extended, and in certain cases may have to be abridged below age 16.[15]

The surface appeal of UMT and universal service may be enduring—painted as broad ideals they are not without some attractiveness—but the obstacles and uncertainties endure as well, and, in the end, appear overpowering.

THE MODEST ALTERNATIVES: A DRAFT FOR THE RESERVES

If universal conscription does too much to be useful, options at the other end of the range—those confined to the reserves—appear to do much too little. Confined to military service, a draft for the Selected Reserve or for the IRR avoids the legal and social encumbrances of universal conscription, but, as with all remaining options, it comes with a major handicap of its own: it is necessarily selective.[16]

The traditional device for filling the reserves' manpower requirements was to link reserve service to a compulsory tour of active duty. This was accomplished in two ways. First, while the obligatory tour of active duty was only two years, both the conscript and the first-term volunteer incurred by law a total military service obligation of six years (prior to 1958, the total was eight years). The difference between the active tour and the total obligation was to be spent in the reserves, in either the Selected Reserve for one or two years followed by transfer to the IRR, or entirely in the IRR. Second, after 1957 the draft law permitted a deferment and exemption for individuals of draft age who directly enlisted for six years in the Selected Reserve. (For a time, there was also a "special skills" program allowing some to enlist directly in the IRR as well.) Since reserve service was normally less burdensome than active duty—entailing only 6 months training and 5½ years of one drill per month and two weeks of refresher training per year—the deferment easily produced queues outside reserve recruiting offices, and also meant less need for prior-service inductees to enter anything other than the IRR to satisfy their total service obligation. Apart from the remote and short-lived exception of a Students' Army Training Corps in 1918 (a form of direct IRR draft), and the even more remote exception of colonial and early state militia service, America never conscripted directly for its reserves.[17]

A reserve draft, however, has three potential advantages. First, given the milder terms of reserve service, it is less an intrusion in the lives of individuals subject to it than is a draft for active duty. Second, it has a precise relevance to one major and immediate problem of the force in the next decade: the reserve manpower shortfall. Third, the numbers of individuals needed would be small, and thus, the numbers of lives interrupted by conscription would be relatively few. Assuming the AVF's reserve manning patterns continue roughly as is, a reserve draft would be needed only for the Army Guard and reserve. Even taking the higher number of wartime requirements (distinguished from normal peacetime programmed strength which assumes an underfill), the Army Selected Reserve shortfall *may* not be much more than 50,000 by the late 1980s. More substantially, a reserve draft to cure near-term (FY 1982) shortfalls—102,000 in the Selected Reserve; an additional 148,000 in the Army IRR—would amount to one-time inductions for both of approximately 250,000, and, spread over four years, to not much more than 60,000 per year.[18] At the same time, such inductions would relax considerably (and prudently) the pressures on the standby mobilization draft to reconstitute itself rapidly in an emergency, by increasing the reservoir of already trained augmentation manpower to be drawn-down first.

Also, a reserve draft would preserve a volunteer active-duty force, and an IRR draft, particularly, would quickly begin to alter an imbalance in which, at present, only some 25 percent of IRR augmentees are junior enlisted men with combat arms skills, whereby the wartime need for such runs closer to 90 percent (given current projections about where casualties are most likely to occur and IRR replacements most likely to be needed).

Offsetting this potential, however, are several looming difficulties.

Conscription for the Selected Reserve

In practical consequence, a draft tailored principally for the army reserve components confronts several, virtually insurmountable, obstacles. Unlike the active forces, the reserve components are organized with local geography in mind: the state and its subdivisions in the case of the National Guard; the local region or community in the case of the regular reserves. This geographical dispersion reflects both history and the availability of military facilities for training; it does not reflect per capita concentrations of the draft-eligible population. Yet, for army reserve units particularly, reasonable proximity of training facilities to the reservist's residence is essential to accommodate weekend drills. To man such units with conscripts, then, would almost certainly require state, local, or regional draft calls, since neither the size of reserve units nor the numbers of enlisted vacancies within units would distribute uniformly across the nation, or in parallel with the geographical distribution of the draft-eligible population.[19] Moreover, draft avoidance in such a conscription scheme would probably entail little more than a change of address (from an area with reserve manpower shortages to one without need for manpower), an evasion opportunity not likely to be evenly available across socioeconomic lines. At the same time, the political acceptability of having a reserve unit in a local community could dissipate rather quickly if its presence came to represent a particular tax on local youth. Last, direct conscription would seem to undermine the one putative value associated with Selected Reserve organization: that unit cohesion and regular unit-level training provide a measure of readiness not achievable in the IRR. This, however, is a realizable benefit only when unit members are relatively stable geographically. Unless a Selected Reserve draft were to prohibit inductees from relocating during their 5½ years of reserve service (an unlikely prospect politically), this value would seem to be quite fragile in practice.

While the costs of a Selected Reserve draft should be lower than those required to achieve the same manpower level with volunteers (even were wages kept the same, a saving in excess of $100 million would accrue annually from reduced reserve recruiting costs), the practical difficulties of administering and enforcing such a procedure seem formidable—in light of current assumptions about reserve organization and training.

A Draft for the IRR

Free of these geographical limitations, conscription for the IRR is a much more manageable prospect: following basic training, IRR conscripts would probably not be required to participate in regular drills. Such a draft would respond promptly to current IRR shortfalls. And, because it imposes a minimal peacetime burden on those who are inducted, it may be more politically acceptable than the alternatives.

Still, there are drawbacks. Foremost is the fact that, like UMT (of which it is merely a limited variant), it produces only basically trained soldiers. More important, the utility of even this basic training diminishes every year after it is received: basic skills atrophy over time.

This is especially the case if an IRR draft is wed to the current six-year military service obligation (MSO). One possibility, of course, is to limit the MSO to a point closer in time to the completion of basic training. An MSO of one or two years would, however, increase the numbers of individuals to be trained annually: conceivably a plus from the standpoint of wider distribution of the obligation to train, but a minus in terms of increased strains on the training base. (Some idea of the differences can be gleaned from table 8.2. Assuming a steady-state strength of 150,000 IRR conscripts to be achieved over four years, the difference in annual draft calls thereafter would be 37,500 with an MSO of four or more years, 75,000 with an MSO of two, 150,000 with an MSO of one.) At the same time it would increase training costs. Assuming a trainee man-year cost of $15,000, basic training of three-months' average duration, and one additional trainer for every 40 recruits at $1200 per month on average, the incremental training costs for 37,500 each year would be approximately $27.5 million; for 150,000, approximately $130 million.

Moreover, except for some undeterminable number which might elect active duty following this basic training, these costs would be largely in addition to the costs of training the active force. Here lies the great limitation.

Table 8.2. Annual Inductions to Achieve Steady-State of 150,000 IRR Conscripts after Four Years, by MSO[a].

Year	4 year MSO		2 year MSO		1 year MSO	
	Induct	Strength	Induct	Strength	Induct	Strength
1	37,500	37,500	37,500	37,500	37,500	37,000
2	37,500	75,000	37,500	75,000	75,000	75,000
3	37,500	102,000	75,000	102,500	102,500	102,500
4	37,500	150,000	75,000	150,000	150,000	150,000
5 +	37,500	150,000	75,000	150,000	150,000	150,000

a. These are illustrative counts, which take no account of losses through attrition.

An IRR draft would accomplish little for the total force that an active-duty draft with a residual IRR obligation would not achieve, and in relatively the same time frame. (An annual draft of 75,000 for two-years active duty followed by two years in the IRR, for instance, would yield the same 150,000 in the IRR within four years.) At the same time, conscription for the IRR is unresponsive to qualitative concerns associated with the active forces, and it targets a draft on an uncertain component of the total force.[20]

CONSCRIPTION FOR ACTIVE MILITARY SERVICE

By contrast, a draft for the active forces seems rich with potential precisely because it has the capability to address quantitative and qualitative concerns across all three branches of the total force. Unlike universal compulsion, it is economical: derived not from worries about the abundance of manpower supply, but, instead, targeted on fairly precise (albeit, always debatable) military manpower demands. And, unlike reserve-only drafts, it does not squander the exceptional power to compel service on limited force-manning objectives. A solidly sized Selected Reserve and an abundant IRR accompanied active-duty conscription in the late 1950s and in the 1960s, and largely as inexpensive by-products.

The potential of such a draft is imposing. Unlike the AVF, which has experienced occasional shortfalls in meeting active force recruiting objectives (these have ranged from zero percent in fiscal years 1975, 1976, and 1980 to 7 percent in 1979), it removes first-term force-manning from recruitment fluctuations. And it has proven to be reasonably dependable for force expansion in circumstances short of a full mobilization, both at times when American forces were already engaged in conflict (Korea, Vietnam) and at times of tension when force bolstering was a measure of precaution and resolve (the Berlin crises of 1948 and 1961).[21] Depending on its terms, such a draft can effect substantial changes in the demographic composition of the enlisted ranks, in both the active forces and the reserves. And, again depending on its terms, it can arrest, and conceivably reduce, the escalating costs of first-term defense manpower.

Offsetting this potential, of course, is a fundamental drawback: it is necessarily selective. Moreover, America has demonstrated in the past that it can manage conscription with reasonable fairness, economy, and military effectiveness, but also that it can bungle badly as well. Procedural vagrancy and substantive venality were not lacking in previous drafts: the reasons why some were selected and others were not were often great mysteries; special interests, from agriculture to the ministry to higher education, made successful claim to special allowances and exemptions. Also, the abundant manpower yield to the reserves was a mixed blessing, and of questionable military value.[22]

Whether, and in what respects, the potential of such a draft is realizable greatly depends on the specific forms it might take. The analysis in chapter four underscores correctly that a draft of limited numbers each year would be highly selective, add relatively little to the IRR, cause little discernible change in the demographic characteristics of the force, and could in fact cost more in net budgetary outlay than the AVF. On the other hand, a draft of much larger numbers would necessarily alter these expectations: quantitatively, to be sure; qualitatively, conceivably. By the same token, conscription shorn of loopholes and a draft policy with tight controls on reserve deferments would produce much different equities than did the draft of the mid-1960s.

While one possibility is simply to pick up where the last draft left off (on the theory that conscription had probably evolved to its most equitable and economical terms by the early seventies), there are two problems with such a course. First, America had little experience with its last draft. Changes in 1969 (reversal of the order of call from oldest-to-youngest-first, introduction of selection by lottery), in 1970 (court rulings substantially redefining conscientious objection and altering the ways the draft could be enforced), in 1970 and 1971 (pay increases for conscripts and volunteers, prospective elimination of several traditional deferments and of the so-called "doctor draft") were quickly followed by the termination of draft calls in 1972. We really do not know how well the last draft would have worked over time. More important, with a near-decade's absence of conscription, it is not readily apparent that these terms would satisfy contemporary defense manpower needs. Changing expectations—the AVF experience itself, which has introduced concerns such as racial representativeness that had little currency a decade earlier—may simply have put much of the past beyond recall.

Still, to branch beyond the most recent experience is to encounter near-endless possibilities. A draft for one year of active duty rather than two, one that includes women as well as men, one pegged to minimum mental standards appreciably higher than those currently required of the AVF by the Congress, one which reverses the order of call again to oldest-first—each would produce substantial variations in force composition and cost. To reduce the options to manageable terms, then, requires some arbitrariness, but three principal variants may serve as useful benchmarks of what might be expected differently from the broader range of specific prospects. The first is a draft that, regardless of its specific terms, aims to maximize volunteering and minimize the occasions for direct induction. The second is the precise opposite; the third, a draft which straddles between the two. Each addresses quite different force-manning concerns.

A Tag-On Draft

Here the proposition is to encourage the maximum amount of volunteering by essentially preserving the AVF's status quo and to shore it up as needed with monthly draft calls. Existing first-term pay levels would not be altered, and would be maintained on a generally competitive basis in the labor marketplace. Some trade-offs between reduced recruiting efforts and enlistment bonuses and first-term reenlistment bonuses might be made, but these would not appreciably diminish the level of recruiting effort.

The benefits to be derived from such a course are several. Since compulsions are not generally viewed as good in themselves, they are kept to an absolute minimum. Adequate first-term pay is preserved, not merely to attract volunteers, but as a matter of equity as well. Volunteering is allowed to work, but, simultaneously, not permitted to fail.

The existence of conscription to immediately fill any enlistment shortfalls accomplishes several things. First, it compensates much more quickly than the AVF for cyclical variations in enlistments. Second, it ensures that the less attractive military occupational specialties are not undernourished in the internal competition of the recruitment market. Third, it removes a precarious liability in current mobilization capability by replacing the existing standby draft—which now must be reconstituted virtually from scratch after an emergency mobilization—with a fully operating system of registration, classification, and processing in peacetime. It thus permits a capability to plan for what to expect in a mobilization: how many registered individuals, for instance, would be physically unfit, hardship cases, and conscientious objectors. In short, while maximizing volunteering, it adds several measures of security not found in the AVF standing alone.

However, these benefits do not come without drawbacks. First, if first-term pay is adequately maintained, inductions in such a scheme would be infrequent, highly selective, and a very random event in the lives of those subject to conscription. Had such a fallback been available in the AVF's worst recruiting year, it would have back-filled with not more than 25,000 inductions (or 1 percent of the male 18-year-old cohort of 2 million).[23] Second, given the limited numbers, it would do little to alter the qualitative or demographic composition of the enlisted force, since those who currently volunteer would be expected to continue to do so in much the same proportions and for much the same reasons as now. Third, since the pay of conscripts and volunteers would be the same, it would amount to only marginal reductions in first-term manpower costs.[24] At the same time, it would overlay on the existing AVF the added expense of a fully operational peacetime draft. In 1978, Selective Service estimated the direct, net, annual costs of registering all males, and classifying, testing, and physically examining

300,000 (those whose low lottery numbers would place them within the zone of possible induction) at approximately $70 million, and of classifying, testing, and examining all males (minus those who would be normally tested as AVF volunteers) at approximately $270 million. Costs related to enforcement, administrative appeals, and litigation would need to be added. (It is a draft with these general features that AVF defenders correctly point to as more costly than the AVF itself.)

Moreover, regardless of the objectives animating such a draft, experience is not the parent of optimism that competitive pay scales would be long kept in place, given the added cost and secure manpower flow which come with such a draft. The incentives to pay when compulsion accomplishes the same thing have not been enduring in the past.

Maximizing Compulsions

The second prospect is the near-reverse. Not only would volunteering not be encouraged, it would be explicitly discouraged. The precedents for doing so are fairly limited—volunteering was prohibited in the later years of both World Wars—but the concept enjoys currency in several circles.

The means by which voluntary enlistments would be uninvited differ with the proposal. Voluntary enlistments might be barred outright, tightly limited in numbers, or restricted to those below and above primary draft age.[25] The terms of voluntary enlistments might be sufficiently onerous (minimum enlistment tours of five or six years compared with conscription for two years, for example) to achieve much the same result. Alternatively, conscripts might be rewarded more favorably than volunteers by, for instance, better pay or exclusive access to postservice benefits such as a GI Bill of educational benefits. Or, first-term military pay might be suppressed to severe levels at which it would not attract many volunteers.

Whether an absolute bar of voluntarism or something less draconian is envisioned, the animating interests are several. First, increasing the ratio of random inductions to voluntary enlistments should produce a more demographically representative force. (This assumes, of course, that random selection produces equally random results, across test scores, race, income levels, and the like.)[26] The quality of the force (in terms of test scores and high-school diplomas) would be improved to some extent over current levels (there would be some better yield of mental categories I and II);[27] racial imbalances in the enlisted ranks should be arrested, and, over time, brought more in line with the racial composition of society generally. Second, the burdens of conscripted service should be more broadly distributed across the draft-eligible population; accordingly, the selective draft becomes less selective. The substitution of large numbers of two-year conscripts for three- and four-year volunteers forces larger accession requirements. (Had all of 1980's 390,000 active force accessions been conscripts, for instance, accession requirements by 1983 would nearly double.) Third, there is greater likelihood that the yield of random selection will be distributed across services: a draft, then, not simply for the army, but for the armed forces. The army's ability to compete for better-qualified individuals is thereby improved. While the other services might offer entering conscripts different packages of training and benefits in return for voluntary "extensions" of service, the population from which they would recruit would be more demographically representative at the outset. Last, while large numbers of inductions do not benefit the career force, they do help appreciably the Selected Reserve (the greater the likelihood of being inducted, the greater the attractiveness of a reserve deferment)[28] and the IRR (through increased force turnover).

A complete bar to volunteering, a position advocated by the Association of the United States Army, would have the most dramatic effects. Compared with current black enlistment levels in the army of 33 percent, a random draft should draw between 9 and 11 percent. Some $800 million in annual recruiting costs and $55 million in training costs for recruiters would be saved, and first-term pay could be suppressed to either the minimum wage (a saving in 1982 of approximately $240 million) or to a subminimum. At the same time, the direct costs of administering a full-scale Selective Service System ($270 million) would be incurred. And, while a substantial increase in training costs would be expected given vastly larger numbers of two-year tours, the precise dimensions are difficult to judge: there is no comparable experience base for anticipating the proportion of each entering cohort which would elect extension of service. The same uncertainty applies to reenlistment rates and to the costs of reenlistment incentives.

While the prospect of formally turning away volunteers in order to induct the entire first-term force is a bit extreme, there are less extreme measures to promote inductions over enlistments, and at the same time to reap cost-savings. A sharply suppressed first-term wage, coupled with longer minimum first-term voluntary enlistments, would alter the ratio of conscripts to volunteers.[29] And, the higher the conscript ratio, the earlier and more prominent the effects would be on the racial and socioeconomic composition of first-term ranks.

Still, the difficulties with the proposition increase in direct proportion to the extent it is pressed. The sharper the suppression of military wages, the greater are the costs in equity (and, after a decade of the AVF, in political acceptability as well). While a GI Bill is occasionally offered as a compensating device, at annual steady-state costs of $1.5 to $4.5 billion, depending on its terms, it could quickly obliterate all other savings. The longer enlistment-tour needs of the navy and air force could well be put at risk. Last, there is something fundamentally imbalanced in the idea that volunteers should be aggressively discouraged in order that others may be inducted.

Balancing the Interests

The third alternative neither prolongs nor precipitously undoes the AVF. It assumes a continuation of voluntary enlistments. Unlike the foregoing, however, the incentives are not tilted to produce an extreme result on either side of the volunteer/conscript equation.

The immediate aim is to acquire a security of active-duty manpower supply in times of danger and quiescence. No less important, but less immediate, objectives are to steadily rebuild an emergency reserve, and to put a brake on upward spirals of first-term manpower costs and on a decade-long trend toward high concentrations of minorities in enlisted ranks.

Existing lengths of voluntary enlistments would not be altered. Nor would there be any fundamental changes in housing and other allowances for the families of junior enlisted personnel.[30] The principal changes would lie in a sharp reduction of recruiting efforts, and in a gradual reduction in the comparative value of first-term pay.

Recruiting activities would be promptly curtailed: enlistment bonuses would be eliminated, and recruitment efforts cut back to a comparable pre-Vietnam level (a combined saving in 1982 of approximately $970 million, but this largely offset by the costs of processing some 300,000 draft registrants per year and by increases in reenlistment bonuses). Entry-level wages would not be suppressed from their current AVF levels (nor would they be different for conscripts and volunteers of the same rank and length of service), but they would not rise in future years as rapidly as civilian wages or career military pay. At the same time, it seems essential to establish a "floor" below which junior enlisted pay would not be permitted to fall in any instance.[31]

The expectation is that draft calls would be relatively small (on the order of 10,000 to 20,000) in the first year or two, but would steadily grow to pre-Vietnam levels (40 to 60 percent of first-term accessions either draftees or draft-motivated) by mid- to late decade.[32] And, as inductions grow in numbers, they will fuel additional inductions by substituting two-year terms for current three-year enlistments.

The advantages of a draft so configured are several. First, of course, it represents no quick or radical departure from current force-manning patterns, and, accordingly, allows the military services some opportunity for paced adjustment. Second, as in the preceding alternatives, it removes the mobilization draft from the uncertainties of standby status. Third, while immediate cost-savings are modest, it does put a brake on future escalations in first-term manpower expenditures, and works over time to contain over-all defense manpower cost increases.[33] Fourth, while in the first several years no dramatic alteration of the demographic or "quality" composition of the force (and especially of the army) would be expected, there should over time be less imbalance by race and test scores as random inductions steadily replace the self-selections of voluntary enlistments.[34]

The limitations and uncertainties, however, are equally apparent. While a gradual transition to larger numbers of conscripts may be beneficial for the armed forces, it comes at the expense of very selective draft calls and elaborate draft machinery in the near term. The political acceptability of such a transition is not assured. Estimating changes in the demographic complexion of the force is a risky exercise in any circumstance. (The wide-of-the-mark predictions of the Gates Commission concerning the racial composition of the AVF is a bracing illustration.)[35] And, once reaching a steady-state overall first-term force mix of 35 to 40 percent conscripts (the proportion of conscripts in the army's first-term ranks would be in the range of 45 to 55 percent), such a draft could be expected to increase annual accessions by as much as 40 percent and the size of the first-term force by 15 to 20 percent, and to produce a higher turnover rate than the current AVF.[36] Last, of course, absent upward adjustments in manpower requirements or an unexpectedly sharp decline in voluntary enlistments, even in a steady-state such a draft would produce only between 150,000 and 180,000 inductions a year, if past peacetime experience holds true.

These effects are illustrated in table 8.3, a projection of likely steady-state manpower flows once such a draft reached comparable pre-Vietnam terms of compensation and service.[37]

Still, of the three points on the spectrum of active-duty alternatives, this third alternative is the stronger policy choice chiefly because it offers, over time, the greater promise of balancing several important and competing objectives—as between security of manpower supply, economy in manpower utilization, minimizing compulsions, and curtailing too great a social unrepresentativeness in military service.

TERMS OF AN ACTIVE-DUTY DRAFT

Still, to arrive at the foregoing judgment is to dispose only partially of the pertinent concerns. Up to this point, the examination has concentrated chiefly on one question: a draft for what? Equally salient, of course is the corollary: a draft of whom? While it is not possible to array in the limited space here the full panoply of policy options embodied in this second question, it is useful to touch briefly on those few which provoke notable discussion. These concern the selection features of selective service: induction

Table 8.3. An All-Volunteer Force and a Pre-Vietnam-like Draft in Steady-State Analysis: An Illustrative Comparison of Effects on the DoD Enlisted Force.

	All-Volunteer Force[a]	Draft	Difference	Percent Change
Trained Strength	1,719,900	1,719,900	0	–
End Strength	1,833,400	1,876,400	+ 44,000	+ 2.4%
Accessions				
Volunteers	340,600	195,700	– 144,900	– 42.5%
Draftees	0	164,600	+ 164,600	–
Draft-Motivated	0	109,700	+ 109,700	–
Total	340,600	470,000	+ 129,400	+ 38.0%
First-Term Force	1,100,500	1,280,900	+ 180,400	+ 16.4%
Accessions Entering Career Force				
Number	100,300	81,500	– 18,800	– 18.7%
Percent	29.4%	17.3%	– 12.1%	– 41.2%
Career Force	732,900	595,500	– 137,400	– 18.7%
Turnover Rate	18.6%	25.0%	+ 6.4%	+ 34.4%

a. Predicated on Fiscal Year 1983 force levels and expected behavior
Source: Gary R. Nelson, former Deputy Assistant Secretary of Defense.

criteria, the idea of draft excusals for "selective" national service, and the matter of draft deferments for reserve duty.

Selection Devices

Two propositions from recent draft experience seem particularly unassailable as matters of public policy, and, accordingly, are treated as givens here. First, selections for military induction would be done on a national basis by random means (the so-called "lottery"). While not all would be selected for service, individual liability to selection would be as broadly and fairly distributed as is reasonably possible. Second, most historical draft deferments (for parenthood, studenthood, priesthood, "critical" occupations, and the like) would be explicitly abolished.[38]

Age, Sex, and Fitness

Apart from a minimum age below which it would not reach (age 18) and a maximum beyond which it would not go (in World War II, age 45), America never did settle conclusively on a single, preferred age of induction.[39] Whether a 19-year-old makes a better soldier than a 24-year old, and vice versa, remains a matter of disagreement within the defense community itself. Still, a draft which inducts the youngest-first (youngest in this context meaning 19 or 20) has the compelling virtue of putting behind the uncertainties of conscription at a relatively early point in life—and for this reason alone, it seems likely (and prudent) to prevail.

Gender is a much more knotty proposition, although a strong case can be made for the extension of draft liability to women.

The male-only draft derived much of its historical rationale from the fact that military service itself was almost exclusively a male experience. Before 1970, less than 1 percent of military personnel were women. However, the AVF introduced new facts. Women were actively recruited in the 1970s; by 1980, they accounted for 8 percent of the active-duty force. Moreover, while women are still barred from assignments which might expose them directly to combat, military jobs available to women have expanded greatly since the late 1970s.[40] Herein stalks a provocative question: if sexual criteria no longer prohibit numbers of women from voluntarily joining and taking a host of military assignments, can sexual criteria any longer be rationalized to prohibit the conscription of similar numbers of women for the same assignments?

It is important to underscore that to answer in the negative does not require abandonment of the nation's long-standing prohibition of women in combat (this bar does not preclude female volunteers). Nor does it require dubious judgments that the sexes are interchangeable from the perspective of military effectiveness, or that women can perform as well as men in certain military environments and assignments. Rather, to reach a judgment that women should assume a liability to conscription requires little more than a certification of the status quo. If a volunteer force comprised of 8 to 10 percent women is a reasonable military policy, a drafted force with a similar composition would seem to be reasonable as well.

To obtain such a force would necessarily require differently sized military requisitions for each gender (and thus separate draft pools by sex), but this is done routinely in the AVF.[41] And, while there are administrative costs and complexities associated with maintaining two gender-based pools, these are not likely to be formidable in practice.[42]

Still, the logic notwithstanding, the choice is, at bottom, a political one, and, therefore it is by no means an easy matter to dispose of.[43] The essential point is that military effectiveness can be maintained by either a single-sex or a dual-sex draft. The essential political question concerns what constitutes equity and sound social policy in this context.

Fitness standards in the context of a draft raise yet another set of questions. Some suggest that minimum standards should be raised to take advantage of the fact that service can be compelled. Raising minimum test score requirements so as to exclude or sharply reduce in numbers category IVs has been offered as one means to dramatically alter the "quality" of the force.

However, this comes with several costs of fairly significant dimensions. To exclude category IVs entirely, the nation would have to assert something that it is incapable of demonstrating: that no military jobs exist which can be adequately performed by the lower scoring 25 percent of the youth population. Enforcement of such a scheme would be difficult precisely because it reinforces incentives to deliberately score poorly. Equity concerns are equally imposing. Random selection from a pool with broad liability loses much of its integrity when a substantial proportion of the population is freed from liability on the basis of quality standards of no conspicuous military necessity. Moreover, aptitude test scores appear to distribute unevenly by race and ethnic grouping (table 8.4). To arbitrarily draft from the higher mental categories would probably skew induction results by race (45 percent of the blacks joining in 1981 would have been rejected were category IVs excluded, compared with only 14 percent of the whites).

And, to attempt inductions differently by mental category, or by possession of a high-school diploma, adds not only complex administrative difficulties, but risks, as well, deliberate low-scoring and conceivably more high-school dropouts.

The sounder policy would seem self-evident: a fair draft should capture a fair distribution of the aptitudes of the population subject to it, tempered only, as in the past, by rejection of individuals who are unlikely to perform adequately in most plausible circumstances (historically those in mental category V and low-scoring mental category IVs separately tested and found unadaptable to training).

Selective National Service

A different question surrounds those who would opt out of a draft by choosing alternative civilian service. One recurring idea has been that individuals otherwise subject to conscription should be permitted to perform nonmilitary service if they prefer: in effect, to allow a limited form of self-selection as to who will be inducted. Such an allowance, it is assumed, would accomplish several things. By allowing civilian as well as military service, the obligation to serve would be more broadly distributed, although still selectively imposed. Nonmilitary public service would be performed by more persons if there were such an outlet. The armed forces, at the same time, would be relieved of the management and supervision of persons who do not want to be in the military. Past drafts permitted such an allowance to certain conscientious objectors, but while there were recurring proposals in the 1960s to extend the status to others, it remained the particular prerogative of the CO.

Two quite different concerns have animated and shaped proposals to expand the option. The first derives from the Supreme Court's rulings in 1965

Table 8.4. Fiscal Year 1981 Nonprior Service Accessions by Racial/Ethnic Groups.
(Percentage)

	AFQT Category			
	I	II	III	IV
White				
Army	3	27	46	24
All DoD	3	35	48	14
Black				
Army	0	5	34	61
All DoD	0	9	46	45
Hispanic/Other				
Army	0	7	38	55
All DoD	1	14	50	35

and 1970 that broadly opened access to conscientious objector status, so much so that conscientious objection became more a matter of assertion than of demonstration in their aftermath. Concerns that these rulings have created the incongruity of a future "voluntary" draft, and that further applications of the historic "belief" tests only invite further, confounding litigation, lead some to want to abandon all such tests in favor of granting the traditional "CO" status to all who are willing to perform alternative civilian work, regardless of their religious beliefs or affiliations. Because this would provide an escape from induction, the terms of civilian work would be sufficiently rigorous so as not to actively encourage its selection.

The second formulation is oriented quite differently: it would use the risk of induction as leverage on the draft-age population to encourage (channel) the widest numbers to choose nonmilitary service. The terms of alternative service, accordingly, would be more attractive than those of military induction.

While there are considerable variations within each, the prevalent characteristics of both of these "selective national service" ideas are the following:

1. acceptable civilian service would have to be in an approved field or activity, these almost always in the delivery of social service;
2. the individual electing this nonmilitary service would have to make the election before he or she receives an induction notice, commonly at the time of the initial draft registration (in some versions, however, the individual may delay actual commencement of service for up to four years);
3. failure to elect civilian service subjects the individual to liability to induction by random lottery for an active tour of military duty;

4. failure to complete satisfactorily such service subjects the individual to another period of lottery exposure;
5. satisfactory completion of service is not cause for a draft exemption per se, but the individual is placed low enough in the order of call of any future draft, in peacetime and in war, to make it unlikely he will be called.

By tying the service to a draft excusal to be voluntarily applied for and enforced simply by revocation of the excusal, the option avoids the constitutional difficulties of universal national service.

As with its universal counterpart, the costs of selective national service are largely non-defense outlays and vary according to different compensation levels and terms of service. Unlike universal service, however, the numbers which would participate are difficult to anticipate and are likely to vary greatly over time.

The two general formulations of selective national service admit between them three programmatic possibilities. The historical CO exemption required two years of nonmilitary service at no direct cost to the federal government. The CO was to locate an acceptable public service position with a government or private sponsor. Selective Service provided some placement assistance and monitored that the service had been performed, but, otherwise, the individual was supervised and paid by the employing sponsor. An expanded program with such terms would add some administrative expenses, but still would be largely at no cost to the federal treasury.

A variation on this was proposed by Congressman Jonathan Bingham in 1971. The Bingham plan would require sponsoring employers to pay the federal government for each participant the same wage paid to other employees doing similar work or the minimum wage, whichever is greater; the government in turn would provide the participant a subsistence allowance based on geographical cost-of-living differences. (In theory, the net costs to the government would be modest.) Civilian service would be for not less than two nor more than four years, with the exact term determined by the value and difficulty of the work performed. Only draft-age, draft-eligible individuals would be expected to participate.

In contrast to these "expanded CO" formulations, the "channeling" alternatives commonly provide for direct and unreimbursed federal subsistence allowances to participants. An illustration is a measure proposed by Congressman Paul ("Pete") McCloskey in 1979. Only one year of civilian service would be required in the McCloskey plan as a satisfactory alternative to two-years active military duty. Women, as well as men, would be required to register and declare their intentions concerning civilian service, but whether women not doing so would be subject to military induction is not clear in the McCloskey proposal. (The McCloskey plan would also reduce entering military wages, but compensates for this by a package of postservice educational benefits.)

Interestingly, both the Bingham and the McCloskey proposals totally exempt from all obligations persons who conscientiously oppose national service. (This would not be so in a simple expansion of the traditional CO program.) Both also provide additional subsistence for civilian participants whose families would suffer economic hardship as a result of their service; but no such special benefits for military participants.[44]

A key unknown in all three alternatives is the participation rate, since this would be a factor in the first instance of how extensive draft calls are likely to be at any given time. (The variations in the preceding section are obviously pertinent in this respect.) Participation is also likely to be highly sensitive to international tensions. And, since all three programs leave the individual to find a qualifying position on his own (the Bingham plan provides for government employment as a last resort), the better qualified will presumably find the outlet more easily managed than will those with less to offer to prospective sponsors. The effects on the armed forces, then, could range from the very negligible (in the absence of large draft calls) to a quality-drain-off were the prospects for induction to increase significantly.

As with universal national service, there is little specificity as to what work individuals would do, how they would be organized, and how such a program would be monitored and compliance enforced. Nor is it evident that adequate numbers of civilian service opportunities exist to accommodate those who might participate. (By 1971, the traditional CO program had a backlog of some 34,000 awaiting placement in civilian service, many for several years.) The Bingham-McCloskey plans speak generally of work in government agencies; public, private, and parochial schools; law enforcement agencies; penal and probation systems; and private, nonprofit organizations whose principal purpose is social service—and of work that will not unreasonably displace wage earners—but there is not much information about how many specific jobs would be available. And, while as much as four years of poorly compensated social service (the Bingham notion) may approximate the burdensomeness of two years of peacetime active duty, it is not easy to find great equity in plans that call for just one year of service (as in the McCloskey proposal).

Of the three (expanding the traditional no-cost CO program to all who apply, the Bingham-like alternative, and the McCloskey-type program), the first two are the more plausible on several grounds. First, they proceed from practical necessity, not grand social vision. Short of abolishing CO status entirely, or attempting to muddle through the vagaries of existing CO case law—there seems little choice except to permit an outlet of rigorous work for those willing to accept its burdens. An expanded CO program assists the workings of a draft, whereas the channeling proposals do precisely the reverse by using military conscription to manipulate civilian behavior. Second, placement problems are less likely to be aggravated in a program which does not encourage large numbers to opt for civilian service than in one which does. Third, given the many uncertainties about national service in practice, a program with limited numbers provides an opportunity for necessary experimentation. Last, direct budgetary costs should be almost nonexistent in an expansion of the traditional CO program, and modest in the Bingham-like variant.

The Reserve Deferment

Turning to the last prominent draft selection matter, it is by no means essential that a draft deferment be allowed in order to man the Selected Reserve in peacetime, or, if one is granted, that the considerable abuses of the past in employing the procedure need be repeated.[45] Much depends on setting a realistic reserve manpower requirement in the presence of an active force draft. This in turn depends on answers to two prior questions: (1) whether the reserves have become critical in AVF force augmentation because it is preferable that they do so, or because the absence of the draft has made this essential; and (2) whether a resumption of conscription would not logically force changes in the size, organization, and missions of the reserve establishment. Both are beyond the scope of this examination, but, in the absence of answers, the case for allowing a draft deferment for Selected Reserve service is not self-evident.

A GI BILL

A prevalent assumption is that a renewed draft would necessarily be accompanied by a large package of postservice educational benefits, on the scale of some $2.8 billion to $3.2 billion annually in steady state. Equity is the animating rationale: because draft calls would be selective, inductees (and volunteers as well) should be afforded a postservice adjustment to restore them to a competitive footing with those who have not served. The proposition is not without merit, and one plausible means to fund such a GI Bill would be to divert some or all of existing "free" federal educational assistance (grants and guaranteed student loans, these totaling some $6.24 billion in fiscal year 1981) for exclusive use of those who serve in the armed forces. (Another plausible device is to provide to conscripts and volunteers priority access to existing grants and loans, or preferential terms of loan pay-back.)

Still, while the equity arguments are strong, they are not conclusive. Peacetime drafts, in the past, operated both with and without a GI Bill. Educational assistance for military service would appear to be sound social policy in the context of conscription. The essential point, however, is that such assistance is not an automatic and indispensable feature of a military draft.

THE OPTIONS AND THE ESSENTIAL OBJECTIVE

Several facts are evident from the preceding sections. First, much has been put forward in the name of obligatory service, most of it not especially convincing when examined closely. Second, conscription can clearly accomplish a host of nonmilitary social objectives; the terms of a draft need merely be configured so as to influence civilian behavior. Third, a draft could be tailored to produce striking changes in the demographic complexion of the armed forces.

Still, the power to compel service is so awesome in potential that it begs for restriction to national defense purposes in practice. And among the military applications, it makes little sense to invoke this power for limited and uneconomical objectives, or to exaggerate its use in campaigns to cure rapidly the perceived social sins of the AVF. The essential purpose of a military draft should be singular: to provide a predictable and secure flow of manpower into the armed forces in times of peace and war, and to do this with a steadfast regard for the precepts outlined at the beginning of this chapter. This certainty of manpower supply is the one capability that most distinguishes a draft from a wholly volunteer force.

The type of draft most likely to meet this objective would have several features. It would coexist with voluntary enlistments, and indeed induce some portion of them. It would strive to be neither a nonexistent nor a totally overwhelming factor in force-manning. First-term military wages would not in future years be ratcheted upward to maintain competitiveness with civilian pay. At the same time, a near-ironclad indexing device seems essential to prevent junior enlisted pay from falling to the levels allowed in the past.

Such a draft would select randomly, and would draw chiefly from 19- and 20-year-olds. There is no great reason why women should not be liable to induction, although there are powerful countervailing political and social instincts which may make the issue simply not worth the effort. Optional selective national service, in the form of broader access to the traditional CO program of alternative service, seems an essential element. How rigorous and how long this alternative need be in order to be a fair equivalent of induction are matters in need of a much overdo debate. Selective national service whose principal purpose is to use the threat of induction to channel large numbers of the young into public service seems wrong-headed as a matter of policy and ghastly as a matter of administration.

Resumption of such a draft forces to the fore a set of issues earlier generations had great difficulties coming to terms with: what to make of the reserves. This, too, is a subject of long overdue debate.

While the probable costs, benefits, and effects of conscription can be articulated with reasonable particularity and confidence, the unknowns are not insubstantial. But then, the risks and uncertainties involved in abandoning the draft for the AVF were, by comparison, far more imposing.

NOTES

1. It is useful to recall that all that actually expired with the adoption of the AVF was the president's authority to issue induction notices. The Military Selective Service Act (50 U.S.C. App. 451 et. seq.) is permanent legislation, and, until amended or revoked, governs the terms of any resumed draft. That law, among other things: (1) requires the registration of all males between 18 and 26; (2) permits, but does not require, that selections for induction be made randomly; (3) provides for active-duty military service of not more than 24 consecutive months; (4) explicitly defers or exempts conscientious objectors, certain government officials, and reservists; and (5) authorizes, but does not require, deferment of students, parents, hardship cases, and persons in occupations or research thought valuable to the national health, safety, or interest.

2. Only national service possibilities that, by their terms, are linked to obligatory military service are examined in this chapter. Not examined are national service ideas that, variously: (1) presuppose the continuation of the AVF; (2) prefer national service participants who are either younger or older than military age; or (3) are strictly divorced from military manpower concerns. Among the third are national service schemes which, even in coexistence with a military draft, would seek no special draft status for civilian service. As regards voluntary national service in the context of an AVF, some "voluntary" national service proposals can be as coercive as the concepts examined here (note, for instance, the proposition in chapter six to precondition receipt of federal educational assistance on performance of civilian service), but they venture considerably beyond the purview of this chapter.

3. Specific documentation is not meant here to imply the embrace of a particular mathematical formulation or model, for such intimacies with singular mathematical exercises have been the persistent pitfall of military manpower analyses (the Gates Commission's 1970 predictions about the AVF are a notable, but not uncommon, illustration). Assumptions about enlistment behavior are invariably tenuous. The best (and most prudent) that can be attempted in a volume such as this is to establish the order of magnitude and ranges of likely behavior, results and attendant costs.

4. Several explanations for the decline in strength have been put forward: civilians have taken over military jobs, thereby reducing the need for military members; greater retention of first-term volunteers means less need for large numbers of first-term personnel; technology has rendered the armed forces more capital-intensive and less labor-intensive; the rupture in Sino-Soviet affiliation has lessened the need for a force capable of fighting a major war with two powerful enemies at the same time; forces of allies are now factored into the equation, whereas before they were not; military manpower is simply better managed now; the reserves now take up much of the slack. While each is probably true (on this there are doubters), neither singly nor in combination do they account for an AVF which began in 1973 with the smallest force in 23 years and which then steadily decreased in size every year for the rest of the decade.

5. A difficult question is whether the reserves became central to the AVF because this is a desirable circumstance, or because the end of the draft made it an unavoidable necessity.

6. There are countervailing views, of course. The point is not that conscription is inevitable. It is, rather, that circumstances render it pertinent enough to require a prudent assessment of what is at stake.

7. Indeed, the debate tends not to be whether conscription can do such things, but rather, whether its societal costs are worth the gains.

8. Some, of course, have worried that, far from being a benefit, this flexibility to respond to international situations represents a great danger by investing in the president the power to commit U.S. forces without popular consent. The proper answer, however, would seem to lie in congressional restrictions on the *use* of forces, not in a national policy which risks insufficient *procurement* of forces.

9. As noted in chapter three, the CCC eventually did involve military training, but it began quite differently. In the early years, it was chiefly a temporary work-relief program managed by the army and supervised by the Departments of Agriculture and Interior. After 1937, the program's emphasis shifted to providing remedial training and education. In 1941, military drill without weapons was introduced.

10. One great difficulty in conscripting individuals for civilian public service is that the political legitimacy of the kind of work to be done tends to be a matter of fierce dispute. Individuals who view the provision of social services and an activist federal government as important "goods" view such things from one perspective. Others, who place less value on direct governmental provision of social, environmental, health care, and similar services are not likely to view such programs with much favor.

11. Some have suggested that UMT might be fitted into the academic year (high school or college) by being done at summer and other recesses, and thus minimize disruptions of the standard educational regime. While this is plausible, it merely transfers disruptions from schools to the military, by forcing a seasonal concentration on the military training base.

12. Indeed, there is the further concern that obligatory public service by massive numbers of the young would displace current and potential wage-earners from jobs they might otherwise claim. As well, there is the matter of opportunity costs for the young themselves: delayed schooling, withdrawal from jobs and job-apprentice programs, and the like.

13. On this score, there were a few legislative proposals in 1979 and 1980 to establish a presidential commission to examine these national service questions in depth, but these did not pass the Congress. In the wake of congressional impasse, a project with interesting potential for addressing these matters was funded by the Ford Foundation in mid-1981, but results are not expected before late 1982 or early 1983.

14. These do not, of course, take account of supervisory, administrative, or enforcement costs, nor do they account for costs associated with potential job displacement (and attendant loss of tax revenues), disruptions of higher education and the labor market, or the shifting of current costs of public service by youth from private sponsors and state and local governments to the general treasury. At the same time, they do not take account of some conceivable budgetary offsets, as perhaps in a reduction or elimination of the Peace Corps, VISTA, and numerous job training programs. (It is not clear whether a compulsory national service program would supplant or merely supplement these existing programs.)

15. *Wisconsin v. Yoder*, 406 U.S. 205, 92, S.Ct. 1526 (1972). Interestingly in this context, the court's majority found state-required school attendance until age 16 justified in part on grounds that it kept youth *out of* the labor market: "(t)he requirement of compulsory schooling to age 16 must therefore be viewed as aimed not merely at providing educational opportunities to children, but as an alternative to the equally undesirable consequence of unhealthful child labor displacing adult workers or, on the other hand, forced idleness." 406 U.S. at 228, 98 S.Ct. at 1540.

16. For some, of course, the selectivity of induction is not a handicap as long as two conditions are present: (1) a universal (or near universal) liability to selection; and (2) a random and unbiased means of selection.

17. See, in this regard, the historical material on reserve utilization in chapter two.

18. These numbers would rise, of course, were the current mix of prior-service and non-prior-service army reserve accessions altered in favor of greater reliance on fresh inductions.

19. One possibility, of course, is to eliminate weekend drills in favor of longer annual summer training. Another is to realign the locations of reserve units to better conform with the geographical distribution of the youth population. While the first is more plausible than the second, it would require a major (and politically cranky) reassessment of the assumptions underlying reserve training. See note 45 *infra* and accompanying text concerning the merits of such a general reappraisal.

20. Recall that the standard mobilization "show-rate" for the IRR in time of mobilization — variously, 70 to 90 percent — has never been put to the test.

21. The AVF has not been tested in either circumstance.

22. See, for example, the historical materials on the reserves in chapter two.

23. Assuming present force levels, fixed recruiting resources (in real terms) and constant relative pay, the Department of Defense currently expects army active force recruiting shortages to average not more than some 10,000 to 20,000 between 1985 and 1987, a relatively small shortage compared with some 350,000 accessions per year.

24. Indeed, such a scheme might actually *increase* marginal costs, by substituting some number of two-year inductions for three-year enlistments.

25. Existing law (50 U.S.C. App. 465 [d]) provides limited authority for such a step: "whenever the Congress or the President has declared that the national interest is imperiled, voluntary enlistment or reenlistment . . . may be suspended by the President to such extent as he may deem necessary in the interest of national defense."

26. See, in this regard, note 34 *infra*, and accompanying text.

27. This can be illustrated fairly simply. When mental category V is excluded (no one has been drafted from this category since World War II), approximately 56 percent of the draft-age male population falls within mental categories I, II, and IIIA. Were all first-term recruits randomly inducted, one would expect to see this proportion reflected in first-term ranks (compared with 37 percent in these categories entering the army in fiscal year 1978, for instance, a reasonably good AVF recruiting year). Were half inducted and half volunteers, the army in 1978 would still have had 42 percent — versus 37 percent — in these higher categories.

28. This, of course, assumes that reserve service would be grounds for draft deferment. The assumption is examined at note 45 *infra* and accompanying text.

29. The draft in several pre-Vietnam years yielded more conscripts than volunteers in the army. The conscript-to-volunteer ratio was in 1954, 75:25; in 1958, 64:36; in 1964, 57:44. Even for DoD as a whole, the pre-Vietnam draft accounted for approximately 40 percent of all accessions (through inductions and draft-induced enlistments).

30. Some have suggested that a curtailment of family housing privileges and allowances would benefit the military services and yield considerable savings, but the prospect is doubtful. As a general proposition, the families of junior personnel (below grade E-4 with under two years of service) have traditionally been denied "command sponsorship" and access to on-post housing in overseas locations. Junior personnel do qualify for on-post family housing in some stateside locations, but only in "inadequate" housing stock, for which they are required to pay a rental not more than 75 percent of their Basic Allowance for Quarters (BAQ) and not less than the operating costs of maintaining the housing. In effect, they pay their way. Little would be gained by lifting the privilege, since by law and custom career personnel cannot be required to live in inadequate on-post quarters. The same is largely true for off-post family housing allowances. In 1981 approximately 69,000 junior personnel received a BAQ "with dependents" allowance, an outlay of roughly $175 million. Had all been cut back to an individual-only BAQ, the outlay would have only dropped to $110 million — a savings of $65 million at best.

31. The necessity of establishing a basic first-term "wage," through some form of indexing device, is evidenced by the niggardly levels of first-term compensation which past drafts tol-

erated. What this "floor" should be is endlessly disputable, but one standard for which there is some precedent might be to index it to a level the equivalent of two-thirds of the federal minimum wage (all hours after a 40-hour week to be excluded from the calculation of equivalency, however). This is the wage currently paid to VISTA volunteers ($385 per month in 1981; $440 per month when benefits and allowances are included). An alternative would be to index future first-term pay increases to a set percentage of future career force pay raises. Less important for present purposes than the specifics is the establishment of the principle and of a certain procedure for maintaining such a "floor."

32. How rapid this transition would be is difficult to predict for several reasons. The differential "lures" of enlistment bonuses and aggressive recruiting, on the one hand, and current levels of first-term pay, on the other, are imperfectly understood. Thus, the short-term effects of curtailing the first while preserving the second are difficult to gauge. Also, fluctuations in youth unemployment are an elusive, but influential, variable, as are future rates of wage inflation in the civilian economy.

33. This last observation may strike some as suspect, but there is the force of considerable logic and history behind it. A draft, by its nature, forces an increase in the numbers of accessions (and a concomitant increase in training costs) in order to maintain the same end-strength as an AVF, and requires, as well, increased levels of expenditure (in the form of reenlistment bonuses) to maintain the career force. (Several studies suggest that a draft with pre-Vietnam terms would cause a decline in the career force of nearly 20 percent unless separate intensive efforts at retention are made). Still, retention in the AVF is an enduring problem and has been a costly proposition at the same time that recruitment has been costly. While an active force draft contributes to retention concerns, it also steadily frees resources from recruitment for use in retention.

34. The racial "production" of a random draft has already been noted. Of note is that expected "qualitative" results may not satisfy some concerns. While 39 percent of the youth population currently falls into mental categories I and II (i.e., when category V is excluded), 26 percent falls into mental category IV. Truly random selection would presumably carry these proportions into first-term inductions, producing among inductions a higher proportion of category IV's than the 20 percent overall level mandated by the Congress for each service beginning in 1983. To reconcile random selection with congressional standards would probably then require upward adjustments in the minimum standards for voluntary enlistment.

35. See, chapter two.

36. Higher turnover, of course, does add manpower to the Selected Reserve and the IRR through the operation of the six-year MSO.

37. Table 8.3, prepared by Gary R. Nelson, former deputy assistant secretary of defense, and used here with permission, was originally constructed for other purposes, but it illustrates well the steady-state consequences of the draft described here. Like all such projections, it is based on several assumptions about behavior, in this case mostly historically derived. (Alterations of assumptions, of course, produce different tabulations.) To serve the purpose here, table 8.3 need only be read as establishing the general order of magnitude of likely effects, rather than as a precise statement of detailed consequences.

38. Since discretion to revive these draft excusals remains in the Military Selective Service Act, an affirmative act of legislative purging remains necessary to assure this second count. See note 1, *supra*. Preserved would be dispensation for hardship and certain technical situations (e.g., nonresident alien status, participation in officer procurement programs, and the like).

39. The last draft applied to men aged 18 to 26 (and, in some cases, to age 35), but, with a youngest-first order of call, the most likely ages of induction were 19 and 20. By contrast, the earlier, oldest-first order of call yielded conscripts at various ages between 18½ and 25. In World War II and its immediate aftermath, draft age fluctuated widely, from 18 to 45, 20 to 44, 21 to 35, 21 to 27, 18 to 37, 20 to 37, 20 to 30, and 19 to 44.

40. In 1964, only 7 percent of enlisted women were in military occupations of a "nontradi-

tional" character ("nontraditional" in the sense that women historically had not entered, or been allowed to enter, these occupations in significant numbers). In 1972, only 10 percent were in these nontraditional assignments. By 1979, however, the figure stood at 46 percent.

41. Were women to volunteer in sufficient numbers, there would, of course, be no need to draft women at a given time, but the same would hold true for men. Given lower requisitions for women generally, the statistical probabilities of being drafted would differ according to sex, but any associated inequity would seem dwarfed by the inequities of a male-only draft.

42. While registration costs would roughly double, the numbers of classifications and examinations of women registrants would still be small. At an estimated unit cost of $150, the classification and examination of 30,000 women (those with low lottery numbers) might add $4.5 million to overall Selective Service outlays. Pregnancy need be treated no differently than other temporary disqualifications; motherhood, no differently than other grounds for hardship exemption.

43. While the Supreme Court has sanctioned the Congress' preference for male-only conscription when such a draft's purpose is to provide mobilization manpower for combat, it has not yet ruled on a peacetime draft in which inductions would fill, as well, military assignments normally removed from direct exposure to combat. In all likelihood, a strong statement of congressional preference would not be overturned by the Court.

44. No cost estimates were produced for the Bingham-type proposal. The Congressional Budget Office (CBO), underscoring the "substantial uncertainty about the respone of the youth labor market," did attempt, in 1980, to place a range on the McCloskey plan. Assuming a definite resumption of conscription and civilian stipends of approximately $440/month, the CBO pegged the net five-year addition to the federal budget of a program with 230,000 youths at $700 million, and one with 1 million participants at $13.1 billion.

45. See, in this regard, the material on reserves in chapter two. Alternatives to the reserve deferment include incentives or requirements to participate in Selected Reserve drills as satisfaction of the residual obligation after active duty. Alternatives to abuse of the reserve deferment would include random selection of applicants and increases in the annual drilling and training requirements.

9

Military Service in American Society*

Mark J. Eitelberg and Martin Binkin

MARK J. EITELBERG, Senior Scientist, Human Resources Research Organization, and MARTIN BINKIN, Senior Fellow, Brookings Institution, examine social and ethical issues that have colored the historical American debate over how the nation should raise its armed forces in peacetime, including individual freedom versus duty to country, citizen-soldiers versus professional armies, racial representativeness, the role of women. As to the current public debate on such issues, the authors doubt that peacetime conscription has gained general acceptance, at least among those who might be called upon to serve, and suggest that "the citizenry in general, and American youth in particular, must be given a better idea of what U.S. national interests are, of how U.S. foreign and domestic policies are designed to support those interests, and of the role that the military institution serves to protect those interests."

It may be laid down as a primary position, and the basis of our system, that every Citizen who enjoys the protection of a free Government, owes not only a proportion of his property, but even of his personal services to the defence of it. . . .[1]

George Washington

Where is it written in the Constitution, in what article or section is it contained, that you may take children from the parents, and parents from their children, and compel them to fight the battles of any war, in which the folly or wickedness of Government may engage it?[2]

Daniel Webster

*Portions of this paper were adapted from Mark J. Eitelberg, *Military Representation: The Theoretical and Practical Implications of Population Representation in the American Armed Forces*, AD-AO93-391 (Alexandria, Va: Defense Technical Information Center [DTIC], October 1979); Martin Binkin, "Military Manpower in the 1980's: Issues and Choices," *International Security Review* 5, (1980); and Martin Binkin and Mark J. Eitelberg, with Alvin J. Schexnider and M. Martin Smith, *Blacks and the Military* (Washington, D.C.: Brookings Institution, 1982).

How the United States should raise its armed forces in peacetime is an issue that rests at least as much on ideological as on strict military effectiveness grounds. Indeed, in the absence of conclusive evidence that a peacetime military establishment raised either through voluntarism or through conscription can defend the nation more effectively or efficiently than the other, social and political considerations have become all the more important.

The issue has long pitted against one another traditional values of citizen obligation and individual freedom and competing concepts of citizen-soldiers and professional armies. More recently, prompted by fundamental changes in American society, questions of social representation in the armed forces have come to the forefront. These factors, along with the temperament of contemporary American society, and particularly its younger generation, form the context within which the nation must consider the issue.

THE AMERICAN "TRADITION"

Some argue that the right to bear arms is as much a duty as a prerogative of citizenship. Others contend that the blessings of liberty in a democracy include the right but not the obligation for armsbearing. And still others seek to define the limits of citizen service in the military according to situational criteria. Yet, it is the absence of a firm, guiding principle in our nation's founding code that has promoted the persistent controversy over how and when Americans should be called to serve their country.

Article I, Section 8 of the Constitution of the United States declares that Congress shall have the power "to raise and support Armies . . . ; to provide and maintain a Navy; to provide for calling forth the Militia to execute the Laws of the Union, suppress Insurrections and repel Invasions; [and] to provide for organizing, arming, and disciplining, the Militia, and for governing such part of them as may be employed in the Service of the United States. . . ." Article II of the Bill of Rights also provides for "the right of the people to keep and bear arms" since "a well-regulated militia . . . [is] necessary to the security of a free State."

Beyond these broad declarations, there is no guidance within the Constitution concerning the precise framework or figuration of the nation's military forces, no prescription or instruction about the means or methods of assembling an army. A testament to the enduring character of the issue is the simple fact that, after 200 years of theory and practice during wars and peace, the basic precepts of citizen service in the American military are still being debated with distinctive passion in public forums.

Whenever patriotic citizens gather to discuss the form and substance of the nation's military forces, they typically venture to uncover the truth and justice that reside in the spirit of 1776. For whatever reason, the answers to difficult questions concerning the manner of military recruitment are often sought in American folklore and the sacred words of the Founding Fathers.

U.S. history with its own peculiar brand of democratic postulates is cited with all but obsessive reverence in the rhetoric of All-Volunteer Force (AVF) critics and apologists alike. Because history functions as a polemical crutch in the continuing war of words, a brief examination of the evolution and significance of early American military thought is appropriate.

The Roots of American Military "Tradition"

The Founding Fathers were strongly influenced in their writings and oratories by the heritage of classical antiquity. The political history of Rome played a prominent role in forming colonial views of the Revolutionary experience, serving as a sort of classical analogy for their own time. Colonial perceptions were also guided by the tradition of English common law, the social theories of New England Puritanism, as well as the social and political thought of the English Civil War and the Commonwealth period. The ideas and attitudes of the European Enlightenment were especially pervasive in the political literature of the American Revolution. Nevertheless, actual knowledge and understanding of the classical works was often superficial, even among the best colonial writers; references to the Great Works were commonly presented as window dressing, and passages were frequently pulled from the classical literature with careful selectivity.[3]

Several founders of American democratic thought were more than enamored of the writings of Rousseau and his glorification of the military spirit. "Every citizen must be a soldier as a duty," Rousseau proclaimed, "and none may be so by profession." Professional armies are typical of despotic regimes. Equality and the armed citizenry, on the other hand, are impartible; inequality encircles the existence of professional armies. Military service is a part of the civic education. And the social contract, Rousseau and his followers argued, makes it a right and duty of each citizen to defend the polity. Just as citizens must pay their debts, they must fight for their country and preserve it from destruction.[4]

Many colonial thinkers also discovered "truth" in the works of seventeenth-century English spokesmen for extreme liberalism, such as John Trenchard, who held that standing armies were no more than gangs of restless mercenaries, beholden to the desires and demands of the self-serving rulers who kept them.[5] They were the praetorians, the janissaries, the bogymen of the American Revolution — prime movers of the process by which improvident nations lost "that precious jewel liberty." They were — as seen in the collective and separate histories of Turkey, France, Poland,

Spain, Russia, India, and Egypt — the power capable of snuffing out right, law, and freedom. They were, in the words of one declaimer, "a number of men paid by the public to devote themselves wholly to the military profession," and "the means . . . of overturning the constitution of a country and establishing the most intolerable despotism."[6]

From the nation's beginnings, then, discussions of how best to achieve national security (from within and without) took the form of a two-sided controversy: Should the American military be a "professional force," prepared to encounter the highly skilled and disciplined armies of Europe; yet forever cast as a threat to liberty; or, should it be a nonprofessional force of citizen-soldiers, prepared to fight primarily out of duty to country and constitution.[7]

In fact, the American Revolution was fought by a mixture of both "amateurs" and "professionals." A universal military obligation for nearly all males of appropriate age appeared in the statutes of all the British colonies (with the exception of Quaker Pennsylvania), and this obligation was enforced in the Indian Wars and in the American Revolution (though exceptions or exclusions from service were common). General Washington was not particularly pleased with the process of raising armies, dissolving them, and then raising them again. And he expressed his irritation and frustration in a letter to the president of the Continental Congress in 1776. "To place any dependence upon the Militia," Washington wrote, "is assuredly, resting upon a broken staff":

> Men just dragged from the tender Scenes of domestick life . . . when opposed to troops regularly train'd, disciplined, and appointed . . . makes them timid, and ready to fly from their own shadows. . . . The Jealousies of a standing Army; and the Evils to be apprehended from one are remote; and in my judgment, situated and circumstanced as we are, not at all to be dreaded . . . ; for if I was called upon to declare upon Oath, whether the Militia has been most serviceable or hurtful upon the whole; I should subscribe to the latter.[8]

The framers of the Constitution, confronted with the problem of devising a permanent military establishment at the conclusion of the American Revolution, sought the learned opinions and recommendations of the Revolution's leading generals. In May 1783, General Washington offered his famous "Sentiments on the Peace Establishment" — proclaiming a universal military obligation as the concomitant of the ballot, an idea that is the foundation of the modern mass army.

Washington's "Sentiments" were framed on a philosophical cornerstone of democratic thought: citizenship entails positive rights as well as negative rights (or responsibilities). For Washington and his like-minded contemporaries, it was but one step from the general notion of civic responsibility to the specific application of a citizen army. This linkage between citizenship and military service was again set forth in a plan for universal militia training, submitted to Congress in 1790 by Secretary of War Henry Knox. The so-called Knox plan envisioned universal military training for all males between 18 and 20 years of age. At 21, soldiers would be given certificates acknowledging the attainment of full citizenship. President Washington approved the plan, but it was never enacted by Congress. Congress did, however, pass the Uniform Militia Act in 1792—granting that "each and every free, able-bodied, white, male citizen" be enrolled in the militia.[9] The Militia Act, designed to provide uniformity and universality to state militias, was unrealistic in practice. Although it remained the theoretical law of the land for over 100 years, it produced only a paper army. The president's powers to call up the state militias were strictly limited to defense against invasions and the protection of domestic order.

During the War of 1812, for example, the enrolled militia had a strength of over 700 thousand men—but it was poorly armed and poorly trained and confined to service within the separate states. When James Monroe, then secretary of state, proposed a national military conscription, he encountered strong opposition. "Who will show me," pleaded Daniel Webster, "any constitutional injunction, which makes it the duty of the American people to surrender every thing valuable in life, and even life itself, not when the safety of their country and its liberties may demand the sacrifice, but whenever the purposes of an ambitious and mischievous Government may require it?"[10]

Currents of Thought through History

From the American Revolution onward, the philosophical debate about the proper form of the nation's military has persisted between the partisans of professional soldiery and adherents to the concept of obligatory service. On the side of a citizen army were several political and military figures, including Thomas Jefferson, Andrew Jackson, John A. Logan, John M. Schofield, John McAuley Palmer, George C. Marshall, and Leonard Wood.[11]

Wood, an outspoken evangelist for universal military service who campaigned vigorously for "preparedness" during the period just prior to World War I, held that: "Every good American honors the real voluntary spirit, but it is difficult to understand how any man who is familiar with our country's history can advocate the continuance of the volunteer system, with its uncertainties, unpreparedness and lack of equality of service. We have been warned repeatedly by the experiences of others of the folly of depending on the volunteer system."[12]

Even though national circumstances and sociopolitical priorities are quite different, Wood's words in support of a universal military obligation might very well have been extracted from a recent editorial in the public press or the latest edition of the *Congressional Record*. Wood's fundamental position concerning "manhood obligation" and his criticism of inequity in the volunteer military are virtually the same arguments used today by some critics of all-volunteer recruitment. Senator Sam Nunn of Georgia, for example, considers the "alarming decline" in acceptance of the obligation for citizens to serve the nation's needs. "The fundamental question that must be answered," Nunn writes, "concerns the citizen's duty. Neither Congress nor the executive branch nor the American people have come to grips with this question."[13] "I believe we must distinguish between a career and a citizen force in the military services," Congressman Robin Beard of Tennessee similarly observes, "because every citizen has an obligation to devote a period of time in service to his or her country."[14]

Advocates of a volunteer or professional military through the years have included Alexander Hamilton, John C. Calhoun, Dennis Hart Mahan, Henry W. Halleck, Emory Upton, and Robert Taft.[15] The draft, Taft remarked in 1945, "is far more typical of totalitarian nations than of democratic nations. It is absolutely opposed to the principles of individual liberty which have always been a part of American democracy." The principle of a compulsory draft, he concluded, is "basically wrong."[16]

The case against government intrusions into private lives was again expounded on the floors of Congress during the AVF debates of the late 1960s and, more recently, when the reinstitution of draft registration was proposed in 1979. Senator Mark Hatfield of Oregon, for instance, stated that he was "opposed to the coercion of the draft . . . to the character of the draft which represents a totalitarian system of Government rather than a democratic system." "From the beginning of the draft programs of this Nation," Hatfield continued, "the draft has been considered contrary, alien, and foreign to the democratic American ideals, and there have been forceful actions taken to resist its imposition of involuntary servitude."[17] "Patriotism, devotion, wisdom, conviction, commitment, idealism, which we all seek, cannot be achieved by conscription," Congressman Ron Paul of Texas likewise remarked. "This tool, used by the state for centuries, has never built a free society, nor can it be used to preserve this society. Consider freedom and volunteerism — reject compulsion and conscription. Freedom cannot be preserved by tyranny."[18]

Philosophical debate aside, actual American experience belies the popular conception of so-called democratic "tradition" in this country. Indeed, despite ample discussion of the universal obligation for armsbearing in the history of American military thought, it was not until March 1863, two years after the Civil War had begun, that Congress enacted the country's first draft law. The law was intended to stimulate the flow of Union troops in geographic areas that did not produce their quota of volunteers, and, unlike the theoretical premise of universal service, the law openly favored conscription of the poor.

The draft was invoked again in 1917, with the ostensible purpose of reducing the voluntary enlistments of the nation's most talented men; government policymakers feared that a brain-drain would cripple U.S. industries and "disturb the domestic and economic life of the nation."[19] In 1940, it was apparent that the country could not meet the manpower demands of the impending war, and Congress once more turned to the mechanism of Selective Service. The draft of World War II continued (with a brief period of interruption) until the last draft call went out in December 1972. Yet, in the customary application of conscription, the last period of selective service was hardly a model of democratic justice. An array of deferments and disqualifications, exemptions and exclusions testified to the fact that the rights and duties of citizen service in the American military differed greatly from idealistic principles to practice. The fundamental standards espoused by the Founding Fathers were, in practice, malleable and duly tied to temporal values and prevailing prejudice.

The tradition of the American military can thus be described as that of a small, professional, cadre force in peacetime, and a citizen army (in some form) during periods of war. The effort to describe an overall, American tradition is, however, complicated by the understanding that the American nation of the past scarcely resembles that of the present. The same pragmatic considerations that overshadowed idealistic concepts in the earliest days of the republic likewise dominate our approach to manning the military today. The fact that this nation has had conscription for only 30-odd years supports neither the citizen-soldier nor the professional (or "career" or "all-volunteer") description of a national tradition.

The underlying rationale of a "nation-in-arms"—and the belief that a universal military obligation is the concomitant of the ballot—has periodically cradled conscription in democratic countries everywhere from revolutionary France to twentieth-century United States. The essential irony, perhaps, lies in the fact that the customary form of military establishment in civilized nations has been a tax-supported professional army.[20] Even in Plato's *Republic*, it was the Guardians, a select group of "spirited" and proficient specialists, who were charged to protect the state and ward off invasion. In Plato's century, as in those that followed, it was the professional force that prevailed for basically practical reasons: citizen militias required special conditions and they were no match for professional soldiers. In all of recorded history, then, citizen standing armies are the rarity; the militia system worked well as a local function, organized by small units of the local government for short periods of time to defend homes and farms in adjoining areas. Yet, the militias were hardly suited for any extended campaigns or long expeditions in distant territories.

The balance of the draft years in American history occurred during a time when the country stood firmly opposed to Communist aggression, and exercised that opposition by fighting in two Asian wars, committing large forces to foreign shores, and accepting a new responsibility to stand as the leader of the free world. General Washington, in all his wisdom, probably never conceived of the day when his army's muskets would be replaced by nuclear missiles, and the once-almighty nations of Western Europe would turn to the North American colonialists for protection. If there is an American tradition to be found in the theory and practice of the military establishment, it can be most accurately characterized as pragmatism — guided, but not led, by the nation's own transitory interpretations of the principles of democracy.

The Evolution and Conflicting Nature of Current Issues

The changing perspective of discussion concerning military manpower and methods of recruitment reflects changing politics and national circumstances. Since 1945, for example, manpower issues have focused on national security, budgetary considerations, and practical expediency (i.e., compulsory service). "Equality of service" grew out of the citizen-soldier concept around the period just prior to World War I; yet, before the 1960s, equity was seldom ever a major factor in manpower policy decisions.[21] A combination of civil rights and antiwar protests, quota consciousness, and the public response to inequities in the Selective Service System led to extensive draft reform, the draft lottery, and the eventual demise of conscription. At the same time, as a result of these social forces, a new public awareness of the military establishment developed — an awareness and interest in the *means* as well as the outcomes of defense manpower policy. Moreover, it was the concern for the social consequences of manpower policy decisions that helped to reshape methods of recruitment and to popularize the concept of "military representation."

"Representation" perhaps means more in the United States than in any other nation. *E Pluribus Unum* (From Many One) is more than just a motto of the Great Seal. It signifies and typifies the American self-image: a nation where unity can be achieved while all diversities of society and the polity are preserved. The U.S. armed forces have always emphasized the diversity of their membership; it is the nature of the organization that consciously brings together persons from varied backgrounds to serve for a common cause. Popular literature and the mass media have helped to create this image of the American military as a sort of miniature melting pot, a faithful reflection of all distinctive traditions and cultural patterns in the nation. And the recent spread of interest in military representation has functioned to convert the image into a national policy goal.

The seeming paradox lies in the fact that the American armed forces have never been truly representative of the civilian population. Class privilege and racial injustice in society, faithfully reflected in the historical policies of the military, have operated in the past to deprive certain groups from "equality of service" and to protect others from the draft. Even now, there are major dissimilarities between military membership and the civilian population. Women, for example, form a relatively miniscule portion of the armed forces. In addition, because of physical job requirements, the military has always been overrepresentative of the young (but not the *very* young) and underrepresentative of everyone over the age of 40.

Conscription has never produced representation in the American military, and it is even less likely that representation can occur under the all-volunteer format. Of course, the ideal of a perfectly representative military—a so-termed "microcosmic replica" of the general population—is an illusion. Besides the myriad differences between subgroups within gross classifications of groups, and subgroups within subgroups of groups, it is clear that a sample of individuals in any corresponding subdivision of the population would be *at least* biased by those who have certain skills, attributes, interests, and personality traits. The ideal of perfect representation within any highly specialized institution is probably not even desirable.[22]

Even the concept of "approximate" representation is difficult to grasp in the abstract. It has been observed that democracy tends to treat its objects numerically, subject to determinations of magnitude—and "our most adequate understanding of things is to be gained by their correlation with, or translation into, terms of commensurable quantities."[23] Thus, we strive to achieve a state of mathematical exactness—using ratios and statistical computations—where our institutions contain the same elements, in the same proportion, as are found in the standard or reference group. Representation problems are looked upon as mathematical puzzlers, equations in which the unknown quantities are the policy decisions necessary to achieve a state of numerical similitude. But once the ideal of perfect correspondence is abandoned, and the notion of "approximate representation" is accepted in its place, the presumed certainty of outcomes associated with exact likeness is lost. Approximate representation can mean one inch or a thousand miles, depending on the perspective of the beholder. Ultimately, we establish a boundary of roughly acceptable proportions beyond perfection with subjective standards that are tied to contemporary public attitudes, the politics of the moment, personal values and biases, and particular views of reality.

The task of defining representation is further complicated by the absence of a precise definition of "representation." The concept is neither self-evident nor universal. There is no common set of criteria, no clear consensus through history concerning important population subgroups. There is an endless variety of characteristics that may be said to affect the goals of proportional participation. The variables, scales of measurement, and inter-pretations of recruiting results consequently vary from study to study—from AVF naysayer to advocate—depending largely on individual principles, perceptions, values, and expectations. Identical statistical data can therefore be found to inspire often contradictory conclusions in the literature and commentary on military recruiting results.[24] Nevertheless, the term has become a permanent part of the military manpower vernacular, and no discussion of the armed forces is complete today without some men-tion of social demography and "proportional distributions."

Although the notion of representation (as applied to the military) is relatively modern, the basic concept has been a part of political thought for hundreds of years. Indeed, in this country it has become a keystone of democracy—an assurance of constitutional behavior and political equilib-rium in the pluralist society—spreading slowly from the political sphere throughout the social setting of the nation. In the 1940s, representation theory was applied to the bureaucracy, and during the 1960s, within the military context.[25] Today, representation manifests itself in "affirmative ac-tion" and related numerical policies in employment and education, in balanced political party tickets, in public concern over ethnic, racial, and female appointments to public office, in symbolic portrayals of the American population, and in the minority and female rights movements.

Proponents of population representation in the American armed forces call upon three basic principles to argue their positions: (1) There is a need to have a legitimate military of "citizen-soldiers" who can "re-present" (or "present again") the variety of community interests and recreate the social fabric of American life; (2) Military membership must ensure a capable, cohesive, and effective fighting force (in symbol as well as in deed); and (3) There must be a fair or equitable system of military service, where the benefits and burdens (or the rights and responsibilities) of national defense are distributed justly (or proportionately) throughout society. It is these three areas of national policy—political legitimacy, military effectiveness, and social equity—that presently frame a core of concern over military manpower recruiting under the AVF.

Political Legitimacy

At the heart of the issue of military representation in this country is the con-cept of "citizen-soldier" and the democratic notion of full citizen participa-tion. Proponents of this view claim that the armed forces can only be con-sidered a truly "legitimate" extension of the citizenry if the military is a citizen's institution, rather than the preserve of career-oriented "regulars." An army that employs mercenaries, professional killers, and "hired guns" to do its bidding commits the "suicidalness of militarism."[26] An army that pulls from the nation's populace the poor and socioeconomically disadvantaged, while excusing the wellborn and the privileged, the rich and the educated, defies the fundamental principles of democratic government and obligatory service by each and every member of the body politic.

Disposal of the right to defend the nation by the full citizenry is thus perceived as an abandonment of liberty. Some observers insist that the shift away from forms of compulsory service "maligns the character" of the American citizen by saying to him: "Give anything but yourself." The national character suffers, as the dual role of military and civilian responsibilities vanishes from our community life. Those who are no longer responsible for serving their country by taking arms never gain a full appreciation of civic duty, and a leadership elite that has no military experience eventually emerges, set far apart from the profession of arms. Inevitably, widespread public apathy and acquiescence concerning the military affairs of the nation are seen to result in the growth of a relatively autonomous, monolithic, military-industrial complex. As the military turns its sights inward, advocates of compulsory service warn, it will necessarily gravitate toward its industrial counterpart in civilian society, seeking bigger and more elaborate defense budgets, taking the nation headlong down the road to endless military adventures. Eventually the military establishment emerges with its *own* professional concerns, ideology, powerful pressure groups, and brand of politics. In the most severe instance, this complex of military and industrial forces — isolated from community values and less concerned about the ethics of its own use — sets in motion a "Seven Days in May" conspiracy.

One school of thought on the subject subscribes to the hypothesis that a military force integrated with its host society provides an informal social network to "ensure that civilian sensibilities are incorporated within the military." This, so the argument goes, can be accomplished through the presence in the military of "in-and-outers" who maintain their identities as civilians rather than as military professionals. As Morris Janowitz, one of the leading advocates of the integration theory, summed it up:

> it would be in error to overlook the fact that self-selection into the volunteer force is already recruiting men with an inclination towards conservative thinking. An in-bred force, which could hold resentments toward civilian society and could, accordingly, develop a strong and uniform conservative political ideology, would in turn influence professional judgments.[27]

This view, however, has been questioned on at least four counts.

First, it has been noted that "no simple link between military professionalism and military intervention in politics has to date been shown to exist." Although instances can be found where highly professional armies have seized political power, these have been largely in the third world, suggesting that such action is also influenced by "the level of political culture."[28]

Others contend that even if the military's link with society is considered important, it is maintained through the professional contacts that the growing corps of military specialists and technicians have with their civilian counterparts. Besides, so the argument goes, "the Defense Department employs more than one million civilians, and many officers serve tours of duty which require daily contact with the business community, academic institutions, and other civilian organizations."[29]

Third, it has been pointed out, the preponderantly conservative officer corps has always been the dominant influence on military values. It has always been this elite, and not the rank and file, that has made decisions about political action and social pressure.

Finally, at the extreme, some argue that whether military forces are representative of, or closely integrated with, the broader civilian society has little bearing on the issue of civilian control. In fact, promoters of "objective civilian control" advocate "autonomous military professionalism"; civilian control exercised through a formal chain of command "achieves its end by militarizing the military, making them the tool of the state," as opposed to the integration approach, which "achieves its end by civilianizing the military, making them the mirror of the state." The benefits of the "objective" approach, according to Samuel P. Huntington, are that it "produces the lowest possible level of military political power with respect to all civilian groups," while preserving "that essential element of power which is necessary for the existence of a military profession."[30]

"Political legitimacy" stands out as one of the oldest, most deeply rooted themes of military representation. Compulsory service follows on the heels of legitimacy arguments, since it is the only manpower recruitment system capable of ensuring universal citizen participation. Yet, conscription violates the precepts of free choice, and forms of conscription in this country have been characteristically unfair, drawing from limited, nonuniversal manpower pools.

Interestingly, while theories of political legitimacy date back (at least) to the birth of the nation, an array of exclusionary practices, inequitable standards, and quotas have historically prohibited military participation by certain segments of the population. Black Americans, for example, were restricted from full participation and subject to special enlistment quotas until only 30 years ago. Today, participation by women is regulated for the stated purposes of military effectiveness and practical expediency (the same reasons once used for limiting participation by blacks). Nevertheless, the special exclusion of women implies that women are "second-class" citizens, and it is difficult to argue that political legitimacy objectives — or universal citizen service — can ever be fully realized unless women are treated and accepted in the armed forces on an equal basis with men.[31]

Military Effectiveness

Military representation—especially when it pertains to measures of "quality"—is often considered in context with "military effectiveness." The end of the draft and advent of volunteer service in the early 1970s operated to make the education and aptitude levels of the general military-age population the criterion of recruiting success. However, it is not clear that "quality" representation, though often included in military manpower analyses and public commentary, necessarily affects overall military performance or organizational efficiency. The military services are, for example, charged to provide the strongest and most capable force. "Perfect" representation, by definition, implies that the *worst* as well as the best elements of society be present in the ranks of the military. In practice, this would mean that restrictive standards on mental aptitude, moral background, and physical condition (and any other standards, such as age and gender-related prohibitions) be completely removed to allow *everyone* the right to participate. It would mean that the armed forces actively seek and recruit, not the most "qualified," but, the most "representative" members of society, however defined. Although the elimination of entry standards is not impossible, it is highly impractical and obviously contrary to the goals of national security.

Military needs are thus used to justify the "quality mix" of individuals in the armed forces as well as the standards for acceptance and placement. "Quality" generally refers to those characteristics and attributes of military personnel that are deemed desirable and that contribute to a more productive, capable, and better-motivated force. Because of the difficulty in constructing individual profiles and predictors of performance, military quality objectives are now defined in the shorthand terms of standardized entry test scores and high-school graduation status.

Still, the disproportionate representation of certain social or economic categories of individuals may negatively influence the effectiveness of the armed forces. The Defense Manpower Commission addressed this point in 1975 and found no evidence to suggest that socioeconomic composition affects the capacity of an armed force to fulfill its mission. Rather, the commission concluded, performance is more influenced by "dynamic factors" such as leadership, training, morale and discipline, and material readiness than by socioeconomic composition.[32]

Even without hard evidence on the requirements for population representation, questions of effectiveness are raised. And these questions are often just enough to stimulate public uncertainty and anxiety about the capability of the armed forces. For example, scholars, military leaders, public officials, and concerned citizens may (and do) ask the following:

- To what extent does social or racial imbalance affect the unity, cohesion, and morale of military units? That is, does social or racial imbalance exacerbate internal tensions and provoke discontent and unrest within the military?

- Does intergroup diversity reduce or improve field effectiveness?
- Is a military force composed largely of the poor, disadvantaged, and otherwise disaffected members of society a "reliable" force? Will racial or ethnic minorities, for instance, if summoned into action for civil disturbances, decide they owe a higher fealty to their own communities than to the government?
- Since individuals are responsive to their own reference groups, values, group memberships, ethnic origins, and so on, how necessary is a "balance" of diversified interests? For example, what effect will an *un*representative armed force have on civil-military relations? Does civilian control exist primarily in the plurality of thought and conflicting interests of various civilian groups in the armed forces? Will the loss of an identity of thought between the military and society result in a self-serving army of career-minded "employees" — unwilling to pay the price of patriotism in battle?

These concerns have all been expressed at some point either directly preceding or during the operation of the AVF, and each, in its own way, is enough to cast some shadow of doubt upon the effectiveness of an unrepresentative military force. Other questions, then, are these: What influence does a loss of public confidence in the military — created by public perceptions of a socially unrepresentative force — have on civil-military relations and military effectiveness? What effect will public doubt or mistrust of the armed forces have on recruitment, oversight, budgets, and other areas? Will public awareness of inequities in military participation fuel disharmony and social protest, as it did during the period of the Vietnam War?

The composition of the military may equally affect the image of American life and American defense capabilities abroad. It has been suggested, for instance, that combat units overweighted with minorities and the disadvantaged will not have credibility in the world arena; a loss of credibility limits military policy options. On another level, such units may not effectively project (i.e., symbolically represent) the goals of U.S. domestic and foreign policy.[33]

It is likely that the overall effectiveness of the American armed forces is somehow influenced by factors related to the social composition of its membership. The manner and degree of influence, the important social variables, the point at which representational divergency creates effectiveness problems, and related issues are still left mainly to speculation.

Yet, it is important to understand that the goals of military effectiveness are tied to the goals of equity and legitimacy. As an agent of the government, the military responds to the higher criteria of equity, and it conforms to legitimate direction and control. At the same time, in order to effectively protect and defend these national guiding principles, the military must fulfill its own peculiar organizational requirements. Hence, there is a basic conflict of purposes, the classic problem of means versus ends: military effectiveness requires that certain standards be employed to control military enlistments and job placements; however, national principles and priorities simultaneously demand that the armed forces be a reflection of society.

Social Equity

The major reasons for current interest in "social justice" of voluntary recruitment are the increasing overrepresentation of blacks in the enlisted ranks and, to a lesser extent, policies that narrow the participation of women. Ironically, while the exclusion of blacks from the military ignited modern discussion of "equality of service," it is their overrepresentation that dominates most commentary today. Just prior to the end of the draft, black membership in the rank and file of the nation's ground forces was roughly in line with the eligible population (about 12 percent); by 1981, however, the proportion had reached 33 percent in the army and just over 22 percent in the Marine Corps. Growth in the black membership of the air force and navy enlisted ranks was far more modest; by 1981, black representation in the navy was slightly under (at 12 percent), and in the air force slightly over (at 16 percent) the proportion of blacks in the military-age population. At the same time, the proportion of black officers in the armed forces remained noticeably out of balance despite a twofold increase during the period—from about 2 percent in 1972 to just over 5 percent in 1981.

Fielding combat forces composed of an overproportion of blacks, it is said, imposes an unfair burden on one segment of American society, a burden that appears all the more inequitable since blacks have not enjoyed a fair share of the benefits conferred by the state. The prospect that as many as half the combat casualties in the early phases of a military engagement would be black soldiers or marines, so the argument goes, is immoral, unethical, and somehow runs contrary to the precepts of democratic institutions. On the other side of the question are those who contend that a disproportionately black force is not without its benefits; particularly appealing are the employment, training, and social opportunities not otherwise available to many young black men and women.

This equity question impales the nation on the horns of a particularly difficult dilemma: Does the legitimate concern that young blacks will probably die in grossly disproportionate numbers, at least initially, in defense of national interests outweigh the concern, equally legitimate, that the armed forces provide many black youth with their only bridge from the "permanent underclass" to the mainstream of American life? That countless blacks have chosen to bear the burden in order to reap the benefit, and in so doing have enabled the nation to maintain a volunteer army, nevertheless begs the question of equity.

The thorny issue of participation by women in the armed forces also poses a question of social equity. As the controversy over military registration attests, the role of women in the armed forces has become an important consideration in military manpower planning and in the volunteer versus draft debate. In contrast to 1972, when women constituted but 2 percent of all military personnel, by 1981 they made up over 8 percent of the uniformed force. This expansion — partly in deference to the women's movement and partly to facilitate the transition to an all-volunteer force — may have run its course, however, as the military services pause to evaluate its implications. Many traditionalists feel that the expansion has gone far enough while feminists contend that that surface has barely been scratched.

In fact, except for the air force, the capabilities for additional expansion beyond present levels appear quite limited, unless the nation is ready to accept — and impel the military services to accept — women in "combat" roles. Critics contend that women lack the physical characteristics for combat, that they would adversely affect combat unit cohesion and hence performance, and, besides, women in warrior roles conflict with the nation's deeply rooted traditions. While the Supreme Court's decision sustaining the constitutionality of male-only registration might appear to settle the issue, the "will of the American people" toward the question is yet to be determined. In fact, public attitudes and values concerning women's military roles are elusive; recent opinion polls indicate that if conscription became necessary, a majority (51 percent) of the public favors drafting women as well as men but that most of those (55 percent) oppose women in combat roles.[34]

There has been a conspicuous lack of interest in pursuing the issue, in part because of its complexity, but also because of ambivalence in each of the opposing camps. Many proponents of mandatory service, it turns out, also favor maintaining traditional sex roles and worry that the adoption of the former would threaten the latter. Many of the staunchest proponents of women's rights are also pacifists and stop short of pressing the combat question to avoid seeming to dignify the military institution.[35] Finally, there appears to be less enthusiasm among young women for entering nontraditional military jobs than some feminists had earlier predicted.[36]

Equity perceptions are greatly influenced by the assumed ratio of benefits to burdens. When the burdens of enlistment are seen to outweigh the benefits, attention is focused on social class distinctions, and, any overrepresentation of individuals from the lower social strata is perceived as evidence of systemic inequity. In cases where the benefits of military service overbalance perceived burdens, however, it has been suggested that the achievement of true social equity occurs through the *over*representation of the disadvantaged poor and racial minorities.

Added to this is the understanding that benefits and burdens are value-laden, culture-bound concepts, which may bear no relationship to the conditions of war or peace. For example, it is seen that American immigrants, the sansei (during World War II), and blacks have valued the "right to fight" and wartime service; exclusion from combat duty was a denial of full citizenship and, therefore, equality. On the other hand, even during peacetime, under the volunteer format—with opportunity for technical training, education, social development and mobility for the disadvantaged, personal fulfillment, and employment—military service is described by some in largely negative terms. In fact, present discussions of military representation have not concentrated on disproportionate black enlistments because whites are being *refused* a fair share of the benefits—but, rather, because depressed minorities are viewed as "accepting" (due to hidden, economic pressures) an unfair share of the burdens in order to obtain the opportunities.

Moreover, because the voluntary military is gaining an image as "employer of last resort"—a haven for the disadvantaged and the "losers" of society—it is failing to advance or improve its attraction for a wider cross section of society. The resocialization of poverty youth, it is said, depends on public acceptance of the military as a legitimate activity for everyone, not just special segments of the population.[37] So, while the disadvantaged find certain opportunities and an outlet for unemployment in the armed forces, the full value of any opportunities for these individuals may be lost without cross-sectional representation.

Yet another area of conflict is found between the objectives of equal opportunity and proportional representation. "Equal opportunity" (i.e., treating every*one* alike) and representation are often perceived in context with particular minority groups, women, and the struggle for civil rights. But equal opportunity is a concept that relates to the *individual*: rights attach to the individual, and individual opportunity (as opposed to group opportunity) means that all persons are judged on the basis of their personal qualifications. Representation conversely classifies individuals according to groups; it draws attention to stereotypical qualities (i.e., statistics are segregated according to distinctive group traits or qualities), and it encourages, rather than obviates, consciousness of innate group differences. So, too, just as conscription offers no certain promise of proportional group participation, voluntary service does not necessarily ensure equal opportunity. To the contrary, even though the military services currently boast of being an "equal opportunity employer," institutional discrimination remains. The opportunities for initial selection and later assignment are not totally free from bias—unless one dismisses the existence of women and disregards the fact that education and aptitude standards have a disproportionate effect on racial and ethnic minorities.[38]

A reasonable balance of opposing objectives is the key to reconciling differences between benefits and burdens, internal organizational needs and external national goals, equal opportunity and equal representation, compulsions and freedoms, and other areas of discord. A trade-off or compromise is similarly needed to mitigate the fundamental conflicts between the goals of equity, legitimacy, and effectiveness. Yet, the search for a reasonable balance to guide military manpower policy, even though it offers a means for reconciling differences between sometimes conflicting objectives, is ultimately an exercise in subjective reasoning. After all, how *does* one strike a balance between realistic military needs or requirements and the perceived social good? Can one, or *should* one, even attempt to balance and trade between separate categories of demands on the nation and the body politic? Indeed, what *is* "reasonable?"

These are all questions that have characteristically followed the history of manpower policy in the U.S. armed forces—and questions that may well be as old as the very origins of organized armies. During the past few years, the search for an equitable and effective recruiting policy has been urged on by the swelling proportion of blacks and other minorities in the armed forces. At the same time, a new awareness of the interrelationship between the military and society has helped to draw the lines of discord between the proponents of conscription and the defenders of voluntary service. The military has thus become a symbol of the society, a manifestation of equity, and as a public institution, its composition is seen to symbolically reflect social justice or social injustice.

THE CONTEMPORARY SETTING

That a majority of the American people support the adoption of military conscription and an even larger proportion support national service has been confirmed by virtually every public opinion poll taken in recent years. Yet, as is the case in other national issues, the influence of minority interest groups—in this case the younger generation—must be reckoned with. Alienation of American youth, as the Vietnam era attests, exacts a large and enduring toll on society.

Many national leaders fear that the adoption of military conscription today would reawaken campus activism that has been relatively dormant since the last chorus of "Hell no, we won't go!" By some accounts, the "protest generation" of the 1960s, alleged to have caused the demise of the draft, has been replaced by a new generation—less idealistic, more inward looking, but just as likely to oppose compulsory service, albeit on different grounds.[30] This should come as no surprise. As products of one of the most disillusioning eras in U.S. history marked by Vietnam, Watergate, and Abscam, today's youth appear to harbor a healthy measure of skepticism—if not distrust—of the nation's political institutions. Moreover, having grown up in a decade marked by apparent U.S. national security failures and the ensuing self-flagellation conducted largely as a media event, young Americans appear to have less understanding—if not less appreciation—for the military establishment and its role in American society.

Finally, ambiguous national goals and inconsistent policies—that warn of a dangerous "window of vulnerability" while selling grain to the adversary; that make the United States appear more interested in protecting Western Europe than those nations are in protecting themselves; and that cherish civil liberties but support repressive regimes and condone racist governments—can only add to the confusion. While such inconsistencies may be difficult to avoid in today's complicated world, they may also undermine popular support of the nation's military establishment.

How deep or widespread these feelings might run is debatable, but it is clear that the threshold for acceptance of peacetime conscription has not been reached, at least among those who might be called upon to serve. The scenario that would galvanize their support is difficult to predict and the willingness of the national leadership to proceed without that support is even more uncertain. It is tempting to believe that the current generation of young Americans would respond in the face of a distinct danger, but there is no clear conception of just what would constitute such a threat. It is unlikely that the cold war rhetoric that sustained peacetime conscription without major dissent during the 1950s and early 1960s would be sufficient today; indeed, there is widespread agreement that the political and social costs of resuming peacetime conscription merely to alleviate shortfalls in quantity or quality or to redress the social imbalance of today's volunteer forces are prohibitive. These costs, however, would lessen should a crisis develop, such as a Soviet incursion into Poland or their direct involvement in the Persian Gulf.

Some contend that entering the 1980s young Americans—startled by events in Iran, Afghanistan, and Poland—have become more defense-minded and more receptive to traditional democratic values. But conflicting evidence suggests that the measurable increase in support for U.S. military superiority and for increases in military spending and influence has been accompanied by a declining interest among youth to register for a draft, much less to serve in the military institution. Moreover, if confronted with a choice of mandatory military or civilian service, one-third of surveyed high-school seniors indicated an intent to avoid both.[40] These reactions cannot be taken lightly; the legitimacy afforded conscientious objector (CO) status during the Vietnam era appears to have become institutionalized in American society and the adoption of any mandatory military service program in the United States (as is the case in West Germany) would likely be accompanied by significant numbers of resisters.

Largely because of the CO problem and the potential for reopening old social wounds, many critics of the status quo stop short of proposing a return to a conscription system that merely meets the needs of the armed forces. A program that would call for all qualified youth to serve the nation in one capacity or the other, not only is attractive to those interested in filling the ranks of the military, but also to those with broader interests in improving American society. And while concern about military recruitment may have prompted recent discussions about national service, the movement has been joined by veterans of the Peace Corps and VISTA programs of the 1960s who see a new opportunity to rekindle the spirit reflected in President John F. Kennedy's dictum: "Ask not what your country can do for you — ask what *you* can do for your country."

National service in one form or another has been discussed for decades. But given the current economic predicament of American youth and the dim prospects for improvement, particularly among disadvantaged minorities, the case for linking the capabilities of the armed forces to the social good becomes even more compelling. With its vast training establishment, the military has a comparative advantage in upgrading the status of the nation's underclass. But employing the military as an engine of social reform, attractive as it might appear, is not without costs, both in financial and in readiness terms. So, although national service is instinctively appealing and appears to enjoy widespread support, no one has yet been able to translate the broad concept into a feasible program that deals with the military, social, political, and economic realities of the 1980s.

There is probably little disagreement in the American conscience that all citizens, in their own way, hold some moral obligation to come to the aid of their country. To serve or not to serve is not the question. The contemporary wrangle centers on the type, timing, manner, degree, and, above all, instrumentality of the obligation. During periods of peace, citizens will ultimately ask: Should service to my nation be given voluntarily or taken by government compulsion? Whatever answer the state provides, it will have to be grounded on firm principles and — if the answer is compulsory service — a clearly visible and overriding necessity. But even the most resolute of draft resisters could be assuaged to accept the reality of compulsion in the face of a "great threat," where liberty or life itself may be on the line. A requisite call to arms has a way of bringing out patriotism and a sense of duty in the nation's populace.

The next decade will see the American people struggle to resolve anew the difficult issues and conflicting priorities that embrace the demands of national security and go right to the heart of our national purpose. In the end, it will be the old philosophical balancing act of benefits against burdens, equal opportunity against disguised quotas and institutional discrimination, national defense needs against the social role of military service, the principles of free choice against government intrusions into private lives, civil rights against civic responsibilities, and so on through the familiar list of clashing values. That a large portion of the population is ambivalent about the issues is understandable since arguments on both sides are powerful, and honorable differences of opinion are difficult to reconcile.

It falls on the nation's leadership to guide the body politic through this thicket, to articulate clear and commanding principles on which to base the nation's foreign and domestic policies. To begin with, the citizenry in general, and American youth in particular, must be given a better idea of what U.S. national interests are, of how U.S. foreign and domestic policies are designed to support those interests, and of the role that the military institution serves to protect those interests.

Admittedly, this is a tall order — but the risks of not taking it on may be high. To avoid aaopting conscription only for fear of political or social consequences could run a risk to national security. Conversely, to reinstitute peacetime conscription without the support of the major elements of American society invites national divisiveness. The task is to find a compromise that promotes both a strong military and a healthy society.

NOTES

1. George Washington, "Sentiments on a Peace Establishment," in *American Military Thought*, ed. Walter Millis (Indianapolis: The Bobbs-Merrill Company, Inc., 1966), p. 23.

2. Daniel Webster, "Speech Against the Conscription Bill," U.S. House of Representatives, December 9, 1814, in *Conscience in America*, edited by Lillian Schlissel (New York: E. P. Dutton and Co., Inc., 1968), pp. 64–71.

3. Bernard Bailyn, *The Ideological Origins of the American Revolution* (Cambridge, MA.: The Belknap Press of Harvard University Press, 1967), pp. 22–54.

4. Judith N. Shklar, *Men and Citizens: A Study of Rousseau's Social Theory* (Cambridge: Cambridge University Press, 1969), pp. 189, 203–204; Alfred Vagts, *A History of Militarism* (New York: Meridian Books, Inc., 1959), pp. 75–77.

5. John Trenchard, "An Argument, Shewing, That a Standing Army Is Inconsistent with a Free Government" (1697). This particular piece was highly popular among colonial writers of the Revolutionary period.

6. Bailyn, *Ideological Origins*, p. 63.

7. Russel F. Weigley, *Towards an American Army: Military Thought from Washington to Marshall* (New York: Columbia University Press, 1962). "Profession" in this context means the opposite of "amateur"—that is, a person who has experience and competence in the art of fighting and participates primarily for financial gain or livelihood.

8. George Washington, Letter "To the President of Congress," in *American Military Thought*, ed. Millis, pp. 12–14.

9. John L. Rafuse, "United States Experience with Volunteer and Conscript Forces," in The President's Commission on an All-Volunteer Armed Force, *Studies Prepared for the President's Commission on an All-Volunteer Armed Force*, Vol. II (Washington, D.C.: Government Printing Office, November 1970), p. III-1-7.

10. Webster, "Speech Against the Conscription Bill," in *Conscience in America*, ed. Schlissel, pp. 67–68.

11. See Weigley, *American Army*.

12. From Leonard Wood, "Our Military History: Its Facts and Fallacies (1916)," in *American Military Thought*, ed. Millis, p. 213. Wood's remarks, it should be noted, came at a time when the nation faced an ever-increasing likelihood of entrance into world war. But Wood's basic theme was not tied to current events; universal military service is a democratic principle, he asserted, a firm part of the American military tradition.

13. Sam Nunn in an article appearing in the *Chicago Tribune*, December 30, 1977. Quoted in "U.S. Defense Policy: Weapons Strategy and Commitments," *Congressional Quarterly*, (Washington, D.C.: Congressional Quarterly, Inc., April 1978), p. 76.

14. Robin Beard, Letter to Fellows of the Inter-University Seminar on Armed Forces and Society, Washington, D.C., n.d. (December 1978), p. 3.

15. See Weigley, *American Army*. See also, James M. Gerhardt, *The Draft and Public Policy* (Columbus: Ohio State University Press, 1971); John O'Sullivan and Alan M. Meckler, eds., *The Draft and Its Enemies: A Documentary History* (Urbana: University of Illinois Press, 1977).

16. Robert Taft quoted in Harry A. Marmion, *The Case Against a Volunteer Army* (Chicago: Quadrangle Books, 1971), p. 37.

17. Mark O. Hatfield in remarks before the U.S. Senate during consideration of S. 109, a bill to reinstate registration procedures under the Military Selective Service Act, September 21, 1979. In "Controversy Over Proposed Draft Registration: Pro and Con," *Congressional Digest*, April 1980, p. 113.

18. Ron Paul in remarks before the U.S. House of Representatives during consideration of H.R. 4040, the proposed Department of Defense Authorization Act for FY 1980, September 12, 1979. In "Controversy Over Proposed Draft Registration: Pro and Con," *Congressional Digest*, April 1980, p. 127.

19. Rafuse, "United States Experience," pp. III-1-22 to III-1-25.

20. William H. McNeill, "The Draft in the Light of History," in *The Draft*, ed. Sol Tax (Chicago: University of Chicago Press, 1967), p. 118..

21. See Gerhardt, *The Draft and Public Policy*.

22. The case of the lunatic is the favorite example used by political philosophers to illustrate this point, but there are many others. There is an opposite view, however. A former U.S. senator, for example, once remarked during the confirmation hearings of a 1970 nominee to the Supreme Court of the United States that justices of the Supreme Court should "represent mediocrity." A.H. Birch, in *Representation* (New York: Praeger Publishers, 1971, p. 59), quotes a similar statement by a British Lord during a television interview: "Ideally, the House of Commons should be a microcosm of the nation. The nation has a great many people who are rather stupid, and so should the House."

23. Marie Collins Swabey, "A Quantitative View" (from *The Theory of the Democratic State*, 1936) in *Representation*, ed. Hannah F. Pitkin (New York: Atherton Press, 1969), p. 83. Ferdinand A. Hermens, in *The Representative Republic* (Notre Dame: University of Notre Dame Press, 1958), p. 205, observes it is no accident that virtually all of the inventors of the various systems of proportional representation in government have been *mathematicians*: "Authorities in the fields of public law and of political science have, at times, felt that *this* fact alone should make everyone think twice before accepting conclusions derived from premises not related to those of political life."

24. The *manner* in which the military is perceived often determines the choice of statistics for comparison and subsequent appraisals of force content. The current controversy over the representativeness of the volunteer force illustrates how conceptions of the military organization may guide assessments of recruiting results. The so-termed "occupational model" in the

volunteer military suggests that distinctions between enlisted and officer positions in the armed forces are analogous to the distinctions between blue-collar and white-collar jobs in the civilian labor force. On the other hand, the "institutional model," which describes military service as a universal obligation of citizenship (or a "calling"), sets the armed forces apart from civilian occupations and draws no occupational or class lines. Obviously, the social demography of the labor force and its various sectors differs from the demographic distributions of the general population (especially among the younger, "military-age" group). Entirely opposite conclusions can thus result in evaluations of the same military data—depending on conceptions of the military, and the selection of "appropriate" variables and population standards for comparison.

25. Eitelberg, in *Military Representation*, examines the concept of representation in political theory and traces its spread or expansion from the political origins through recent applications concerning citizen participation in the bureaucracy and in the military. Other recent treatments of this include Hannah F. Pitkin, *The Concept of Representation* (Berkeley, CA.: University of California Press, 1967); Hannah F. Pitkin, ed., *Representation* (New York: Atherton Press, 1969); A. H. Birch, *Representation* (New York: Praeger Publishers, 1971); the first examination of bureaucratic representation, J. Donald Kingsley, *Representative Bureaucracy* (Yellow Springs, Ohio: Antioch Press, 1944); Harry Kranz, *The Participatory Bureaucracy* (Lexington, MA.: Lexington Books, 1976); Samuel Krislov, *The Negro in Federal Employment* (Minneapolis, MN.: University of Minnesota Press, 1967); Samuel Krislov, *Representative Bureaucracy* (Englewood Cliffs, N.J.: Prentice-Hall, Inc., 1974); and William A. Niskanen, *Bureaucracy and Representative Government* (Chicago: Aldine Publishing Company, 1971).

26. The term, "suicidalness of militarism," is from Arthur A. Ekirch, Jr., *The Civilian and the Military* (New York: Oxford University Press, 1956).

27. Morris Janowitz, "The U.S. Forces and the Zero Draft," *Adelphi Papers*, no. 94 (London: International Institutional Institute of Strategic Studies, 1973), p. 27.

28. S. E. Finer, *The Man on Horseback: The Role of the Military in Politics* (New York: Praeger, 1962), pp. 86–88.

29. *The Report of the President's Commission on an All-Volunteer Armed Force* (Washington, D.C.: Government Printing Office, 1970), p. 138.

30. Samuel P. Huntington, *The Soldier and the State: The Theory and Politics of Civil-Military Relations* (Cambridge, MA.: The Belknap Press of Harvard University Press, 1957), p. 83.

31. An extended treatment on "The Legitimacy of Female Representation" can be found in Eitelberg, *Military Representation*, pp. 316–348.

32. U.S. Defense Manpower Commission, *Defense Manpower: The Keystone of National Security* (Washington, D.C.: Government Printing Office, April 1976), pp. 156–157.

33. A staff-written article in a British magazine observes that, apart from purely military concerns, "the social and political implications of an all-black army defending a 12 percent black country are staggering." "It is a brittle Army," the article finds. "Beneath a hard surface, the core is soft and spongy. The American army's weaknesses have to be cured, soon, if it is to face the challenges of the 1980s." See "Today's American Army," *The Economist*, April 25, 1981, pp. 23–25.

34. *The Gallup Opinion Index*, Rept. No. 175, February 1980, pp. 5–6.

35. A sample of opinions (from a selection of magazines) on the question of whether women should face the selective service draft on an equal basis with men appears in Jason Berger, ed., *The Military Draft, The Reference Shelf*, 53, no. 4 (New York: The H. W. Wilson Company, 1981): 135–169.

36. A number of surveys suggest that, for a variety of reasons, women who enlist in the military are "tradition-oriented." A *Washington Post* reporter also noted in 1979 that

"American women, it turns out after one year of experimenting, are not wild about joining the Army or doing the jobs formerly restricted to men if they do sign up." See George C. Wilson, "Army Programs for Women Falter During Fiscal-Year Test," *Washington Post*, April 23, 1979, p. A-6.

37. Charles C. Moskos, "Making the All-Volunteer Force Work: A National Service Approach," *Foreign Affairs* 60 (Fall 1981): 20.

38. In FY 1981, for example, women who did not have high-school diplomas or equivalency certificates were not eligible to enlist in either the navy or the Marine Corps; women with equivalency certificates were also barred from entering the Marine Corps. Females who qualified on the basis of their education in these services were required to meet different (i.e., higher) aptitude standards than those established for men with similar education. Until recently, the army used a different test composite for male and female applicants in determining Armed Forces Qualification Test (AFQT) scores. The net effect of this practice was a relative reduction in the supply of qualified female applicants—even though it appeared, ostensibly, that males and females were being evaluated equally in terms of mental aptitude standards. All services still preserve quotas (or "ceilings") on the enlistment of females.

Differences in the measured mental aptitude between blacks and whites have been used to justify segregation, racial restrictions, and quotas in the military. Historically, the military's aptitude tests have also served as a convenient device to regulate the enlistment of blacks. The predictability of average race differences on certain test items and subtests permits the creation of test composites that, with a fair degree of confidence, can be used to "favor" one race over another. In 1950, the army agreed to an abolition of the racial quota based on the belief that (1) blacks could be "counted on" to score well below whites on mental qualifying examinations and, therefore (2) the minimum mental aptitude standards could be manipulated, if necessary, to keep the proportion of blacks below 10 percent. In 1975 and, again, in 1979 the navy was accused by Congress of using a disguised racial quota in the form of restrictions on the percentage of recruits scoring in AFQT Category IV (the lowest acceptable category). In 1980, Congress itself imposed a ceiling on the percentage of AFQT Category IV recruits who are permitted to enter military service between FY 1981 and FY 1983.

Based on FY 1981 aptitude/educational standards, about 44 percent of all black males in the general population (aged 18 through 23) would be expected to qualify for enlistment in the army; 41 percent would qualify for the navy; 34 percent would qualify for the Marine Corps, and 21 percent would qualify for the air force. In sharp contrast, over eight out of ten white male youth would qualify for service in the army, navy, or Marine Corps; and about seven out of ten would be expected to qualify for the air force on the basis of FY 1981 aptitude/educational standards. Fewer than 10 percent of black male youth without a high-school diploma or equivalency certificate—compared with 40 percent of white males—would qualify for enlistment in the army. About 12 percent of white high-school dropouts would qualify for the air force, compared with fewer than 1 percent of blacks without a diploma. See Mark J. Eitelberg, Brian K. Waters, and Janice H. Laurence, *Profile of American Youth Qualified for Military Service: The Effects of Aptitude and Education Standards on the Enlistment Eligibility of Contemporary Youth*, Professional Paper (Alexandria, Va.: Human Resources Research Organization, 1982).

One lingering effect of racial differences in performance on tests of mental aptitude is the existence of a definite pattern of black participation in the military's occupational areas. Historically, blacks have been relegated to service and supply units—a trend that can be traced back as far as the American Revolution. Recent experience exposes the enduring social class and color lines of the military's occupational placement system: in 1964, the last peacetime year before the Vietnam conflict, blacks were greatly overrepresented in the Service and Supply Handler occupational area in all four services; in every succeeding year, blacks have remained overrepresented in this occupational area.

39. For an excellent overview of the current generation of college students, see Arthur Levine, *When Dreams and Heroes Died: A Portrait of Today's College Student* (San Francisco: Jossey-Bass, 1980).

40. Samuel S. Peng, William B. Fetters, and Andrew J. Kolstad, *A National Longitudinal Study for the 1980s: A Capsule Description of High School Students* (Washington, D.C.: National Center for Education Statistics, April 1981), pp. 23-27.

10: The Policy Paper:
Toward a Consensus on Military Service*
The Atlantic Council's Working Group on Military Service, J. Allan Hovey, Jr., Rapporteur

INTRODUCTION

In a dangerous world, nations have limited choices. First and essential is to pursue all reasonable measures to preserve peace among nations and to reconcile inevitable differences by diplomatic and other means short of armed conflict. Failing this, where vital interests are at stake, few choices remain. One is to offer no resistance to acts of aggression. The other is to deter the threat or use of armed force or, failing that, to defend against it.

The United States has vital interests in the Western Hemisphere, Western Europe, Japan, South Korea, the oil reservoirs of the Middle East, and still other places with which we are allied and/or upon which we depend for trade and essential raw materials. The United States thus seeks freedom of the seas and a global environment that is reasonably free of war, terrorism, and any imposed hegemony—a world conducive to economic, social, and political progress.[1]

Agenda for a Safer World

Absent an effective international peacekeeping agency, both peace and the security of vital interests depend upon maintaining the balance of power between East and West. Essential equivalence of nuclear power is indis-

---

*This Policy Paper is the sole "collegial" product of the Atlantic Council's Working Group on Military Service. It seeks to record the consensus that emerged within the group over more than a year of discussions and includes the group's final conclusions and recommendations. Members' individual comments, reservations, and dissents appear in footnotes or in Appendix I, as appropriate. The Policy Paper was prepared by J. Allan Hovey, Jr., International Relations Specialist, U.S. General Accounting Office; formerly Vice-President, Radio Free Europe, and Adjunct Associate Professor, City University of New York.

pensable to minimize the risk that such weapons will ever be fired in war or brandished for political blackmail. The other military requirement for peace and security is adequate *conventional* forces.

All the wars of the nuclear age have been nonnuclear. As one authority points out:

> It is probably safe to say that no one at present can spell out with authority how, short of being able to execute a disarming first strike, either the United States or the Soviet Union could prosecute a strategic nuclear campaign to anything like a favorable conclusion.

And as to theater nuclear war:

> The power of nuclear weapons, so far, has outstripped the ability of both the United States and the Soviet Union to adapt to it. . . . It requires the suppression of much information and an enormous effort of the imagination to believe that, in [a nuclear] environment, units could hold together and fight with anything like the cohesion and coordination they achieve with such difficulty in the face of non-nuclear fires.

> Admittedly, the Soviet Union could simply leapfrog the nuclear battlefield with its peripheral attack forces, as it has been in a position to do for twenty years, and destroy all or part of Western Europe from a distance. But the United States could wreak similar vengeance, however pointless it might be, on all or parts of Eastern Europe. What either side would gain from such massive barbarism, or how the threat of it could be turned to political profit, escapes comprehension.

> Threats, to be more than bluffs, must have the potential for something greater than self-defeating action in back of them. This being the case, most nuclear threats are bound to be empty under present conditions.[2]

Thus, given nuclear parity, the adequacy of conventional forces will be the key to effective deterrence. As former Secretary of State Henry Kissinger wrote recently: "We must seek to avoid nuclear war. The only way to do this without jeopardizing freedom is to build up immediately the conventional forces on both sides of the Atlantic."[3]

A complete "agenda for a safer world" would extend far beyond the scope of this Policy Paper. Our purpose is to examine the nation's peacetime military volunteer force, to evaluate alternative means of dealing with important manpower problems, and to recommend specific steps designed both to strengthen our all-volunteer system and to prepare the way, should circumstances require it, for a resumption of compulsory military service. In so doing, we also seek to provide enough background information to help the interested public put these urgent issues in some perspective.

The national security requires much more, of course, than armed forces.

It requires a coherent and realistic foreign policy, including leadership in the Atlantic Alliance, and a serious effort to negotiate for both arms reduction and the resolution of disputes. It requires due care for the needs of our intelligence services, of our international information and exchange programs, of our bilateral and multilateral economic assistance operations. It requires a healthy U.S. and world economy, and much more.

Beyond and above those concerns, the defense of the nation requires a firmness of purpose of the sort that has always guided the American people once they understood what was required.

Arms and Men in America[4]

Historically, however, Americans have generally been slow to concern themselves with the gathering international storms and to make the necessary defense preparations.

Insulated by oceanic moats, preoccupied for generations with achieving their continental destiny, imbued with historic traditions against standing armies and "entangling alliances," the American people maintained the minimum forces thought necessary for continental defense. In 1789 the regular army consisted of 718 officers and enlisted men. The Federal army prior to the Civil War barely exceeded 16,000. The volunteer army of 1914 was less than 100,000. Indeed, the largest wholly volunteer American Army before World War II was a mere 190,000, in 1939, ranking seventeenth in size in the world.

In the past, it was possible to prepare the defense after a war began and still protect vital interests. Few who have seriously considered the matter believe this to be the case any longer. The need for peacetime alliances between the United States and like-minded countries is no longer in serious dispute. And while the need for a peacetime draft remains a matter of controversy among Americans, their history has left no reasonable doubt that the draft is indispensable in major conflicts and that the country must at least be in a position to resume conscription rapidly and effectively in a national emergency. The United States relied on the draft in the Civil War, in both World Wars, and indeed during most of the years since World War II.

Recent Experience with the Draft

In 1941, fully a year after World War II began in Europe, Congress approved a selective service draft. In the early fall of 1941, the Congress voted — by a one-vote margin in the House — to keep the one-year draftees in service beyond their term. A public opinion divided between those who favored intervention in the war, lest Britain go under, and those who supported a policy of neutrality and "America First" had made it impossible, as in World War I, to make timely military preparations. The "great debate" was resolved only by the Japanese attack on Pearl Harbor, December 7, 1941. After that the draft was for the duration.

By May 1945, America had close to 12 million men and women in uniform. Ten million men had been drafted; 5.4 million had been deployed overseas. When the war ended a few weeks later, we moved, as we had always in the past, pell-mell to demobilization. In 1947 we terminated the draft. By 1948 total armed forces were down to 1,374,000, of which ground forces numbered 631,000.

The Soviet coup in Czechoslovakia in early 1948, putting an end to the last democracy in Central Europe, shocked the West into a prompt reexamination of its defenses. The United States in that year reenacted Selective Service and joined in creating the North Atlantic Alliance. It was a draft that would be needed to supply only a small margin of additional manpower not available through recruitment of volunteers.

Unlike the three relatively brief periods of conscription that preceded it, the Selective Service system that was enacted in 1948 endured, with certain modifications, for nearly a quarter of a century. Unlike the others, its termination was occasioned less by a cessation of hostilities than by a groundswell of public opposition to the war in Vietnam and to the discriminatory ways in which the draft had selected men for service in that war.

Until that point, public support for this "peacetime" conscription was consistently high—some 77 percent at its peak in 1956 and more than 60 percent even as late as 1969. Thereafter, such support quickly evaporated, and by 1972, according to one survey, only 13 percent believed conscription should be continued.

In December 1972, the last of the 1.7 million draftees of the Vietnam War era were inducted into the U.S. armed services. (After that date, although the law permitted inductions for another six months, only deferrals and draft evaders were taken.) During the entire 31-year period of conscription (1940–1973 minus 1947–1948), nearly 15 million men had been inducted.

Toward the end of that conscription era several reforms were adopted to correct discriminations in the selection of draftees. These reforms, among other things: terminated deferments for post-high-school students other than those in medicine and related fields; instituted a lottery to reduce the discretion of local draft boards; authorized inductions on a youngest-first rather than oldest-first basis; and terminated the possibility of occupational deferments, under which the government could influence the career decisions of draft-age men.

The American experiments with conscription had certain important features in common. Whenever we conscripted, we did so only for the active forces. A draft for the reserves was periodically proposed after World War II, but the nation settled on an easier, if more controversial, device to maintain a reserve force: it exempted reservists from conscription, thereby offering an effective lure to voluntary part-time reserve service.

In both world wars the nation augmented its armed forces almost exclusively by conscription. That is, for the most part, volunteers were not accepted, except as they volunteered to be drafted and were inducted as conscripts. After World II, the United States settled on a defense manpower scheme that was neither wholly voluntarism nor purely conscription, but an unequal mixture of the two. Voluntary enlistments would be induced by the draft (for, to volunteer was normally to get a more desirable military assignment than to be drafted); inductions would simply make up for any shortfalls in volunteering.

All of the American drafts were selective in at least five respects. They took: (1) only men; (2) only young men; (3) only those "qualified" for military service (including some classified for "limited service"); (4) only those who were not certifiably "deferred" or exempted; and (5) only as many as were needed at a given time. The means of selection varied with the times: fishbowl drawings, discretionary judgments by local draft boards, random computer-sequencing of birthdates. The selectivity of conscription was often a source of fierce dispute. It gave rise to periodic calls for a draft that would be "universal" in its distribution of burdens. (The merits of such "universal military service" alternatives are considered in a later section of this Policy Paper.)

Advent of the All-Volunteer Force

In the end, this selectivity of conscription, together with the unpopularity of the war it was then serving, led to a political judgment under President Nixon that the draft had to be abolished. A Presidential Commission (the Gates Commission) asserted the feasibility of a volunteer force and provided guidance for the new course.

In the ensuing decade, the civilian and military leadership accomplished a difficult transition and developed what is by far the largest military force this country ever raised without conscription.

It is no denigration of that achievement to ask today, as many have done, whether the force can be manned to meet the nation's defense needs in the 1980s and 1990s. Conditions are changing. And the experience of the past decade poses urgent questions about the assigned missions of the armed forces and about their readiness to carry them out.

The first question about readiness is of course: Readiness to do what?

DEFINING TODAY'S SECURITY REQUIREMENTS[5]

Determining national security requirements for protecting vital national interests is at best an inexact science. Defense planners must first make judgments about the worldwide level of organized hostility to those interests and the extent to which like-minded nations share them and are likely to contribute to their defense.

Defense Planning Concepts

To determine prospective manpower and other needs, defense planners must then make assumptions about possible or probable military involvements. In the 1950s and 1960s, planners worked on the assumption that the United States should be prepared to cope simultaneously with "two and a half wars" — for example, an attack by the Soviet Union in Europe, an attack by China in Korea or in Southwest Asia, and hostile action elsewhere by a smaller country such as Cuba. This assumption was scaled down during the Nixon administration when the Sino-Soviet estrangement — and the U.S. defense budget — were reassessed.

The Defense Department then postulated that the U.S. must be ready to support our allies in fighting one major war in Europe while coping simultaneously with one smaller crisis elsewhere. From that assumption, at least in theory, were derived the missions or tasks assigned to the three services and their various commands. Recently, however, Secretary of Defense Caspar W. Weinberger repudiated these planning concepts, saying that such "mechanistic assumptions neglect both the risks and the opportunities that we might confront." That is, the United States should have the capability not only to deter and defend in NATO Europe but also to deploy armed forces rapidly against an attacker's interests in other theaters. This would seem to imply a larger increase in military requirements than the administration has yet requested.[6]

What is the optimum "force structure" or size and make-up of the military services needed to carry out whatever missions are established? The question is fraught with imponderables, and different planners inevitably reach quite different judgments. Present policy calls for about 2.1 million active-duty personnel, about 900,000 in the Selected (i.e., organized) Reserves, and some 480,000 in the Individual (i.e., unorganized) Ready Reserves. (See table, AII-10.1)

The Carter administration, while calling for annual 5 percent real increases in defense spending over fiscal years 1982–1986, contemplated essential improvements in the effectiveness of existing forces rather than their enlargement. The task thus viewed was primarily one of making sure the existing forces could respond to contingencies in a timely manner with particular attention being given to the rapid deployment of forces to Europe and the Persian Gulf. The Reagan administration, while maintaining that goal, has also proposed an increase of some 200,000 in the size of the active force.

The ability of the U.S. and allied forces to hold the line against a major attack will depend on the size, composition, readiness, mobility, and morale of the available forces. Present and alternative means of providing the manpower for those forces are examined in the next two sections of this chapter. What needs to be noted here is that the present plans place an unprecedented and crucial reliance on the timely availability of the reserves and depend for the longer pull on the timely induction, training, and deployment of conscripts, particularly for the ground forces.

The "Total Force" Policy

The advent of the All-Volunteer Force coincided with the adoption of what is called the "total force" policy and with that a major new role for the reserves in the event of an emergency.

The total force policy was developed in 1970–72 when it became clear that the draft would be terminated and that the AVF, at any foreseeable budget levels, would not attract enough people to maintain the pre-Vietnam active force structure.

Under this policy, the first months of intensive combat in Europe would have to be fought with the active *and reserve* forces that existed before the war started. Nine of the 16 active army divisions depend upon augmentation by affiliated reserve units, from battalion to brigade size, to reach deployment strength. The commitments for deploying the reserves are thus very nearly as demanding as for the active forces. Pentagon plans call for deploying some 1,525,000 combat-ready troops, plus 200,000 replacements for casualties, during the first 120 days after mobilization. The Army National Guard and Reserve would have to provide some 52 percent of U.S. infantry and armor battalions in Europe, some 57 percent of field artillery, 65 percent of combat engineers, and 65 percent of all tactical support units.*

It is far from clear that the reserve forces as presently organized, equipped, and trained can meet that requirement.

---

*Lawrence J. Korb comments: "The Total Force concept, first promulgated by Secretary of Defense Laird in 1970, grew partially out of a need to assure the Reserve Components that they would play an important role in the national security. They had not been involved to any appreciable degree in the Vietnam conflict and needed such assurance . . . There was no great shift in manpower or units to the Army Reserve Components: There was, however, an increased reliance on the Army Guard and Reserve due primarily to the army's adding three partially-structured active divisions to its force. These new divisions needed not only roundout units from the Reserve Components to make them fully structured organizations in time of war but demanded more logistics support from the Reserve Components and from Host Nation Support. Reliance on reserve units has increased over time as deployment schedules have been accelerated to accommodate strategic mobility improvements."

Mobilization

Mobilization manpower can be thought of as being available in two echelons: One is the Selected Reserve and the Individual Ready Reserve; the second is conscripts delivered by the Selective Service System after Congress passes the legislation necessary to reactivate the draft. The Selected Reserves are those organized into units. They have equipment, train regularly, and are scheduled in mobilization plans for specific roles. Many Selected Reserve units, for example, would deploy to Europe within 30 days of mobilization.

The Individual Ready Reserves (IRR) are persons who have served in the Active or the Selected Reserve forces, have residual military obligations, but are not organized into units. In theory, they are liable for immediate callup and may be deployed to the combat zone without further training. The IRR would be used to fill out the active and Selected Reserve units being deployed, and to replace casualties after the fighting begins. The IRR and the Selected Reserve are usually grouped under the term "pre-trained manpower," to distinguish them from conscripts, or "untrained manpower," to be called upon when mobilization begins.

Untrained manpower will be delivered by the Selective Service System to the training base at some time after the draft is reinstated. By law, no individual may be sent to a combat zone with less than 12 weeks military training. Thus, the stream of untrained manpower does not represent a useful source of augmentation to the active and reserve forces until at best 100 days or so after the decision to start the draft. The worst-case planning scenario is generally taken to be one in which war breaks out suddenly, with minimal warning time, requiring mobilization to take place while the fighting is going on. In such a case, then, the active and reserve forces cannot look for augmentation until the war has gone on for some time. Many believe that the critical stages of the war would be over well before that time. In any case, it is clear that the combined active and reserve forces must be deep enough to last until conscripts can be inducted, trained, and deployed.

The Gates Commission specifically provided that its AVF should be backed by an on-going registration and a standby draft. However, in 1975 the Ford administration terminated registration and placed the Selective Service in deep standby, i.e., reduced to a planning and training organization of fewer than 100 full-time persons supported by reservists. This meant that time to reactivate the system, which some had estimated at six months to a year, would have to be added to the mandatory 12-week training period in calculating when new recruits would be available to augment forces in battle.

On January 23, 1980, President Carter, primarily impelled by the Soviet invasion of Afghanistan, announced a decision to resume registration of draft-eligible young people. In spite of some resistance in the Congress, funds were made available to expand and revitalize the Selective Service to accomplish this task. Between July 21 and August 2, 1980, men born in 1960 and 1961 were registered. On September 4, the Director of Selective Service announced that registration was complete, with a 91 percent response rate, or about 3.5 million young men registered. (The rate was lower in 1981, and the considerable number who have violated the law by failing to notify Selective Service of a change of address is unknown.)

The Department of Defense's stated requirements for draftees are for 100,000 to be delivered in the first 30 days after mobilization starts, and 650,000 within the first six months. At present about 8 million young men are registered; DoD estimates that some 600,000 failed to register, thus putting the compliance rate as of April 1982 at 93 percent. About 2 million 18-year-olds will be added each year.

Problems for the Selective Service System now focus on reconstitution of local boards as avenues of appeal; on meshing the system of calling draftees with the Military Enlisted Processing Command, which will receive, induct, examine, and deliver draftees to the training base; and on what to do about conscientious objectors.

THE ALL-VOLUNTEER EXPERIENCE

On the question of the viability of the All-Volunteer Force, close observers are seriously divided. Its partisans argue that in both size and quality the numbers show the AVF essentially measuring up to expectations, and that its admitted shortcomings could be corrected if we would stop shortchanging it. Critics say that the numbers are often misleading; that field tests, unit commanders, and other numbers tell a different story; and that in any case the changing requirements and demographics of the 1980s and 1990s call for a new approach.

Active Forces[7]

November 1981 marked the tenth anniversary of the military pay raise that helped make the volunteer force possible. As proposed by the Gates Commission, compensation for junior military personnel was raised from the then subsistence wage to a level commensurate with that earned by their peers in civilian life. During the years 1973 to 1980, military pay was allowed to fall somewhere between 5 and 15 percent below that standard, but with pay raises in October 1980 and 1981, military compensation is now roughly comparable to civilian sector pay.

Strengths. Over the past decade, the defense establishment attracted some 379,000 new recruits each year and sustained an active military force of about 2.1 million. Except for one year, all services have stayed within 1.5 percent of their active force strength objectives. That is an achievement unprecedented in U.S. history without conscription and unequaled elsewhere in modern times.

The overall figures for the defense establishment, however, are considerably more satisfactory than they have been for the army, where the limitations of voluntarism have had the greatest impact.

Total active uniformed personnel strengths in the AVF as a whole declined from nearly 2.7 million in 1964 to about 2.1 million in the AVF years. The army's totals in that period declined from 972,000 to 767,000. (Army recruits sign up today for a minimum of two years* plus four years in the reserves.) While it is true that the active army came close to meeting its annual recruitment goals, it is also true that its goals were substantially reduced.** (The bulk of the active force reductions resulted from transfers of force structure into the reserves and were justified on the grounds that under the total force policy the reserves would provide combat-ready units and individuals on short notice. As we explain in the next section, that assumption is open to question.)

Moreover, during much of the AVF period, military recruitment was the beneficiary of a sluggish civilian economy and high levels of unemployment. If the economy picks up, and/or if the manpower requirements are increased—and both objectives have been high on the present administration's agenda—the army could find itself unable to maintain requisite total numbers.***

Quality and Representativeness. Quality of personnel, as measured by aptitude tests and educational levels, has also declined in the AVF era, although by how much and with what meaning are matters of considerable controversy. The services use educational attainment (specifically, whether the applicant has a high-school diploma) as a general indication of his/her

---

*Only a few two-year options are offered. The great bulk of army enlistments are for three and four years.

**Dr. Korb comments: "The decline in active military strength was primarily due to:
- Elimination of unnecessary overhead, particularly base closures and management headquarters reductions.
- Reductions in the training establishment associated with reduced turnover and therefore fewer accessions.
- Some civilianization.

When military personnel became more costly, more attention was devoted to making the force structure more efficient."

***The Reagan administration's five-year defense program calls for increasing overall active forces by 182,517 of which the army's share would be 38,158.

adaptability to the military environment. High-school graduates, the Pentagon has found, are twice as likely as high-school dropouts to complete their enlistments. Through written tests known as the Armed Services Vocational Aptitude Battery, applicants are ranked in five categories. Applicants falling in the top 7 percent are Category I, while those in the bottom 10 percent are Category V. The latter are legally ineligible to be drafted and by policy ineligible to enlist. The services generally accept all or most of Category I–III high-school graduate volunteers who meet the medical and moral fitness requirements and try to limit the numbers of Category IV accepted.

It is the army again that suffered the most notable "quality" decline under the AVF, although with much smaller accession requirements, a remarkable turnaround has occurred, starting in FY-1981. During the 1977–1980 period, the proportion of army recruits with a high-school diploma dropped from 67 percent to 57 percent, but jumped to 80 percent in FY-1981. Its Category IV intake was 52 percent in fiscal 1980, an increase of 35 percentage points over the lottery draft experience, but again, dropped to 31 percent in FY-1981 and is running at only 18 percent in FY-1982. Its combined Category I and II intake dropped during 1977–1980 from 33 percent to 15 percent, but rose to 23 percent in FY-1981, dropping in FY-1982 to 16 percent. Perhaps even more serious, those recruits above the average for all youth (Categories I, II, and III A) fell from 56 percent in 1972 to 26 percent in 1980 before recovering to 40 percent in 1981. Since the start of the AVF an average of 45 percent of male recruits did not have a high-school diploma, compared with 29 percent of draftees and 39 percent of volunteers in 1964—this during a period when the number of male 18–19-year-old high-school graduates in the population as a whole was rising from 65 percent to 74 percent. In 1981, the army high-school graduate intake rebounded to 80 percent. As for recruits with some college, the decline has been even sharper. In 1964, one in six draftees and one in eight enlistees had some college. For the army today the figure is about one in twenty-five.* Quality trends in the army in various years over the past two decades are shown in table AII-10.2.**

---

*However, enlisted men have the opportunity while in the service to continue their education, and many do. Counting both the first term and the career force, 2 percent have a college degree, and 9 percent have some college.

**Dr. Korb comments: "To put the quality issue in better perspective [it should be noted that] the enlistment test in use from January 1976 through September 1980 was miscalibrated. This error inflated Armed Forces Qualification Test (AFQT) percentile scores for low-scoring enlistees. New conversion tables which corrected the calibration problem were developed in July 1980. Application of these corrected conversions to data on 1976 through 1980 accessions showed a significant decrease in percentages of Category III personnel and an increase in

In FY-1981, for a variety of reasons—including congressionally imposed quality requirements, improved pay and benefits, economic conditions, dramatic gains in reenlistment (reducing the army's annual accession requirements), and what appear to be improved recruiting practices—the army showed significant gains in the various measures of quality. There has been further improvement in 1982. These results, however, do not necessarily establish a new pattern which can be sustained over the decade. Given the country's demographic trend, it is questionable whether they can be maintained in the event of increased manpower requirements and/or improved economic conditions.

The other services generally seem to have at least maintained the quality that characterized their personnel in the draft era.

During the AVF years, as during the draft era, the army has generally assigned recruits with the lower aptitude scores to the combat arms. With major increases in the sophistication of weapons, however, some believe the standards for assignment to the combat arms will need to be raised. Moreover, studies of combat soldiers in World War II and the Korean War have shown that in general soldiers with higher education were rated as better fighters by their peers and immediate supervisors.

As one authority has observed, although many outstanding soldiers in the AVF have come from underprivileged backgrounds, "our concern must also be with the chemistry of unit cohesion which requires an optimum blend of talents and backgrounds. Research evidence confirms the observations of commanders and NCO's who remember the draft period: middle-class and upwardly mobile youth helped to enrich the skill level and commitment of military units in peace as well as in war."[8]/*

Perhaps the single most controversial issue to emerge during the AVF decade concerns the racial composition of the forces. By 1980, minorities accounted for 41 percent of all army enlisted personnel. Thirty-three percent of army enlisted personnel were black (versus 13 percent of the population), 4 percent Hispanic (versus 6 percent of the population), and 4 percent other minorities. Blacks are even more disproportionately represented in some army combat units, which may run as high as 40 percent in battalion-size units and even higher in smaller units. To an extent this phenomenon,

Category IV. During that period, the Department of Defense and the Military Services believed that the test scores of new recruits were considerably higher than they in fact were. If the test had been correctly calibrated, the efforts of recruiters might have resulted in the enlistment of more highly-qualified individuals, and the average AFQT scores might not have been so low as now recorded."

*Dr. Korb comments: "The overriding quality criterion for accessions should be the mix of aptitudes the Services need for junior enlisted people and for future entrants to the career force."

which amounts to a social transformation in the AVF enlisted ranks, can be attributed to the fact that a proportionately larger number of young blacks were becoming qualified educationally for enlistment, and the fact that the armed services have been in the forefront of those American institutions moving to eliminate racial discrimination. But basic to this racial "unrepresentativeness" of Army enlisted personnel is what some have called "conscription by poverty." In November 1981, black teen-aged unemployment was 41.3 percent nationally, more than twice that for white teen-agers.*

The situation is different with respect to blacks in the officer corps. In 1970, blacks comprised only about 1 percent of new officer accessions. By the mid-1970s the figure was 7 percent, which is closely representative of the pool of black college graduates, although the proportion in the more senior grades remains low.

Whether this unrepresentativeness, both economic and racial, is healthy in an institution whose members are expected to accept special risks and hardships in defending the society as a whole is a question the society needs to ponder deeply.

Role of Women. Until comparatively recently, the United States, like most countries, took it for granted that war was essentially a man's job. The military has been mostly a world designed by men for men, and many involved ardently want to keep it that way. But World War II and subsequent developments have called that view into question. In that war, the Soviet Union drafted some 1 million women and used women in combat. Britain also drafted women. The United States had 300,000 women in uniform in a wide range of assignments throughout the world, including combat zones.

The value of women in many service positions has been increasingly recognized both within and outside the military and their career opportunities have grown accordingly. In the draft years 1948–1973, nearly all servicewomen were assigned to the traditional medical, dental, and administrative fields. Today 55 percent are so assigned. More than 173,000 women were on active duty in 1981, representing 8.5 percent of total active

---

*Dr. Moskos comments: "The white component is even more unrepresentative. Since the end of the draft, white army entrants have had lower high school diploma rates than blacks."

Dr. Korb comments: "In regard to racial mix, no race is unduly burdened by military service, if its members individually and voluntarily choose to accept those burdens in return for the benefits and opportunities provided. . . . The paper fails to consider that many minorities see the military as a means of upward mobility. Perhaps the benefits of military service (i.e., income, education, job experience and training, leadership, and social mobility) far outweigh the 'burdens,' especially during peacetime. As a minimum, this side of the argument should be incorporated into the discussion of the report at this point."

military strength, as compared to 1.1 percent in 1964. In 1972 for the first time, women were made navy pilots. Four years later they could enroll in the service academies. The test scores and educational level of female recruits have been as good as or better than those of males.*

In proposing to revive peacetime registration for the draft, President Carter recommended that women be included. When Congress adopted the legislation requiring the registration of 18-year-olds, however, it excluded women. This exclusion was challenged as a violation of the equal protection guarantees of the Fifth and Fourteenth Amendments but was upheld in 1981 by the Supreme Court. The Court deferred to Congress's view that this exclusion served an important governmental interest. One argument that influenced the Court was that under existing law and regulation, women are excluded from combat. Since mobilization under the draft was intended to make available troops for combat, Congress was deemed within its rights to exclude them from the draft. This issue can be expected to emerge again if peacetime conscription is reinstituted.

Reserves[9]

During the AVF era the major share of the army's manpower for use in an emergency in Europe shifted from the active to the reserve forces. Under the total force policy[10] the active forces will provide only about 44 percent of the manpower required in a major war in Europe. Moreover, as noted earlier, many active army units, including nine of the sixteen divisions, require Selected Reserve augmentation, in units up to brigade size, to reach full combat strength. The army's ability to perform its basic mission will thus depend largely on the strength and readiness of the organized units in the Selected Reserve. But in both components of the Army Selected Reserve—the National Guard and the Army Reserve—manning levels have fallen substantially short of their wartime requirements, and equipment and training have been far short of adequate.

The reserves have been in many ways the stepchildren of the All-Volunteer Force. During the last draft era, and especially during the Vietnam War, the reserves had no trouble filling their ranks with the pick of America's youth. Reserve duty offered automatic deferral from being drafted for active service. Similarly, the problem with the pool of pretrained individuals in the Individual Ready Reserve was, not too few, but too many. The IRR is created by the residual obligation of people who flow through the active forces and Selected Reserve, leaving before six years' service.

---

*Dr. Moskos comments: "Females have much higher attrition rates than comparably educated males and there is increasing reluctance of women to enter the non-traditional assignments. Female utilization is not going to be any long-term answer to AVF problems."

Under the draft, about a third of new accessions and about 15 percent of total active-duty forces were short-term (two-year) conscripts.

In the period of the AVF, the reserves experienced a startling decline in strength. From 1973 to 1978, the total number in the reserves (Selected Reserve and IRR) fell from 2.2 million to 1.2 million. The Army National Guard's end strength (trained and untrained)* in fiscal year 1981 was 387,000 (against a wartime trained strength requirement of 446,000) and that of the Army Reserve was 226,000 (trained and untrained, against a wartime requirement of 286,000 trained). This shortfall of 120,000 could absorb nearly two-thirds of the entire Army IRR, leaving a pool of only about 80,000 to fill out the active forces and to replace combat casualties. But the shortfall in fact is nearer 160,000 counting trained strength only, and this would require all but about 40,000 of the Army IRR.**

Army IRR strength in fiscal year 1981 was 200,000 against stated requirements that have varied from 400,000 to 750,000. The army and the Office of the Secretary of Defense in 1979 compromised differences and agreed on a requirement of about 480,000, making the shortfall about 280,000. (The reason for the decline in the IRR is that the AVF has a reduced active force and has required fewer new recruits — who serve longer terms, tend more often to reenlist, and when separated more often join reserve units.) By fiscal year 1985, a variety of administrative and recruiting devices may reduce the shortfall to less than 200,000. Some believe that concerted action — requiring, however, additional resources — could make it less than 100,000. In fact, however, it may be difficult to locate members of the IRR, many would be unfit, and the remainder probably would require some refresher training in any case. Today, only 29 percent of the IRR are in the combat arms.

For the army reserves as a whole, it appears on balance that there will be significant shortfalls from stated requirements for the foreseeable future under present manning policies.

With respect to the issues of quality, balance, and equity the AVF reserve forces appear quite similar to the active forces. To the extent recruit quality for the active forces is adequate, for example, it should be so for the

---

*On December 31, 1981, there were 65,684 guardsmen and army reservists untrained, of whom 21,022 were in training. None of the 65,684 were deployable.

**Dr. Korb comments: "This paragraph grossly misrepresents what is happening today to the strength of the Army Reserve Component units. . . . The Army Selected Reserve increased its strength by 40,000 in FY-1981; that trend is continuing . . . The Army should have no trouble, subject to funding availability, in reaching its wartime requirements for Selected Reservists by 1986 . . . We expect to have the largest Army Guard and Reserve in our history. The problems in the Army Selected Reserve are not numbers of people, it's training and equipment. The so-called 'wartime requirement' was introduced as a planning goal last year to make room for a growing Selected Reserve strength and to compensate for shortages in the IRR."

reserves. More important, measures to redress active force problems could bring solutions to related reserve force problems. Reserve force quality would appear to be bound up even more in the issues of training and equipment than in changes in manpower policies.

In testimony before a Senate subcommittee, in July 1981, a senior army official summed up the army's manpower mobilization deficiencies as follows:

> "Significant manpower shortages exist in several forms: shortage of immediate trained replacements for combat losses, shortage of personnel in existing Reserve Component units, and substantial shortage of units to meet identified requirements. The result is the current Reserve manpower pool cannot sustain mobilization requirements until manpower can be supplied by a post mobilization draft, trained by a CONUS [continental U.S.] base, and shipped to a theater of operations.

> "At mobilization plus 90 days and fighting a NATO only war, the Army trained military manpower shortfall computed for end FY 1980 was 249,000."[11]/*

It is clear that the army's reinforcement capability is much less than that needed to provide confidence in a successful conventional defense.

THE OPTIONS

An enlightened national debate should take into account a broad range of possible options for correcting present deficiencies in U.S. defense posture. Several such options or variants of them have been tried or debated in the past. All can be examined under the general headings "voluntary service" or "compulsory service."

Voluntary Service[12]

The voluntary options entail alteration rather than replacement of the present system. No set of options can guarantee the success of the AVF. It has some difficult challenges ahead, with a shrinking pool of potential enlistees and a manpower program whose requirements may grow but are not likely to be decreased.

Civilianization of previously military positions or spaces has been tried as

---

*Dr. Korb comments: "The paper in many cases ignores the constrained fiscal environment in which military manpower decisions must be made. For example, in seeking the needed quantity and quality of active reserves and IRR manpower, decisions are often made to delay full realization of manning objectives until equipment can be purchased in sufficient quantities to support the higher manning levels."

a concept for reducing military requirements, but prospects for further increase appear limited. Civilians are less generally deployable and contribute little to the rotation base needed to sustain careerists overseas. Furthermore, they tend to get compressed against arbitrary strength ceilings that appear periodically when new ways to find budget savings are sought. Adding more women to the military is a possibility that is now under official study. The full potential remains to be clarified.

Beyond this and maintaining military-civilian pay comparability, what now remains to be done is to expand the available enlistment options, and to show how—if supported enthusiastically by the government and if found to be attractive by the nation's youth—they might help to overcome impending problems. The heart of the new options would be shorter terms of service and generous educational benefits offset by reduced compensation.*

The pages that follow introduce a series of options, first dealing with the major quantitative problem in the IRR, and then with the basic enlistment program for active and reserve forces. The army is chosen both because the army has experienced the greatest difficulties under the AVF and also because the army probably requires the greatest array of options.

Mobilization Needs: The IRR. Despite inherent weaknesses of the Individual Ready Reserve, it is necessary and needs to be better managed. A permanent (though long-term) solution of the problem of the IRR is available and would cost virtually nothing. It is to increase the statutory military service obligation (the total of active plus inactive service) from the current period of six years to ten years. The change would be in keeping with the volunteer concept, and indeed was suggested as long ago as 1976. It is not logical to depend on volunteers to meet only *some* categories of military manpower needs; the "all-volunteer" concept must meet *all* needs, including those of the IRR pool of trained and experienced veterans. A six-year total obligation does not "fit" the AVF concept because it does not

---

*Dr. Korb comments: "The paper contains a number of findings/recommendations that address the youth decline, strength increases and probable recruiting problems in the future. I agree that we must be concerned about all these things. However, the paper should discuss some of the factors that would tend to mitigate these effects. These factors include the large and growing 30 to 55 year-old cohorts that will probably exclude youth from civilian employment even as the economy improves, the continued influx of women into the labor force and the Army's proportion (38,000) of the 200,000 active force increase.

"Also, there are many AVF ideas that are still open to fruitful investigation. These ideas include: developing an enlistment package that is competitive with civilian opportunities; lateral entry programs; and linking military acquired occupations to civilian requirements in a national labor market information scheme (one that possesses a job search feature)."

meet all of the needs. Nor does the eight-year obligation recently proposed by the administration. A ten-year obligation would. It might increase the army's IRR by about 80,000 per year after the sixth year, adding by the end of the tenth year some 320,000 and substantially erasing the deficit. The steady-state size of the IRR might then approach 500,000. Most major countries (and many small ones) impose a much longer military service obligation than does the United States, extending even beyond age 40. The ten-year obligation proposed here would be over by age 28 or 30 for most enlistees.

Some have said that to lengthen the period of obligation might inhibit volunteer enlistments and thus endanger the viability of the AVF. We believe that concern has little validity. The recall of IRR obligors would occur *only* under a dire national emergency. Most potential enlistees would probably assign that a low probability and would heavily discount it in a decision to enlist. Other factors, such as their near-term employment prospects, would undoubtedly be far more influential in their decision.*/**

In the near term, the army should be authorized to pay current IRR obligors a substantial bonus to reenlist in the IRR. It appears to be the only practical short-term fix based on a voluntary approach. Another possibility that has been experimented with, in a limited way, over the past two years is recruitment for basic training and direct enlistment in the IRR. This has been found to be extremely costly and in any case merely stockpiles graduates of basic training who have never served in military units and trained as team members.

Quality: Careerists. Great care is needed in the selection and retention of those who become military careerists. This requires due attention to such considerations as career progression, promotion opportunity, grade distribution, and cost. The major concern in recent years has been the premature loss of technical specialists and seasoned leaders with 8–12 years of experience. Along with essential improvements in responsiveness to the legitimate needs of the men and women in uniform, recent pay increases for the middle enlisted grades and incentive pays for specialists may solve the problem at that level. If they do not, further increases will be in order. No other options appear feasible as far as careerist retention is concerned.

---

*James L. Lacy comments: "Four principal flaws in the IRR that this 'option' ignores are: (1) only 29 percent are in combat specialities; (2) all the rest would need cross-over training; (3) the show-rate on mobilization is highly uncertain; and (4) the country has had no experience in rapidly integrating it into active and reserve forces."

**Julius Debro comments: "I believe that the ten year obligation is excessive and that the increase would meet with considerable opposition on the Hill. It would also inhibit volunteer enlistments and thus endanger the viability of the AVF."

First-Term Enlistment Quantity, Quality, Representativeness and Personnel Management. If, as we believe, one goal should be to attract a larger number of higher quality and college-bound youth into the army and to reach those socioeconomic groups not participating in the AVF in roughly proportional numbers, significant changes will be needed in the enlistment conditions and incentives now being offered.

There are at least two things that can be done: Shorten active-duty enlistment terms, and substantially increase educational benefits through a new "GI Bill of Rights".* At the same time, to reduce cost, to mitigate some significant personnel management problems, and to avoid attracting career enlistees into the short-term enlistments, compensation for new enlistees (those not contemplating a military career) should be drastically reduced, and skill and assignment options severely curtailed for the short enlistments. Active-duty enlistment terms should be matched to assignment tours. Enlistees on short enlistments, say those of less than three years, would not be granted allowances for dependents. Reducing pay levels in exchange for postservice educational benefits would create a "two-track" system of career soldiers and short-term soldiers.

Those attracted to this high educational benefit plan would enlist for one to two years of active duty preceded by as much active-duty time as is needed for basic and skill training. Alternatively, the recruit would take two to four years in the organized reserves, plus basic and skill training, and would serve a year of active duty following his educational program. Such recruits would be assigned to the combat arms and other labor-intensive tasks. These are the kinds of assignments in today's military where recruitment shortfalls, attrition, and desertion are most likely to occur. Active-duty pay for these short-term soldiers would be at a subsistence level. Other than the GI Bill, they would receive no entitlements, such as off-base housing or food allowances. This would discourage the frequency of marriage and single parenthood at junior enlisted levels and help restore unit cohesion in the barracks. With no presumption of acquiring civilian skills in the

---

*The GI Bill, a program of housing, unemployment, and educational assistance for returning veterans, was enacted in 1944. It not only rewarded past military service but encouraged returning veterans to seek schooling instead of immediate employment, thereby easing the transition to a civilian economy. In its first 12 years the GI Bill assisted 7.8 million veterans (half of the 15.6 million who were eligible) at a cost of $4.5 billion. The impact on universities was substantial. In 1939–1940, American colleges and universities awarded 216,521 degrees; in 1949–1950, the number was more than double: 496,661. The GI Bill was terminated in 1956. Those who had already qualified for its benefits, however, continued to receive them. While there were various proposals to reinstate the bill, the Department of Defense opposed them on several grounds. Defense worried that the bill lured people out of service and thus hurt retention. Also, the bill had been a reward for veterans of armed conflict (World War II and Korea) and should not be available for peacetime service. A "Cold War GI Bill" was nevertheless enacted in 1966. It was terminated in 1976.

military, the terms of such service would be unambiguous, thus alleviating a major source of postentry discontent in the AVF.

It is sometimes asked whether such a system would cause dissension and invidious comparisons and thereby compound leadership problems. This concern is seldom raised by military commanders and NCOs. If the short-term soldier feels so put out by his lower pay, he can easily rectify matters by joining the career track. More likely, the short-term soldier will accept the army on its own terms because military life is viewed as a hiatus. The AVF must attract middle-class and upwardly mobile youth who would find a temporary diversion from the world of school or work tolerable, and perhaps even welcome.

Table AII-10.3 presents illustratively some possible enlistment options for the army. These are designed to do several things:

1. Provide a group of limited-length active-duty enlistment options and a reserve enlistment option aimed at attracting college-bound or trade-school-bound youth. Assignment to skill and location would be at the convenience of the service.

2. Provide generous postservice educational benefits for the short active-duty enlistments in proportion to time served. Educational benefits for the reservists would be earned simultaneously with satisfactory performance in an Army National Guard or Reserve unit. The benefit would include tuition (up to a maximum amount), fees, and a modest subsistence allowance at an accredited school of choice. Educational benefits for the three- and four-year active enlistments would not be changed, i.e., the Veterans Educational Assistance Program (VEAP)* would remain as an incentive for the longer terms.

3. Match active-duty terms of service with the imperatives of personnel management, particularly those having to do with regulated tours overseas, such as the 12-month tour in South Korea or the desired 18-month tour in Europe for first-termers.

4. Offset the cost of (somewhat) higher turnover and educational benefits by reducing the compensation level for the short terms and by excluding from short-term service (less than three years) those having dependents.

To meet those objectives, the enlistment options must break with the long-standing but outdated tradition of keying enlistments to integral numbers of years. Instead, for those enlistments of less than three years of active-duty service, the training time, whatever its length, should be additive

---

*Under the Veterans Educational Assistance Program, the enlistee deposits part of his earnings to an educational fund, and additional funds are deposited by the government. The army has now been authorized to offer an "enhanced" VEAP that it hopes will attract high-school diploma graduates in Categories I, II, and IIIa. The enhanced VEAP is available, however, only to relatively small numbers of recruits and exists only on a year-to-year basis.

to the basic active term, permitting the service to gear personnel rotation to an annual cycle and to avoid charging training time against the active-duty commitment.

Because the preponderance of those electing to enlist for the shorter periods would go into the combat arms—the skills that have the shortest training schedules—the training time would fit into the summer time frame. Thus, a high-school graduate could go immediately into a training program following graduation, complete training by the end of the summer, begin the effective period of active-duty service in a unit, and complete the ensuing 12-month, 18-month, or 24-month period of service in a unit, in time to begin postservice education in the fall or spring semester. This works to the convenience of both the service and the individual.

A side benefit of the these short enlistments would be an earlier buildup in the IRR. For example, enlistees selecting the one-year (plus training time) option would enter the IRR as early as 15 months after enlistment. The buildup rate would of course depend on the mix of enlistment terms.

The enlistment option shown in table AII-10.3 for the reserve components would have to be carefully designed to be compatible with the ROTC program now carried out on many college campuses. For example, a cross-over option from one to the other might be desirable.

The army's training base capacity (or at least, annual throughput) would have to be expanded to meet the somewhat higher training load associated with the shorter terms of service. Offsetting this need to some degree would be an expected reduction in failure rates during training as a result of faster-learning recruits. Also, because the higher load would occur during the summer months, a surge capability might be available using the Army Reserve Training Divisions more extensively during their summer training periods.

Projected quantitative effects of the new enlistment options in a steady-state situation may be summarized as follows: Army annual nonprior service (NPS) enlistments would increase from 120,000 to about 140,000. Of the total, 41,000 would be in the new short-term options. Army total strength would increase about 22,000. The percentage of NPS enlistees who are above average (Categories I, II, and IIIa) would increase to 55 percent and there would be many more of them in the the first-term force because annual accessions would be higher as well. And the percentage of NPS enlistees who have high-school diplomas would be maintained at 80 percent, much higher than the average achieved in recent years, and as mentioned previously, there would be many more in the force.[13]/*

---

*Dr. Korb comments: "The only reason one would want to consider such a radical [two-track enlistment] proposal is if Army could not recruit enough quality people under the current system of incentives. I think we can demonstrate that Army can recruit enough quality people using VEAP with kickers and enlistment bonuses. [I question] the estimates of the number of high quality recruits who would be attracted under [this proposal]."

Contrary to some analysts, we believe that the expected increase in accession requirements that would result would have *desirable* consequences by leavening the active force. Nor do we agree that this plan would reduce retention—the plan should appeal essentially to those not contemplating a military career. Differences of view on this proposal derive from differences over the importance of recruiting more college-bound youth. The possible appeal of this lower-pay, short-enlistment, GI Bill track should now receive systematic evaluation at the Department of Defense. We believe this plan entails no risk and is eminently worth trying.

Voluntary National Service. Under the arrangements examined, quality short-term enlistments in the active forces or longer tours in the reserves would be encouraged by offering a graduated scale of attractive educational benefits. Under present conditions, however, such incentives to military service would be in competition with a variety of federal student aid programs to which no requirement of service, military or civilian, attaches. We have today a system that in effect offers more to those who do not serve their country than to those who do. Under the Veterans Educational Assistance Program, a contributory scheme which replaced the liberal post-World War II GI Bill, government expenditures are less than $90 million annually. In comparison, federal aid to college students exceeded $5.2 billion in 1980 and is estimated at $6.3 billion for 1981 and $7.0 billion for FY 1982. In effect, we have a GI Bill without the GI.*

Some, like Professor Moskos, have proposed that all or most federal student aid be made conditional on a variable period of service to the nation in either a military or a civilian capacity. Other inducements, such as hiring preference in federal, state, and private sector jobs, have also been proposed.

Under the Moskos proposal for a voluntary national service program, the civilian component of the program would make specified levels of student aid available to young men and women in exchange for a short period of unpaid or low-paid service. Recruitment would be handled by voluntary associations, welfare agencies, local governments, nonprofit institutions, schools, and recreational facilities. The range of tasks could include grooming care for the aged in nursing homes, day care for the elderly, serving in hospices, monitoring safety on public transit systems, and library and museum cataloguing. An important criterion would be useful services not entailing displacement of the gainfully employed.

Determination as to whether or not a specific task would meet service

---

* Dr. Korb comments: "This statement that 'we have a GI Bill without the GI' is misleading. Those who join the Army can participate in VEAP and depart with a $20,000 educational benefit. While in service they can take college courses on-base, with 75 percent of the tuition costs paid by Army. Those who do not participate in VEAP are in effect indicating that they have no interest in post-service education. If they change their mind after they return to civilian life, they will still be eligible for the educational benefits available to all civilians."

criteria would be the responsibility of local national service boards, whose members themselves would be volunteers (albeit not youth). Salaries would be received only by clerical help at local, regional, and national levels, and staff personnel at regional levels and at a headquarters office. The decentralized system of the old selective service boards is the obvious parallel.

Advocates of such a program believe it could go far to advance the idea and habit of peacetime service to the nation as a normal and desirable part of growing up in America. By creating a climate of expectation that young people will normally give time to national service, such a program could, its advocates argue, improve military recruiting.

Such a program would also provide an alternative means by which those not qualified for military service, or opposed to it on grounds of conscience or religion, could qualify for service-related student aid.

The military component of this proposal for a voluntary national service program would provide postservice educational benefits for members of the AVF along the lines described above. This proposal, like the related options considered in the preceding section, would provide the "functional equivalent of conscription" by establishing a noncareer enlistment category.

Current proposals for voluntary national service (like their compulsory counterparts discussed below) come in numerous other variations.[14] Our local and national experience with volunteer civilian service projects provides at best an ambiguous indication of the prospects for success. Much remains unclear about the costs, problems of administration, and prospective impact on the military. Some advocates recommend that such a program be phased in gradually over a period of years.[15]

Actual practice can provide the only test of feasibility and utility. Considering the dilemma of Americans coming of age in the 1980s, some find this option particularly appealing today. Of that dilemma, Dan Morgan wrote in a nationwide survey of teen-agers for the *Washington Post*:

"If caring and concern is measured by what is asked as well as by what is given, society has not served this generation of Americans as generously as it seems. What's missing? Skeptical adults would be surprised by the answer from scores of young people: The lack of challenging responsibilities against which they can shape their character, their values and their commitment to society. A sense of purpose, of inspiration, of fruitful connections, not only to parents but also to other elements of the larger society."[16/*]

---

*Dr. Korb comments: "The National Service proposals have a tenuous connection with military recruiting. The Moskos plan established a voluntary national service scheme to enable those who do not enlist to still qualify for educational benefits of an unspecified amount. First Moskos creates an equity problem for those not getting benefits, then proposes a national service scheme to solve it. The philosophy of the Reagan Administration is to minimize government interference in the lives of our citizens."

Compulsory Service[17]

If changes in the present all-volunteer system prove unable to provide the manpower to support the U.S. defensive posture necessary to deter war or to protect vital national interests, and if the nation desires to have such a posture, its only alternative, as a matter of definition, would be to adopt some form of compulsory military service.

The American people as a whole have accepted conscription in the past when they have perceived the existence of circumstances requiring it. In this century we have thus drafted young men for service not only in two world wars and two limited wars but in most of the "peacetime" years following World War II. In such circumstances, conscription served the nation well, and no other system would have served adequately. In today's world, all of our principal NATO allies except Britain and Canada—and virtually every conceivable adversary—employ compulsory military service in one form or another. By international standards, defense capability tied to the whims of the labor marketplace is an idiosyncrasy.*

Yet it does not necessarily follow that the United States needs to reinstate the draft today. Whether and when to do so are issues that can reasonably depend on judgments about the prospects for correcting the defects of the all-volunteer system. We address that subject in our concluding section. It is useful meanwhile to ask: If and when the nation decides it needs conscription, what are the options and their respective merits?

The compulsory service options can be either universal or selective in scope. Some leading options of both kinds are considered below.

Universal Conscription. Those who have advocated one form or another of peacetime universal conscription for this country—and it is a distinguished roster beginning with George Washington—have relied on two kinds of argument. One is that the alternatives are inherently less effective in providing for the common defense. The other is that universal conscription can improve the society by contributing to the moral and physical development of young people.

Universal conscription may take three forms: universal military service, universal conscription but only for military training in peacetime, and universal national service in which some would enter the armed forces but most would perform obligatory nonmilitary public service. Most of the sporadic debate about peacetime universal conscription has been notable more for its emphasis on philosophical and sentimental considerations than for its concern with the practicalities.

---

*A number of our NATO allies having conscription, however, contribute no higher a proportion of their populations to active service than does the United States (at 0.9 percent).

Proponents commonly concede that universal conscription in peacetime, if used to fill the active forces, would produce a military establishment out of all proportion to needs. In 1981, for example, some 2 million men and 2 million women turned 18. Had each been required to serve two years, and assuming all were eligible to serve and none were COs, first-term ranks would have swelled to over 8 million (or over 4 million, were such a draft confined to men).*

Accordingly, proponents of universal conscription offer two alternative avenues to a universal obligation. First, all (or nearly all) youth (or only male youth) would be required to undergo basic military *training*, but in peacetime actual military *service* would be expected only of volunteers. The alternative would be universal national service, incorporating compulsory civilian public work as well as military service. This would enlarge the "demand" for manpower to approximate the size of its supply without having to enlarge the armed forces. Both alternatives come in numerous versions. Neither has ever been attempted in the United States.

The Truman administration campaigned for universal military training (UMT) for six years following World War II but was unable to convince the Congress that rotating an entire generation through training and into the reserves satisfied any modern military requirement. When President Eisenhower raised the idea in the mid-1960s, the Defense Department examined it briefly and concluded that it would cost $2.5 billion annually in added operating expenses alone, and would offer no increase in military effectiveness.

Whatever one may think of the moral and social potential of UMT, it is clearly a costly and ineffective way to provide defense manpower:
- It would create very large pools of reservists with limited training and no active-duty experience.
- It would require an enormous military training base, with substantial dislocations of men and matériel from the "tooth" to the "tail" of the force structure.
- Unless UMT graduates were to be drafted selectively for active duty (which is not commonly proposed), the United States would still have to maintain and support a wholly volunteer active-duty force.
- Finally, while the courts have interpreted the constitution liberally in allowing the national government to conscript for military service, both UMT and universal national service go considerably beyond all past constitutional interpretations. The authority of the national government to

---

* In practice, at least during the Vietnam draft period, only about 40 percent of those called made it through both physical examinations and 10 percent of those were conscientious objectors. Thus only about 36 percent were actually inducted. Even so, the numbers inducted under universal conscription would remain vastly out of proportion to needs.

compel service, the courts have held, is found in the enumerated power to raise and support armies and provide and maintain a navy. The courts have yet to wed such authority to any other enumerated power of the Congress (the commerce power, for instance) or to any general provision (such as to promote the general welfare). Absent a strong case on security grounds, the courts would be unlikely to do so. At the same time, "involuntary servitude" is proscribed by the Thirteenth Amendment, a prohibition from which the Supreme Court rescued the military draft (and some limited forms of obligatory civilian service for some citizens subject to the military draft). The courts have allowed very few other exceptions— jury service, for example, and in an earlier era a few days' compulsory work each year on state and local roads.

Selective Service. If then the voluntary system were to be abandoned and no form of universal conscription is deemed practical, the only remaining option is the one the nation has always chosen: compulsory service for which some, but not all, will be selected. Any selective service system invites two broad objections: it involves compulsion, and its burdens fall only to some.

On the other hand, a peacetime draft (for the active forces) has several distinct advantages:

First, a draft, however designed, would fully man the force structure of all services, active and reserve, and this would be true even if there were increases in the structure and in manpower requirements. Whether or not the draft would also correct the 280,000 shortfall in the Army Individual Ready Reserve would depend on the size of the draft and manpower management policies.

Second, a draft could, over time and at all times (even in prosperous times and periods of diminished eligible population) improve the quality and representativeness of nonprior service accessions in the ground forces, although it might well have little impact on the other components. The very fact of a draft and its pressures permit all services to establish more rigorous entrance requirements for volunteers, as indeed they did in the past. The draft could deliver a more representative sample of American youth remaining after the volunteers, COs, and those excluded for cause. (Since, however, reenlistment rates for draftees are normally low and minority reenlistment rates are relatively high, minority representation, now about 41 percent in the army, would probably not fall much below 25–30 percent even with the draft.)

Third, a peacetime draft, again however designed, would force timely resolution of several difficult issues left hanging when the draft was ended in 1972:

• Can men but not women be drafted?

- If both must be drafted, can men but not women be drafted for all positions in the combat arms?
- What is the size and nature of the conscientious objector problem? What solutions are acceptable to the courts?
- Will there be mass failure to accept draft calls? If so, what actions are feasible? (This is especially important in an ambiguous emergency.)
- What policy should be adopted for self-admitted drug users and homosexuals?

Finally, a draft would put the country in a more ready mobilization posture by revivifying the Selective Service System, by requiring a larger training base, and by assuring a fully manned force, active and reserve.

In considering what if any kind of selective service may best serve for the future, one should be familiar with the present Military Selective Service Act. (All that actually expired with the adoption of the All-Volunteer Force was the president's authority to issue induction notices.) This "permanent" legislation, until revoked or replaced, governs the terms of any resumed conscription. Among other things, it (1) requires the registration of all males between 18 and 26, (2) permits, but does not require, selections for induction to be made randomly, (3) provides for active-duty military service of not more than 24 consecutive months, (4) explicitly defers or exempts conscientious objectors, divinity students, ministers, surviving sons and brothers, certain government officials, and reservists, and (5) authorizes, but does not require, deferment of students, parents, hardship cases, and persons in occupations or research thought valuable to the national health, safety, or interest.

Five possible forms of selective service have gained considerable attention and are examined below—two for the reserves and three for active duty.

Conscription for the Reserves. One proposal has been to conscript only for the Individual Ready Reserves. Any such draft would of course eliminate an important part of the reserve manpower shortfall. It would also alter a serious imbalance in the IRR. At present, only some 25 percent of IRR augmentees are junior enlisted men with combat arms skills, whereas the wartime need for such reserves runs closer to 90 percent, given current projections about where casualties are most likely to occur and IRR replacements most likely to be needed.

The disadvantages of this kind of draft, however, appear decisive. Conscripting for the IRR would, like UMT (of which it is merely a limited variant), produce only basically trained soldiers whose skills diminish every year without the benefit of participation in organized units. Above all, an IRR draft would accomplish little for the total force that an active-duty draft with a residual IRR obligation would not achieve, and in relatively the same time frame.

Conscription for the Selected Reserve, on the other hand, presents a different sort of difficulty. The units of that reserve are organized on the basis of state and local geography. Their viability as training entities for weekend drills depends on their being in reasonable proximity to the reservists' residence. To man such units with conscripts would require state, local, or regional draft calls, since neither the size of reserve units nor the numbers of enlisted vacancies within units would correspond with the geographical distribution of the draft-eligible population. The political acceptability of a reserve unit in a community would erode rapidly if it thus became the vehicle for disproportionate burdens on local youth.

Conscription for Active Duty. Of the compulsory service options, this would seem to leave some form of selective conscription for active military service. There are essentially three.

The first would be a "tag-on" draft designed to encourage the maximum amount of volunteering by essentially preserving the AVF's status quo, but shoring it up as needed with monthly draft calls. In this variant, existing first-term pay levels would not be altered and would be kept generally competitive in the labor marketplace. This would have the advantage of keeping compulsions to an absolute minimum, of meeting recruitment shortfalls in the most expeditious manner, and of providing sufficient manpower for the less attractive military occupations specialties. It would also eliminate a dangerous weakness in current mobilization capability by replacing the existing standby draft with a fully operating peacetime system of registration, classification, and processing. The drawbacks, on the other hand, are equally clear. The tag-on draft would induct so few that it would inevitably seem discriminatory. Had it been available, for example, in AVF's worst recruiting year, it would have taken no more than 25,000 draftees out of the 18-year-old male cohort of 2 million. Second, given the limited numbers called, it would do little to improve the qualitative or the demographic composition of the enlisted force. And it would save little in first-term manpower costs, while superimposing on the AVF the expense of a fully operational peacetime draft.

The second variant of selective peacetime conscription for the active forces would be the near-reverse. Here, a far larger proportion of the active forces would be obtained through the draft by discouraging volunteering. (Enlistments could be barred outright or limited, or voluntary enlistment tours could be lengthened, for example.) The substitution of large numbers of two-year conscripts for three- and four-year volunteers would mean larger accession requirements. This should produce demographically more representative forces. The quality of the first-term force (in terms of test scores and high-school diplomas) would improve to some extent over current levels.

Finally, while the larger numbers of inductions would not increase the career force, they would help appreciably the Selected Reserve (the greater the likelihood of being inducted, the greater the attractiveness of a reserve deferment) and the IRR (through increased force turnover).*

A third variant of selective peacetime conscription would entail a sharp reduction of recruiting efforts and a gradual reduction in the relative value of first-term pay. Like the others considered above, its purpose would be to assure an adequate supply of active-duty manpower and to rebuild the reserves. This variant would also be expected to put a brake on upward spirals of first-term manpower costs** and on a decade-long trend toward higher concentrations of minorities in the enlisted ranks.

Under this variant, enlistment bonuses would be eliminated and recruitment efforts cut back to the pre-Vietnam level. The expected result is that ensuing annual draft calls would rise steadily from not more than 20,000 in the first year or two to some 165,000 thereafter. Forty to sixty percent of first-term accessions would be either draftees or draft-motivated volunteers. As such inductions (for two-year tours) grow in numbers, they will fuel additional inductions by cutting into the current level of three-year enlistments.

Costs-savings in the first year from reduced recruitment efforts would be substantial but would be largely offset by the increased costs of processing draft registrants and possibly by increases in reenlistment bonuses. Entry level wages would not be suppressed from their current AVF levels (nor would they be different for conscripts and volunteers of the same rank and length of service), but they would not rise in future years as rapidly as civilian wages or career military pay. It would be essential, however, to establish a floor below which junior enlisted pay would not be permitted to fall. Past drafts tolerated excessively low rates of pay, which might better be indexed, for example, to the equivalent of two-thirds of the federal minimum wage. This is the wage currently paid to VISTA volunteers ($385

---

*Richard V. L. Cooper comments: "Perhaps the greatest shortcoming of this variant, though, is the potentially disastrous effect that it would have on re-enlistment. Draftees historically had re-enlistment rates of less than 10 percent. This means that making draftees the predominant source of first-term manpower could make it extremely difficult to man the career enlisted ranks—i.e., the senior non-coms so crucial to effective leadership."

**Dr. Cooper further comments: "I take exception to the viewpoint that a draft would have a significant impact on manpower costs. The cost of first-termers only comprises about 10 percent of total manpower costs, and about 5 percent of the total defense budget. Manpower costs are high, not because of the wages paid to first-termers, but because of the costs of career manpower, military retirement, and civilian employees of the DoD—none of which would be affected by a return to the draft. Thus, the draft provides only limited leverage over costs that comprise about 5 percent of the defense budget (after all, the wages of first-termers cannot be reduced to zero), and no leverage at all over the remaining 95 percent."

per month in 1981; $440 per month when benefits and allowances are included).

The advantages of this variant are that (1) it permits a less precipitous departure from present manpower procedures; (2) as with the preceding variants, it removes the mobilization draft from the uncertainties of standby status; (3) it works over time to contain overall defense manpower cost increases; (4) it would produce after the first several years a better balance by race and test scores as random inductions steadily replace the self-selection of voluntary enlistments.

While a gradual transition to larger numbers of conscripts may be beneficial for the armed forces, however, it comes at the expense of highly selective draft calls and elaborate draft machinery in the near-term. Of those called, such a draft would produce only modest yearly inductions. Finally, this option would increase annual accessions by as much as 40 percent and the size of the first-term force by 15 to 20 percent, with a higher turnover rate than in the AVF. (Higher turnover would, on the other hand, add manpower to the reserves through the operation of the six-year Military Service Obligation.)

Selective National Service. Selective national service differs from the other variants of selective peacetime service discussed above by adding a component of nonmilitary service.

In 1965 and 1970, the Supreme Court expanded the definition of "religious" objection to include secular views as long as they were held with a fervor comparable to that with which traditional COs maintained their views. The decision has the potential for greatly enlarging the pool of conscientious objectors.

Concerns that these rulings have created a future "voluntary" draft, and that further applications of the historic "belief" tests only invite further, confounding litigation, lead some to want to abandon all such tests in favor of granting the traditional "CO" status to all who are willing to perform alternative civilian work, regardless of their religious beliefs or affiliations. Because this would provide an escape from induction, the terms of civilian work would be sufficiently rigorous so as not to actively encourage its selection.

The second formulation is oriented quite differently: It would use the risk of induction as leverage on the draft-age population to encourage (channel) the widest numbers to choose nonmilitary service. The terms of alternative service, accordingly, would be more attractive than those of military induction.

While there are considerable variations within each, the prevalent characteristics of these "selective national service" ideas are the following: acceptable civilian service would have to be in an approved field or activity, these almost always in the delivery of social service; the individual electing this nonmilitary service would have to make the election before he or she receives an induction notice, commonly at the time of initial draft registration (in some versions, however, the individual may delay actual commencement of service for up to four years); failure to elect civilian service subjects the individual to liability to induction by random lottery for an active tour of military duty; failure to satisfactorily complete such service subjects the individual to another period of lottery exposure; satisfactory completion of service is not cause for a draft exemption per se, but the individual is placed low enough in the order of call of any future draft, in peacetime or in war, to make it unlikely he will be called.

By tying the service to a draft excusal to be applied for voluntarily and enforced simply by revocation of the excusal, the option avoids the constitutional difficulties of universal national service. The numbers which would participate are difficult to anticipate and are likely to vary greatly over time.

The historical CO exemption required two years of nonmilitary service at no direct cost to the federal government. The CO was to locate an acceptable public service position with a government or private sponsor. Selective Service provided some placement assistance and monitored that the service had been performed, but otherwise, the individual was supervised and paid by the employing sponsor. An expanded program with such terms would add some administrative expenses, but would still be largely at no cost to the federal treasury.

A variation on this was proposed by Congressman Jonathan Bingham in 1971. The Bingham plan would require sponsoring employers to pay the federal government for each participant the same wage paid to other employees doing similar work or the minimum wage, whichever is greater; the government in turn would provide the participant a subsistence allowance based on geographical cost-of-living differences. (In theory, the net costs to the government would be modest.) Civilian service would be for not less than two nor more than four years, with the exact term determined by the value and difficulty of the work performed. Only draft-age, draft-eligible individuals would be expected to participate.

In contrast to these "expanded CO" formulations, the "channeling" alternatives commonly provide for direct and unreimbursed federal subsistence allowances to participants. An illustration is a measure proposed by Congressman Paul ("Pete") McCloskey in 1979. One year of civilian service only would be required in the McCloskey plan as a satisfactory alternative to two years active military duty or six years in the reserves. Women as well as men would be required to register and declare their intentions concerning civilian service, but whether women not doing so would be subjected to military induction is not clear in the McCloskey proposal. Those choosing none of these options would be liable to the military draft if and when the authority to induct is reinstated. (The McCloskey plan would reduce entering military wages, but compensate for this by a package of postservice educational benefits.)

A key unknown in all three alternatives is the participation rate, since this would be a factor in the first instance of how extensive draft calls are likely to be at any given time. Participation is also likely to be highly sensitive to international tensions. And, since all three programs leave it to the individual to find a qualifying position on his own (the Bingham plan provides for government employment as a last resort), the better qualified will presumably find the outlet more easily managed than will those with less to offer to prospective sponsors. The effects on the armed forces, then, could range from the very negligible (in the absence of large draft calls) to a quality-drain-off were the prospects for induction to increase significantly.

As with universal national service, there is little specificity as to what work individuals would do, how they would be organized, and how such a program would be monitored and compliance enforced. Nor is it evident that adequate numbers of civilian service opportunities exist to accommodate those who might participate. (By 1971, the traditional CO program had a backlog of some 34,000 awaiting placement in civilian service, many for several years.)

Short of abolishing CO status entirely, or taking the risk that recent CO case law will not greatly expand the CO pool, it will be necessary to provide a rigorous civilian alternative to military service. The historical CO exemption system and the Bingham alternative would do this without encouraging large numbers to opt for civilian service. A civilian program of limited size, in turn, would reduce the uncertainties of placement, facilitate necessary experimentation, and cost the government far less than the other selective national service options. How rigorous and how long this alternative need be in order to be a fair equivalent of induction are matters that now invite study and debate.[18]

* * *

After nearly a decade of "zero-draft" force-manning, American armed strength entering the 1980s was at its lowest ebb since 1950. Few today believe that force size could be substantially increased through reliance on volunteers alone. Conditions that have favored the AVF in much of the 1970s, such as demographic trends and the state of the economy, will change. At some point in this decade, resumption of the draft may well become necessary to national security.

The power to compel service should be restricted to national defense purposes. Whatever form a future draft may take, its basic purpose should be to provide a predictable and secure flow of manpower into the armed forces in time of peace and war.

The type of draft most likely to meet this objective has several features. It would coexist with voluntary enlistments, and indeed induce some portion of them. It would strive to be neither a very small nor a totally overwhelming factor in force-manning. First-term military wages would not in future years be ratcheted upward to maintain competitiveness with civilian pay. At the same time, a near-ironclad indexing device seems essential to prevent junior enlisted pay from falling to the deplorable levels allowed in the past.

Such a draft would select randomly, and would draw chiefly from 19- and 20-year olds. There is no great reason why women should not be liable to induction, although there are powerful countervailing political and social instincts which complicate the issue.

Broader access to the traditional CO program of alternative service seems an essential element. How rigorous and how long this alternative need be in order to be a fair equivalent of induction are matters overdue for debate. Selective national service whose principal purpose is to use the threat of induction to channel large numbers of the young into public service seems wrong as a matter of principle.

If and when the nation is obliged to resume conscription, it should understand that there can be no flawless draft, just as there can be no flawless AVF. The proper question is: Which combination of arrangements will best promote peace and security in this decade and the next?

CONCLUSION: FINDINGS AND RECOMMENDATIONS

The Stakes and the Risks

Over the past decade and a half—while we indulged the luxury of democratic disarray over errors and misfortunes at home and abroad and let our investment in defense decline in real terms—a totalitarian superpower with a disquieting record in international relations accelerated its modernization of essentially every element of military force structure and weaponry. Today the Soviet Union appears to have achieved strategic nuclear parity. In Europe the Soviets have gained a preponderance of both nuclear and conventional military power. In strategic regions of the Third World, they and their Cuban surrogates have been on the move.

Such objective realities are not in serious dispute. What is in dispute is what this implies for U.S. policy.

In this matter, Americans would be well advised to avoid speculating about what the Soviets may intend to do. Rather, we should put into focus what they are now politically and militarily able to do. We believe that the record of Soviet repression at home and expansion abroad, coupled with their unparalleled buildup of nuclear and conventional arms over the past 15 years, constitute a serious threat to international stability and the security of the West.

In the absence of a world peacekeeping agency with "teeth" in it, the security of the Atlantic Community must continue to depend on maintaining the world balance of power. As Andrei Sakharov, the Soviet Union's most famous scientist and social activist, wrote (in an article recently smuggled into the West from his internal exile), maintaining world peace today means making the Soviet Union "realize that any attempts to alter the equilibrium existing in the world, no matter what considerations are used as a cover, are inadmissible."[19]

Many Americans are understandably baffled by the complexity and appalled by the enormity of today's strategic issues. Their confusion and dismay sometimes translate into public demonstrations against nuclear weapons and the North Atlantic Alliance and in favor of unilateral disarmament. Yet a reasonably clear public understanding of deterrence, and a willingness to accept its costs, have become indispensable to the West's prospects of averting its own decline and fall.

In the past, Americans as a whole have always been willing to pay the cost, once they perceived the need. But in all previous crises involving our national security, we had time to create the required force after the hostilities had begun. Few who have considered the matter carefully believe we have that luxury any longer. Whatever armed forces we may need initially to deter aggression or defend against it we must keep in being or be able to bring to bear within weeks of an attack. The cost of effective deterrence or defense is far higher than ever before.

We believe most Americans, including most young Americans, like their predecessors back to colonial times, do appreciate what is at stake and are willing to do what may be necessary to protect the national interest — on two perfectly reasonable conditions: first, that the threat be real; second, that the burdens of deterrence and defense be fairly shared.

For those who agree with our assessment of the stakes and the risks, the remaining question is, "What must we do about it?" As a reader of the preceding pages will appreciate, there is no simple or infallible answer. The findings and recommendations that follow reflect a hard-won consensus among a group of private citizens of diverse professional experience and personal predilections.*

---

*Comments, dissents, and reservations of Working Group participants are recorded in footnotes or in Appendix I, as appropriate.

A Policy for the 1980s and 1990s: Findings and Recommendations

FINDING #1: ROLE OF CONVENTIONAL FORCES

Assuming current U.S. efforts will maintain general nuclear parity between East and West, the one other indispensable requirement for decisive deterrence or defense is the prompt availability of adequate, mission-ready conventional forces. Recent proposals for a U.S. declaration of "no first use" of nuclear weapons would, if adopted, make the case for strong conventional forces even more compelling. Conventional forces are the key element in reducing the likelihood of nuclear confrontation and avoiding nuclear war without jeopardizing Western freedom. And adequate manpower is a key element of adequate conventional forces.

FINDING #2: FORCE STRUCTURE AND READINESS

Decisions following the war in Vietnam have resulted in an active U.S. Army force of 16 divisions that is smaller by nearly 200,000 than before the war. It is heavily unbalanced toward combat forces, and must rely extensively on mobilized reserves for combat units and for combat support and combat service support at the very outset of any major emergency.

The reliance placed on Army Reserve components demands a readiness for them far higher than any ever achieved before. Yet, the resources of manpower, equipment, and training needed to bring the Army Reserve components to the required combat readiness have not been made available to them. Despite impressive gains in the Army Selected Reserve strength recently, we find no program that will bring it to adequate training strength before about 1990.

In addition, the Individual Ready Reserve, the pretrained manpower pool needed by the army prior to the time that emergency actions could produce trained strength from recruits, has been reduced to an unacceptable level, and no action thus far undertaken or announced will fully correct the problem.

The combination of these conditions—unbalanced active army force structure, unready reserve units, and inadequate numbers of pretrained manpower—means that U.S. conventional forces are not in a position to carry out the full range of established missions.

A significant number of the Working Group members believe that the only adequate remedy would be to increase the authorized strength of the active army force from the present 786,000 to about the pre-Vietnam (1964) level of 972,000. Moreover, some who propose this believe it would require an immediate return to peacetime conscription. (See, "Comments and Dissents," Appendix I.)

FINDING #3: THE CHANGING CONDITIONS

In this decade and the next, some increase in U.S. manpower requirements is likely (and some has been programmed), and it will have to be obtained from a diminishing manpower pool. Economic recovery and a consequent drop in unemployment will further reduce the numbers of qualified young people who will enlist.

FINDING #4: BASIC CRITERIA OF MANPOWER POLICY

Whatever military manpower system we employ for the present decade and the next, it needs to meet four fundamental criteria:
- produce the size of forces required for all components of the uniformed services to carry out assigned missions;
- provide personnel who are mentally, physically, and attitudinally equipped to serve effectively;
- see that no racial segment of American society is grossly over- or under-represented in sharing the burdens of deterrence and defense;*
- provide a rapid, effective means for mobilizing the manpower needed to meet a major military contingency.

FINDING #5: ACHIEVEMENTS OF THE ALL-VOLUNTEER SYSTEM

In several respects the all-volunteer system has been a notable success. The authorized size of all active forces for all services (albeit reduced by more than 500,000 from the pre-Vietnam level) has been nearly achieved each year. Over the AVF years, the quality of recruit accessions for the Department of Defense as a whole (the army apart), as measured by educational background, has consistently been at least as high as during the draft years. The reserve components of the navy, Marine Corps, and air force have been kept at or near their authorized peacetime strengths, and the Army Guard and Army Reserve have now recovered most of the strength lost in the earlier AVF years.

FINDING #6: SHORTCOMINGS OF THE ALL-VOLUNTEER SYSTEM

In other important respects, however, the present all-volunteer system has serious deficiencies:

1. Quality as measured by test scores and high-school diplomas has been shown in numerous studies to correlate with soldierly effectiveness.[20] Com-

---

*Perfect representativeness is neither necessary nor possible. Gross unrepresentativeness has both philosophical and practical difficulties. The possibility, for example, under present conditions, that blacks would take disproportionately high casualties in the early phase of hostilities is a matter of legitimate concern. At the same time, some are concerned that increasing representativeness may have the effect of denying some qualified members of minority groups the opportunity to serve.

manders testify that within reason "smarter is better," a view that has gained much ground with the rapidly increasing sophistication of weaponry. The quality of active army recruits has varied from year to year and has often fallen far below that of the draft years, with fiscal years 1977 through 1980 so consistently low as to be unacceptable. It is true that part of the quality problem in 1977–1980 was due to an error in norming the aptitude tests and that the army has since made a strong comeback in recruit quality. It remains to be seen whether this can be maintained under the projected conditions that will make recruiting more difficult in coming years.

2. The ground elements of the All-Volunteer Force have not drawn anywhere near proportionally from white middle-class America. Particularly this is true in the army, where minorities make up 41 percent of the enlisted force, including 33 percent black enlistees (as compared to a population of about 13 percent black).*

3. Under the AVF emphasis on military service as an occupation, the armed forces have lost some of their unique qualities as an institution. This drift cannot be fully measured but is evident in such conditions as attrition, the erosion of unit cohesiveness, moonlighting, the separation of workplace and residence, and feelings of disillusionment among junior enlisted personnel.[21] Several of our recommendations should help correct this.

FINDING #7: RETAINING SKILLED PERSONNEL

Although not caused by the all-volunteer system, all services in varying degrees have had trouble retaining mid-level career officers and enlisted men, particularly in the costly-to-train, highly technical skills. As a result of recent pay raises, however, retention has improved dramatically. Since the career force is the key element around which recruits will coalesce into an effective military force, it is essential that any military service program (draft, volunteer, or combination) provide adequate institutional and material incentives to retain a quality career force.

FINDING #8: PEACETIME REGISTRATION

Peacetime registration for the draft gives the nation, at minimal cost and inconvenience, an important time advantage in the event of a crisis requiring rapid mobilization. Perhaps more important, it is also a clear statement

---

*Dr. Cooper comments: "I believe that it is difficult to attribute the rising minority content in the military to the All-Volunteer Force, as much of this increased participation of minorities would have occurred even had the draft been retained. I believe, rather, that the increased minority participation can be attributed largely to two factors. First, the proportion of black youth found qualified for military service has increased dramatically over the past two decades. Second, black youth faced especially poor civilian job prospects in the 1970s. As a result, simply returning to the draft would do little to alter the racial content of the enlisted ranks."

to allies and adversaries of national resolve about the U.S. and Western security. Compliance with present registration requirements has been unsatisfactory but is now much improved. Absent evidence to the contrary, it is reasonable to believe that noncompliance has more to do with a lack of public information (and until recently the lack of administration urging) than to defiance of the law.

FINDING #9: POLICY ON CONSCRIPTION

Several possible developments could trigger the need to reinstate conscription. These include a failure to maintain needed force levels, a large upward revision of military manpower requirements, an external provocation (including one short of a direct military attack on American interests), and a return to the low average quality of personnel taken by the army from 1977 to 1980.

Given the anticipated increase in manpower needs, the diminishing manpower pool, and the prospect of economic recovery, it is only prudent that the nation prepare now to resume a form of the draft later in the 1980s.

Whatever form it may take, if and when reinstated, the draft should be designed first to provide economically and reliably whatever additional manpower is needed. It must also be designed so as to select from the draft-eligible population fairly and randomly and with few exemptions, deferments, and excusals. And it should balance equities between those who are selected and those who are not through a variety of postservice benefits that are reserved for those who serve.

FINDING #10 ROLE OF WOMEN

The value of women in many service positions has been increasingly recognized both within and outside the military, and their career opportunities have grown accordingly. The question of further increasing the role of women in military service is complex and is under serious study in the Department of Defense. We believe that a greater role for women should be a continuing objective and an important part of the national discussion of military "manpower" issues.

FINDING #11: POLICY ON VOLUNTARY NATIONAL CIVILIAN SERVICE

The idea of a voluntary national service program, incorporating civilian as well as military service options, has much to commend it but requires a more thorough analysis of purposes, costs, benefits, and administrative arrangements than has yet been undertaken. Under the proposals we noted above, voluntary youth service in approved civilian activities for stipulated periods of time and subsistence wages, as well as in the active and reserve armed forces, would be encouraged through the provision of suitably scaled educational benefits and other inducements such as preference in federal, state, and private sector employment.

What is needed is a comprehensive, dispassionate analysis of the prospects and problems. A proposal to establish a Presidential Commission on national service is pending in the Congress. Recent studies such as that currently sponsored by the Ford Foundation are other important steps in this direction.

The present array of federal student aid programs offers more to those who do not render such services than to those who do. A substantial restructuring of such programs to favor those volunteering for brief periods of noncareer military service is now in order and is the subject of Recommendations #4 and #5 which follow. This should attract increasing numbers of middle-class and upwardly mobile youth who may find in the active or reserve forces a tolerable and perhaps even welcome temporary diversion from the world of school or work.

Whether student aid incentives should be extended to voluntary civilian service is an issue that deserves wider and more intensive consideration. Such a program might go far to advance the ideal and habit of peacetime service to the nation as a normal and desirable part of growing up in America. To that extent it should improve the climate for voluntary enlistment in peacetime military service. Such a program would have the additional advantage of providing an alternative means by which those not qualified for military service or opposed to it on grounds of conscience or religion could qualify for student aid.

Even if national civilian service did not significantly benefit military recruitment, it might well be worth trying. The dilemma of millions of Americans coming of age in the 1980s is serious. A voluntary national service program could be a major part of the answer.

RECOMMENDATION #1: FORCE STRUCTURE AND READINESS

Purpose: To achieve better balance between commitments and capabilities.

In light of our Finding #2, the United States should either alter its defense commitments and plans to match realistically the resources we seem willing to provide, *or*—as we believe—it should provide the resources to permit altering force structure and manning to match present commitments. In particular, the Department of Defense should reexamine the army's immediate and major reliance on its reserve components in a defense emergency to determine whether established mobilization and deployment goals can be met.

RECOMMENDATION #2: THE RESERVES

Purpose: To correct shortfalls in Army Reserve strengths.

1. The secretary of defense should develop and press for legislation in-

creasing the military service obligation (total of active plus reserve duty) for the first-term from six to ten years.*/**

2. As an interim remedy for the shortfall in the Individual Ready Reserve, the army should offer a bonus for extending one's tour of duty in the IRR. The army should also introduce a management program for the IRR that permits a thorough knowledge of the IRR's requirements by skill, inventory by skill, and member availability and that preassigns IRR members to active and reserve units.

3. Recruiting and retention incentives for the Army Selected Reserve should be designed to correct manning deficiencies within the next four years.***

4. The secretary of defense should require, and seek the resources for, all measures necessary to bring the training and equipment of reserve units up to standard.

RECOMMENDATION #3: QUALITY

Purpose: To assure adequate quality of recruits for the All-Volunteer Force and to preclude a repetition of the 1977-1980 unacceptable quality of army nonprior-service accessions.

1. The services should establish quality goals and quality floors so that accessions avoid a gross unrepresentativeness of the educational background and mental capacity of the population.

2. We recommend that the following minimum standards be established for all services:

	AVF Minimums (in %)	
	AVF accessions	Base population
High-school diploma graduates	65	74
Above average mental categories (I–IIIa)	50	50
Maximum lowest mental category (IV)	25	23

---

*The Department of Defense has proposed legislation to extend the MSO from six to eight years for new recruits and to offer an IRR reenlistment bonus of $900 for three years of service. We believe this will help but will not prove adequate.

**Dr. Korb comments: "Our analysis indicates that a two-year extension together with other low-cost programs would provide sufficient numbers and skills in the Army IRR. Further, market research shows that a 10-year service obligation would probably adversely affect recruiting—64 percent of males surveyed opposed a 10-year obligation."

***The army has recently taken promising steps in this direction with a series of enlistment and reenlistment bonuses which it projects will bring the Army Reserve and National Guard to wartime strength by 1987. We believe this should be achieved more rapidly, and that the projection is too high (by some 60,000) because it reflects total strength levels, not trained strength levels.

If these minimum levels are not maintained during any particular years, new programs (see number 3) to increase incentives should be started immediately.*

Quality goals or standards, as distinct from minimum goals, should also be set by each service each year with the concurrence of the secretary of defense. They should, of course, be considerably higher than the minimums.

3. The Department of Defense should be prepared with an in-place program of flexible incentives to be used by any service unable to meet the minimum quality standards established. Congress should support such flexibility.

RECOMMENDATION #4: ACTIVE SERVICE ENLISTMENTS AND EDUCATIONAL BENEFITS

Purpose: To improve the representative character and the quality of accessions and to alleviate the IRR problem.

1. The administration and the Congress should restructure present student aid programs to promote voluntary enlistment in the services, particularly the army.

2. The services should be authorized to offer a new active-duty enlistment program, to supplement regular options, that consists of an enlistment term of one to two years of active service preceded by as much active-duty time as is needed for basic and skill training. Legislation should be enacted to reward successful performers in this program with two to four academic years of postservice education (at a ratio of two years of education for each year of active duty served after completion of training) at an accredited institution, with the government paying tuition support (up to a maximum amount), fees, and a modest subsistence allowance. Active-duty pay for these enlistees should be reduced by law to a minimum subsistence level,

---

*Dr. Korb comments: "The recommended quality standards are arbitrary and based on a representativeness policy. No explicit analysis of the most appropriate standard has been conducted. The paper suggests floors which almost perfectly match the aptitude in the general society. We do not believe that those floors are appropriate for several reasons:

—The enlisted force is primarily 'blue collar' in nature. Thus it is composed of jobs which require a smaller proportion of individuals in the upper-ability ranges.

—The representativeness standard is inappropriate, military need should govern.

—The costs to achieve those standards would be prohibitive and there would be substantial risk they could not be achieved, notwithstanding the new proposals for short term enlistments made in the paper.

—Any representative comparison should be made against the entire force, officer and enlisted.

—Each Service has different jobs to be performed; those jobs translate into different percentages of mental categories needed.

"Recommend the paper delete any specific minimum standards for enlistment."

and dependent allowances should not be authorized for them. Such enlistees while on active duty should have the option, if qualified, of switching to the regular longer-term enlistment options with regular pay and benefits, and to retain whatever educational benefits had been earned at the time of transfer. Such a program should be limited, at least initially, to the army and to low-skill, easy-to-train positions (such as combat arms) and should fit into the service overseas rotation scheme. The law regarding military enlistments should accordingly be changed to permit enlistment for terms other than an integral number of years.

RECOMMENDATION #5: RESERVE ENLISTMENTS AND EDUCATIONAL BENEFITS

Purpose: To raise the quality of the reserves.

The services should be authorized to offer a new reserve enlistment program, to supplement current options, that requires two to four years of effective service in a reserve unit preceded by as much active-duty time as is needed for basic and skill training. Legislation should be enacted to reward successful performers in this program with two to four academic years of concurrent education or training at an accredited institution, with the government paying tuition (up to a maximum amount), fees, and a modest subsistence allowance. Active-duty pay for these reserve component enlistees should be reduced by law to a minimum subsistence level, and dependent allowances should not be authorized for them. Following completion of the educational program, the enlistee should serve one year on active duty at full pay and allowances, in whatever grade and specialty were earned in the reserve component. Such enlistees should have the option, if service needs permit, of shifting to ROTC, with a possible active-duty obligation.

RECOMMENDATION #6: EVALUATION OF MILITARY COMPENSATION

Purpose: To facilitate comparison of military and civilian pay levels.

The government should strive to end the piecemeal attacks on military fringe benefits by completing a comprehensive evaluation of these benefits and including their value in a new index of total military compensation. This is needed not only to educate service members as to the real potential value of the military compensation program (including retirement), but also to permit reasonable comparisons with similarly constructed civilian pay indices, if civilian pay levels are to continue to be used as a basis for adjusting military pay.

RECOMMENDATION #7: PEACETIME REGISTRATION

Purpose: To improve peacetime registration for the draft.

The administration should foster better public understanding of the importance of peacetime registration and take further steps to assess and correct noncompliance. To that end, the president should require that the registrant have and use a Social Security number when registering. Both Social Security and IRS records should be used to determine compliance, as the administration recently announced it intends to do.

The Congress and the president should enact legislation to revise the penalties for noncompliance so that they are commensurate with the gravity of the offense, that is: are less severe and more enforceable.*

RECOMMENDATION #8: DRAFT WHEN NECESSARY

Purpose: To cope with the possibility that such measures will prove inadequate.

If all reasonable programs fail to satisfy minimum standards for either quantity or quality within a reasonable period of time for the army's active and reserve forces, peacetime conscription should be resumed.*

RECOMMENDATION #9: PREPARATION FOR CONSCRIPTION

Purpose: To be ready for resumption of the draft, in either peace or emergency.

1. The president should prepare the ground for seeking induction authority as a supplement to voluntary enlistments. The risks of not doing so are unacceptable.

A presidential commission, in conjunction with the Selective Service System, should design the criteria which a future draft must meet and, from them, specify the details of such a draft, including all policies as to the selection process, conscientious objection, whether or not to permit volunteers, age, sex, order of call, deferrals, exemptions, organization, operations, etc.

We believe such plans should include among others the following provisions: (1) state quotas should be eliminated to permit a uniform national call; (2) resumption of the draft should not prohibit enlistments; (3) the president should have authority, when necessary, to induct women in the numbers required by the services; (4) service of those conscripted should be two years or less on active duty with the remainder of the ten-year military obligation in the IRR; (5) if one is called for service in the armed forces but qualifies as a conscientious objector, that person may serve in an alternate

---

*Dr. Korb comments: "The law should be easier to enforce if the penalty is a felony. Judges can make the punishment fit the severity of the crime. A lesser penalty might not be as effective in improving compliance."

*Dr. Korb comments: "This recommendation is both naive and bad policy. Presumably, much more should be considered in a decision to return to conscription than simply the failure to meet an arbitrary set of quality standards over an equally arbitrary time period. A decision to return to the draft should not be dictated by such artificial constraints.

service role (defined as in the present law) or in a program established by an agency of the Federal Government, for a term of three years (as compared to two years in the armed services) but with no further vulnerability for call (as compared to eight years in the IRR); (6) the call should be based upon random selection of the eligible pool of 18-year olds, with induction in the nineteenth year; (7) the local boards should continue to have the right to excuse registrants from preinduction physical examinations for obvious reasons (blind, lame, incompetent); (8) medical doctors should be subject to the doctors' draft, regardless of prior vulnerability for selection.

This "model" draft should then be compared to the draft law now on the books and changes, as necessary, should be proposed to the Congress for enactment before the need arises.

2. In conjunction with such advance planning, the Selective Service System should estimate the size of the potential conscientious objector problem if and when a draft is resumed and should continue to develop a program to deal with it, including a narrow, workable legal definition of conscientious objection and a civilian conscription/service alternative for COs.

3. Emergency legislation should be drafted permitting the recall of recent but unobligated veterans to meet, in case of a severe national emergency, any needs for pretrained individuals not met by the IRR.

4. The president should be given limited authority to induct a limited number of men and women into the armed forces in a situation in which there is an emergency short of the outbreak of general war. This authority should require declaration of a national emergency, and be limited to some reasonable number (say 100,000) and to a period of six months without explicit congressional extension. It should also be subject to the other kinds of controls and limitations such as presently affect the president's authority to call up reserves and deploy forces under the War Powers Act.*

---

*Dr. Korb comments: "There is no need for this recommendation:

"Recent improvements in Selective Service capabilities, including the reinstatement of peacetime registration for all young men born in 1960 and thereafter, have enabled the Selective Service System to achieve a much more satisfactory level of responsiveness to mobilization manpower requirements. The Selective Service can now produce the first inductees in 13 days after mobilization and the 100,000th inductee by M + 30.

"In bringing the SSS out of deep-standby status we began the lengthy process of operational planning for wartime conscription—a process that continues today. Many of the concerns expressed in the policy paper have been addressed in this process. In addition, issues of conscientious objection, pre-induction screening, state quotas, and continuation of enlistments up to the point at which the military training base is at capacity, are all being resolved in the current planning process.

"Other features of the recommendation differ only slightly from current procedures. These include: induction of 19-year-olds (current policy is induction of youngest first, beginning with 20-year-olds); military service obligation (MSO) of 10 years (proposed legislation would give the Secretary of Defense the authority to extend the MSO up to two years beyond current statutory limits); and development of a health professional draft.

RECOMMENDATION #10: THE CAREER FORCE

Purpose: To retain quality officers, noncommissioned officers and technical specialists in the career force.

Any plan for military service (draft, volunteer, or combination) must include steps to insure retention of needed skills in the career force. Specifically, the DoD should, with the support of the Congress, continue to use differential pays to the extent required to retain the appropriate number and quality of officers and noncommissioned officers in the career force. The services should also review and improve personnel management policies directly related to retention. In particular, more individual choice and assignment lead time should be a goal for key-skills personnel.

RECOMMENDATION #11: NATIONAL SERVICE

Purpose: To develop and evaluate plans for a program of voluntary national service.

The president should appoint a commission of qualified citizens to evaluate current proposals for a program of voluntary national service and to develop, if it appears feasible, recommendations for such a program together with an assessment of its prospective costs and benefits, its relationship to federal student aid, and the modalities by which it would be implemented. The commission should carefully address the prospective impact of such a program on the problems involved in meeting the nation's military manpower requirements.

Study alone, however, will not answer all the relevant questions. We further recommend that the government promote national service pilot projects of different types to provide empirical data for such studies and to make more visible to the public the national service idea in practice.

Getting from Here to There

The first objective of the United States and its Atlantic allies is to prevent war by deterring aggression. To achieve this objective in the 1980s and 1990s, as this Policy Paper has sought to show, we will have to do two

---

"The recommendation for Presidential authority to resume a 'limited' draft should be withdrawn. A limited draft may be irreversible. Once induction begins in a crisis situation, volunteer motives will change, i.e., some may seek jobs far removed from hostile fire, some may seek the adventure of combat. Few, however, will be joining to learn a skill or to visit foreign countries. The numbers volunteering might initially increase, but will probably decline in the long run. We most probably would not be able to stop the 'limited' draft without a serious decline in force manning.

"For this reason and because the Administration would probably want to gain the support of the Congress on such an important policy, it is likely that, even were such authority available to the Administration, it would seek some formal approval of the Congress to resume induction."

things: adopt several measures to strengthen the All-Volunteer Force, and prepare detailed plans to resume conscription if and when that becomes necessary later in this decade. Both kinds of effort should prove mutually reinforcing. Both will require public understanding and support.

FINDING #12: PUBLIC OPINION

On the strength of available evidence, one may reasonably conclude that "getting from here to there," in the sense of correcting a sagging military posture, should not be as politically difficult as many commentators have suggested. Opinion polls in this country have been generally reassuring. They may reflect very limited knowledge of pertinent details, but they confirm the prevalence of sound instincts, a readiness to follow credible leadership, and a firmness of spirit. Judging from their history as well as surveys of their current opinion, the American people will support whatever level of defense is needed once they perceive the need.* Perceiving the need is of course the key.

If the draft becomes necessary, the case for resuming it must be clearly and persuasively presented. While opinion polls consistently indicate broad receptivity to the idea of peacetime conscription, it is clear that respondents generally have only the vaguest notion of what kind of draft they say they would support. Only a detailed debate on the costs and benefits of alternative manpower systems can yield a meaningful consensus — or a workable system.

At the same time, we believe it is urgent that the American people as a

---

*A Gallup Poll in June 1981 reported that 71 percent of the American people favored "requiring all young men to give one year of service to the nation, either in the military forces or in non-military work here and abroad." In an Associated Press/NBC poll in July 1981, respondents favored reinstatement of the draft by 59 percent to 33 percent, with 8 percent undecided. In a Washington Post/ABC poll in October 1981, 86 percent said the United States should spend whatever is necessary to be either equal or superior to the Soviet Union in military strength (40 percent for superiority and 46 percent for rough equality). In the same poll, incidentally, 57 percent agreed the United States should enter into a new round of arms limitations talks with the Soviet Union.

The data on the attitudes of younger Americans is somewhat less conclusive. One poll in 1981 indicated that support for resumption of the draft is to a degree a function of age: 65 percent of those over 50 favoring it, as compared to 46 percent of those between 18 and 29. On the other hand, a Gallup poll in 1980 found more than three-fourths of the 18–24-year-old respondents in support of reinstating the draft. The National Coalition of Independent College and University Students no longer takes a position against the draft, having found that its membership was divided on the issue. "Overall," writes public opinion analyst Daniel Yankelovich (in *Psychology Today*, March 1982), "it is clear that the vast majority of Americans want the United States to be strong, at least as strong as the Soviets, if not more so, and that to a large majority of young and old, a newly fashioned draft involving military and non-military service and a degree of choice is a serious option."

whole gain a fuller understanding of their military establishment and its role in deterring war and protecting their vital interests.

Getting from here to there on any issue in a democracy is preeminently a matter of public education and understanding—with, on the issue of military service, the accent on youth.

RECOMMENDATION #12: TALKING IT OVER

Purpose: To promote a better public understanding of national security needs, the role of conventional military forces, and the manpower alternatives.

We urge that World Affairs Councils, educational and student organizations, history and social science classes, and youth groups put on their agenda for study and discussion the question of the West's defensive needs, the role of military forces in a democracy, and the rights and duties of citizens in manning those forces—making use for that purpose of this Policy Paper as well as other materials expressing different points of view.

Further to that end, the Atlantic Council of the United States should undertake within the limits of its resources to provide such groups with qualified speakers and to make available without charge reasonable quantities of this Policy Paper. The Council, through its Working Group on the Successor Generation and in cooperation with other educational organizations, should also promote a series of national seminars on military and civilian service in the United States, with the participation of high-school and college students.

APPENDIX I: COMMENTS AND DISSENTS

By Members of the Atlantic Council Working Group

George S. Blanchard, Robert G. Gard, James L. Lacy, David E. McGiffert, Bruce Palmer, Jr., Paul D. Phillips, and Stanley R. Resor. In our opinion, the United States should reinstitute conscription for active-duty military service as soon as possible because of the immediate need to increase nonnuclear force capabilities and thus reduce reliance on nuclear weapons. The task force Policy Paper concludes that it is probable that the United States will need to resume military conscription by the mid-1980s. We believe that this conclusion does not go far enough.

There is widespread agreement today that it is imperative for the United States to increase its conventional force capability to put the United States and its allies in a better position to deter and, if necessary, withstand a nonnuclear attack without resort to the use of nuclear weapons. We do not believe that conventional force adequate for this purpose is achievable so long as the United States relies on all-volunteer forces.

The factual information presented in the Policy Paper seems to us to lead inescapably to the conclusion that the All-Volunteer Force has not been a reliable source of army manpower, qualitatively in the case of the active forces and both quantitatively and qualitatively in the case of the reserve forces. The current favorable recruiting environment, driven by high levels of unemployment, should not obscure this fact. The problem will grow as the relevant age cohort shrinks over the rest of this decade.

Moreover, the army's active forces have been reduced by almost 200,000 as compared to 1964, the last peacetime draft year, even though requirements have increased. This has forced the army to transfer from its active forces to the Selected Reserve 100,000 positions in units which, in the event of a European conflict, would be required to deploy in the first 30 days. As the Policy Paper points out, however, the army reserve forces are incapable of adequately fulfilling their rapid reenforcement role. The Policy Paper implies that this deficiency may be remedied without changing the current distribution of units between the army's active and reserve forces. This is wishful thinking. The problem is not fixable without structural change because the problem is congenital, and because it stems from the limitations on training and facilities which necessarily characterize the reserves. These limitations particularly apply to certain types of combat units, especially (but not exclusively) those of more than battalion size.

Past experience with the callup of army reserve forces confirms without exception that it is wholly unrealistic to expect the Selected Reserve Force units to attain the level of readiness required by current deployment plans. To avoid such unrealistic reliance on the reserves, units comprising 100,000 to 200,000 should be restored to the active army force structure. Given the erratic performance of the all-volunteer approach to date in meeting reduced active force requirements, we see no way this can be done without reinstating conscription.

Conscription of active-duty military manpower would also assure that the shortage of deployable manpower in the Selected Reserve Force would be filled, that the shortage in the Individual Ready Reserve would also be filled more promptly, that a tested and operative Selective Service System would be put in place and that a brake could be placed on the upward spiral of first-term manpower costs. These consequences all would make essential contributions to creating an adequate conventional force deterrent.

A return to conscription in peacetime would be selective, requiring only one of several to serve. However, any perceived inequity would be fully justified by the significant and necessary contribution to a credible conventional force, which will reduce the risk of nuclear as well as nonnuclear war, provided that the method of conscription met two conditions; namely: (1) a near universal liability to selection, and (2) a random unbiased means of selection. A lottery draft with minimum exemptions would satisfy these conditions.

Robert Komer and Robert B. Pirie, Jr. We cannot accept the Paper as presently written. It implies that the country will be compelled to return to peacetime conscription in this decade. We disagree. If pay comparability is maintained, and human resources are managed effectively, there is no reason why the nation's military manpower requirements cannot continue being met with volunteers. Large increases in force sizes predicted a year ago do not now appear feasible, not because of manpower constraints, but because of cost. Moreover, are such increases in force structure strategically desirable, or should the United States concentrate instead on readier, more modern, and more effective forces—relying mainly on our allies for most manpower extensive force structure increases?

The Paper as now written is also resolutely wrong-headed about the significance of the so-called quality measures: high-school diplomas and entrance test scores. In particular, the assertion that "Higher quality means increased soldierly effectiveness" is seriously misleading. The quality measures are used in entrance screening. Experience has shown that there is correlation between success in initial military training and the quality measures. Test scores are also used to screen candidates for technical training. Soldierly effectiveness in subsequent military jobs, however, is an immensely complex matter, and influenced by many more variables than educational attainment and scores on aptitude tests. Little, in fact, is known about the relationship between the quality measures used for screening and late performance. For example, many of the individuals who would have been screened out in 1977–1980 if the tests in use had been properly normed, are now in service and are performing well. The summary Paper states that the quality of accessions in 1977–1980 was "unacceptable," but produces no evidence to show why or how, other than the screening measures themselves. Again, there is no evidence that we know of to the effect that quality was more of a problem with the 1977–1980 accessions than it was with the 1973–1977 accessions.

Recommendation #2, "Quality" should be deleted. Nobody knows whether the minimums recommended are right, necessary, feasible, or appropriate— least of all the Atlantic Council Working Group. Further, the Paper ought to acknowledge explicitly that such quotas tend to screen out minorities to a much greater degree than the rest of the population. Where they are arbitrarily fixed they are vulnerable to charges of discrimination.

The summary Paper is unwarrantedly pessimistic with respect to army reserve strength. The assistant secretary of defense (Manpower, Reserve Affairs and Logistics) has testified that he expects army selected reserve end strength to be 650,000 by the end of this fiscal year and 702,000 by the end of fiscal 1984, at which time it will be larger than in any other peacetime year. It is absurd for an Atlantic Council Working Group (no matter how prestigious) to assert, in the face of that evidence "we find no program that will bring [the Army Selected Reserve] to adequate trained strength before 1990."

Concern over the IRR is better warranted, but here the Policy Paper is very confused. Either there is a low cost/no cost fix for the IRR, as the Paper asserts early on, or there isn't. If there is, we should advocate it, and we can then remove mobilization manpower from the list of concerns that motivates us to consider a return to peacetime conscription. We note that DoD is proposing a program to rebuild the IRR that contains the major elements of the proposed Atlantic Council program: increase in the military service obligation and reenlistment bonuses. The major difference is that the council would increase the MSO to ten years; Dod is proposing eight. Does the Working Group believe that this difference is so crucial as to make DoD's resulting IRR unacceptable, and thus warrant the tone and content of the proposed recommendations?

We further disagree with recommendation #6, "Draft When Necessary." Nobody knows what minimum standards are appropriate, either for quantity or quality, and nobody knows whether two years is the right period of time. Presumably the international situation has some influence on whether one would want to wait two years for recruiting to improve. On the other hand, under the proposed rule we would probably have returned to conscription in 1978–1980, a step that now appears unwarranted.

Finally, we believe that now is the wrong time to divert attention from the crucial issue of greater U.S. defense spending by dragging the red herring of conscription across its trail. We believe that it is important to work out in advance what kind of peacetime conscription system would be used if it were necessary. However, that is not the same as engaging the administration, Congress, and the public in a major debate on whether to return to conscription now. Such a debate would be very untimely, strongly divisive, and would shift attention and support from much needed increases in defense programs. The national consensus on more for defense is rapidly dissipating. It would not be helped by proposals to reinstitute the draft at a time when all the armed services are meeting their quotas, turning away volunteers, and raising reenlistment standards.

By Additional Participants in The Regional American Assembly

By Mark Blitz and Barbara Wyatt. In the draft version of the Policy Paper entitled "Toward a Consensus on Military Service," the Atlantic Council recommends that the president appoint a citizen commission to study the concept of a "national voluntary service" program, and that the concept be tested in a series of pilot projects.

The council evinces particular interest in the idea of offering student aid incentives, like those in the GI Bill, to citizens volunteering for civilian "national service." "Such a program might go far to advance the ideal and habit of peacetime service to the nation as a normal and desirable part of growing up in America. To that extent it should improve the climate for voluntary enlistment in peacetime military service," the council states.

There is reason to believe that neither the military nor the nation at large would benefit from the establishment of a national voluntary service, or even from further study and testing of the concept.

The national service concept has already been studied exhaustively by private groups and has been considered at the federal level since the early 1960s. The ACTION agency tested the concept, most notably in 1977–1980 with the $11 million Youth Community Service (YCS) project in Syracuse and Oswego, New York. The outcome of the YCS project, which offered participants both stipends and student aid incentives, did not show the national service idea in a favorable light. Indeed, although YCS was given a high degree of attention and support by the ACTION leadership, and was staffed and funded generously, it is now regarded as a textbook case of an ill-conceived and poorly run project.

There is no compelling reason to spend millions more testing the national service concept, especially in a time of budget stringency. The Atlantic Council rightly directs its recommendations toward the problems of the military. It offers no evidence to support its assertion that a national civilian service offering student aid incentives would encourage enlistment in the armed forces. Logic would suggest the contrary, civilian service being, presumably, less onerous than military.

There are a number of strong objections to the National Service concept itself. First, it is based on the underlying assumption that a young person's volunteering for some type of social work is more beneficial to the nation than the same youth's pursuing an education or entering productive private sector employment. This implies a concept of the common good at odds with that traditionally held by most Americans.

Furthermore, the National Service concept ignores the innumerable existing opportunities for volunteer service by Americans of all ages. It is difficult to conceive of any benefit to such activities for the establishment of a "national service."

Finally, one of the most frequently raised objections to the All-Volunteer Army is the cost of attracting and keeping quality recruits. Yet defense is an essential function of government. The objections on grounds of cost alone that could be raised against the far less essential civilian service proposed in the report are insurmountable at present, and are likely to remain so. To study and plan for the establishment of such a national service corps, would be, under the circumstances, a frivolous exercise.

By Donald J. Eberly. A study group aimed at reaching a consensus on military service will, understandably, not give center stage to the subject of national service. Quite properly, national service will be examined for its relationship to and effect on military service. All the same, I must dissent from the description of national service put forth under the heading "Selective National Service."

This section seems to be predicated on the viewpoint that selective national service would be very different from the voluntary national service described in an earlier section. It fails to recognize that national service could and should become a cornerstone of our national youth policy. As such, there would be civilian service opportunities for all young men and women who volunteered for them regardless of whether there was a military draft, a volunteer army, or no army. The only exception would be a period of such a high degree of mobilization that there would be no civilian service option.

The organization of national service would be the same regardless of whether conscription was in effect. The only changes would be that civilian service participants would move toward the end of the draft queue and Congress might set a minimum period of service to qualify such persons for this place in the draft queue. Under national service, the number of persons in the draft pool would be the same as without national service.

This section also errs in seeming to blur the fairly sharp distinctions between national service and conscientious objection. In national service, the government would tell young men and women that they are needed to help preserve the forests, conserve energy, care for the very old and very young, and provide for the national defense. It would then invite them to contribute a period of federally underwritten service as a responsible citizen. Each young person would make an individual choice. In conscientious objection, the government would tell young men and women that if they sincerely hold moral, ethical, or religious views which do not permit them to take part in war or military service in any form, and if they can convince their draft board or appeal board of their position, then they will be required to serve in a civilian capacity for two years.

Whether we are in a period of the All-Volunteer Force or of conscription, national service has more to do with national security than with military service. Toynbee's study of history revealed that some 90 percent of the civilizations he examined fell from within rather than from external aggression. National service would help to repair some of the social fabric that has given way in the past two decades. It would give young people an investment in the country and in the future; it would give them work experience and career exploration; it would acquaint them with the rewards of service to others, and it would accomplish a great deal of work that, although it happens to be outside the market economy, is still vitally important.

APPENDIX II: TABLES

Table AII-10.1. Defense Manpower: the Baseline Force.
(in thousands)

	1964	1968	1975	1980	1981	1982
Active Military						
Army	972	1,570	784	777	775	786
Navy	667	765	535	527	540	555
Marine Corps	190	307	196	188	191	192
Air Force	856	905	613	558	569	587
	2,685	3,547	2,128	2,050	2,075	2,120
Selected Reserves						
Reserve Personnel						
Army	269	244	225	207	217	237
Navy	123	124	98	87	87	88
Marine Corps	46	47	32	35	37	39
Air Force	61	43	51	59	61	64
National Guard						
Army	382	389	395	367	386	398
Air Force	73	75	95	96	98	98
	954	922	896	851	886	924
Civilians						
Army	453	542	401	361	371	382
Navy/Marine Corps	346	433	326	309	317	313
Air Force	338	357	278	244	243	247
Defense Agencies	37	74	73	77	82	83
	1,174	1,406	1,078	991	1,013	1,025

Source: Adapted from William W. Kaufman, "U.S. Defense Needs in The 1980's," Lt. Gen. Brent C. Scowcroft, ed., *Military Service in the United States* (New York: The American Assembly, 1981), p. I.4.

Table AII-10.2. Active Army Enlisted Nonprior Service Recruit Quality Distribution as Measured by Mental Groupings and Educational Level. (Percentages)[1]

	Pre-War Draft		War Peak	Post-War Draft	PMVF								
	(1960) 60	(1964) 64	(1969) 69	(1972) 72	73[2]	74	75	76	77	78	79	80	81
Mental Categories													
I & II (highest)	32	34	35	33	32	31	35	31	21	21	17	14	24
IIIA (just above avg.)	20	22	18	23	24	21	23	22	15	16	13	12	16
Subtotal (above avg.)	52	56	53	56	56	52	58	53	36	37	30	26	40
IIIB (just below avg.)	31	25	20	26	27	30	31	36	24	23	24	22	29
IV (lowest accepted)	17	19	27	18	17	18	10	11	41	39	46	52	31
Educational Attainment													
College Degree	5	5	6	4	3	1	2	2	1	2	1	1	1
Some College	26	15	19	11	11	4	5	3	5	4	3	2	3
High-School Diploma	36	50	45	46	48	45	51	54	53	68	60	51	76
Subtotal (At least HSDG)	67	70	70	61	62	50	58	59	59	74	64	54	80
Nongraduate	33	30	30	39	38	50	42	41	41	26	36	46	20
Total NPS Accessions (000)	185	268	455	187	215	182	185	180	168	124	129	158	118
At least High-School Diploma Accessions (000)	124	187	319	114	133	91	107	106	100	91	83	86	95

1. Numbers may not add to 100% due to rounding.
2. Year of transition to the Peacetime Military Volunteer Force.

Table AII-10.3. Army AVF Enlistment Options.

Enlistment Term	Total Obligation	Specialty Or Skill	Tour Assignment	Dependents Permitted	Educational Benefits	Compensation	Housing
Active							
1. 12 mos. plus training	10 yrs.	Service convenience	12 mos., Korea	No	2 academic yrs. postservice	Subsistence level	Barracks
2. 18 mos. plus training	10 yrs.	Service convenience	18 mos., Europe	No	3 academic yrs. postservice	Subsistence level	Barracks
3. 24 mos. plus training	10 yrs.	Service convenience	12 mos., CONUS plus 12 mos., Korea; or 24 mos., Europe or CONUS	No	4 academic yrs. postservice	Subsistence level	Barracks
4. 3 yrs.	10 yrs.	Limited options	Options	Yes	Current VEAP	Regular	Regular options
5. 4 yrs. or more	10 yrs.	Full options	Options	Yes	Current VEAP	Regular	Regular options
Reserve Components							
6. 6 yrs.	10 yrs.	Service convenience	5 yrs. in a unit	Yes	4 academic yrs. concurrent with satisfactory service in a unit	Subsistence level during drills and annual training	N/A
7. 6 yrs.	10 yrs.	Limited options	6 yrs. in a unit, less training time	Yes	None	Regular	N/A

NOTES

1. For a discussion of the geopolitical background, see chapter 1, "The Setting," by Joseph J. Wolf.

2. William W. Kaufmann, "U.S. Defense Needs in the 1980s," in *Military Service in the United States*, ed. Brent Scowcroft (Englewood Cliffs, N.J.: Prentice-Hall, Inc. for The American Assembly, 1982), pp. 28–29.

3. *Washington Post*, December 21, 1981.

4. For a more extensive discussion of this subject, see chapter 2, "Military Manpower: The American Experience and the Enduring Debate," by James L. Lacy, and chapter 9, "Military Service in American Society," by Mark J. Eitelberg and Martin Binkin.

5. For a more extensive discussion of this subject, see chapter 3, "U.S. Security Requirements: Missions, Manpower, Readiness, Mobilization, and Projection of Forces," by William J. Taylor, Jr.

6. *Annual Report to the Congress*, February 8, 1982, pp I-15ff.

7. For a more extensive discussion of this subject, see chapter 4, "The All-Volunteer Force: Status and Prospects of the Active Forces," by Richard V.L. Cooper.

8. Charles C. Moskos, "Social Considerations of the All-Volunteer Force," in *Military Service in the United States*, Brent Scrowcroft, ed., The American Assembly, op. cit., p. 136.

9. For a more extensive discussion of this subject, see chapter 5, "The All-Volunteer Force Today: Mobilization Manpower," by Robert B. Pirie, Jr.

10. See above, p. 266.

11. Acting Assistant Secretary of the Army, Manpower and Reserve Affairs, Senate Armed Services Committee, Subcommittee on Manpower and Personnel, February 26, 1981.

12. For a more extensive discussion of voluntary service options, see chapter 7, "Peacetime Voluntary Options," by William K. Brehm, and chapter 6, "Beyond the Marketplace: National Service and the AVF," by Charles C. Moskos and John H. Faris.

13. For further elaboration of the projections and data explaining them, see chapter 7, "Peacetime Voluntary Options," by William K. Brehm.

14. Cf., for example, Committee for the Study of National Service, *Youth and the Needs of the Nation* (Washington, D.C.: The Potomac Institute, 1979).

15. Cf., for example, Michael W. Sherradan and Donald J. Eberly, *National Service: Social, Economic and Military Impacts* (Elmsford, NY: Pergamon Press, 1982).

16. December 27, 1981.

17. For a more extensive account of compulsory service options, see chapter 8, "Obligatory Service: The Fundamental and Secondary Choices," by James L. Lacy.

18. Under existing lower court case law, Selective Service must assign a CO to alternate service as soon as he would be inducted were he not a CO. Thus Selective Service needs programs for assignment and cannot depend on the CO finding his own opportunity.

19. *Parade*, August 16, 1981, p. 5.

20. This point and the relevant studies are discussed in chapter 6, "Beyond the Marketplace: National Service and the AVF," by Charles C. Moskos and John H. Faris.

21. A discussion of the "occupation versus institution" issue appears in chapter 6, "Beyond the Marketplace: National Service and the AVF," by Charles C. Moskos and John H. Faris.

Index

Confederacy, 22
Conscientious objectors
  alternative service, 290–291
  in Peacetime Military Volunteer
    Force (PMVF), 164–165
  present day, 252–254
  and selective national service, 224–
    228
  Supreme Court definition of, 289
  in Vietnam War, 40–41, 45
  in World War I, 29
  in World War II, 32–33
Conscription
  for active duty, 215–221, 287–289
  arguments for, 25–26
  American attitudes toward, 69
  in Civil War, 22
  and contemporary issues, 252–255
  criticism of, 22
  equity of, 209–211
  military effectiveness of, 208–209
  in other countries, 25
  universal, 27, 30, 283–285
  weaknesses of, 207–211
  See also Draft; Universal Military
    Training
Czechoslovakia, 7, 34, 363

Davis, Jefferson, 23
Defense Budget, 72, 97
Defense planning, 265–268
Détente, 6, 13, 14
Deterrence, 63–64
Draft
  vs. All-Volunteer Force (AVF), 200–
    201, 203–205
  bipartisan support of, 47
  and blacks, 37, 224–225
  and Carter administration, 67
  in Civil War, 22–23
  criticisms of, 22–23
  end of, 80
  enforcement of, 42
  future limitations of, 205–207
  non-military, 229–230
  in peacetime, 31–32, 263, 296–97,
    301–302

policy changes in, 79–80
reform, 40–46
for reserves, 211–215
"tag on," 217–218, 287
terms of, 221–228
and Truman administration, 34–35,
  46
and Vietnam War, 263
and women, 37, 229
in World War I, 28–29
in World War II, 262–263
See also Conscription; Universal
  Military Training (UMT)

Educational assistance
  in All-Volunteer Force (AVF), 108,
    115, 141–142, 146–149
  in Peacetime Military Volunteer
    Force (PMVF), 182, 192
  recommendations for, 300–301
  for reservists, 279
Einstein, Albert, 30
Eisenhower administration, 38, 42
Eliot, Charles, 25, 27
Ethiopia, 8
European allies, 12–16

Ford administration, 267
Foreign trade, 3–4
Forrestal, Secretary of Defense, 34
Franco-Prussian War, 25
Frank, Stanley, 37

Gandhi, M. K., 30
Gates, Thomas Jr., 80
Gates Commission
  and All-Volunteer Force (AVF), 43–
    44, 80, 86, 102, 133, 267
  and reserves, 115–116
Germany, 25
GI Bill
  and All-Volunteer Force (AVF), 108,
    141–143, 149, 278
  future of, 219–220
  post war, 46
  proposal for, 228–229
  in World War II, 33, 36

National Grange, 27
National Guard, 28–29, 38, 46, 266
National Manpower Task Force, 62
National service, 26–28
  compulsory, 283–291
  cost of, 210–211
  model for, 146–149
  proposals for, 44–46, 304
  selective, 289–291
  voluntary, 281–283
  See also Conscription; Draft;
    Universal Military Training (UMT)
National Student Association, 45
Nifty Nugget, 65–66
Nixon administration, 40, 42, 43, 45
North Atlantic Treaty Organization
  (NATO), 5–11, 53, 62, 63, 265
North Korea, 8
Norway, 71
Nuclear weapons, 9–16, 261
Nunn, Sam, 240

Oakes, James, 24
Oil reserves, 3, 4, 8, 13, 260

Pacifism, 26
  See also Conscientious objectors
Palmer, John McAuley, 239
Paul, Ron, 240
Peace Corps, 44, 45, 254
Peacetime draft, 31–32, 263, 296–297,
  301–302
Peacetime Military Volunteer Force
  (PMVF), 152–153
  enlistment options, 179–180, 182–186
  and Individual Ready Reserves
    (IRR), 180–182
  manpower of, 153–160, 165–173
  quality of life in, 176–179
  recommendations for, 186–188
  unresolved issues of, 161–165
Peacetime preparedness
  American attitude toward, 16–19
Peacetime service
  logistics of, 188–199
Perry, Ralph Barton, 25
Persian Gulf, 4, 8, 55, 56

Pirie, Robert B., 62
Poland, 6, 7
Prepositioned Organizational Material
  Configured in Unit Sets
  (POMCUS), 70–71
Proud Spirit, 68, 116

Quakers, 27

Rapid Deployment Joint Task Force
  (RDJTF), 71, 72
Reagan administration, 56, 57, 146, 265
Reserve Forces Act of 1955, 38–39
Reserves
  deployment of, 114
  effectiveness of, 113–114
  in Korean War, 37–39
  and Peacetime Military Volunteer
    Force (PMVF), 187–188
  See also Individual Ready Reserves
    (IRR); Selected Reserves
Revolutionary War, 21, 237–239
Rogers, Bernard D., 62
Roosevelt, Franklin D., 30
Roosevelt, Theodore, 25
Root, Elihu, 25
Rousseau, Jean Jacques, 237
Russell, Bertrand, 30

Schmidt, Chancellor, 25
Schofield, John M., 239
Selected Reserves, 115–124
Selective Service, 128–129
  criticisms of, 285–286
  inequities of, 242–244
  mobilization of, 66
Seymour, Horatio, 23
Singapore, 8
Social equity, 249–252
  See also Blacks; Women
Socialist Party, 27, 31
Somalia, 8
South Korea, 260
South Yemen, 8
Soviet Union
  defense policy, 4–8
  forces, 9–11, 54

About the Co-Chairmen and Rapporteur

Andrew J. Goodpaster received his Ph.D. from Princeton in International Relations. A retired U.S. Army General, he was formerly the superintendent of the U.S. Military Academy, a professor of government and international studies at the Citadel, and a Senior Fellow at the Woodrow Wilson Center for Scholars. He was also the Supreme Allied Commander in Europe from 1969-74 and Vice-Chairman of the Atlantic Council of the United States.

Lloyd H. Elliott, President of George Washington University, was formerly President of the University of Maine. He received his Ed.D. from the University of Colorado.

J. Allan Hovey, Jr. has been an international relations specialist with the U.S. General Accounting Office since 1976. He was vice president and secretary of Radio Free Europe from 1968 to 1976, during which period he was also adjunct associate professor of international relations at City University of New York. He has an M.A. and Ph.D. from Columbia University and is the author of numerous scholarly articles, GAO reports to the Congress, and a book on interparliamentary assemblies.